The Macroeconomics
of Populism in
Latin America

D0878773

A National Bureau
of Economic Research
Conference Report

The Macroeconomics of Populism in Latin America

Edited by   Rudiger Dornbusch and
Sebastian Edwards

The University of Chicago Press

Chicago and London

RUDIGER DORNBUSCH is the Ford International Professor of Economics at the Massachusetts Institute of Technology and a research associate of the National Bureau of Economic Research. SEBASTIAN EDWARDS is the Henry Ford II Professor of Business Economics at the University of California, Los Angeles, and a research associate of the National Bureau of Economic Research.

The University of Chicago Press, Chicago 60637
The University of Chicago Press, Ltd., London
© 1991 by the National Bureau of Economic Research
All rights reserved. Published 1991
Printed in the United States of America

00 99 98 97 96 95 94 93 92 91   5 4 3 2 1

ISBN (cloth): 0-226-15843-8
ISBN (paper): 0-226-15844-6

Library of Congress Cataloging-in-Publication Data

The Macroeconomics of populism in Latin America / edited by Rudiger
  Dornbusch and Sebastian Edwards.
      p.   cm. — (A National Bureau of Economic Research conference
  report)
    Papers of a conference held at the Inter-American Development
  Bank in May 1990.
    Includes bibliographical references and index.
    1. Latin America—Economic conditions—1945-   —Congresses.
  2. Latin America—Economic policy—Congresses.   3. Populism—Latin
  America—Congresses.   I. Dornbusch, Rudiger.   II. Edwards,
  Sebastian.   III. Series: Conference report (National Bureau of Economic Research)
  HC125.M255   1991
  339.5'098—dc20   91-25305
                                                                        CIP

♾ The paper used in this publication meets the minimum requirements of the American National Standard for Information Sciences—Permanence of Paper for Printed Library Materials, ANSI Z39.48–1984.

National Bureau of Economic Research

Officers

George T. Conklin, Jr., *chairman*
Paul W. McCracken, *vice chairman*
Martin Feldstein, *president and chief executive officer*

Geoffrey Carliner, *executive director*
Charles A. Walworth, *treasurer*
Sam Parker, *director of finance and administration*

Directors at Large

John H. Biggs
Andrew Brimmer
Carl F. Christ
George T. Conklin, Jr.
Kathleen B. Cooper
Jean A. Crockett
George C. Eads
Morton Ehrlich

Martin Feldstein
George Hatsopoulos
Lawrence R. Klein
Franklin A. Lindsay
Paul W. McCracken
Leo Melamed
Michael H. Moskow
James J. O'Leary

Robert T. Parry
Peter G. Peterson
Robert V. Roosa
Richard N. Rosett
Bert Seidman
Eli Shapiro
Donald S. Wasserman

Directors by University Appointment

Jagdish Bhagwati, *Columbia*
William C. Brainard, *Yale*
Glen G. Cain, *Wisconsin*
Franklin Fisher, *Massachusetts Institute of Technology*
Jonathan Hughes, *Northwestern*
Saul H. Hymans, *Michigan*
Marjorie B. McElroy, *Duke*

James L. Pierce, *California, Berkeley*
Andrew Postlewaite, *Pennsylvania*
Nathan Rosenberg, *Stanford*
Harold T. Shapiro, *Princeton*
Craig Swan, *Minnesota*
Michael Yoshino, *Harvard*
Arnold Zellner, *Chicago*

Directors by Appointment of Other Organizations

Rueben C. Buse, *American Agricultural Economics Association*
Richard A. Easterlin, *Economic History Association*
Gail Fosler, *The Conference Board*
A. Ronald Gallant, *American Statistical Association*
Robert S. Hamada, *American Finance Association*
David Kendrick, *American Economic Association*

Ben E. Laden, *National Association of Business Economists*
Rudolph A. Oswald, *American Federation of Labor and Congress of Industrial Organizations*
Dean P. Phypers, *Committee for Economic Development*
Douglas D. Purvis, *Canadian Economics Association*
Charles A. Walworth, *American Institute of Certified Public Accountants*

Directors Emeriti

Moses Abramovitz
Emilio G. Collado
Frank W. Fetter

Thomas D. Flynn
Gottfried Haberler
Geoffrey H. Moore

George B. Roberts
Willard L. Thorp
William S. Vickrey

Since this volume is a record of conference proceedings, it has been exempted from the rules governing critical review of manuscripts by the Board of Directors of the National Bureau (resolution adopted 8 June 1948, as revised 21 November 1949 and 20 April 1968).

Contents

Preface

The papers collected in this volume are the final product of a research project organized by the National Bureau of Economic Research. Earlier versions of the papers were presented at a conference held at the Inter-American Development Bank in May 1990.

We are indebted to the Tinker Foundation, and especially Ms. Renate Rennie, for enthusiastic research support. The Inter-American Development Bank helped make the conference possible and graciously provided the facilities. We acknowledge gratefully the interest of Miguel Urrutia, with whom we first established contact, and of Nora Rey de Marulanda and Enrique Iglesias, who carried the project forward. We thank the Rockefeller Foundation, the Tinker Foundation, and the Inter-American Development Bank for financial support.

Our special appreciation goes to the National Bureau of Economic Research, whose staff have been indispensable at each stage and, as always, wonderfully efficient. Julie McCarthy and the staff of the University of Chicago Press were immensely helpful in making a speedy publication possible. We also acknowledge the assistance of Beth Anne Wilson and Guy Debelle.

Any opinions expressed in this volume are those of the respective authors and do not necessarily reflect the views of the National Bureau of Economic Research or any of the sponsoring organizations.

Rudiger Dornbusch and Sebastian Edwards

Introduction

Rudiger Dornbusch and Sebastian Edwards

Macroeconomic instability has long been a salient feature of the Latin American economies. Inflationary outbursts, balance of payments crises, and painful stabilization attempts have dominated the economic history of the region since, at least, the early twentieth century. The magnitude of macroeconomic convulsions in Latin America is particularly startling when compared with the tranquility that has characterized the macroeconomic environment in other parts of the world, especially Southeast Asia.

How can we explain Latin America's proclivity toward macroeconomic mismanagement? Is it deeply rooted ignorance on the mechanics of deficit financing, or is it the deliberate consequence of Machiavellian politics or, is it, perhaps, the unavoidable outcome of distributional struggles? The papers and commentary collected in this volume constitute an effort to answer some of these questions. These articles address issues related to income inequality and political institutions at the regional level and analyze, in great detail, important episodes of macroeconomic crises in Argentina, Brazil, Chile, Colombia, Mexico, Nicaragua, and Peru.

The papers in this book take as a point of departure the description of the broad characteristics of the economics of populism that we set forward in chapter 1. In that chapter we argue that, although we clearly recognize that populist episodes have had specific and unique characteristics in different nations, they tend to have some fundamental common threads. In particular, populist regimes have historically tried to deal with income inequality problems through the use of overly expansive *macroeconomic* policies. These policies, which have relied on deficit financing, generalized controls, and a disregard for basic economic equilibria, have almost unavoidably resulted in major macroeconomic crises that have ended up hurting the poorer segments of society. As the case studies collected here clearly show, at the end of every populist experiment real wages are lower than they were at the beginning of these experiences.

The devastating effects of the Great Depression on the Latin economies, the vast income inequalities in almost every country in the region, a naive confidence in the ability of governments to cure all social and economic ills, and the ideas of the United Nations Economic Commission on Latin America in the 1950s are among some of the most important doctrinal and historical roots of traditional populist views in Latin America. Although a number of the chapters in this volume address these issues in detail, the main emphasis of the collection is on macroeconomic policy. In a way this has been deliberate, since we are persuaded that it is precisely because of macroeconomic misman-agement that populist experiences have failed. We are, in fact, convinced that the concerns for poverty and inequality are not only legitimate but clearly of great urgency. The issue is not whether these distributional problems should be addressed by policymakers, but how to better tackle them. In this respect the message emerging from the papers in this book is clear: the use of macro-economic policy to achieve distributive goals has historically led to failure, sorrow, and frustration. The articles in this volume do not deal with the eval-uation of alternative programs for dealing with extreme poverty situations nor do they deal with detailed ways of coordinating macroeconomic management with poverty alleviation programs. We think, however, that these issues should be high on the list of priorities for the research agenda of the next few years.

An Overview of the Volume

The first part of the volume includes two chapters that address some of the most salient aspects of populist economics' doctrine and policies. In chapter 2, Robert R. Kaufman and Barbara Stallings address some political angles of Latin American populism, emphasizing the relationship between political and economic goals, as well as the role of unequal income distribution and class conflict in the genesis of populism. Kaufman and Stallings also inquire on the possible future prospects for populist policies, arguing that in an increasingly global world economy individual populist adventures will become more and more rare. Chapter 3, by Eliana Cardoso and Ann Helwege, deals with in-come distribution and populism in Latin America, using cross-country evi-dence. They show that, in spite of their stated purposes, populist experiments have failed to benefit the poorest segments of population; in classical populist episodes income redistribution has run from the agricultural and export sec-tors to workers and capitalists in the urban area. Cardoso and Helwege also argue that the inability of populist regimes to make corrections to their poli-cies, once they become clearly unsustainable, resides in those regimes' lack of social cohesion and powerful political parties. When the time comes to implement a macroeconomic adjustment package, politicians hesitate and are unable to decide on which groups to place the costs of stabilization.

Part two of the book deals with populist experiences in six countries—Argentina, Chile, Brazil, Mexico, Peru, and Nicaragua—and with the absence of populism in recent Colombian history. Chapters 4 and 5 deal with (some of) Argentina's bouts with populism. In chapter 4, Federico A. Sturzenegger analyzes the Argentinian economic experience during the second Peronist administration of 1973–76. He points out that although this Argentinian episode fits our general paradigm, the different phases were extremely long. Sturzenegger shows that during this period a number of stabilization attempts—both abrupt and gradual—were initiated only to be rapidly abandoned. At the end, the Peronist experience had the fate of so many other episodes: political unrest and economic collapse. In a more general perspective, Roque Fernández looks in chapter 5 at the way in which recurrent episodes of populist expansive macroeconomic policies have affected the strategy to combat hyperinflation in that country. In his discussion Fernández deals with some important theoretical aspects of stabilization, including time consistency and credibility. He argues that the lack of credibility has indeed been related to Argentina's failed stabilizations. In chapter 6, Paulo Rabello de Castro and Marcio Ronci argue that modern Brazilian economic history can be better understood as the succession of populist governments. They contest the notion of a causal relationship going from poor income distribution to populist policies and that populism is related to macroeconomic disequilibrium. In their view, Brazil's traditional populism—Getúlio Vargas's brand of populism—was characterized by a marked absence of macroimbalances; according to them the main feature of Brazilian traditional populism was the reliance on very strong interventionist policies. According to the authors' interpretation, the inflationary saga of the last 35 years in Brazil has been the direct consequence of Vargas's populist and interventionist development strategy.

In chapter 7, Felipe Larraín and Patricio Meller analyze the economic policy of Allende's Chile (1970–73). They make a clear distinction between Allende's structural reform program—which had an important, if not dominant, socialist orientation—and his short-run macroeconomic policies. The latter, they claim, had important populist elements, and followed closely the euphoria to doom phases discussed by Dornbusch and Edwards.[1] Carlos Bazdresch and Santiago Levy evaluate, in chapter 8, Mexico's economic policy from the late 1950s through the eruption of the debt crisis in August of 1982, in the light of the populist paradigm. They argue that in contemporary Mexico there have been two populist episodes: the Cárdenas and the Echeverría–

1. R. Dornbusch and S. Edwards, "The Macroeconomics of Populism in Latin America," *Journal of Development Economics* 32, no. 2 (April 1990): 247–77.

Lopez Portillo administrations. They go on to show that the cycle of redistribution, growth, and economic collapse is largely applicable to these episodes. Indeed, the debt crisis, and its concomitant effects, is the most visible manifestation of the failure of these policies.

Chapter 9, by Ricardo Lago, deals with Peru's populist policies under Alán García. He shows how the motivation for policies, as well as their implementation, followed neatly the populist paradigm presented in this introduction. Lago also illustrates vividly the way in which populist goals handicapped, from the very beginning, every attempt to stabilize the economy and correct the most serious macroeconomic disequilibria. In chapter 10, Jose Antonio Ocampo evaluates the economic policy in Nicaragua under the Sandinista rule. As in the case of Allende's Chile, this experience provides a combination of socialist oriented reforms with classical populist macroeconomic management. However, the existence of armed conflict makes the analysis of the Sandinista experience diverge from other populist episodes.

Finally, in chapter 11, Miguel Urrutia analyzes the evolution of economic policy in Colombia in the last four decades. Urrutia forcefully argues that, contrary to most other Latin American countries, Colombia has not experienced populist policies. In making this point, he shows that the most important characteristics of populist regimes, as presented above in this introduction, have been absent in Colombia. In particular, he notes that inflation has not exhibited abrupt bursts, and that, since 1967, the real exchange rate has remained at a "realistic" and stable level without suffering overvaluation interludes. Urrutia argues that the absence of populism in Colombia can be explained by a number of political and institutional factors, including the existence of a well-established two-party political system, the clientelistic nature of politics, and the professionalism of civil servants engaged in economic advice.

I   The Framework

1 The Macroeconomics of Populism

Rudiger Dornbusch and Sebastian Edwards

Latin America's economic history seems to repeat itself endlessly, following irregular and dramatic cycles. This sense of circularity is particularly striking with respect to the use of populist macroeconomic policies for distributive purposes. Again and again, and in country after country, policymakers have embraced economic programs that rely heavily on the use of expansive fiscal and credit policies and overvalued currency to accelerate growth and redistribute income. In implementing these policies, there has usually been no concern for the existence of fiscal and foreign exchange constraints. After a short period of economic growth and recovery, bottlenecks develop provoking unsustainable macroeconomic pressures that, at the end, result in the plummeting of real wages and severe balance of payment difficulties. The final outcome of these experiments has generally been galloping inflation, crisis, and the collapse of the economic system. In the aftermath of these experiments there is no other alternative left but to implement, typically with the help of the International Monetary Fund (IMF), a drastically restrictive and costly stabilization program. The self-destructive feature of populism is particularly apparent from the stark decline in per capita income and real wages in the final days of these experiences.

Accounts of these populist episodes by sympathizers often highlight politics and, especially, external factors as central to the demise. We do not pretend to belittle these factors. There is no question in our minds that external destabilization can be an important part of the unraveling of an economic program. But we want to emphasize that the extreme vulnerability that makes destabilization possible is, by and large, the result of unsustainable policies.

Rudiger Dornbusch is the Ford International Professor of Economics at the Massachusetts Institute of Technology and a research associate of the National Bureau of Economic Research. Sebastian Edwards is the Henry Ford II Professor of Business Economics at the University of California, Los Angeles, and a research associate of the National Bureau of Economic Research.

This is one more reason to focus sharply on the *macro*economics of populist programs.

How can we explain this recurrence of mistakes and ill-conceived development strategies that span so many countries at different points in time? Is it just the lack of "memory" of policymakers, or is it, perhaps, a deeply rooted ignorance of the mechanics of economic populism? An alternative interpretation, based on the new political economy approach to economic policymaking, is that the engineers of these populist episodes have some kind of (dynamic) strategic considerations in mind.

Our purpose in organizing this conference was to bring together a group of experts on Latin America to analyze general systemic features of macroeconomic populism in Latin America and to document the regularities, and peculiarities, of a large number of populist episodes. The case studies collected in this volume show the striking similarity of populist policies in a score of Latin American countries. Policymakers in Argentina, Brazil, Chile, Mexico, Peru, and Nicaragua had comparable views on the objective conditions of their economies, on how they proposed that strongly expansionary policies should and could be carried out, and how they rationalized that constraints could be dealt with. More impressive perhaps, is the fact, so clearly illustrated throughout the volume, that in the end, foreign exchange constraints and extreme inflation forced, in every country, a program of violent real wage cuts that ended, in many instances, in massive political instability, coups, and violence. There is no doubt in our minds about the sincerity of the policymakers who embarked on these programs, and we share their concern for income distribution and poverty alleviation. It is, however, the very sincerity of these policymakers that makes the necessity of laying out exactly how and why the programs go wrong particularly urgent.

In this first chapter we present what we consider to be the most salient features of the populist paradigm, and we discuss the circumstances that lead policymakers to repeatedly undertake these type of policies in spite of abundant historical evidence on their harmful consequences.[1] Our emphasis is on the macroeconomics of populism, not because we think that other aspects of the phenomenon are uninteresting, but because we believe that it is in the macroeconomic sphere that populist experiences have been particularly weak. An earlier version of this paper was distributed to the different participants in this project and was used by most of them as a general framework in preparing their own contributions to the conference. In that regard, then, this chapter provides a somewhat unifying framework used by the majority of the authors.

1.1 The Populist Paradigm

Populism is, in many ways, a controversial concept. In fact, for many years political scientists have struggled to provide a meaningful and precise defini-

---

1. Parts of this chapter draw on our paper on the populist experiences of Peru and Chile. See Dornbusch and Edwards (1990).

tion. Drake (1982), for example, has emphasized three elements of a tentative definition: populism uses "political mobilization, recurrent rhetoric and symbols designed to inspire the people," it draws on a heterogeneous coalition aimed primarily at the working class, but including and led by significant sectors from the middle and upper strata, and, third, populism "has connoted a reformist set of policies tailored to promote development without explosive class conflict." He notes that the programs "normally respond to the problems of underdevelopment by expanding state activism to incorporate the workers in a process of accelerated industrialization through ameliorative redistributive measures" (p. 218).

Conniff (1982, p. 5) has argued that "populist programs frequently overlapped with those of socialism." We emphasize that the redistributive objective is the central part of the paradigm. Whether they are motivated by a strategy of massive social reform is important and consequential, but it is not central to our discussion.

For us "economic populism" is an approach to *economics* that emphasizes growth and income redistribution and deemphasizes the risks of inflation and deficit finance, external constraints, and the reaction of economic agents to aggressive nonmarket policies.[2] The purpose in setting out this paradigm is not a righteous assertion of conservative economics, but rather a warning that populist policies do ultimately fail; and when they fail it is always at a frightening cost to the very groups that were supposed to be favored. A central thesis we advance is that the *macro*economics of various experiences is very much the same, even if the politics differed greatly.

The most important features of the populist paradigm can be summarized as follows:

1. *Initial conditions.*—The populist policymakers—and the population at large—are deeply dissatisfied with the economy's performance; there is a strong feeling that things can be better. Typically, the country has experienced very moderate growth, stagnation, or outright depression as a result of previous stabilization attempts. This previous stabilization experience often, though not necessarily always, has been implemented under an IMF program and has resulted in reduced growth and lower living standards. In addition, a highly uneven income distribution usually presents a serious political and economic problem, providing the appeal for a radically different economic program. The preceding stabilization would generally have improved the budget and the external balance (through the accumulation of international reserves) sufficiently to provide the room for, though perhaps not the wisdom of, a highly expansionary program.

2. *No constraints.*—Policymakers explicitly reject the conservative paradigm and ignore the existence of any type of constraints on macroeconomic policy. Idle capacity is seen as providing the leeway for expansion. Existing international reserves and the ability to ration foreign exchange create addi-

---

2. See Sachs (1989) for a discussion of some aspects of populism in Latin America.

tional room for expansive policies without the risk of running into external constraints. The risks of deficit finance emphasized in traditional thinking are portrayed as exaggerated or altogether unfounded. According to populist policymakers, expansion is not inflationary (if there is no devaluation) because spare capacity and decreasing long-run costs contain cost pressures and there is always room to squeeze profit margins by price controls.

For example, the script for Peru's populism, *El Peru Heterodoxo: Un Modelo Economico* (Carbonetto et al. 1987, p. 82) notes: "An examination of the Peruvian record reveals that periods of moderate inflation are associated with expansionary fiscal policies. And periods of major inflation are associated with fiscal restraint. Thus, the record shows exactly the opposite of what is predicted by a theory which explains inflation by fiscal deficits." And:

> If it were necessary to summarize in two words the economic strategy adopted by the government starting in August 1985 they are *control* (meaning control of prices and costs and recognizing that this could be done only temporarily for the first twelve months) and *spend,* transferring resources to the poorest so that they increase consumption and create a demand for increased output, thus "justifying" that idle capacity be put to use.
>
> It is necessary to spend, even at the cost of a fiscal deficit, because, if this deficit transfers public resources to increased consumption of the poorest they demand more goods and it will bring about a reduction in unit costs, thus the deficit is not inflationary, on the contrary!

3. *Policy prescriptions.*—In light of the initial conditions described above, the populist programs emphasize three elements: reactivation, redistribution of income, and restructuring of the economy. The common thread here is "reactivation with redistribution." The recommended policy is to actively use macroeconomic policy to redistribute income, typically by large real-wage increases that are not to be passed on into higher prices. However, even if inflationary pressures do develop, the populist policymaker rejects devaluation because of a conviction that it reduces living standards and because it will have further inflationary impact without positively affecting the external sector. The economy is to be restructured to save on foreign exchange and support higher levels of real wages and higher growth. In Allende's Chile, Vuskovic (1973, p. 50) argued:

> The urgent need to achieve rapid recovery of the economy, and to extend the benefits to the mass of the working population, cannot be undertaken in isolation from the structural changes; they are all necessarily interdependent. It is not possible to make deeper changes without broadening the Government's political support, and economic reactivation and income redistribution will provide an impulse to these fundamental changes.

In Garcia's Peru, a strikingly similar program was articulated in the *Plan Nacional de Desarrollo, 1989–90:*

> The new economic policy seeks to pass from an economy of conflict and speculation to one of production and consensus. In this economy it is pos-

sible to make compatible stability, growth, distribution, and development in a context of national planning which finds concrete expression in dialogue and social and economic agreement. We need to reconcile economic efficiency with social equity in a productive system which is fundamentally sustained by domestic resources. (Presidencia de la Republica 1986, p. 63).

1.2   The Phases of Populist Economics

Once in power, and armed with the above paradigm, populist policymakers rapidly move to implement ambitious economic programs aimed at redistributing income, generating employment, and accelerating growth. Although each historical populist episode exhibits some unique features, it is still possible to distinguish four phases common to the vast majority of experiences.[3]

Phase 1.—In the first phase, the policymakers are fully vindicated in their diagnosis and prescription: growth of output, real wages, and employment are high, and the *macro*economic policies are nothing short of successful. Controls assure that inflation is not a problem, and shortages are alleviated by imports. The run-down of inventories and the availability of imports (financed by reserve decumulation or suspension of external payments) accommodate the demand expansion with little impact on inflation.

Phase 2.—The economy runs into bottlenecks, partly as a result of a strong expansion in demand for domestic goods, and partly because of a growing lack of foreign exchange. Whereas inventory decumulation was an essential feature of the first phase, the low levels of inventories and inventory building are now a source of problems. Price realignments and devaluation, exchange control, or protection become necessary. Inflation increases significantly, but wages keep up. The budget deficit worsens tremendously as a result of pervasive subsidies on wage goods and foreign exchange.

Bitar (1986, chap. 5) portrays very clearly the Chilean government's inability to control events, to shift from redistribution to accumulation: "It turned out to be very difficult to contain the forces unleashed in 1971. The sequential conception of redistribution followed by accumulation assumed that basic political and social conduct could be altered and popular expectations changed virtually instantaneously. In the next few months [early 1972] it proved impossible to apply this thinking with the facility that had been hoped for."

Phase 3.—Pervasive shortages, extreme acceleration of inflation, and an obvious foreign exchange gap lead to capital flight and demonetization of the economy. The budget deficit deteriorates violently because of a steep decline in tax collection and increasing subsidy costs. The government attempts to stabilize by cutting subsidies and by a real depreciation. Real wages fall massively, and policies become unstable. It becomes clear that the government is in a desperate situation.

---

3. Sturzenegger (1990) develops a dynamic intertemporal model that traces out the dynamics of populism described in this section.

Phase 4.—Orthodox stabilization takes over under a new government. More often than not, an IMF program will be enacted; and, when everything is said and done, the real wage will have declined massively, to a level significantly lower than when the whole episode began. Moreover, that decline will be very persistent, because the politics and economics of the experience will have depressed investment and promoted capital flight. The extremity of real wage declines is due to a simple fact: capital is mobile across borders, but labor is not. Capital can flee from poor policies, labor is trapped.

The ultimate dismantling is often accompanied by major political change, including violent overthrow of the government. The middle-class sanctions these developments because of the economic threat of populism. Rosenstein-Rodan (1974, p. 7) has captured this middle-class "legitimization" of the coup in the crass expression, "Salvador Allende died not because he was a socialist, but because he was an incompetent."

1.3   Policy Mistakes, History and Memory

With the exception of Colombia—where populist macroeconomic policies have been largely absent during the last four decades—the episodes with populist economics in Argentina, Brazil, Chile, Peru, Mexico, and Nicaragua, analyzed in this book, have followed quite closely the four phases we identify above. Although the final outcome of these experiments was not always the total collapse and destruction of the economy (as in Chile, Peru, and Nicaragua, for example), in all cases there were disastrous effects for those groups who were supposed to be the beneficiaries of the policies.

At the end of the road one cannot avoid wondering whether the mistakes of past populist regimes can be internalized by policymakers, politicians, and the population at large and, thus, be avoided in the future. Quite clearly, the detailed case studies collected here suggest that, in general, there is very little capacity (or willingness) of learning from other countries' experiences. Indeed, one of the most striking regularities of these episodes is the insistence with which the engineers of the populist programs argue that their circumstances are *unique* and thus immune from historical lessons from other nations.

A slightly different question, however, is whether countries have an economic and political *memory* that allows them to learn from their *own* mistakes. Recent developments in Chile, where the new democratic government that took power in March 1990 faced urgent and immediate pressures to improve the social conditions of the poor, provide some new light on this subject. Both the writings of the economic team of the new Chilean government, as well as the economic program of the governing coalition—which includes many of the parties in Allende's Unidad Popular, suggest that some of the more important lessons regarding the design of economic policy have indeed been absorbed in that country. The new authorities have, in fact, emphasized repeatedly the need to maintain fiscal balance and to pursue redistributional goals through focussed microeconomic policies.

The central question is whether populist policies are outright unsustainable, or whether there is a variant that, properly executed, can in fact succeed. We leave to further research the elaboration of the thesis that (short-term) expansionary policies can succeed provided they stay far clear of foreign exchange constraints, emphasize reactivation only for a brief initial period, and then shift to growth policies. Most important for success, expansionary policies need to be aware of capacity constraints and for their financing must rely on an extremely orthodox fiscal policy and rigorous tax administration.

References

Bitar, S. 1986. *Chile, Experiments in Democracy.* Philadelphia: Institute for the Study of Human Issues.

Carbonetto, D., et al. 1987. *El Peru Heterodoxo: Un Modelo Economico.* Lima: Instituto Nacional de Planificacion.

Conniff, M. 1982. *Latin American Populism in Comparative Perspective.* Albuquerque: University of New Mexico Press.

Dornbusch, R., and S. Edwards. 1990. The Macroeconomics of Populism in Latin America. *Journal of Development Economics* 32: 247–77.

Drake, P. 1982. Conclusion: Requiem for Populism? In *Latin American Populism in Comparative Perspective,* ed. M. L. Conniff. Albuquerque: University of New Mexico Press.

Presidencia de la Republica. 1986. *Plan Nacional de Desarrollo, 1986–1990.* Lima: Instituto Nacional de la Republica.

Rosenstein-Rodan, P. 1974. Why Allende Failed. *Challenge* 17 (May-June): 1–14.

Sachs, J. 1989. Social Conflict and Populist Policies in Latin America. NBER Working Paper no. 2897. Cambridge, Mass., March.

Sturzenegger, F. 1990. Fiscal Policies in an Open Economy: A General Equilibrium Approach. MIT. Mimeograph.

Vuskovic, P. 1973. The Economic Policy of the Popular Unity Government. In *The Chilean Road to Socialism,* ed. J. A. Zammit. Austin: University of Texas Press.

2

The Political Economy of Latin American Populism

Robert R. Kaufman and Barbara Stallings

The crisis of the 1980s has brought into stark relief the economic and political limitations of populist policy cycles, in which governments seek to spur economic growth by the expansion of domestic demand and the redistribution of income. Such approaches have been recurrent features of Latin American political economies since the 1930s. Although moderate versions have arguably played a positive role in fostering industrialization, they sooner or later run into serious external bottlenecks. In their more radical incarnations—those, for example, associated with Perón, Allende, and Alán García—they have led to major (and predictable) economic and political collapse. These are characterized by very high levels of inflation, stagnation of growth and exports, capital flight, and political polarization.

There are four questions that need to be asked about populist policy cycles in Latin America. (1) Why have they been so prevalent in Latin America, as opposed to other parts of the world? (2) What accounts for variations in the intensity and frequency of populist policy cycles within Latin America? (3) What accounts for persistence in these policy cycles over time, notwithstanding predictable limitations? Under what conditions is there a "learning process" that can lead to positive modifications in such approaches or to the adoption of others? (4) What are the prospects for the future? Have populist cycles ended and, if so, why?

2.1 Definitions: The Economic and Political Context of Populism

Before beginning to address these questions, we need to make clear what we mean by populism. Our definition is more specific than most others; it

Robert R. Kaufman is professor of political science at Rutgers University. Barbara Stallings is professor of political science at the University of Wisconsin–Madison.

The authors would like to thank Paul Drake and Alberto Alesina for helpful comments on an earlier draft of this chapter.

involves a set of *economic policies* designed to achieve specific *political goals*. Those political goals are (1) mobilizing support within organized labor and lower-middle-class groups; (2) obtaining complementary backing from domestically oriented business; and (3) politically isolating the rural oligarchy, foreign enterprises, and large-scale domestic industrial elites. The economic policies to attain these goals include, but are not limited to: (1) budget deficits to stimulate domestic demand; (2) nominal wage increases plus price controls to effect income redistribution; and (3) exchange-rate control or appreciation to cut inflation and to raise wages and profits in nontraded-goods sectors.

To further specify our definition, a few additional comments may be helpful. First, we are referring to the political and economic characteristics of *governments,* not just to isolated *policies* or to the *movements* or parties associated with political leaders.[1] Second, the political characteristics of the alliances described eliminates "right-wing populism," whether of the Reagan or Latin American military variety.[2] The definition also excludes from consideration certain historical populist experiences with a rural focus. In fact, it should be emphasized that we are referring specifically to Latin American versions of populism in the twentieth century. Third, we are including here both "classical" and "new" populism, to use the distinction put forward by Cardoso and Helwege (in this volume). We are not saying that the set of macroeconomic policies discussed are the only policies followed, nor are we specifying the ultimate goals of the governments.[3]

Using our definition, it is possible to rank and compare various experiences of Latin American populism. One attempt to do so is shown in table 2.1. The cases included are Salvador Allende (Chile, 1970–73), Juan Perón (Argentina, 1973–76), Alán García (Peru, 1985–90), José Sarney (Brazil, 1985–90), Luis Echeverría (Mexico, 1970–76), and Carlos Andrés Pérez (Venezuela, 1974–78). The table suggests that Allende, Perón, and García rank high on both the political and economic components of populism. Echeverría and Pérez represent less intense populist episodes. Sarney is in-between; his economic policies are more like the first group, but his political alliance was more similar to that of Echeverría and Pérez.

In the Allende, Perón, and García periods, labor and other low-income

---

1. This distinction was introduced by Paul Drake of the University of California, San Diego, one of the commentators on an earlier version of this paper at the conference held at the Inter-American Development Bank, Washington, D.C., May 18–19, 1990.

2. The notion of right-wing populism is suggested in Williamson (1990, p. 3).

3. Cardoso and Helwege (in this volume) also draw a distinction between populism and "socialism," claiming that Allende's Chile and Sandinista Nicaragua should not be considered populist. While we agree with them about Nicaragua (although because of its policies and the war, rather than the supposed socialist character of the government), we strongly disagree about Chile. Regardless of the ultimate goals of the Allende government, even its own participants did not claim the government was socialist but "preparing for a transition to socialism." More important, as a way of increasing political support, a multiclass coalition was sought and distinctly populist policies were followed.

Table 2.1   Latin American Governments Ranked according to Populist Tendencies

	Political Goals			Economic Policies		
Government	Labor Base	Business Alliance	Anti-oligarchy, Foreign Capital	Budget Deficits	Wage Increase/ Price Controls	Overvalued Exchange Rate
Allende (1970–73)	+ +	+	+ +	+ +	+ +	+ +
Perón (1973–76)	+ +	+	+	+ +	+ +	+ +
García (1985–90)	+ +	+	+ +	+	+ +	+ +
Sarney (1985–90)	+	+ +	+	+ +	+ +	+
Echeverría (1970–76)	+	+ +	0	+	+	+ +
Pérez (1974–78)	+	+ +	0	+	+	+ +

Note: + + = very important/large; + = moderately important/large; 0 = not important/large. Entries represent peak of populism during given presidential period

groups constituted the primary support base of the governments in power. This reflected the historical origins of the parties or coalitions led by Perón (*Justicialista*) and Allende (Socialist and Communist). The APRA (Alianza Populara Revolucionavia Americana), García's party, has a more complicated history. It was never the main representative of organized labor, but García, as a candidate of the party's left wing, attracted much labor and "popular-sector" support from outside the party. Within the parties themselves, there were already substantial numbers of white-collar workers and professionals. Beyond this inherent multiclass character, the decision was made to seek support from most domestically oriented business. These were broad coalitions that targeted only a small group as being outside: the largest domestic business firms with close international ties ("the monopolies," as they were labeled in Allende's Chile), foreign business itself, and the landed oligarchy. It was clearly recognized that these cross-class alliances would place limits on the policies that could be followed, but their numbers were necessary to win elections. Thus the macroeconomic policies of all three governments focused on the populist elements outlined above. The package of budget deficits, nominal wage increases, and controls was designed to produce growth and distributive effects that would appeal to the disparate elements of the coalitions.

Both economic and political factors distinguished Echeverría and Pérez from the three governments just discussed. Their coalitions were of the same multiclass type, but the relative weight of the popular class and business elements varied. Specifically, business groups were more dominant, while labor was relatively weaker. The negative targeting of big business/foreigners/oligarchy *in general* was not very important, although specific actions were directed against individual elements of these groups. For example, Pérez nationalized the oil industry, and Echeverría encouraged takeovers of large farms in certain regions. In terms of macroeconomic policies, the same package of measures was followed, but demand stimulation was weaker in Mexico and Venezuela.

In economic as well as political terms, Sarney fell between the two groups of governments just discussed. The business/labor relationship in Brazil was similar to that in Mexico and Venezuela. In terms of the "enemy," however, it should be noted that Sarney not only initially advocated an agrarian reform (from which he later retreated), but Brazil also initiated a moratorium on debt payments at two points during the Sarney administration. Macroeconomic policies during the Sarney administration were similar to those of Allende, Perón, and García with respect to budget deficits and wage increases, although the exchange rate was never allowed to become as overvalued.

Why these coalitions and policies? Our primary hypothesis is that populism is rooted in the distributive political struggles that have characterized Latin America since the beginning of the century. Although such distributive struggles are ubiquitous in the region, variations in institutional arrangements across countries and time periods determine the extent to which they are expressed through populist policies. A move away from populism seems to have occurred in the late 1980s, but we have doubts about how to interpret this trend. On the one hand, despite the fact that most governments have abandoned populism, important groups in society still support such policies. On the other hand, populist politics—where workers play a key role—seem to have been displaced by struggles among sectors of capital. Although the macroeconomic results are superficially similar, the processes are quite different and require more analysis.

2.2 Latin American Social Structure: Class and Sectoral Inequalities

Most countries of Latin America are distinguished from those of other regions by two sets of structural characteristics, each rooted in the formation of strong traditional export oligarchies during the second half of the nineteenth century.[4] The first is a very high concentration of income and assets. Table 2.2 shows the differences in income distribution in comparison to some of the principal Asian countries. It suggests that income inequality is two and a half times as great in Latin America. The average ratio between the highest and lowest quintiles of household income is 21.1 in Latin America and only 8.7 in East Asia.

The second structural feature is a sharp division between employers and workers in industry and services versus the primary products export sector controlled by the traditional oligarchy. Sectoral antagonisms became particularly pronounced after the 1930s, when the shocks of the Depression encouraged an acceleration of the import-substitution industrialization (ISI) processes begun earlier in the century, and paved the way for the formation of influential new development doctrines—widely associated with the UN Economic Commission for Latin America—which emphasized inward-oriented strategies of development. At the same time, the capacity of most export oligarchies to block significant land reforms meant that, in contrast to countries such as Korea and Taiwan, the political weight of urban popular groups was not typically counterbalanced by the presence of a large class of independent farmers or small export-oriented manufacturing firms.[5]

Sharp class and sectoral divisions may encourage populist policy approaches in several ways. In the first place, there is probably some link between income/asset inequality and redistributive pressures on the government, although objective disparities in income rarely constitute a very satisfying explanation for the mobilization of such pressures.[6]

A more important aspect of highly unequal societies is that upper-income groups are generally in a good position to resist direct taxation. This has

4. Similar points are raised by Sachs (1989).
5. For comparisons of the situation in Latin America and East Asia, see Haggard (1990) and Gereffi and Wyman (1990).
6. On the relationship between income distribution and politics, see Dahl (1971, pp. 81–105).

Table 2.2   Comparison of Income Distribution in Latin America and East Asia[a]

Countries	Lowest Quintile	Highest Quintile	Ratio
Latin America:			
Argentina	4.4	50.3	11.4
Brazil	2.0	66.6	33.3
Chile	4.5	51.3	11.4
Colombia	2.8	59.4	21.2
Costa Rica	3.3	54.8	16.6
Ecuador	1.8	72.0	40.0
Mexico	4.2	63.2	15.1
Panama	2.0	61.8	31.0
Peru	1.9	61.0	32.1
Trinidad/Tobago	4.2	50.0	11.9
Uruguay	4.4	47.5	10.8
Venezuela	3.0	54.0	18.0
Average	3.2	57.7	21.1
East Asia:			
China	7.0	39.0	5.6
Hong Kong	6.0	49.0	8.2
Korea	6.6	49.4	7.5
Malaysia	3.5	56.0	16.0
Philippines	3.9	53.0	13.6
Singapore	6.5	49.2	7.6
Taiwan	8.8	37.2	4.2
Thailand	5.6	49.8	8.9
Average	6.0	47.5	8.7

Source: Adapted from Sachs (1989, table 1).
[a]Based on national household surveys in the late 1960s or early 1970s

placed a major limit on the capacity of Latin American governments to deal with distributive pressures within the context of growth-oriented export models. In small open European economies, for example, the expansion of the welfare state has been an important political concomitant of liberal trade policies. Transfer payments negotiated through corporatist bargaining institutions have typically been employed to even out the differential gains and losses associated with economic adjustments to shifts in the international market (e.g., see Katzenstein 1984, 1985). Since Latin American states had much more limited capacity to tax income and assets directly, such open-economy welfare state models were far less feasible. During the 1930s and 1940s, it was politically easier to turn to ISI, rather than welfare transfers, in order to protect politically mobilized working- and middle-class constituencies from international market shocks, notwithstanding the higher economic costs.[7]

Urban-oriented populist policies, in turn, can be linked directly to the sharp sectoral divisions that emerged within the context of ISI and the primary ex-

7. On the issue of sectoral clashes in general, see Mamalakis (1969, 1971).

port sector. Although there is no *necessary* connection between populism and ISI, and the latter was accompanied by fairly orthodox macroeconomic policies in some instances (e.g., Chile and Colombia in the 1960s), in practice there usually has been a link. On the one hand, ISI provided the intellectual justification for policies that, if carried to extremes, resulted in populism. For example, the emphasis on the domestic market justified large wage increases and higher government spending. In addition, high tariffs and/or overvalued exchange rates were allowed in order to protect the new industries.

On the other hand, the industrialization process itself created groups that supported such policies. The ISI industries, together with the public sector, provided the main source of employment for the groups in the best position to mobilize distributive pressures against the government in power: the urban middle classes and blue-collar unions. As producers of nontraded goods, these groups could capture substantial short-term gains from policies that combine fiscal expansionism and an overvalued currency. Since small groups dominate commodity exports in Latin America, governments seeking popular support had relatively little to lose in the short term by policies that transfered income from the traded goods sector, even though the export elites frequently passed the costs of such policies onto the unorganized rural workers under their control.

Class and sectoral divisions may suggest some important answers to the question of why populist policies appear more frequently in Latin America than in other regions, but they do little to account for cross-national or over-time differences within Latin America itself. There is little or no intraregional correlation between populist policy cycles and income distribution. Such cycles have been more frequent in societies with relatively equal income distributions, such as Argentina and Uruguay, than in countries with greater income concentration, such as Colombia and Venezuela.

A focus on sectoral divisions, rather than class conflict, provides a somewhat better fit with populist experiences. In the cases of Argentina and Uruguay, several familiar aspects of the traditional wheat and livestock sectors have exacerbated conflicts with groups in services and ISI. Since export proceeds are generated by only a small fraction of the total population, they offer an especially tempting target for urban-oriented politicians. Moreover, since wheat and livestock are also important wage goods, the distributional effects of exchange-rate policy are almost immediately evident to the urban population.[8] Nevertheless, intense populist policy cycles have also been played out in countries with very different types of export structures (e.g., Allende's Chile) as well as in societies with comparatively large rural populations (e.g., Brazil under Sarney or Peru under Alán García).[9]

8. For an analysis of these relationship in the Argentine case, see O'Donnell (1978).

9. See accounts of Allende, Sarney, and García in Larraín and Meller (in this volume), Rabello de Castro and Ronci (in this volume), and Lago (this volume). See also the comparative analyses by Sachs (1989) and Dornbusch and Edwards (this volume).

To understand more fully the conditions under which governments adopt populist policies, we need to look at the institutional mechanisms through which characteristics of the social structure are translated into political behavior and policy choice. We examine the impact of two of these in the following sections: the influence of the party system and of political regime in determining cross-national differences in the intensity and frequency of populist policies.

2.3   Party Systems and Cross-national Differences in Populist Policies

Party systems in Latin America vary widely across countries, sometimes reflecting regional, religious, or personal conflicts that date back to the late nineteenth or early twentieth century. A full elaboration of the historical origins or contemporary workings of these systems would take us well beyond the scope of this essay.[10] For our purposes, however, the crucial question to ask is the extent to which long-term partisan alignments offer incentives for politicians to attempt to form anti-elite coalitions of unions, white-collar employees, and import-substituting industrialists. We argue that these incentives are relatively weak in systems where one or two multiclass parties have provided governmental elites with stable electoral majorities. They have been much stronger in societies where popular-sector groups have been linked to parties that have been systematically excluded from electoral competition and/ or in multiparty systems where competing political elites are unable to organize stable electoral majorities.[11]

Systems characterized by stable electoral blocs include Mexico's dominant party system and those of Colombia and Venezuela, where two parties have either shared power or rotated in office for the last several decades. In Mexico, the dominant party, the PRI (Partido Revolucionario Instituto) has until very recently encompassed virtually all sectors of the electorate and maintained close organizational links to the union movement. The two-party systems in Venezuela and Colombia also aggregate a wide range of interests, although in somewhat different ways. In Venezuela, the AD (Accion Democratica) and COPEI each incorporate similar multiclass electoral constituencies and, like the Mexican PRI, maintain close links to the labor movement. This has encouraged the two parties to adopt roughly similar macroeconomic approaches and has reduced broad swings in policy when governments change hands. In Colombia, the more traditional Liberal and Conservative parties have much weaker ties to the organized labor movement than the parties in either Mexico or Venezuela and are much more extensively influenced by economic elites. As in the other two countries, however, each of the major parties maintains

10. For such a historical analysis, see Collier and Collier (1990). We have relied heavily on this volume for descriptions of party systems.
11. Arguments in this section parallel those in Haggard and Kaufman (1990).

strong electoral roots among popular-sector voters, whose partisan allegiances have been passed on from one generation to the next.[12]

A second pattern is one in which substantial portions of the popular-sector
support parties are periodically barred from entering the electoral competition
by economic and military elites. The most important examples in this category are the Perónists in Argentina and the Aprista party in Peru.[13] Even during periods of civilian government, these parties frequently suffered prolonged military bans on electoral participation and/or winning control of the
presidency. Because these parties had gained the allegiance of broad portions
of the electorate, the bans—or the ongoing threat of them—made it virtually
impossible to establish systems based on stable governing majorities.[14]

The final pattern is one in which fractionalization of the system into a large
number of narrowly based parties impedes the formation of stable governing
coalitions. The Chilean party system, with its sharp ideological divisions,
falls into this category. Prior to the military coup of 1973, shifts in coalitional
alignments caused control of the presidency to shift between the right, center,
and left. Brazil's multiparty system provides a second example, although in
this case, regionalism and personal political rivalries have weighed much
more heavily in the divisions among the parties.[15]

The Uruguayan system, finally, should be mentioned as a special case that
combines several of the patterns discussed above. On the one hand, as in Colombia and Venezuela, two multiclass parties, the Colorados and Blancos,
have traditionally dominated electoral contests. At the same time, the "double
simultaneous voting system" has allowed both of these parties to field three or
four presidential candidates, who frequently represented widely divergent
policy positions.[16] By the early 1970s, moreover, a new center-left coalition,
the Frente Amplio, had begun to make major advances as a third electoral
force, especially within the capital city of Montevideo.[17]

It is not surprising that Argentina, Chile, Brazil, and Peru—the systems
with exclusionary and/or unstable multiparty patterns—have been the countries most prone to populist policy cycles. Several of these cycles (Allende,

12. For an analysis of political parties in Mexico, Venezuela, and Colombia, see the following
sources, respectively: Levy and Szekely (1987), Levine (1989), and Hartlyn (1988).

13. It should also be noted that there have been extended bans on left or populist parties in other
systems as well—including the Chilean Communists between 1948 and 1958 and the Brazilian
Communists from 1946 to 1964. Unlike the Perónists and the Apristas, however, these were more
narrowly based parties that would not have been able to capture the presidency or to dominate the
legislature if they had been allowed to run.

14. Peronism and the APRA are discussed, respectively, in Rock (1987) and Bonilla and Drake
(1989).

15. On parties in Chile and Brazil, see Cavarozzi and Garretón (1989, pp. 139–242, 335–465).

16. The double simultaneous voting system functions as a primary and general election rolled
into one. Voters select both a party and competing candidates within the party. The candidate with
the most votes of the party with the most votes becomes president.

17. On parties in Uruguay, see Cavarozzi and Garretón (1989, pp. 243–96).

Perón, García, and Sarney) have been discussed earlier in this paper and elsewhere in this volume, but there have been many others as well—including the first Perón government in Argentina, Vargas and Goulart in Brazil, Ibáñez in Chile, and Velasco in Peru.

Several types of political incentives help to account for these tendencies. On the one hand, for the leaders of periodically excluded multiclass parties such as the Perónists and the Apristas, broad distributive appeals to workers and industrialists have been a way to mobilize the support necessary to regain entry into electoral politics and to consolidate power on occasions in which they have been allowed to take office. More narrowly based working-class parties such as the Chilean Communists and Socialists face similar incentives. Cross-class distributive appeals to middle-sector groups and industrialists were perceived by many leaders of Allende's Popular Unity government as crucial means of avoiding political isolation and stabilizing the governing coalition. Finally, in highly fragmented multiparty systems such as Brazil's, one or more of the competing segments of the divided "political class" typically faces a strong temptation to strengthen its electoral position by appealing to the distributive interests of politically available working-class groups.

Political leaders in countries with more stable electoral blocs have sometimes engaged in similar strategies. Compared to Argentina, Brazil, Chile, and Peru, however, populist politicians in these systems have generally had a harder time winning office and face greater constraints when they do arrive. It is more difficult for populist challengers to win office precisely because they must compete within the framework of broadly based governing parties that already claim substantial support among working-class voters. Once in office, political leaders such as Echeverría or Pérez, who are inclined to cultivate popular-sector support, face opposition within their own ruling coalitions from factions that seek closer ties with economic elites. A brief survey of the macroeconomic experiences of these countries illustrates these points.

Venezuela experienced a brief period of distributive populism under Carlos Andrés Pérez in the mid-1970s; since the late 1970s, however, both AD and COPEI governments have exercised tight monetary and fiscal controls. Indeed, since his reelection to the presidency in 1989, Pérez himself has backed very tough stabilization policies and a wide-ranging program of liberal reforms in the Venezuelan economy.[18] In Colombia, traditionally cautious fiscal and monetary policies were challenged by the nearly successful populist campaign of Gustavo Rojas Pinilla in 1970 as well as by the demand-expansion policies initiated by Belisario Betancur in the early 1980s. Nevertheless, with both major parties still heavily influenced by coffee and financial elites and a high priority on consensus, macroeconomic policy has been consistently more conservative than in most of the other countries.[19]

18. Populist policies under Carlos Andrés Pérez are analyzed in Karl (forthcoming).
19. Economic policies in Colombia, and the absence of populism, are discussed in Urrutia (in this volume).

Mexico has exhibited more extensive political polarization and policy swings than Colombia and Venezuela, but these have still been relatively mild compared to those of the South American populists. Expansionist policies pursued under Echeverría—intended to deflect growing left-wing militancy among unions, students, and the peasantry—did lead to serious macroeconomic disequilibria during the 1970s. After 1982, however, the capacity of the PRI to dominate both the electorate and organized labor made it possible for more orthodox factions of the party to engineer a sharp change in policy direction without major political upheavals. Such a shift might possibly have come even earlier if the oil boom of 1978–1981 had not temporarily alleviated the exchange crisis of the mid-1970s.[20]

Long-term macroeconomic experience in Uruguay, finally, appears to reflect the complex mix of features within its party system. On the one hand, institutionalized factionalism within each of the major parties made it difficult for civilian governments of the 1950s and 1960s to deal effectively with inflationary pressures and external accounts problems rooted in conflicts between agro-export elites and urban-based popular-sector groups. By 1973, these conflicts had culminated in political polarization and a military coup. On the other hand, the nonideological character of the two major parties does appear to have had an effect on economic policy. From the early 1950s to the 1973 coup, all civilian presidents represented centrist or right-wing factions of their respective parties. Although none was able effectively to stabilize the economy, none systematically used expansionist policies to mobilize support from a popular-sector coalition. Centripetal tendencies within the major parties also appear to have played a role during the democratic transition of the 1980s. Centrist factions predominated in both parties in the presidential contest of 1984, and there was a greater emphasis on wage and fiscal restraint than was the case during comparable transitions in Argentina and Brazil.[21]

2.4   The Role of Political Regimes and Regime Change

We consider the nature of the principal sociopolitical cleavages in society, as reflected in the political party system, to be the single most important factor in explaining differences in populist tendencies across Latin American countries. Nevertheless, the rules that govern political interaction—such as type of political regime, characteristics of institutions, and timing of elections (if any)—are also important. They can reinforce the influence of party structure; they can also temporarily mute it. As will be discussed in the next section, however, these rules are more easily changed than the cleavages themselves. Of course, the two are not completely independent, as seen in the Uruguayan case, but it is usually possible to separate their role for the purposes of analysis.

20. On economic policies in Mexico, see Bazdresch and Levy (in this volume).
21. Uruguayan policies are discussed in Noya and Rama (1988).

In the Latin American context, observers have tended to separate political regimes into the categories "authoritarian" and "democratic." In an earlier study, we found it useful to add the category of "transitional democracies" (Kaufman and Stallings 1989). We defined authoritarian regimes as those that do not permit competitive elections; they restrict the space allowed to either oppositional or interest group activity. Democratic regimes, by contrast, were characterized as ones where a government must win and retain power through competitive elections, tolerate opposition challenges to its incumbency, and deal with relatively independent interest groups. A transitional democracy is one that has recently changed from authoritarian to democratic; several turn-overs of government need to be accomplished before a democracy can safely be considered as consolidated.

An authoritarian regime affects a political system by preventing underlying divisions from manifesting themselves for a certain period. Elections can be suspended, parties and interest groups outlawed, and congress closed. Also the conditions that led to a military intervention (the most frequent type of authoritarian regime) can themselves submerge societal divisions in the short run. Under these circumstances, populist policies are unlikely, since the government is not primarily reliant on public support. Nevertheless, the end of an authoritarian period may produce populist-like policies aimed at softening the military's reputation before they return to the barracks.[22]

In the longer run, an authoritarian regime will inevitably be replaced, leading to a transitional democracy. There are several reasons why a transitional democracy will be especially susceptible to populist policies. First, authoritarian regimes (and thus transitional democracies) are most likely to occur in countries with exclusionary or unstable multiparty systems, which have already been identified with populist tendencies. Second, transitional democracies face considerable pent-up economic demand from their constituents. Third, in the new democracies, institutional uncertainties tend to shorten the time horizons of both the incumbent governments and their opponents. For such governments, there is a premium for meeting distributive expectations early in the administration and a substantial discount for the political risks attached to later problems with the balance of payments and inflation. Institutional uncertainty and shortened time horizons likewise affect the calculus of opposition political parties and other economic actors. Without some expectation that they will be able to share in future gains from growth, it may make sense for labor and other popular-sector groups to seek "unrealistic" nominal wage gains even if they know that these will later be wiped out by inflation.

Finally, like authoritarian systems, consolidated democracies are less likely than transitional democracies to experiment with populism. The reasons are

---

22. Argentina in 1982–83 would be an example of this phenomenon. It should be pointed out, however, that these are populist *policies*, not a populist *government*. The political coalition of the Argentine military clearly did not resemble a populist coalition.

essentially the opposite of those prevailing in transitional situations. Consolidated democracies tend to be found in systems with stable governing electoral blocs; by definition, abrupt changes of regime are less likely. Also, with longer time horizons, it may pay for a newly elected president to impose unpopular policies early in his or her term in order to reap the political payoffs of later success. Moreover, unlike an authoritarian regime, a consolidated democracy does not rely as heavily on satisfying material demands, since its legitimacy derives from political as well as economic factors.

Some empirical support for these propositions was found in our study referred to above. At least for the 1980s, we found a high correlation between type of regime and choice of economic policies. These relationships are shown in table 2.3. The analysis showed that authoritarian regimes (Chile and Mexico) were most likely to choose orthodox macroeconomic policies and to take significant steps toward liberalization and privatization. Established democracies (Venezuela, Colombia, and Costa Rica in our study) were also associated with orthodox macro policies but did little with respect to structural change. It was the transitional democracies (Peru, Argentina, and Brazil) that followed populist policies. Uruguay was the exception to our analysis. It was a transitional democracy but behaved more like the consolidated democracies. Our explanation was focused on the nature of the political system, a two-party system, similar to those of Venezuela, Colombia, and Costa Rica.

2.5   Repetition of Populist Cycles and Problems of Political Learning

Countries vary not only with respect to the intensity of populist policy cycles, but with respect to the recurrence of those cycles. As suggested above, Argentina, Chile, Brazil, and Peru have each experienced several episodes that approximate the populist policy cycles outlined by Dornbusch and Edwards, whereas other countries discussed in this essay have experienced no more than one. The most severe episodes, in terms of macroeconomic disequilibria and political polarization, are listed in table 2.4. The table does not include a fairly large number of briefer or less extreme populist initiatives—for example, those of Frondizi in 1958 or Alfonsín in 1984.

Such patterns are not necessarily immutable. In principle, they may change either because social actors learn from earlier experiences and/or because they are forced to adapt to new conditions in the present. In the final section, we examine the influence of some of the comparatively new international conditions that emerged during the decade of the 1980s. Here we offer some hypotheses about the possibilities for learning from the past.

There are two variants of the argument that the lessons drawn from earlier experiences can eventually bring an end to populist policy cycles. The first is that repeated iterations of cycles in which "everyone loses" will eventually encourage more cooperative attempts to find nonpopulist policy alternatives. The second relates to the severity of the cycles: support for macroeconomic

Table 2.3 Economic Policies by Type of Regime in Latin America, 1980s

Country	Administration Dates	Political Regime Type	Stabilization Type	Trade Liberalization	Relations with International Monetary Fund (IMF) and Banks
Chile	Pinochet, 1982–90	Authoritarian	Orthodox	Substantial	Collaborative
Mexico	de la Madrid, 1982–88	Authoritarian	Orthodox	Substantial	Collaborative
Costa Rica	Monge, 1982–86 Arias, 1986–90	Established democracy	Moderate orthodox	Limited	Collaborative with IMF, but suspended interest payments
Venezuela	Lusinchi, 1984–89	Established democracy	Moderate orthodox	Limited	Broke with IMF, but collaborative with banks
Colombia	Betancur, 1982–86 Barco, 1986–90	Established democracy	Moderate orthodox	Limited	Broke with IMF, but collaborative with banks
Brazil	Sarney, 1985–90	Transitional democracy	Heterodox	None	Broke with IMF, moratorium
Peru	Belaunde, 1980–85	Transitional democracy	Moderate orthodox	None	Broke with IMF, moratorium
Argentina	García, 1985–90 Alfonsín, 1983–89	Transitional democracy	Heterodox Moderate heterodox	None None	Broke with IMF, moratorium Collaborative with IMF, but suspended interest payments
Uruguay	Sanguinetti, 1985–89	Transitional democracy	Moderate orthodox	Limited	Collaborative

Source: Robert Kaufman and Barbara Stallings. 1989. Debt and Democracy in the 1980s: The Latin American Experience. In *Debt and Democracy in Latin America*, ed. Barbara Stallings and Robert Kaufman, p. 211. Boulder, Colo: Westview.

Table 2.4   Populist Episodes in Eight Latin American Countries

High Populist Countries	Low Populist Propensities
Argentina	Colombia
Perón (1946–55)	Betancur (1982–86)
Perón (1973–76)	
Brazil	Mexico
Vargas (1951–54)	Echeverría (1970–76)
Goulart (1961–64)	
Sarney (1985–90)	
Chile	Venezuela
Ibáñez (1952–58)	Pérez (1974–78)
Allende (1970–73)	
Peru	Uruguay
Belaunde (1963–68)	Batlle (1954–58)
Velasco (1968–75)	
García (1985–90)	

discipline is likely to be greater if the consequences (or perceived consequences) of populist policies have been especially bad.

Although both of these hypotheses are plausible, the empirical support for them is ambiguous. In Chile since 1984, there are preliminary indications that some social learning has occurred. Most of the major party leaders of the Left and Center have indicated that they intend to avoid the mistakes of the Allende years by adopting a much more cautious macroeconomic approach. "Social learning," however, does not account fully for these changes in orientation. The changes must also be explained in terms of the global and regional pressures that have operated throughout Latin America during the 1980s, and— even more important—by the structural changes imposed during the Pinochet era. The latter include a severe economic weakening of the urban-industrial base of leftist support, and the emergence of new commercial-agricultural groups with strong interests in the maintenance of export-led growth models.[23]

In other countries, particularly prior to the 1980s, there is even less evidence that past experiences in themselves have been sufficient inducements for changes in policy orientation. Neither the Perónist episodes in Argentina nor the experience with Goulart in Brazil inoculated those countries against the subsequent resurfacing of populist "temptations." The same is true with respect to the relation between Velasco in the early 1970s and Alán García a decade later.

What have been the impediments to more effective long-term adjustments in policy behavior? Before turning in the next section to conditions that might diminish the likelihood of repeated populist cycles, it is important to highlight

23. On political changes in Chile, see Cavarozzi and Garretón (1989, pp. 395–465).

several factors that have contributed to a maintenance of the pattern. First, and most obvious, many of the same political and institutional factors that help to explain the intensity of populist policy episodes have also encouraged their recurrence. The possibility of new rounds of populism has been highest in systems where severe electoral rivalries encourage an emphasis on redistributive issues and/or the exclusion of partisan adversaries. Similarly, where tenure insecurities have limited the time horizons of governments, officials have tended to discount heavily the longer-term costs of populist policy choices.

The second concerns the way in which social actors have perceived the alternatives to populist macroeconomic policies. Although some countries (e.g., Colombia) have had considerable success with mixed economy models, a great deal of the ideological debate in Latin America has focused on the relative merits of more orthodox approaches urged by international lending agencies and developed-country governments. Evidence about the positive social welfare effects of this alternative, however, has been mixed at best and has in general provided governments with very little incentive for abandoning comparatively activist fiscal and monetary policies. The most notable exception is Chile where—despite the extraordinary hardships imposed under Pinochet—the post-1984 recovery did contribute to a reorientation of economic policy perspectives. In most cases (including Chile itself), the most visible short-term effect of this alternative has been to transfer resources from urban wage earners to exporters and financial elites.[24]

Finally, it should not be surprising that iterations of populist/orthodox policy cycles have been as likely to reinforce self-fulfilling zero-sum assumptions as to encourage a convergence around common welfare interests. Especially in countries like Argentina, the historical record itself has placed competing sociopolitical groups in prisoner's dilemma situations, in which the groups must choose between the possibility of achieving mutual gains from cooperative behavior and the high costs they must bear if they cooperate and others defect. Even after repeated iterations, there is no single "equilibrium solution" to this game. It may be just as rational to seek short-term distributive advantages as to collaborate in support of more disciplined fiscal and monetary policies.

2.6   Prospects for the Future

What are the possibilities that such vicious circles can be reversed over a longer time period? Events in the last few years suggest a changing policy climate in the region. On the one hand, voters in a number of countries have elected leaders who openly ran on antipopulist platforms. These would include Aylwin in Chile, Collor in Brazil, Lacalle in Uruguay, and Chamorro in

24. Negative outcomes of orthodoxy are analyzed in Sheahan (1987), Pastor (1987) and Weeks (1989).

Nicaragua. On the other hand, several new presidents who had been expected to follow populist policies—Meném in Argentina, Pérez in Venezuela, Manley in Jamaica, and Borja in Ecuador—changed their stance once in office. It appears that Fujimori in Peru will do the same. But how enduring are these policy trends, and what are the chances that they will continue to receive public support?

Within the international system, there have been changes at both the economic and ideological levels that have reduced the viability of populist policies operating within an ISI framework. The most important economic change is the cutoff of external finance to Latin American governments. The availability of public-sector funds in the 1960s, and especially private bank loans in the 1970s, made it possible for governments to run trade and budget deficits. When this financing dried up following the Mexican crisis of August 1982, they had to choose between populist policies and debt service. It is not surprising that the choices generally followed the pattern outlined earlier. That is, Mexico, Venezuela, Colombia, and Uruguay squeezed their populations in order to maintain debt service, while Brazil, Argentina, and especially Peru took the opposite path. The exception was Chile, whose military government had made substantial changes in that country's political alignments and economic policy choices in comparison with the Allende administration and earlier years.[25]

The change in material conditions was reinforced by a significant shift in the intellectual climate in many parts of the world during the 1980s. The most important was in the United States, where the Reagan government not only changed U.S. priorities (or at least rhetoric) but also put pressure on other governments to carry out tight fiscal and monetary policies as well as to limit the role of the public sector. The U.S. voice in the international financial institutions was influential in forcing similar policies to be incorporated into those institutions' programs for Third World countries. At least as important, however, was the demonstration effect of different parts of the Third World. As Latin America and Africa became mired in recession with no end in sight, the Asian newly industrialized countries (NICs) suffered only small fluctuations in their growth patterns and then continued their upward trajectories. Although it was recognized that some misrepresentations were being made in the analysis of the policies followed in Asia, it was nevertheless clear that populism and ISI were much less prevalent in that region. The lesson extracted was that the latter two characteristics were responsible for many of Latin America's problems.[26]

A second important change has been the shift in the intellectual and political discourse within Latin America itself in favor of greater fiscal restraint,

25. On different responses to the debt crisis, see Frieden (1989).
26. On the East Asian cases and the lessons drawn by Latin America, see Haggard (1990) and Gereffi and Wyman (1990).

trade liberalization, and privatization. Although this shift was conditioned by the international developments just discussed, by the end of the 1980s it had been buttressed by sharp contrasts in the experience of specific countries within the region itself. On the one hand, in Chile, where the Pinochet government had pursued highly orthodox economic strategies, there was substantial growth and comparatively low inflation after 1984. Conversely, new democratic governments in Argentina, Brazil, and Peru had all engaged in heterodox experiments aimed at protecting popular-sector incomes, and these countries were mired in the worst economic crises in their modern history. Although the policy implications are far from clear, lessons have nevertheless been drawn.

Among competing economic interests, finally, there have been important changes in access to resources and new divisions that cut across old class and sectoral lines. Even before the debt crisis, the liberalization of capital markets had opened up major new opportunities for the growth of the financial sector. At the same time, although there is still considerable uncertainty about the distributional consequences of the debt crisis, the cutoff of external financing appears to have seriously weakened important components of popular-sector coalitions. Public employees have generally been hit hard, with wages declining at a faster rate than in the private sector. Business groups that are especially dependent on state subsidies or contracts have also been particularly disadvantaged. Such changes alter the balance of power among segments of union and business organizations and diminish the capacity of such organizations to mobilize strong political opposition to market-oriented adjustments. The weakening of "rent-seeking" groups, in turn, increases the political latitude available for governments seeking to push through stabilization measures and market-oriented reforms.

What does this analysis suggest about future outcomes? There seem to be four possible scenarios on the horizon. First, the market-oriented policies might yield significant improvements in growth rates, employment opportunities, and price stability over the medium run. If this were to happen, public support for such policies would increase. For long-run stability and continuity, of course, it would still be necessary to mobilize the beneficiaries into political support groups and to establish institutional arrangements within which they could operate.

Even if reasonably positive results do occur in terms of growth, however, opposition is likely to increase if the benefits are distributed in a very skewed manner. This was clearly part of the reason for the defeat of the military government and its presidential candidate in Chile. A second strategy, then, is a set of policies that maintain the emphasis on balanced accounts and competitiveness but place equal weight on policies geared toward increased equity. These include social policies as well as wages and benefits. The potential support for such a coalition is vast, but the economic policies would be extremely difficult to manage.

If the new market-based policies do not produce positive medium-term results, opposition will increase and, in spite of the weakening of the traditional support bases of populism, a return to populist cycles could occur in at least some countries. In the recent Brazilian presidential election, the candidate of the left, running on a very traditional populist platform, was only narrowly defeated by the antipopulist Fernando Collor. And in Mexico, Cuauhtémoc Cárdenas, also running on populist principles, mobilized the most serious electoral challenge ever launched against a candidate of the dominant PRI. Whether such candidates, once in office, would actually implement populist policies cannot be determined in advance. Like Meném and Pérez, they might betray the voters' expectations. If they did try to implement populist policies, the situation could quickly degenerate into chaos as seen in recent years in Peru.

New populist experiments in a world where international finance is not readily available is one route to a fourth alternative: a disintegration of civil society and a steady deterioration in the capacity of state authorities to frame and implement policy alternatives of any sort. In circumstances where popular-sector groups have been badly weakened, and a coalition around market-based policies has not been mobilized, this final alternative cannot be ruled out. At the present time, contemporary Peru perhaps best approximates this situation—although it is by no means the only country where it could happen. As the 1990s begin, the problems faced by this society is rooted not so much in conflicts between populism and orthodoxy as in the institutional fragmentation of parties and political coalitions, atomized competition among business groups, and self-fulfilling bets against the government's capacity to control prices or guarantee order. In other words, the problem is no longer class or sectoral conflict, but a decline in the capacity for collective action of any sort.

Prediction about the relative likelihood of the four scenarios for the region as a whole is impossible. On the contrary, it seems clear that Latin America will see ever-greater differentiation among countries. Indeed, each of the scenarios is likely to appear somewhere in the region. For any individual country, the situation will depend on political organization as well as economic outcomes.

References

Bonilla, Heraclio, and Paul Drake, eds. 1989. *El APRA: De la ideología a la praxis.* Lima: Nuevo Mundo.
Cavarozzi, Marcelo, and Manuel Antonio Garretón, eds. 1989. *Muerte y resurreción: Los partidos políticos en el autoritarianismo y las transiciones del Cono Sur.* Santiago: FLACSO.

Collier, Ruth Berins, and David Collier. 1990. *Shaping the Political Arena: Critical Junctures, Trade Unions and the State in Latin America.* Princeton, N.J.: Princeton University Press.

Dahl, Robert A. 1971. *Polyarchy: Participation and Opposition.* New Haven, Conn.: Yale University Press.

Frieden, Jeffry. 1989. Winners and Losers in the Latin American Debt Crisis: The Political Implications. In *Debt and Democracy in Latin America,* ed. Barbara Stallings and Robert Kaufman. Boulder, Colo.: Westview.

Gereffi, Gary, and Donald Wyman, eds. 1990. *Manufacturing Miracles: Patterns of Development in Latin America and East Asia.* Princeton, N.J.: Princeton University Press.

Haggard, Stephan. 1990. *Pathways from the Periphery: The Politics of Growth in Newly Industrializing Countries.* Ithaca, N.Y.: Cornell University Press.

Haggard, Stephan, and Robert Kaufman. 1990. The Political Economy of Inflation and Stabilization in Middle Income Countries. Working Paper no. 444. Country Economics Department, World Bank.

Hartlyn, Jonathan. 1988. *The Politics of Coalition Rule in Colombia.* Cambridge: Cambridge University Press.

Karl, Terry. Forthcoming. *The Paradox of Plenty: Oil Booms and Petro-States.* Berkeley and Los Angeles: University of California Press.

Katzenstein, Peter J. 1984. *Corporatism and Change: Austria, Switzerland and the Politics of Industry.* Ithaca, N.Y.: Cornell University Press.

————. 1985. *Small States in World Markets: Industrial Policy in Europe.* Ithaca, N.Y.: Cornell University Press.

Kaufman, Robert, and Barbara Stallings. 1989. Debt and Democracy in the 1980s: The Latin American Experience. In *Debt and Democracy in Latin America,* ed. Barbara Stallings and Robert Kaufman, pp. 201–33. Boulder, Colo.: Westview.

Levine, Daniel. 1989. Venezuela: The Nature, Sources, and Prospects of Democracy. In *Democracy in Developing Countries: Latin America,* ed. Larry Diamond, Juan Linz, and Seymour Martin Lipset. Boulder, Colo.: Lynne Rienner.

Levy, Daniel C., and Gabriel Szekely. 1987. *Mexico: Paradoxes of Stability and Change.* Boulder, Colo.: Westview.

Mamalakis, Marcos. 1969. The Theory of Sectoral Clashes. *Latin American Research Review* 4 (3):9–46.

————. 1971. The Theory of Sectoral Clashes and Coalitions Revisited. *Latin American Research Review* 6 (3):89–126.

Noya, Nelson, and Martín Rama. 1988. *La política económica en la transición democrática: Uruguay (1982–1987).* Montevideo: CINVE.

O'Donnell, Guillermo. 1978. State and Alliances in Argentina, 1956–76. *Journal of Development Studies* 15.

Pastor, Manuel, 1987. *The International Monetary Fund and Latin America: Economic Stabilization and Class Conflict.* Boulder, Colo.: Westview.

Rock, David. 1987. *Argentina, 1516–1982: From Spanish Colonization to the Falklands War,* rev. ed. Berkeley and Los Angeles: University of California Press.

Sachs, Jeffrey, 1989. Social Conflict and Populist Policies in Latin America. NBER Working Paper no. 2897. Cambridge, Mass.

Sheahan, John. 1987. *Patterns of Development in Latin America* Princeton, N.J.: Princeton University Press.

Weeks, John, ed. 1989. *Debt Disaster? Banks, Governments, and Multilaterals Confront the Crisis.* New York: New York University Press.

Williamson, John. 1990. *The Progress of Policy Reform in Latin America.* Washington, D.C.: Institute of International Economics.

Comment   Paul W. Drake

To understand the political economy of populism in Latin America, it is necessary to explore the forces driving that phenomenon. Robert R. Kaufman
and Barbara Stallings provide an excellent beginning for that task. Their work
can be complemented with a longer historical perspective. As they suggest,
Latin American populism cannot be explained as an irrational set of self-
destructive economic measures to redistribute income through deficit spending. Behind those policies is a political logic that propels the emergence and
recurrence of populist programs despite the cautionary advice of orthodox
economists.

Historical Definition

Populism is not new in Latin America. To the contrary, the heyday of populism is past. Historically the term referred to a reasonably definable category
of political actors and proposals. To illuminate that record and its current manifestations, it is important to distinguish among populist movements, policies,
and governments.[1]

Populist Movements

As a political movement, populism has been quite common since World
War I and will continue to surface in some countries. Prime examples would

Paul W. Drake is the Institute of the Americas Professor of Political Science and History at the
University of California, San Diego.

1. For standard sources on Latin American populism, see Michael L. Conniff, *Latin American
Populism in Comparative Perspective* (Albuquerque, N.M., 1982); Torcuato Di Tella, "Populism
and Reform in Latin America," In *Obstacles to Change in Latin America*, ed. Claudio Veliz
(London, 1965), pp. 47–74; Thomas Skidmore, "A Case Study in Comparative Public Policy:
The Economic Dimensions of Populism in Argentina and Brazil," *The New Scholar* 7 (1979):129–
66; Jeffrey Sachs, "Social Conflict and Populist Policies in Latin America," NBER Working Paper
no. 2897 (Cambridge, Mass., 1989); Rudiger Dornbusch and Sebastian Edwards, "Macroeco-
nomic Populism in Latin America," NBER Working Paper no. 2986 (Cambridge, Mass., 1989);
Guillermo O'Donnell, *Modernization and Bureaucratic-Authoritarianism* (Berkeley, Calif.,
1973); Fernando Henrique Cardozo and Enzo Faletto, *Dependency and Development in Latin
America* (Berkeley, Calif., 1979); Guita Ionescu and Ernest Gellner, *Populism: Its Meaning and
National Characteristics* (New York, 1969); Ernesto Laclau, *Politics and Ideology in Marxist
Theory: Capitalism, Fascism, Populism* (London, 1977); Aníbal Quijano and Francisco Weffort,
Populismo, marginalización y dependencia (San Jose, Calif., 1973); Francisco Weffort, *O popu-
lismo na política brasileira* (Rio de Janeiro, 1978); A. E. Van Niekerk, *Populism and Political
Development in Latin America* (Rotterdam, 1974); Octavio Ianni, *A formaçao do estado populista
na América latina* (Rio de Janeiro, 1975) and *Crisis in Brazil* (New York, 1970); Paul W. Drake,
Socialism and Populism in Chile, 1932–52 (Urbana, Ill., 1978); Heraclio Bonilla and Paul W.
Drake, *El APRA de la ideología a la praxis* (Lima, 1989); Steve Stein, *Populism in Peru* (Madi-
son, Wis., 1980). Rafael Quintero, *El mito del populismo en el Ecuador* (Quito, 1980); Candido
Mendes, *Beyond Populism* (Albany, N.Y., 1977); Christopher Mitchell, *The Legacy of Populism
in Bolivia* (New York, 1977); Robert J. Alexander, *Prophets of the Revolution* (New York, 1962);
Lars Schoultz, *The Populist Challenge: Argentine Electoral Behavior in the Postwar Era* (Chapel
Hill, N.C., 1983).

include Victor Raúl Haya de la Torre and the American Popular Revolutionary Alliance (APRA) in Peru from the 1920s to the 1970s, the Chilean Socialist party in the 1930s, Jorge Eliécer Gaitán in Colombia in the 1940s, Rómulo Betancourt and Democratic Action in Venezuela prior to the 1950s, and some aspects of the campaigns of José María Velasco Ibarra in Ecuador over several decades. Most of these movements were characterized by three key features: (1) paternalistic, personalistic, often charismatic leadership and mobilization from the top down; (2) multiclass incorporation of the masses, especially urban workers but also middle sectors; and (3) integrationist, reformist, nationalist development programs for the state to promote simultaneously import-substituting industrialization and redistributive measures for populist supporters.

These three essential ingredients of populism were logically interconnected. Ideally, a charismatic leader welded together a polyclass coalition to compromise on the coterminus expansion of industry and social welfare. Such a movement fitted the historical circumstances and structural conditions in highly agrarian countries that had not yet used the government significantly to foment industry and to assimilate emergent urban groups into national politics. Populism provided a coherent political response to the dislocations caused by the increasing tempo of industrialization, social differentiation, and urbanization.

By the same token, such movements might be expected still in the poorer countries of Latin America that have not advanced very far in the elaboration of national industry and an inclusive political system, for example, in Central America. It will still be tempting for politicians to create a new constituency by galvanizing the urban underprivileged. Elsewhere, echoes of populism may reverberate in nations that have already gone through such experiences, because of the continuing inadequacies of development and the maldistribution of income. Populist rhetoric and promises retain widespread appeal, as seen with the electoral surge of Cuauhtémoc Cárdenas in Mexico in 1988 and Luís Inácio da Silva ("Lula") in Brazil in 1989.

In countries that have already had a lengthy history of populism, however, "bait-and-switch" populists have now become more common. They reflect the contradiction today between the immiseration of the majority of the population and the imperatives for neoliberal economic restructuring to favor market mechanisms and to honor the foreign debt. These putative populists awaken hopes of massive redistributionist policies on the campaign trail but implement free-market austerity packages once in office. "Baiters and switchers" may sincerely desire to revive an emphasis on social justice, but current resource constraints frequently consign such plans to the dustbin. Recent examples would include Carlos Andrés Pérez in Venezuela, Michael Manley in Jamaica, Rodrigo Borja in Ecuador, Jaime Paz Zamora in Bolivia, and Carlos Meném in Argentina.

Populist Policies

Like Populist movements, populist policies have been fairly common in the twentieth century. A certain set of initiatives and instruments has become associated with populist attempts to ram through rapid industrialization and redistribution. Traditional populist policies have included tariff protection and subsidized credits for industry, discrimination against agriculture and exports, wage hikes, deficit spending, and proliferation of state planning, employment, and welfare agencies. However, some combinations of these policies have also been tried by many Latin American governments without a populist leadership, social base, or reform agenda; they have been enacted for reasons other than the incorporation of neglected urban sectors, including foreign exchange constraints, revenue shortages, and pressures from organized interest groups. Although the policy outcomes may have been quite similar, the policy causes were quite different.

Populist Governments

In contrast with populist movements or policies, full-blown populist governments with a magnetic inspirational leader, a multiclass urban clientele, and a hothouse program to raise domestic demand and production have been rarer. The classic models are Argentina under Juan Perón (1946–55, 1973–76), Brazil in the democratic period of Getúlio Vargas and his heirs (1951–64), and Peru under Alán García (1985–90). Other contenders might include many facets of Lázaro Cárdenas in Mexico in the 1930s, the Popular Front in Chile before World War II, the National Revolutionary Movement in Bolivia in the 1950s, and Juan Velasco in Peru, 1968–75.

The quintessential populist administrations have undergone fairly predictable experiences. They enjoyed a couple of years of successful redistribution and expansion through Keynesian deficit spending. That buoyant moment was followed by demand exceeding supply, as investment and growth declined because of bottlenecks constricting capital, government revenues, and foreign exchange. As a result, deficits and inflation ballooned, eroding the initial gains for the poor. While scarcities dimmed the luster of the popular leader, conflicts erupted among his or her multiclass backers, especially between industrialists and laborers. On the heels of the spiraling economic and political crisis often came authoritarian repression of popular expectations, demands, and mobilization. The state clamped down on the lower classes in order to facilitate macroeconomic stabilization, government austerity, and capital reaccumulation for renewed growth. Although failing to achieve their higher objectives, populists bequeathed a residue of greater industrial capacity and enhanced leverage for organized labor. Moreover, the memories of their early good years, in contrast with the harsh period that followed, left a reservoir of popular support.

These populists must be differentiated from superficially similar nonpopulist cases. Neither more leftist governments pursuing socialist aspirations nor more rightist administrations failing to hold the line on deficits and inflation really belong in the populist camp. Their policies are not a result of reformist movements energized by efforts to accelerate capitalist industrialization and worker integration.

Salvador Allende in Chile (1970–73) led a socialist, not a populist, movement and government, though he employed some populist policies his first year. He sought to move the country toward socialism, not just to reform the capitalist system to incorporate workers. Allende's leadership was neither paternalistic nor charismatic. His social base concentrated far more on the working class than any multiclass movement, stretching from dissident industrialists to the lumpenproletariat; class conflict was far more pronounced than class collaboration. Allende's government preferred to expropriate, not foment, industry. Whereas populism signifies redistribution of income, socialism denotes redistribution of property and wealth.

José Sarney of Brazil (1985–90) is an even more unlikely candidate for any pantheon of populists. This accidental president was scarcely the fiery champion of an aggressive mass movement dedicated to economic modernization and social justice. Rather, Sarney was a conservative who proved too weak to impose a stabilization program in the face of concerted opposition from vested interests and international circumstances. His inability to surmount the economic crisis of the 1980s was not due to his dedication to populist forces. Sarney's style, coalition, and objectives were a far cry from those of true Brazilian populists like João Goulart and Leonel Brizola.

Historical Phases

Latin American populism has gone through three stages: early, classic, and late. The "early" populists appeared in the opening decades of the twentieth century in the more prosperous countries. As the strains of urban growth eroded upper-class hegemony, populist precursors protested insufficient state attention to disaffected elites, emergent middle classes, and, to a lesser extent, nascent labor groups. These moderate leaders advocated liberal reforms to open up aristocratic political systems to greater participation for the literate few. Examples would include Arturo Alessandri in Chile and Hipólito Irigoyen in Argentina.

Populism flourished following the disruptions of international trade by World War I, the Great Depression, and World War II. In the aftermath of those shocks, discontent with laissez-faire economics and with exclusionary political systems swept the more advanced republics of the hemisphere. The traditional oligarchic order faced a fourfold crisis of growth, distribution, participation, and legitimation. Populism responded to that crisis with industrialization, state welfare, worker mobilization, and mass support for the government.

During the 1930s and 1940s, the "classic" populists took center stage. Compared to their predecessors, they were more dedicated to the urban working class and to socialistic visions of government reform. Their programs mainly resulted in state capitalist promotion of industry and urban welfare. They relied on renegade elite leadership and cooperation, especially from industrialists, intellectuals, and the middle class. For some elites, the costs of excluding segments of the working class—strikes, protests, ideological radicalization, and so on—seemed to exceed the costs of including them through mild reforms. Populists mobilized, enfranchised, and incorporated previously marginal lower-class groups (particularly urban workers) and continued to exclude others (particularly peasants). These classic populists proved most successful when periods of growth generated temporary surpluses after periods of recession and austerity.

After the heady days from the 1930s to the 1960s, populism waned in the leading countries for several reasons. The relatively easy stage of replacing manufactured consumer goods from abroad was exhausted. At the same time as economic resources tightened, the number of organized and voluble contenders—rural-urban migrants, peasants, women, and so on—for incorporation and redistribution multiplied. In several countries, privileged groups concluded that the costs of including the masses—inflation, property transfers, and the like—exceeded the costs of excluding them; many elites opted for expelling previously incorporated lower-class elements from the crowded political arena. Populist coalitions among industrialists and workers unraveled. Rightist groups lashed populists as demagogues who spurred excessive mass expectations and inflation. At the same time, leftists denounced populists as charlatans who duped the workers into settling for reform instead of revolution.

Into this unpropitious environment in the 1970s and 1980s strode "late" populists like Luis Echeverría in Mexico, Juan Perón in Argentina, and Alán García in Peru. They found it increasingly difficult to revitalize the populist alliances and programs of earlier years. The network of entrenched interests and demands had become too thick, the state too cumbersome and burdened, the economy too inefficient, inflation too relentless. Repressed in some countries, spurned in others, populism became less viable as a governing formula, even when it retained favor as an electoral device.

As the 1980s unfolded, populist governments, except for the anachronistic APRA administration in Peru, did not exercise power, despite rumblings at the ballot box. Almost regardless of who got elected president, populist policies were discredited and discarded in most of the hemisphere. As Kaufman and Stallings point out, there are several reasons for the paucity of populist administrations in the eighties and nineties.

The recession of the early 1980s, the debt crisis, and the perceived need for market-oriented restructuring to reignite growth have convinced most leaders that resources are inadequate for swift redress of income inequalities. At the same time, import-substituting industrialization and other policies once promulgated by the UN Economic Commission for Latin America have been eclipsed by neoliberal economic formulas. Free enterprise solutions modeled after the East Asian success stories are in vogue. It has become fashionable and virtually unavoidable to reduce government interference with domestic and international markets. Partly as a result of those economic transformations, the long-standing enemies of populism—capitalist and export elites—have been strengthened, while the stalwarts of populism—organized labor and the urban masses—have been weakened. Furthermore, after years of authoritarian repression of labor and the left, reformist politicians have tried to restrain populist impulses so as not to capsize democratization. Consequently, populism seems unlikely to sweep the Americas anytime soon.

So long as populism is in retreat, the most pressing issue in the 1990s is not how to stamp out the vestiges. Rather, the key question is how to address, better than populism did, the burning issues of severely unequal distribution without sacrificing growth and stability. The problem is how to bridge the gap between the political, electoral logic of speaking to the desperate needs of the deprived majority and the economic, governing logic of adhering to the requirements of investors and entrepreneurs. In democratic political systems, the trick is to design a new winning coalition that can sustain equitable growth. Today, most of Latin America is plagued with poverty, not populism.

Comment   Alberto Alesina

Robert Kaufman and Barbara Stallings have written an interesting paper that emphasizes the effects of income inequality on political polarization and on populist experiments. I quite agree with their approach. In fact, in my view, explaining populism amounts to explaining why is it that economic policy in Latin America has been so polarized; that is, why we observe major swings in the orientation of economic policy in this part of the world.

A crucial characteristic of populist experiments is the use of macroeconomic policy to achieve redistributional goals in favor of certain social groups. Thus, it is not surprising that these experiments are often followed by reactions against those same groups when the latter lose political control. Kaufman and Stallings argue that this political polarization arises from

Alberto Alesina is the Paul Sack Associate Professor of Political Economy at Harvard University, research fellow of the National Bureau of Economic Research, and research fellow of the Center for Economic Policy Research.

income inequality: this phenomenon would explain important differences between Latin American and Asian countries. However, as the authors themselves acknowledge, income inequality alone cannot account for the differences in policy experiments in different Latin American countries.

As additional explanations, the authors refer to various kinds of institutional arrangements. One question, which is not sufficiently addressed in this respect, is whether these institutional arrangements are exogenous or endogenous. More specifically, are these arrangements themselves a function of various socioeconomic forces, such as income inequality, or do they affect the socioeconomic characteristics of different countries? Perhaps the answer is that both directions of causality are important. Examples of institutional characteristics that may affect economic policy-making include different kinds of electoral rules (say, the degree of proportionality of the electoral system, which may affect the degree of fragmentation of the party system), the existence of constitutional rules that are institutionally difficult to change (say, because they require qualified majorities in the legislature), systems of checks and balances between various branches of government, and the degree of independence of the Central Bank.

Different degrees of political polarization can also be the result of different histories. A country history may be the result of two types of equilibria. One is the cooperative equilibrium: when a party or group is in office, it does not pursue extreme redistributive policies, expecting that its opponents will do the same (i.e., they will be moderate) when they will be in office in the future. In the noncooperative equilibrium this implicit cooperation is broken, and when a group controls policy, it pursues radical redistributions, knowing that an economic "revenge" will follow, when political power changes hands. When a country is trapped in the noncooperative equilibrium, it may be very hard to move away from it, since one group has to begin to act in a "moderate" way, even though history indicates that its adversaries have never been cooperative. Different institutional arrangements, such as those mentioned earlier, may affect the likelihood that a country is trapped or not in the noncooperative equilibrium.

The basic problem that underlies much of the discussion on political polarization, is that these radical swings of policy, back and forth, from and toward populism, imply aggregate inefficiencies. It is worthwhile to summarize why it is that political polarization leads to losses in aggregate welfare. Three related arguments can be made.

1. *Political polarization leads to high uncertainty about future policies or even about property rights.* This, in turn, leads to difficulties in making long-run economic decisions such as investments in plants and equipments. Instead, economic agents may find it more profitable to engage in capital flights. The latter reduce taxable resources in the country, leading to a worsening of the fiscal situation. As the fiscal crises deteriorate, political struggle over the distribution of the tax burden may become even harsher, leading to even more

political polarization and instability. The potential for vicious cycles are very clear.

2. *In a noncooperative political equilibrium, politicians view their horizon as short.* They know that when they will be out of office their opponents will show "no mercy." Thus, policymakers may try to redistribute resources not only from currently taxable resources, but they will also borrow abroad to distribute resources to their supporting constituencies. Future governments will be left with the debt burden; in the meantime, the beneficiaries of the foreign borrowing can take advantage of it and may even shelter their resources from future taxation. Note that these kinds of short-sighted partisan policies are not necessarily the prerogative of populist governments, but also of right-wing governments. During the tenure of the latter, one often observes at the same time public borrowing and private capital flight.[1]

3. *Political polarization may lead to costly delays in adjustment to adverse shocks, and to repeated failed stabilization attempts.*[2] If, in the aftermath of an adverse shock, countries need to pursue costly stabilization policies, different politically powerful groups may disagree on the allocation of the burden of the adjustment. In a politically polarized country, these groups may find it hard to agree on a mutually acceptable division of the burden. Instead, they may engage in political struggles to shelter themselves from all or most of the stabilization costs and make the other groups pay for the adjustment. Successful stabilizations are then delayed until one of the groups consolidates its political influence and makes it impossible for its opponent to "veto" its desired stabilization plan. Lacking cooperation, time is needed to resolve the noncooperative "war" over who should pay for the adjustment. Needless to say, in most cases, the more one country waits to stabilize, the higher are the aggregate costs of the stabilization when it is finally implemented. In many cases, these delays take the form of monetary financing of budget deficits in a situation in which a political deadlock makes it impossible to raise noninflationary taxes or cut expenditures.

These views are consistent with the finding of the paper by Kaufman and Stallings that the countries that experienced the largest economic difficulties are transitional democracies. These are in fact cases in which political uncertainty, polarization, and unresolved political struggles between groups are particularly important.

I will close with a general remark concerning the usefulness of the political economy approach. A question is often asked in the discussion of populist experiences, and more generally in the discussion of Latin American economic difficulties: Why is it that certain countries keep repeating the same "mistakes" and never learn? In fact, once the political and institutional incen-

---

1. For a formal discussion of this case, see Alberto Alesina and Allan Drazen, "Why are stabilizations delayed?" NBER Working Paper no. 3053 (Cambridge, Mass., 1989).

2. This case is argued by Alberto Alesina and Guido Tabellini in "External debt, capital flight and political risk," *Journal of International Economics* 27 (November 1989):199–220.

tives and constraints are correctly taken into account, policies that appear to be mistakes are perfectly rational responses to distorted or imperfect political incentives. The political economy approach attempts to explain why certain apparent mistakes repeatedly occur. This approach underscores that one cannot correct the "mistakes" without addressing the institutional features which make these so-called mistakes likely to occur.

3   Populism, Profligacy, and Redistribution

Eliana Cardoso and Ann Helwege

3.1   Introduction

Recent bouts of economic instability, originating in overexpansion and ending in hyperinflation, led economists to describe regimes in power during the past decade in Latin America as populist. Certainly Sarney, Alfonsín, García and the Sandinistas have overseen inflation caused by budget deficits and balance-of-payments crises. The macroeconomic imbalances of these governments show strong similarities with the economic record of Perón, Vargas, and Goulart, three leaders traditionally identified as populists. Yet one should think twice about generalizing the term. Although recent regimes have failed to rein in budget deficits, the economic strategies they pursued and their underlying motivations display considerable heterogeneity and are quite distinct from past populism. This paper discusses these differences.

Why debate terminology? There are lessons that recent leaders should have learned from traditional populists. The most basic is that failure to adjust to constraints imposed by the balance of payments and the internal productive capacity will lead to inflation and disaster (Harberger 1970). Yet, the early warning signs, evident in rhetoric and specific policies, have varied widely. If we broadly identify the disease and lump, ex post, all inflationary failures into the category of populism, we will not understand ex ante the development of crises and avert them. Moreover, because populism is associated with redistribution (although not toward the poorest), it is important to clarify when and why redistribution can lead to inflation.

We begin by describing classical populism, as it has been viewed by Latin

Eliana Cardoso is associate professor of international economic relations at the Fletcher School of Law and Diplomacy, Tufts University, and faculty research fellow of the National Bureau of Economic Research. Ann Helwege is assistant professor at the Urban and Environmental Policy Department, Tufts University.

45

Americanists over the past four decades (Archetti, Cammack, and Roberts 1987) and use the Argentine experience between 1945–52 to illustrate it. We then describe the new economic concept of populism, put forth by Sachs (1989), Dornbusch (1988), and Dornbusch and Edwards (1989). Their analyses stress the repeated willingness of Latin American regimes to push demand beyond economic bounds. We then examine specific cases of populism discussing the diversity of situations. We emphasize that there are at least three distinct roots of inflationary finance:

• excessive optimism about the potential for rapid growth through demand stimulation and inward-looking industrialization, as seen in the Peruvian experience under García;
• market-based socialism, which causes insecure property rights and triggers intervention from the United States and larger defense budgets, as observed in Nicaragua in the 1980s;
• the inability to impose the burden of contractionary adjustment on various groups, as in Brazil after the oil shock and debt crisis.

Far from providing a compelling indictment of redistribution efforts, the history of populism makes conspicuous the paucity of genuine redistribution programs in Latin America. Most regimes failed to target the poor. Urban workers in the informal sector did not benefit from populist increases in the minimum wage, nor did social programs concentrate resources on the indigent. The rural poor suffered both from a deterioration in agriculture's terms of trade and a failure to implement land reform with adequate credit and technical assistance.

3.2 Classical Populism

Social scientists (Baily 1967; Conniff 1982; Germani 1978; Hamilton 1980; Hennessy 1976; Malloy 1977; and Stein 1980) traditionally associate populism with policies pursued by Perón in Argentina between 1946 and 1949, by Vargas in Brazil after 1945, by Cárdenas in Mexico between 1934 and 1940, and by Velasco in Peru between 1968 and 1975.

We refer to these episodes as classical populism, an urban political tradition that opposed the primary-product-export-oriented status quo of the nineteenth century and endorsed accelerated industrial development. It constructed alliances linking the working class to the industrial bourgeoisie and minimized interclass antagonisms through the propagation of a broadly nationalist ideology.

Classical populism favored activist governments committed to a strong role in price determination, to protection of workers and wages, to policies of cheap food, to state ownership of key industries, to state allocation of credit at low interest rates, and to favors for private industry. It rejected any appeal to the need for overall restraints on spending. The consequences were an extensive growth of government relative to the private sector and the pervasiveness of corruption in varied forms, including tax evasion. Growing budget deficits resulted in rising dependence on foreign savings. Import substitution associated with trade restrictions resulted in dependence on foreign capital. The urban bias of economic policy and resource allocation resulted in dramatic rural poverty.

Economists and political scientists from right and left have emphasized the negative sides of populism. The right attacks populists as demagogues who fuel inflation, frighten capital, and provoke political instability. The left accuses them of betraying the masses. But it was not part of populist programs to carry out a social revolution, as in Allende's Chile or Ortega's Nicaragua. Populists hoped to reform the system, not to overthrow it. Their program was to deliver economic growth based on industrialization as the path to sustained employment. Overwhelmed by their mistakes, we now tend to forget the successful role played by import-substitution industrialization (ISI) in Latin American extravagant growth rates, which averaged more than 5 percent per year between 1950 and 1980 (table 3.1). It is worthwhile asking whether there were viable alternatives to the populist import-substitution industrialization of the 1940s and 1950s. Right-wing, coercive regimes in the 1970s did not provide political development, economic growth, and social justice. Neither did socialist governments.

ISI was the pragmatic answer to the problems following the Great Depression of the 1930s and the disruption of the Second World War. Later, structuralists, cepalists, reformists, and developmentalists conceived the economic models that justify the import-substitution strategy pointing to the inadequacy of market mechanisms alone to achieve industrialization (Prebisch 1976; Singer 1984). They built their arguments on two pillars:

- They called attention to the foreign exchange constraint as an important determinant of growth. In a world where the terms of trade moved against traditional primary export products, domestic production would have to substitute for nonessential imports, freeing foreign exchange for the needed inputs. Moreover, while technical progress in agriculture would leave labor unemployed, industry could absorb the growing population with increasing productivity and incomes. Expanding domestic production required protection against imports.
- In the microeconomic sphere, they stressed imperfections and discontinuities, both of which impeded effective operation of price signals. Whether in agriculture, where land concentration was notorious, or in industry, where new privileges provided shelter from market forces, the competitive model was flawed.

These conditions supported a strong state presence. Development was a consequence of policy, not the result of natural evolution (Cardoso and Fish-

Table 3.1   Per Capita Gross Domestic Output and Growth Rates of Latin American Countries[a]

	Share in Total Population, 1980 (%)	GDP per Capita (1975 Dollars)		Growth Rate of GDP per Capita (% per year)	
		1950	1980	1950–80	1981–89[b]
Brazil	35.6	637	2,152	4.2	.0
Mexico	20.2	1,055	2,547	3.0	−.9
Argentina	8.0	1,877	3,209	1.8	−2.4
Colombia	7.5	949	1,882	2.3	1.4
Venezuela	4.3	1,811	3,310	1.5	−2.5
Peru	5.1	953	1,746	2.1	−2.5
Chile	3.2	1,416	2,372	1.8	1.0
Uruguay	.8	2,184	3,269	1.4	−.7
Ecuador	2.3	638	1,556	3.1	−.1
Guatemala	2.0	842	1,422	1.8	−1.8
Dominican Republic	1.7	719	1,564	2.6	.2
Bolivia	1.6	762	1,114	1.3	−2.7
El Salvador	1.3	612	899	1.3	−1.7
Paraguay	.9	885	1,753	2.4	.0
Costa Rica	.6	819	2,170	3.3	−.6
Panama	.5	928	2,157	2.9	−1.7
Nicaragua	.7	683	1,324	2.3	−3.3
Honduras	1.0	680	1,031	1.4	−1.2
Haiti	1.6	363[c]	439	.7	−1.9
Latin America[d]				2.7	−0.8

Sources: Summers and Heston (1984); and ECLA, Preliminary Overview of the Latin American Economy, 1988.
[a]Countries are ordered by average share in regional GDP between 1950 and 1985.
[b]Figures for 1989 are preliminary.
[c]1960 amount.
[d]Latin America except Cuba.

low 1992). Such a model made sense but was far from perfect. It downplayed the market role and confronted three limitations:

- Protection led to overvalued exchange rates and hence to an eventual reduction in the export supply. Industrialization in turn required increased inputs of capital goods and intermediate imports. As trade deficits increased, foreign capital flows became vital, an ironic consequence of a strategy deriving its strong political appeal from its emphasis upon national productive capability.
- In sectoral terms, import substitution policies exaggerated industrial growth at the expense of agriculture. Moreover, relatively capital intensive manufactures absorbed only a fraction of the increment in the labor force, placing pressure on government to serve as an employer of last resort.

• Finally, as the resources taxed away from primary exports failed to increase, subsidies to industrial investment and growing government responsibilities put new pressures upon the budget. Monetization of the deficit led to persistent inflation.

The distributive agenda of populism called for an increase in urban incomes at the expense of rural producers, exporters, and foreign capital. Velasco and Cárdenas promoted agrarian reforms in Peru and Mexico, but their credit and price policies favored the urban sectors. Specific policies included higher minimum wages, price controls on food, and protectionist barriers. While the urban working class served as a primary constituency, domestic industrialists also supported Perón, Vargas, and Velasco.

The classical populist agenda of redistribution was not sustainable for the same reasons that ISI failed in the end. Protectionism did not raise real productivity to create a basis for large gains in urban wages. Nor did tax collections grow enough to finance government subsidization of the industrialization process. Inelasticity of supply in the agricultural and export sectors was overestimated: it did not take long for overvalued exchange rates and price controls to cause stagnation in these sectors. Alienation of foreign capital exacerbated problems. In the absence of a major boom in export prices, classical populism rapidly self-destructed.

The most representative populist was Perón. He came to power in 1946 by building a base of support among unions as Argentina's secretary of labor between 1943 and 1945. Perón promoted the vision of a rapidly industrializing Argentina, free of foreign influence.

Wages rose rapidly as Perón's government settled strikes in favor of workers: real wages rose 25 percent in 1947 and 24 percent in 1948 (Skidmore and Smith 1984). Labor's share of income rose from 40 percent in 1946 to 49 percent in 1949. Social security benefits expanded dramatically (Mesa-Lago 1978). What made this rapid redistribution possible without an immediate collapse of the economy was the boom in Argentina's export prices after the Second World War. Export revenues more than doubled between 1945 and 1948, although volume remained roughly the same (Rock 1975). Industry grew markedly faster than agricultural growth. Control of the state marketing board for agricultural output enabled the government to keep food prices down and reap a surplus from exports. Despite high world prices, agricultural income declined 27 percent between 1946 and 1949. Perón's strong nationalist streak led to nationalization of the railroads, the telephone system, and the ck facilities, with ample compensation of foreign firms.

Problems emerged in 1949. Argentina's terms of trade deteriorated sharply as adjustment in postwar Europe curtailed the region's ability to import food and U.S. agricultural protectionism excluded Argentine goods. The trade balance turned from surplus to deficit. Reserves disappeared. Complicating the situation was the adoption of inconvertible currencies by Argentina's trade partners. "Europe could not pay; the United States would not buy" (Fodor

1975, p. 150). Exchange rate policy and low prices paid by the agricultural marketing board exacerbated the consequences of unfavorable shifts in the world economy.

Internally, expansion had gone well beyond what could be financed by agricultural surpluses. The money supply was increasing rapidly in order to finance industrialization. Inflation doubled to 31 percent in 1949. Perón launched a stabilization program, tightened credit, cut government spending, and capped wage and price increases. He offered incentives to agriculture and made overtures to foreign capital. A severe drought in 1950/51 forced further adjustment.

The multiclass, nationalist alliance needed high growth to sustain political viability. After 1952, "the state's adjudicatory role in the economy ceased to be a matter of allocating relatively higher rates of return to one group or another in the midst of an expanding surplus. Economic recession meant that its role became more coercively redistributive" (Rock 1975, p. 191). The government became increasingly authoritarian to force adjustment on various groups. Growing levels of violence and social tension preceded a military takeover in 1955.

3.3 Economic Populism

Recent economic literature argues that populist policies like those of Perón were repeated in the 1980s, leading to similar crises. Two excellent articles spell out a new, economic definition of populism. Dornbusch and Edwards (1989) define populism as an "approach to economics that emphasizes growth and income redistribution and deemphasizes the risks of inflation and deficit finance, external constraints and the reaction of economic agents to aggressive non-market policies." The belief in excess capacity sets up the expectation that government deficits and higher real wages are feasible. Governments avoid devaluations because of their distributive consequences. As higher wages go into effect, the economy responds with more rapid growth, but it does so by running down inventories and foreign reserves. Bottlenecks become binding constraints and inflation takes off. The failure to reverse redistributive efforts leads into growing government deficits, balance of payments problems and pervasive shortages. The collapse of the economy makes workers worse off than they were at the beginning of the populist period.

In a similar vein, Sachs (1989) blames much of Latin America's inflation on attempts to implement redistributive policies. In an insightful analysis, he argues that Latin America's high level of income inequality creates political pressure to pursue bad macroeconomic policies. In an environment of high social conflict, populist regimes attempt to improve the lot of low income groups, mainly through demand stimulation. The result is a set of unsustainable macroeconomic policies including government deficits and overvalued exchange rates. What perpetuates the cycle of populism is that expansionary policies yield favorable results at first. Because leaders have insecure tenure in office they adopt short-sighted policies that bring immediate gains to their constituencies.

Both articles argue that the politics of each regime and the specific policies are not significant. What needs to be learned is a universally applicable lesson: policies must be consistent with the capacity of the economy to generate foreign exchange for imports and savings to finance investment. In the past two decades, several Latin American regimes have failed to manage their economy within these limits. Nowhere is the sense of déjà vu stronger than in the case of Peru's once charismatic president, Alán García.

García took power in 1985 promising growth at 6 percent per year and the weakening of the *Sendero Luminoso*. A demand-driven expansion was set in motion. Wages were sharply increased, interest rates cut, and taxes reduced. Old style structuralism provided the rationale: inadequate demand prevented the economy from reducing costs through economies of scale; low elasticities of supply in the export sector accounted for balance-of-payments problems; unemployment and unused industrial capacity implied that the economy could grow much faster.

Policies were nationalistic and inward looking. García increased tariff levels, imposed restrictions on capital flows and announced that Peru would not pay more than 10 percent of its export earnings in debt service. To control inflation, he froze prices and fixed the exchange rate. Like Perón, he intended not only to serve labor through higher wages but to raise profits for local industrialists through stimulation of demand and increased protectionism.

The initial results were fantastic. In 1986, inflation dropped to less than half its level in the preceding year and growth shot up to 9.5 percent. Strong growth continued in 1987 (at 6.7 percent), but inflation exploded and the economy moved quickly toward collapse. The public sector deficit had more than doubled, from 4.4 percent of gross domestic product (GDP) in 1985 to 9.9 percent in 1987 (Dornbusch 1988). As reserves evaporated, García continued to raise wages, announcing a generous wage package in April 1987. He executed his own coup de grace in late July by nationalizing the banks. Industrialists immediately withdrew their support and social conflict intensified. By early 1988, inflation was well over 1,000 percent and output was sliding rapidly. For all intents and purposes, García relinquished control to aides.

Like Perón, García did not aim at the very poor. Urban wage earners (especially unionized workers and public employees) and domestic capitalists were the first to gain. These gains were more distributive than redistributive: growth in the size of the pie can benefit all. Initially, the rural sector was hurt by García's exchange rate policies. As shortages of foreign exchange developed, he allowed peasant prices to rise and made credit more readily available, but he never implemented a program to overcome widespread rural poverty. Support for the *Sendero Luminoso* barely wavered.

If Perón served as the model for populism's demise, the shoe fit García fairly well. Neither was serious enough about redistribution to do it without trying to boost growth, and both were more interested in distributive issues affecting the politically powerful than the poor. As Sachs (1989) suggests, lack of consensus about income distribution does indeed cause political tension, and policymakers often try to diffuse this with inflationary spending. The poor, however, are neither part of the political conflict nor prominent in the populist solution. Populism lacks a significant role for redistribution.

Genuine efforts to mitigate poverty do not necessarily lead to hyperinflation: Costa Rica has done fairly well on this score. At the same time, hyperinflationary experiences are not always the result of failed populism. Few authors would be willing to argue that Martinez de Hoz was a populist, but his policies also led to a balance-of-payments crisis and the explosion of inflation in Argentina. The easy access to foreign capital enjoyed by the military in the late 1970s helped sustain bad policies and macro imbalances. Argentina's neoconservative experience indicates that even without populist rhetoric, governments are quite capable of pursing polices that fuel inflation and balance-of-payments crises (Ramos 1986). Procapital policies are not a panacea for instability, nor is redistribution necessarily to blame for economic mismanagement.

3.3.1   Allende and Ortega: Populists?

Two socialist experiences, Allende's regime in Chile (1970–73) and the Sandinista era in Nicaragua (1979–90) have been placed under the broad rubric of economic populism. Both regimes collapsed as hyperinflation created increasingly chaotic economies. Moreover, both governments promoted redistribution and ran deficits that were the proximate cause of inflation. In the case of Allende, there was also excessive optimism about the potential for economic growth through demand stimulation. Nonetheless, the socialist nature of these regimes sets them apart: their challenge to capitalism vitiated any possibility of building a multiclass alliance and set up strong internal and external forces determined to overthrow the regime. The instability caused by uncertain property rights and U.S. hostility figured strongly in the development of macroeconomic imbalances.

3.3.2   Allende

When Allende took power in 1970, Chile was already a highly urbanized, industrial economy. Chileans enjoyed the third highest per capita income in Latin America. An extensive social welfare system kept extreme poverty to low levels relative to the rest of Latin America. In contrast to Perón and Vargas, who introduced import-substituting industrialization strategies and social welfare legislation, Allende came to power after these had occurred in Chile. The economy depended upon imported parts and materials for its heavily protected industry, and agriculture had been neglected for decades. Whereas Perón tried to set up a successful and profitable industrial sector, Allende's program targeted redistribution. The multiclass base of Perón's regime was not evident under Allende. Instead, he took power despite strong opposition from capitalists.

Allende's first step in early 1971 was to increase real minimum wages by 37–41 percent for blue-collar workers and by 8–10 percent for white-collar workers. He expanded housing, food, and educational assistance: public-housing starts were up twelvefold and eligibility for free milk was extended from age 6 to age 15. The government deficit rose from 3 percent to 10 percent of GDP (World Bank 1981).

Initially, idle capacity, high copper prices, and large reserves of foreign exchange helped. Real GDP rose 7.7 percent, and unemployment in Santiago fell from 8 to 4 percent in 1971. Industrial output rose sharply as consumer demand expanded. The hard currency needed for this expansion came from foreign reserves, a drawing down of inventories and reduced capital imports. (Industrialists cut capital imports in part because of wariness about Allende's respect for private property rights.)

Allende attempted to repeat his early success with a new round of wage increases in 1972. Real blue-collar wages were increased by 27 percent and white-collar wages were fully indexed. But shortages of foreign exchange became serious, and it was impossible to increase Chileans' consumption without sustained copper earnings and commercial lending. Working-class consumption in Chile was very import-intensive, as both manufactured goods and food imports required foreign exchange. The country's backward agricultural sector was in no position to absorb growing demand for food. Eduardo Frei's gradual process of land reform was accelerated: takeovers increased eightfold in Allende's first year. Despite rising real food prices, both the area planted and output fell.

Compounding Allende's problems was a sharp decline in receipts of foreign exchange:

- Copper prices fell by a sharp 23 percent in 1971 and did not recover until mid-1973, a few months before the coup. At the time, copper accounted for two-thirds of the country's export earnings. Although volume did not change markedly, export earnings fell 24 percent, between 1970 and 1972.
- The U.S. government, opposing Allende from the start, contributed to his downfall by withdrawing aid, by placing an embargo on exports to Chile, and by financing his opponents. Allende's call to end compensation to foreign firms nationalized in the 1960s was a specific basis for opposition. Socialist ideals were the general cause of antagonism. Net official capital flows from the United States dropped from $172 million in 1969 to −$198 million in 1971. Refusal to repay debt restored capital flows to a negligible positive amount. Commercial lenders also eliminated their short-term credits. It is often noted that Allende received more aid from communist countries than he lost from Western creditors. In fact, almost all of this aid was granted for purchases of industrial plants and technical assistance, which

Chile did not need. It did not provide spare parts for existing equipment or necessary intermediate materials and food. By June 1973, the Chileans had taken up only 21 percent of the credits offered by the East Bloc.

Was Allende a populist? In terms of the new economic definition of populism, three criteria are met: he tried redistribution through wage increases, government deficits rose dramatically, and a balance-of-payments crisis figured prominently in the economy's collapse. By more traditional notions of populism, the case is not clear. The program never aimed at satisfying both capitalists and workers. From the start, it was expected that capitalists would gradually lose. The regime's socialist agenda brought property rights into question. Workers increasingly demanded that the state take over plants, and social tension over property rights turned to near anarchy by the end (Falcoff 1989). The Allende constituency was distinctly not a multiclass coalition, as political scientists so often describe populist regimes. Nor was Allende's long-term strategy to promote capitalist growth with the help of selective state intervention. The Popular Unity platform explicitly rejected the power of industrial monopolists who had gained power during Chile's import-substitution period (Sideri 1979).

The Popular Unity agenda violated basic rules of good macroeconomic management. Allende's problems, however, derived also from his willingness to step into the conflict between superpowers and his challenge to private property rights, two significant factors that cannot be dismissed. Of course, one can also debate just how socialist the Allende regime was. It never controlled the legislature enough to implement a dramatic change in the nature of production or the structure of social classes.

3.3.3 The Sandinistas

The Sandinistas' downfall resulted from weak economic performance, but they followed a different path from the one chosen by Allende. The Sandinistas put no stake on demand-driven growth. They counted the beans in their bag and knew that none were magic. Yet pursuit of a redistributive program (as distinct from distribution with growth) caused an unmanageable political backlash.

When the Sandinistas took power in 1979, the rural sector represented roughly half of the economy. The industrial sector employed a smaller proportion of the labor force than in other Latin American countries. Although some basic industries were in place (food processing, cement, fertilizer, and petroleum refining industries), there were virtually no sophisticated assembly operations. The Sandinista strategy did not have to cater to a highly protected industrial sector, nor did the program call for import-substituting industrialization.

The first years of the revolution brought an energetic attack on urban and rural poverty. During Somoza's last years, Nicaragua had the highest child death rate in Latin America, and 47 percent of the population was illiterate.

The Somoza regime itself estimated that 60 percent of rural Nicaraguans were undernourished. The Sandinistas embarked on a massive literacy campaign, construction of health clinics and schools, extension of water services, and agrarian reform.

Were there resources to finance these revolutionary programs? Initially, yes. Foreign aid was extraordinarily generous during the regime's first three years. Moreover, the government took over land owned by Somoza and his close associates (23 percent of the country's cultivated land) to initiate its land reform program. Taxes increased from an average of 13 percent of GDP in the period 1974–78 to 22 percent in 1980; they peaked at 35 percent in 1984. The government deficit, at 8.9 percent of GDP in 1978, stayed at that level through 1981 and then jumped when Contra activity began in 1982. However, extensive foreign aid mitigated repercussions from this deficit in the regime's first years (Helwege 1989).

The Sandinistas were very careful to avoid across-the-board wage increases. The right to strike was tightly controlled and wage increases were strongly discouraged as early as 1979 in an effort to contain inflation. The hope was that a tight lid on wages would help the private sector to slowly recover from the destruction caused by the war. Inflation was modest in the regime's first years. It was 37 percent in 1980 and dropped down to 12 percent in 1981, 17 percent in 1982, and 11 percent in 1983. It did not get over 100 percent until 1985.

What went wrong? Four factors contributed to the Sandinistas' problems. First, socialist rhetoric and threats to expropriate property created enormous uncertainty for private producers, who were expected to generate most output. Second, world prices of cotton and coffee, which account for about 60 percent of the country's export earnings, fell after 1980. Third, the currency was grossly overvalued as early as 1980. Finally, the war with the Contras, which started in 1982, must take most of the blame.

As a result of civil war, the government deficit soared to 30 percent of GDP in 1983 and stayed in the 15–25 percent range thereafter (Ocampo and Taylor 1989). Half of the government's budget was devoted to the military, squeezing out social spending. The war effort drew scarce resources from the rest of the economy. The draft exacerbated labor shortages and export earnings were diverted toward weapons, forcing industry and agriculture to get along without imported parts and fertilizers. Rebel attacks also destroyed the transportation infrastructure and prevented harvests in the most important agricultural areas of the country.

The war also made distributive issues more critical. Rural peasants could not be alienated for fear they would support the Contras. Both in pursuit of socialist goals and for defense reasons, the government continued to give peasants title to land and to build schools and health clinics in rural areas as budget deficits became unmanageable.

At the same time, it became increasingly important to maintain the presence of large private producers. They not only brought in most of the country's hard currency, but they legitimated the government's claim of respect for private property, blunting European support for a full-scale invasion by the United States. The government paid dearly for their support. Subsidies to this group included a multiple exchange rate system that enabled large producers to buy pesticides and fertilizers at low rates while selling export dollars back to the government at the parallel rate. Credit was also heavily subsidized.

Urban workers were the easiest to control. Although the government courted urban workers with rhetoric, their real wages fell every year after 1981 (and they had increased only minimally before that). Shortages of basic goods were pervasive in urban areas early on and became worse as the economy deteriorated.

Unable to impose the full burden of defense on any group, the government increasingly used the printing press. By 1986 private consumption had fallen to roughly one-third of its prerevolution level. For the next three years, Nicaraguans scrambled to outwit inflation by hoarding and speculating, making matters worse. By 1988 inflation had reached 11,500 percent and output had fallen back to levels of the late 1960s.

Populism was not the problem in Nicaragua, socialism was. It caused too much uncertainty about property rights, and it triggered a war that the country simply could not afford. Although the Sandinistas ran deficits, the reasons for these deficits differed from those one finds in classical populist experiences.

3.3.4   Brazil: Endless Populism?

1945 provides a good starting point for discussing politics in Brazil. Vargas's populist reputation is based on the last 10 years of his political career. Having relied on a ruling coalition of military elites, coffee exporters, and industrialists throughout the 1930s, Vargas began to bid for the support of workers in the mid-1940s. In 1942, he instituted a minimum wage and, in 1943, a labor code. In 1945, a group of radicals in the *Partido Trabalhista Brasileiro* (PTB) called for reform socialism and for special development banks that would provide massive injections of capital in order to broaden the internal market for domestic manufactures. This more radical program greatly influenced the PTB after Vargas's reelection in 1950. Vargas moved to the left within the framework of restrained militancy of organized labor and state control over union financing. With unions extensively supervised, Brazilian industrialists and exporters did not feel threatened and acquired a vested interest in the government subsidies and investment policies. During the decades to come, Brazil was to operate under the legacy of her most notorious populist leader. Continuing expansionist policies attenuated distributional conflicts and blended the interests of business and bureaucracy.

By 1950 the easy phase of populist import-substitution industrialization was over. Adjustment was avoided by violating budget constraints and engendering inflation. Such problems encumbered Vargas in 1954, Kubitschek in

1958, and Goulart in 1964. When Goulart, trapped in deep economic crisis, tried to undertake radical reforms, the military stepped in. National security doctrine provided the ideological justification for intervention by claiming that the survival of a free society depended on putting an end to the popular classes' resistance to authority.

The new military government announced a series of policies aimed at reducing the public-sector deficit, raising taxes, cutting import tariffs, establishing wage controls and allowing foreign investors easier access. The limits of the import substitution strategy were recognized and important modifications to commercial policy introduced in the late 1960s. A crawling peg exchange rate avoided the overvaluation so predominant earlier. Explicit concern for inducing nontraditional exports produced special export subsidy programs. In the context of a more buoyant international market, such reinforcements produced positive results, and export growth and diversification increased.

Still, the commitment to industrialization remained. And that meant an intrusive role for the public sector even under the "orthodox" policies pursued by military governments. Their administrations were a clear descendant of import substitution, not outward orientation. The large domestic market still dominated production decisions and economic austerity did not last long. By 1974 the populist tradition of accommodation staged a comeback.

Mounting indebtedness and deterioration of domestic policy in a more difficult external environment marked the post–oil shock experience. Brazil chose her adjustment strategy badly, relying upon import-substituting investment stimulated by the government rather than upon market-driven responses to changes in exchange rates or the relative price of petroleum. External debt played a central role: it financed investment and large current account deficits, postponing the negative real income effects of the shock. The strategy succeeded in sustaining high rates of growth, but the debt/export ratio almost doubled. At the same time, fiscal disequilibria increased as government pursued its ambitious investment plan. Even on the eve of the second oil shock, Brazil faced the need for a midterm modification of strategy. But the "recessionist" proposal of Finance Minister Mario Simonsen yielded to a more ambitious supply-side plan undertaken by Antonio Delfim Netto in 1979. Priority was given to credit expansion in order to finance investment in the agricultural and energy sectors. Macroeconomic policy was supposed to contain inflation by reducing interest rates (seen as a significant cost component) and by changing expectations through preannounced internal monetary correction and exchange rate devaluation.

Delfim's "populist" strategy did not work. The weakness of the economy only became fully apparent when a new oil price rise, an abrupt increase in real interest rates, and an OECD recession coincided in the early 1980s. The balance of payments registered a record current account deficit in 1980. The inflation rate reached the three-digit level, reflecting excess demand, supply shocks, and the consequences of a new wage law mandating a shorter adjustment lag. In October 1980, a more orthodox package of fiscal and monetary restraint was fashioned and Brazil entered into a period of adjustment through recession that was to last until 1983.

The translation to democracy in 1985 opened the way for popular resistance to austerity measures. Sarney brought in a new populist experiment, the Cruzado Plan. The goal was to stop inflation without imposing contraction. With prices frozen, the budget was allowed to deteriorate while monetary policy turned expansionist. Inflation disappeared temporarily but new stabilization programs were necessary in 1987 and in 1989. Once again, the government froze prices and cut zeros off the face value of the currency. Promises to eliminate the budget deficit were made but not kept. President José Sarney lacked the political will to implement measures of fiscal consolidation.

Was Sarney a populist? He certainly meets all the criteria of the new economic concept of populism. Yet, according to more traditional views, he fell short of the charisma of a populist leader. The heterodox Cruzado Plan reflected his inability to impose contraction on any constituency, for he lacked popular support and allies in the Congress.

The threat of hyperinflation at the end of 1989 coincided with the presidential election that brought Collor to power in March 1990. Collor seems to fit the classical description of the populist leader. During his campaign he spoke to masses of the poorer sectors of society against the existing institutions of the state. His speech had no precise or logically consistent ideology. It appealed to alienated or deprived members of a mass society and directed its energy against existing elites. He attacked traditional symbols of prestige in the name of popular equality. His populist rhetoric was a collection of strands of both left- and right-wing thought, with a heavy stress on his charismatic leadership, often with a highly illiberal and intolerant stand on traditional civic liberties.

His economic program, though, does not fit the new paradigm of economic populism. The plan mixes "free-marketeering" and authoritarian intervention:

• In 1989, the government had tried to reduce liquidity through high interest rates. As real interest rates rose, so did the cost of servicing the government's domestic debt and the debt itself. Because the government debt was almost equivalent to cash, high interest rates only helped to create more money. Collor's plan eliminated the money overhang. After five days during which all banks were closed by order, the government blocked a large portion of new cruzados in bank accounts—ranging from checking accounts and savings deposits to overnight money-market operations and corporate foreign exchange hedges—for a period of 18 months.[1] A monetary reform replaced the cruzado novo by the cruzeiro of equal value in order to distinguish money that remains in circulation from that which is held in the cen-

---

1. Frozen assets will yield monetary correction and 6 percent interest per year. Starting September 1991, the government will return funds in 12-month installments.

tral bank. The central bank estimates that M4 was reduced to one-third its previous level.

- The government counts on increased revenues to revert a deficit of 8 percent of GDP into a 2 percent surplus. Part of the revenue derives from increased taxation on financial investments. Elimination of unidentified investors, ceilings on bearer checks, and a special income tax declaration for blocked funds will cut down on tax evasion. Other taxes rose and new ones were levied. For the first time farmers pay taxes. Fiscal incentives are on hold. But increased taxation and a clampdown on evaders might be offset by the decline in economic activity. Some critics also say that the plan did little to curb the spendthrift state: closing a few useless federal establishments will get rid of only a very small fraction of public employees and the initial privatization program looks timid.[2]
- According to the new plan, Brazil has opened its borders. It abolished import quotas, import licenses, and the list of prohibited items. In their place remain tariff barriers. Export subsidies no longer exist. Port and merchant marine surcharges dropped by 50 percent and will disappear in 1991. The exchange rate for trade transactions will float.
- The government froze prices for 45 days but prices of the public sector, of fuel, electricity, postage, and telephone calls increased. Starting in April, wages are corrected according to the government-projected inflation. For April the correction is zero. Many industries have already negotiated with workers a 25 percent cut in wages and reduced work hours.

Collor's plan combines a liquidity and fiscal squeeze of such austerity that, if it sticks, will not only kill inflation but also create a major recession. Yet, the opinion polls show more than 60 percent support for the president. Congress grasped that message and approved the package. It is still too early to judge whether austerity will prevail or melt down before the October elections. The businessmen who last year hustled to fill Collor's campaign coffer now grieve, moan, and whine. The trade unions are protesting the prospect of mass unemployment. Is Collor a populist?

3.4   Populism, Poverty and Distribution

Redistributive efforts based on government deficits and overvaluation will melt in an inflationary pyre. Despite ample experience from the past, this is a lesson that bears repeating. There is, however, an important distinction to be made between policies of excessive spending and programs aimed at overcoming poverty.

Far from providing an indictment of redistribution efforts, the history of populism makes conspicuous the paucity of genuine redistribution programs in Latin American (see tables 3.2 and 3.3). Despite compelling criticism,

---

2. Banks and financial institutions will be forced to buy privatization certificates.

Table 3.2   **Economic and Social Indicators in Latin America[a]**

	GDP per Capita Index[b] 1980	Urban Population (% of total) 1987	Life Expectancy (Years) 1987	Infant Mortality (per thousand) 1987	Population per Physician (in thousands) 1984	Literacy Ratio 1978
Y > $2,000 in 1980:						
1. Venezuela	100.0	83	70	36	.70	82
2. Uruguay	98.8	85	71	27	.51	94
3. Argentina	96.9	85	71	32	.37	93
4. Mexico	76.9	71	69	47	1.24	83[c]
5. Chile	71.7	85	72	20	1.23	89[d]
6. Costa Rica	65.6	45	74	18	.96	90[c]
7. Panama	65.2	54	72	23	.98	82
8. Brazil	65.0	75	65	63	1.08	76
Y > $1,000 in 1980:						
9. Colombia	56.9	69	66	46	1.19	81[c]
10. Paraguay	53.0	46	67	42	1.46	84
11. Peru	52.7	69	61	82	1.04	80
12. Dominican Republic	47.3	58	66	65	1.76	67
13. Ecuador	47.0	55	65	63	.83	77
14. Guatemala	43.0	33	62	59	2.18	46[e]
15. Nicaragua	40.0	58	63	62	1.50	90
16. Bolivia	33.7	50	53	110	1.54	63[c]
17. Honduras	31.1	42	64	69	1.51	60
Y < $1,000 in 1980:						
18. El Salvador	27.2	44	62	59	2.83	62
19. Haiti	13.3	29	55	117	7.18	23[c]

Sources: Summers and Heston (1984); World Bank, *World Tables*, IMF, *International Financial Statistics*, PREALC, and ECLAC.

[a]Latin America except Cuba; countries are ordered by size of GDP per capita in 1980.

[b]Indices of GDP per capita in 1980, Venezuela = 100. Venezuela GDP per capita = $3,310 in 1975 dollars.

[c]1980

[d]1970

[e]1975

Table 3.3   Percentage of Population Living under the Poverty Line in Latin America, 1970–86

	1970[a]	1981[b]	1986[b]
Argentina	8.0		
Brazil	49.0		
Chile	17.0		
Colombia	45.0		
Costa Rica	24.0	24.8	
Honduras	65.0	68.2	
Mexico	34.0		51
Panama	39.0	53.9	41
Peru	50.0		59
Venezuela	25.0		37
All 10 countries	39.0		

Sources: Altimir (1982); CEPAL (1989).
[a]The national averages of Altimir's poverty line vary between $162 for Honduras and $296 for Argentina (in 1970 dollars).
[b]ECLAC direct estimates follow Altimir's methodology.

changing relative prices was the most common strategy of classical populism. The costs of this policy included significant leakages as well as large government and efficiency costs. Organized, vocal, and visible groups of the modern sector used their political power to press for increases in the minimum wage as well as for food and transport subsidies. Governments, held directly responsible for the earnings of the workers in the modern sector, chose to impose losses on the rural and informal sectors because the administration would be less likely to be held accountable for such losses.

Classical populists distributed the gains from growth among the politically enfranchised. Latin American reformism in the 1960s was based in the alliance between the national bourgeoisie, the middle classes, and urban workers, all aiming at the development of an internal market. The favored groups were urban labor and the middle classes. Industrial workers gained union recognition, electoral power, and welfare benefits. The middle classes received more public jobs, better educational facilities, and decision-making authority in the bureaucracy. *Desarrollo hacia adentro* involved a pattern of growth based on higher levels of consumption by the urban population included in the *pacto social*. But strengthening the labor movement and increasing real wages soon would face its own limits. The *pacto social* supported policies that favored the urban middle class at the expense of the rural population. Thus its contradictory nature: the demand for increased food production by a growing urban population clashed with policies that channeled the bulk of public investment funds to industry.

Regardless of populists' promises to "serve all the people," some sectors were denied access, were ignored or excluded. Although populism favored the urban sector, it barely touched the urban poor. As the cornerstone of populist redistribution, minimum-wage increases promoted the welfare of relatively small groups at the expense of larger groups. When effectively enforced (and often they were not) such laws made wages higher for those fortunate enough to get jobs in the modern, formal sector. They did little to overcome poverty. The reasons are two. First, low income groups do not receive the official minimum wage. Second, the evidence does not support the hypothesis that there is a positive correlation between the official minimum wage and the level of wages below it (see Almeida dos Reis 1989).

In the urban areas, the poorest are self-employed (rather than wage earners), workers in construction (the most likely entry point for immigrants), and people working in public make-work programs such as those in Chile (World Bank 1986). Because the poor have larger families, the incidence of poverty among children is higher than among adults.[3] Programs that could have alleviated urban poverty would have included improved access to birth control and prenatal care, nutrition and sanitation programs, childcare programs for working mothers, and better primary school education. Classical populists expanded the welfare state, but the emphasis was not on poverty. Broad-based social security programs and state support for universities served the middle class and absorbed resources that could have targeted the poor.

The group most seriously neglected by populists—and nonpopulists—is the rural poor. The extent of poverty is markedly higher in rural than in urban areas in all Latin American countries (Altimir 1982). Whereas 26 percent of urban Latin Americans were poor in 1970, 60 percent of rural households were poor. Even in Argentina, Chile, and Uruguay, the most heavily urbanized countries in the region, the extent of rural poverty was not less than 20 percent of rural households. In Mexico, the poorest 30 percent of the population was almost entirely rural. In Brazil, 70 percent of the lowest four deciles in the mid-1970s were rural households. In 1986, the extent of poverty continued to be markedly higher in rural areas (table 3.4).

Both peasants and landless labor comprise the rural poor, although the mix varies among countries. In Brazil, for example, the poorest are mainly temporary laborers, while in Peru, subsistence farmers dominate. In Colombia, about half of poor rural households are small producers, the rest landless labor. Landowners who are poor typically own too little land to subsist on and earn a large share of their cash income as laborers on larger farms.

Where land ownership is concentrated in the hands of a few and large estates are farmed carelessly, agrarian reform can promote economic growth and greater equity. But of the regimes that might be considered populist by econ-

---

3. Selowsky (1982) and Altimir (1984) both estimate that the proportion of small children and school-age children in poverty is larger than the proportion of poor households; there are also more children in poverty among those belonging to households whose heads are female or have little education; Paes de Barros (1989) shows that in the metropolitan areas of Brazil children in households headed by women are overrepresented among the poor.

Table 3.4   Percentage of Population Living in Poverty, 1986

	% of Population below Poverty Line			% of Population below Destitution Line		
	Urban Area	Rural Area	Total	Urban Area	Rural Area	Total
Argentina[a]	11			3		
Colombia	39			16		
Guatemala	60	80	73	31	57	49
Mexico[b]	47	61	51	19	30	22
Panama	36	52	41	16	28	20
Peru[c]	51	71	59	23	53	34
Uruguay		21		5		
Venezuela	34	48	37	11	22	13

Source: CEPAL (1989).
[a]Metropolitan areas only.
[b]Figures from Mexico are from 1984.
[c]Preliminary figures.

omists, only a handful have implemented major agrarian reform: Velasco, Allende, and the Sandinistas. Democratic regimes fail to implement change for two reasons: large landowners still influence government and policymakers fear reform will improve rural diets at the expense of output for urban food and export markets. Plagued by foreign exchange crisis and afraid to alienate urban workers who are sensitive to food prices, populists dragged their heels on land reform. For the most part, it has been the military and revolutionaries who have reformed landownership.[4] The fact that military regimes have also reversed or prevented land reform, as in Chile and Guatemala, reflects the difficulty of achieving social consensus on rural property rights. Table 3.5 shows the impact of redistribution on rural households.

Land reform has yielded both orderly transitions and chaotic disruptions of output in Latin America. The diversity of experiences reflects considerable variation in the nature of redistribution within the region. New rights to land have taken the form of individual ownership, communally organized production, or the allocation of lands to family farms on a semipermanent basis. It also has involved distribution of unused public or private lands to new settlers, varying levels of compensation for expropriation and diverse degrees of protection for the nonreform sector.

In Mexico and Bolivia, land reform was relatively successful in pacifying the countryside and mitigating rural poverty. Peruvian land reform failed in

4. The Mexican revolution redistributed 43 percent of the country's agricultural land, the Bolivian revolution shared out 83 percent of the land. The Peruvian military government redistributed 40 percent of the country's farming area (see table 3.5). A more recent example of radical reform is found in Nicaragua, following the overthrow in 1979 of the Somoza dynasty. The Sandinista regime turned the Somoza family's holdings, covering more than a fifth of the country's arable land, into state farms and gave peasants access to idle land.

Table 3.5   Latin American Agrarian Reforms

Country	Year Initiated, Modified	Beneficiaries as % of Rural Households[a]	% of Affected Forest and Agricultural Surface[b]	Organization of Production[c]
Cuba	1959, 1963	70 (1963)		SF, IH, CO
Mexico	1917, 1971	69 (1971)	42.9 (1970)	43.4 (1970)	Ejidos
Peru	1963, 1969	37 (1975)	30.4 (1982)	39.3 (1982)	CO and some IH
Bolivia	1952, . . .	33 (1970)	74.5 (1977)	83.4 (1977)	IH
Nicaragua	1979, 1981	30 (1983)		SF, IH, CO
Chile	1962, 1970	20 (1973)	9.2 (1982)	10.2 (1982)	Asentamientos
Venezuela	1960, . . .	17 (1970)	30.6 (1979)	19.3 (1979)	IH, CO
El Salvador	1980, . . .	12 (1983)	22.7 (1985)	21.8 (1985)	IH, CO
Colombia	1961, 1973	10 (1975)		IH, CO
Costa Rica	1961, . . .	9 (1975)	5.4 (1980)	7.1 (1980)	IH, CO
Honduras	1962, 1975	8 (1978)		IH, CO
Ecuador	1964, 1973	7 (1972)	10.4 (1983)	9.0 (1983)	IH, CO
Dominican Republic	1962, . . .	3 (1970)	8.5 (1983)	14.0 (1983)	IH, CO
Panama	. . . . . .		13.3 (1977)	21.9 (1977)	IH

Sources: Deere (1985) and Thiesenhusen (1989).

[a]Total number of beneficiaries until the year in parentheses divided by number of rural households in that year.

[b]Affected area as measured until year in parentheses.

[c]SF = state farms; IH = individual holdings; CO = cooperatives.

both economic and political terms. It not only failed to stimulate production and eradicate rural poverty but it did nothing to improve political stability. In part its failure can be blamed on the weaknesses of the reform program but mostly it reflects Velasco's economic policies. The cooperative model also contributed to the poor results. The large-scale cooperatives were met with opposition from the peasantry; imposed from above the cooperatives were perceived as a burden by those they were supposed to benefit. The Peruvian experience indicates that land reform is not sufficient for rural development unless accompanied by proper price, marketing, credit, and investment policies.

Three lessons stand out from past experiences. First, land reform has been most successful from an efficiency perspective when it has involved the takeover of inefficient haciendas or colonization of undeveloped land. There is not much sacrificed on this situation and peasants eager for land are quick to put it into use. The takeover of commercial farms is most tricky: the transition period is damaging due to decapitalization and the existing managerial efficiency is difficult to duplicate.

Second, redistribution of land does not help the most destitute. Land tends to be distributed to those who know how to work with the authorities or those who have been permanent workers on large estates. Temporary workers often find it harder to find employment after land reform. As a welfare measure, land reform needs to be accompanied by programs that target the very poor.

Finally, land reform works best when it is accompanied by credit and technical assistance from the government. It is not a cost-free solution to rural poverty. Governments can proclaim a change in ownership at little fiscal cost. But credit and technical assistance to help land reform succeed is expensive. Past experience has demonstrated that capitalization and market stability are important if small farmers are to participate in the modernization of agriculture. Without credit, adequate irrigation, transportation networks, and reliable markets, access to a small piece of land may be only marginally better than the alternatives open to poor rural people.

In short, a serious land reform program requires broad social acceptance of its inevitable costs. The consequences fall not only on large landowners but also on urban consumers who will face higher food prices (at least in the short run) and taxpayers who must be willing to support credit and technical assistance. Populists have generally not been willing to commit resources to land reform.

Roughly 60 percent of Latin America's poorest people still live in rural areas. Land reform may be the most effective tool in helping these people to survive, because it distributes assets that outlive government jobs programs and minimum wage fiats. Even under the best circumstances, however, land reform will not absorb Latin America's rapidly growing rural population. A long-run solution to rural poverty must involve an expansion of job opportunities in the cities and targeted education programs that enable the poor to qualify for them.

The need for genuine redistribution and economic growth in Latin America is acute. In 1984, Couriel reported that poverty affected more than half of the population in Peru, El Salvador, Guatemala, Honduras, Nicaragua, Haiti, Ecuador, the Dominican Republic, and Bolivia. The Comision Economica para America Latina y el Caribe (CEPAL 1989) shows that, in 1986, more than 70 percent of the population of Guatemala lived below the poverty line (see table 3.4 above).

Attempts to accelerate growth through government deficits fail, as economic populism has amply demonstrated. Redistribution must carry the ball. Average income per capita in most Latin American countries exceeds that in African and Asian countries, but extreme poverty persists as a result of inequitable income distribution. Table 3.6 shows the distribution of income in several Latin American countries. A social consensus to tax, to reduce subsidies to the middle class, and to finance poverty programs and land reform are critical to changing this picture.

Economic stability contributes to the alleviation of poverty. Urrutia (1985) uses the case of Colombia to claim that progress can be achieved through prudent management: "A complete analysis of all existing statistical data shows that the income distribution did not worsen in the 1970s and that the real incomes of the poor improved significantly, especially in the later half of the decade." The Colombian eclectic system used controls but avoided the extreme protectionism of other Latin American countries; its crawling peg kept the exchange rate at reasonable levels, and government avoided inflationary finance. By stimulating housing construction and exports other than coffee, Colombia experienced sustained growth and avoided the spectacular crises found in other Latin American countries.

According to Urrutia, wages of agricultural workers increased faster than national income, while wages of lower-income urban workers grew faster than wages of higher-income urban workers and salaries of white-collar em-

Table 3.6   **Income Shares and Gini Indices for 14 Latin American Countries, circa 1970**

	Income Share of Top 20% as Multiple of Bottom 20%		Gini Index	
	(1)	(2)	(3)	(4)
Brazil	21	15	.574	
Mexico	15	16	.524	.567
Argentina	7	7	.437	.425
Venezuela	24	18	.622	.531
Colombia	17	15	.557	.520
Peru		26		.591
Chile	12	14	.506	.503
Ecuador	16	24	.526	.625
Dominican Republic	13		.493	
El Salvador	18	11	.539	.532
Costa Rica	11	9	.416	.466
Panama	20	24	.557	.558
Uruguay		13		.449
Honduras		21		.612

Sources: For cols. 1 and 3, Kakwani (1982). For cols. 2 and 4, Lecaillon et al. (1984).

ployees. Urrutia also argues that financial liberalization brought about better credit allocation, and that fiscal policy had a positive impact on income distribution. He suggests that the 1960s tax system was slightly progressive and that the reforms of 1974–75 were a factor in improvement. The income of the first decile was twice as high after taxes and government transfers, while the income share of the top decile was reduced. Education, health, and public services such as water, electricity, and government programs benefited the poor in more than a proportional way. Urrutia shows that between 1964 and 1972 the overall distribution improved because of the narrowing rural-urban differential. Londono (1989) calculates an 8 percentage points reduction in Colombia's Gini index between 1964 and 1988 (see table 3.7).

Despite progress, inequality and poverty in Colombia remain acute. But its stable macroeconomic policies certainly did more for the poor than the oscillations observed in Brazil and Chile. In both cases there is evidence that recessions caused dramatic increases in the Gini coefficient. In Brazil, the coefficient jumped from 0.5 in 1960 to 0.6 in 1970, an unusually large deterioration in only 10 years. Fishlow (1972) shows that the stabilization policies that followed Goulart's populism in 1964 were largely responsible for the widening of inequality. Chile also exhibits this extraordinary 10-point increase in the Gini coefficient in one decade (table 3.7). Two extreme recessions certainly played a role in this deterioration.

No doubt, secular growth is a significant factor in reducing poverty, but its effects are relatively small and thus easily washed over by greater earnings inequality and by cyclical conditions. Recessions have a disproportionate impact on the poor and widen the distribution of income. A recession causes more unemployment, a drop in the labor-force participation and slower growth of real earnings. The costs of continuing high inflation are not any smaller. Even where everything is indexed, including wages, prices, interest rates, taxes, and accounting systems, inflation has a profound impact on the lower classes whose subsistence is not protected. The inflation tax also falls more heavily on the poor classes who cannot benefit from indexed deposits accessible to those who can open accounts above a minimum floor. Stop-go policies hurt the poor. Stability might help them.

3.5 Conclusion

In Latin America, a variety of different political agendas have led to economic crisis:

- Classical populists put too much stake on the possibility of demand-driven growth, inward-looking industrialization, and unrealistic expectations. Perón, García, and Allende, to a large extent, failed to realize that Keynesian stimulus falters on foreign exchange constraints.
- Attempts at developing market-based socialism are also to blame for failed economic policy. Insecure property rights make it difficult to sustain private

Table 3.7   Gini Indices for Brazil, Chile, and Colombia

Year	Brazil	Chile	Colombia
1938			.442
1960	.500		
1961			.525
1964			.555
1970	.608		
1971			.527
1974		.45	
1975		.47	
1976		.54	
1977		.53	
1978		.52	.481
1979		.52	
1980		.53	
1980	.597	.52	
1981	.584	.54	
1982	.587	.54	.474
1983	.589	.55	
1984	.588		
1985	.592		
1988			.474

Sources: Hoffmann (1989), Larraín (1990), and Londono (1989).

production, and socialist rhetoric triggers costly intervention by the United States. The Sandinistas may have been overly ambitious in their initial plans to redistribute and their early budget deficits were high, but their downfall is more the result of Contra activity and uncertainty about property rights than of populism.
- Lack of social cohesion and strong political parties make it difficult to impose the burden of contractionary adjustment on various classes. Sarney and Alfonsín could never decide how to distribute the burden of adjustment to the debt shock. As fragile elected regimes without strong political support of any particular group, they were unable to impose contraction on anyone. The result was failure to live within the economy's contraints and hyperinflation.
- Although redistribution marks populism, the poorest have not benefited from it. Classical populism redistributed income from the agricultural and export sectors to capitalists and workers in the formal urban sector. Rural peasants and the urban poor remained marginalized both politically and economically. Modern populists did not serve them better.

Minimum wages, the redistributive centerpiece of populism, are ineffective in overcoming poverty in Latin America. The poor are in the countryside and in the informal sectors where minimum wages are not enforced. Broad-based social security programs have also failed to concentrate resources on the poor.

Solutions to poverty in Latin America lie in a concerted effort to tax and to redistribute revenue to support agrarian reform and programs that aim specifically at the poor. This is only possible if the rest of society accepts redistribution. Experiences with hyperinflation show that the politically enfranchised cannot agree on a distribution of income among themselves, much less on distribution toward an increase in the share of the poor.

Finally, whatever its root, budget deficit booms, however progressive they might sound, hurt the poor. The lesson is that fiscal responsibility, realistic exchange rates, and a stable environment are essential to sustain the basis on which to build a better income distribution.

References

Almeida dos Reis, J. G. 1989. Salario Minimo e Distribuicao de Renda. In *Perspectivas da Economia Brasileira, 1989*. Rio de Janeiro: INPES/IPEA.

Altimir, O. 1982. The Extent of Poverty in Latin America. World Bank Staff Working Paper no. 522. Washington, D.C.: World Bank.

———. 1984. Poverty, Income Distribution and Child Welfare in Latin America. *World Development* 12 (3):261–82.

Archetti, E., P. Cammack, and B. Roberts, eds. 1987. *Sociology of Developing Societies: Latin America*. London: Macmillan.

Baily, S. 1967. *Labor, Nationalism and Politics in Argentina*. New Brunswick, N.J.: Rutgers University Press.

Cardoso, E., and A. Fishlow. 1992. Latin American Economic Development: 1950–1980. *Journal of Latin American Studies*. In press.

Comision Economica para America Latina y el Caribe (CEPAL). 1989. Magnitud de la Pobreza en Ocho Paises de America Latina en 1986. Documento para el Proyeto Regional para la Superacion de la Pobreza, July. Mimeograph.

Conniff, M., ed. 1982. *Latin American Populism in Comparative Perspective*. Albuquerque: University of New Mexico Press.

Deere, C. D. 1985. Rural Women and State Policy: The Latin American Agrarian Reform Experience. *World Development* 13, no. 9:1037–53.

Dornbusch, R. 1988. Peru on the Brink. *Challenge*, November-December.

Dornbusch, R., and S. Edwards. 1989. The Economic Populism Paradigm. NBER Working Paper no. 2986. Cambridge, Mass.

Falcoff, M. 1989. *Modern Chile: A Critical History.* New Brunswick, N.J.: Transaction.

Fishlow, A. 1972. Brazilian Size Distribution of Income. *American Economic Review* 62 (May).

Fodor, J. 1975. Perón's Policies for Agricultural Exports, 1946–48: Dogmatism or Commonsense? In *Argentina in the Twentieth Century*, ed. D. Rock. Pittsburgh: University of Pittsburgh Press.

Germani, G. 1978. *Authoritarianism, Fascism, and National Populism*. New Brunswick, NJ: Transaction.

Hamilton, N. 1980. *The Limits of State Autonomy: Post-Revolutionary Mexico*. Princeton, N.J.: Princeton University Press.

Harberger, A., 1970. Economic Policy Problems in Latin America. *Journal of Political Economy*.

Helwege, A. 1989. Is There Any Hope for Nicaragua? *Challenge*, November–December.

Hennessy, A. 1976. Facism and Populism in Latin America. In *Facism: A Reader's Guide*, ed. W. Laqueur. Berkeley: University of California Press.

Kakwani, Nanak. 1982. *Income Inequality and Poverty: Methods of Estimation and Policy Applications*. New York: Oxford University Press.

Larraín, F. 1990. The Economic Challenges of Democratic Development. Harvard University. Mimeograph.

Lecaillon, Jacques, et al. 1984. Income Distribution and Economic Development: An Analytical Survey. Geneva: International Labor Office.

Lodono, J. L. 1989. Income Distribution in Colombia: Turning Points, Catching Up and Other Kuznetsian Ideas. Harvard University. Mimeograph.

Malloy, J. ed. 1977. *Authoritarianism and Corporatism in Latin America*. Pittsburgh: University of Pittsburgh Press.

Mesa-Lago, C. 1978. *Social Security in Latin America*. Pittsburgh: University of Pittsburgh Press.

Ocampo, J. A., and L. Taylor. 1989. La Hyperinflacion Nicaraguense. MIT: Mimeograph.

Paes de Barros, Ricardo. 1989. Pobreza e Estrutura Familiar. IPEA, Rio de Janeiro. Mimeograph.

Prebisch, R. 1976. Peripheral Capitalism. *CEPAL Review*, no. 1, pp. 9–76.

Ramos, J. 1986. *Neoconservative Economics and the Southern Cone of Latin America, 1973–1983*. Baltimore: Johns Hopkins University Press.

Rock, D. 1975. The Survival and Restoration of Peronism. In *Argentina in the Twentieth Century*, ed. D. Rock. Pittsburgh: University of Pittsburgh Press.

Sachs, J. 1989. Social Conflict and Populist Policies in Latin America. NBER Working Paper no. 2897. Cambridge, Mass.

Selowsky, Marcelo. 1982. Distribucion del Ingreso, Necesidades Basicas y "Trade-offs" con Crescimiento: El Caso de Los Paises Latinoamericanos Semiindustrializados. *Cuadernos de Economia* (April):37–68.

Sideri, S. 1979. *Chile, 1970–73: Economic Development and Its International Setting*. The Hague: Martinus-Nijhoff.

Singer, H. W. 1984. The Terms of Trade Controversy and the Evolution of Soft Financing: Early Years in the U.N. In *Pioneers in Development*, ed. G. Meier and D. Seers. New York: Oxford University Press.

Skidmore, T., and P. Smith. 1984. *Modern Latin America*. New York: Oxford University Press.

Stein, S. 1980. *Populism in Peru*. Madison: University of Wisconsin Press.

Summers, Robert, and Alan Heston. 1984. Improved International Comparisons of Real Product and Its Composition. *Review of Income and Wealth* 30, no. 2:207–62.

Thiesenhusen, William, ed. 1989. Preface to *Searching for Agrarian Reform in Latin America*. Boston: Unwin Hyman.

Urrutia, M. 1985. *Winners and Losers in Colombia's Economic Growth of the 1970s*. New York: Oxford University Press.

World Bank. 1981. *Chile: An Economy in Transition*. Washington, D.C.: World Bank.

———. 1986. *Poverty in Latin America*. Washington, D.C.: World Bank.

Comment   William R. Cline

I find myself in broad agreement with the paper by Cardoso and Helwege, and my comments primarily will seek to highlight and extend rather than refute.

William R. Cline is senior fellow at the Institute for International Economics.

The authors make an important point when they observe that populism is not the same thing as either socialism or equity-oriented redistribution without departure from private ownership of property. Populism purports to raise wages and benefit national capitalists without acknowledging trade-offs at the expense of other groups. Its redistribution is toward politically powerful groups, not those in need, for example, toward organized labor, not the rural poor. A corresponding point that is crucial for this discussion is the authors' correct observation that the failure of populism in Latin America should not be read as evidence that efforts to reduce income inequality are fatally in conflict with economic stability and growth.

I would also stress another point in the paper: inflation is regressive. The poor do not have financial instruments to defend themselves. The authors are correct in indicating that stable growth is the best climate for improving the conditions of the poor.

The experience reviewed in the paper does make one wonder whether there might not be a political inconsistency theorem for efficient redistributive policies: by the time the political situation has become radicalized enough that the new leaders are prepared to take action seriously favoring the poor, the group in power has an ideology antagonistic to efficient economic structures. For example, radical land reformers reject the family farm as petty capitalist and insist on state farms, even though all the evidence suggests the latter will be less efficient because of poor incentives.

Again on the political level, the shift in Brazil from Simonsen to Delfim II exemplified an irony of populist pressures in military regimes. The pursuit of rapid growth at all costs was a consequence of the need to seek legitimacy for a politically illegitimate government. The paradox is that there may be better chances for stability under democratic rule.

I agree with the critiques of import-substituting industrialization and would add the problem of monopoly in a closed economy resulting from the need for scale economies, as well as the loss of efficiency as the economy moves further from its comparative advantage. I generally concur with the criticism of Brazil's move to intensified protection and import substitution after the 1974 oil shock, although it should be kept in mind that Brazil's present export capacity in sectors such as steel is the consequence of investments made under that regime.

With respect to adjustment in Brazil and Argentina in 1990, I would note that both programs sought to exempt the poor by freezing assets above thresholds that caught primarily the middle and upper classes. In both cases, the verdict on whether the poor actually escaped will depend on whether there is severe recession that causes unemployment and job losses and on the long-term growth effects of damage to domestic financial institutions and trust in government obligations. I do think the Brazilian government may be more serious about fiscal adjustment than the paper implies; for example, the Collor administration is talking about dismissing over 300,000 government employees.

The paper is correct in its conclusion that raising the minimum wage is an inefficient means of reducing inequality. Workers in agriculture often do not receive the minimum wage, so that increases can generate intralabor inequality. In Brazil, the new constitution links pensions and social security to the minimum wage, so that increases have a devastating effect on the fiscal balance. Incidentally, the Cardoso-Helwege conclusion on the minimum wage contradicts the Fishlow analysis of Brazilian income distribution in the late 1960s and early 1970s; Fishlow emphasizes erosion of the real minimum wage as a source of growing inequality. Cardoso and Helwege cite recession later in the 1970s as the source of rising inequality. However, the data are so shaky that trends are questionable. Moreover, on the basis of theory one would not necessarily expect recession to concentrate relative income distribution, as profits are likely to be more procyclical than wages.

Let me turn to elaborations of some of the themes in the paper. An implicit issue in this conference is whether income redistribution can be pursed without causing macroeconomic destabilization. I would remind everyone of the rather extensive literature on income distribution and growth in the 1970s. At that time the structuralists argued that, without redistribution of income, Latin America was doomed to stagnation for lack of an adequate domestic market. Related arguments held that basic goods had higher labor intensity and lower import content, so that redistribution would favor growth on these grounds as well. In contrast, the orthodox view had been that premature redistribution would jeopardize growth by reducing saving. And empirical patterns in the "Kuznets curve" seemed to suggest an inevitable concentration of income in the early stages of growth before eventual redistribution.

Simulation analysis carried out by me and others found that the redistributional issue was essentially neutral with respect to growth. Marginal savings propensities did not differ sharply among income classes. There was no simple correlation between income elasticities of demand and labor or import intensity of basic versus luxury goods, and a large bloc of intermediate goods in the economy was necessary regardless of the composition of final demand. Such findings tended to leave the issue of income redistribution as a matter to be addressed on its own merits—neither a precondition for growth nor an obstacle to it.

Instead, attention turned by the late 1970s to a focus on absolute poverty and basic human needs. The principal objective of distributional policy was increasingly seen as a need to set a floor to living standards rather than to focus on relative income distribution. Researchers at the World Bank and elsewhere emphasized the importance of targeted government expenditure (e.g., on health, infant and maternal nutrition, rural potable water) as the efficient way to pursue equity-oriented policies. Unfortunately, the debt crisis of the 1980s meant that attention had to be concentrated on survival of the economy as a whole, and for a time the distributional issue became a luxury that had to be postponed.

What are the lessons of the populist record for policy formation in Latin America today? I think they are not only compelling, but that they have already been learned by key political actors. Consider Carlos Andrés Pérez in Venezuela. His past policies might have led to the expectation of another round of populism. Instead, his new government adopted strong adjustment measures. Or Carlos Menem in Argentina. A Peronist, his relatively orthodox austerity measures came as an even greater surprise to domestic and foreign observers. In Brazil, Fernando Collor also embarked on such nonpopulist measures as a wage freeze and cutback in government employment.

Mexico provides perhaps the best model of this transition. In contrast to the populism of Echeverría in the 1970s, the governments of de la Madrid and Salinas Gortari have carried out massive and painful fiscal adjustment. Salinas has the right diagnosis: it is necessary to slim the state sector so that it can become stronger and focus its activities on the fundamental responsibilities of the state, that is, the social infrastructure. As Salinas puts it, in his travels to Mexican towns he frequently hears pleas for new sanitation projects or irrigation; he never hears demands for additional Boeing 747s for the state airline to facilitate travel to Paris. The new government's budget reflects these priorities: even as it is privatizing airlines and the telephone system, the government is sharply increasing spending on education, health, school lunches, and other social areas after a long period of cutbacks for purposes of fiscal adjustment.

Privatization is in fact a major feature of the new trend in Latin America toward economic realism. As one high official in Brazil put it, the Brazilian state has some $200 billion in state firm assets and $180 billion in domestic and foreign public debt. Interest must be paid on the debt, but very little is earned in the way of dividends on the state firm assets. By reducing both sides of the balance sheet, the government can become much stronger fiscally. Even where state firms are not inefficient, privatization can help macro policy. Incomes policies often force the government to freeze the rates for utilities and other public services, causing them to lag behind inflation and provoke fiscal losses. Then, when the rates are increased, there is a new shock to inflationary expectations. Taking these services out of the state sector helps depoliticize pricing policy. I note that privatization is largely absent in the recommendations of the Cardoso-Helwege paper, but it would seem to be an essential part of successful adjustment and growth in many countries of Latin America.

One negative side of privatization and state-sector adjustment does need to be highlighted. In the past, many Latin American governments used state-sector employment as the means of generating jobs for a rapidly growing labor force. Somehow the private sector will increasingly have to provide these employment opportunities. The answer to this dilemma lies in part in the prospects for more rapid and sustained growth, as adjustment to the debt crisis and, more fundamentally, restructuring of economies under more open, modern strategies lifts Latin America out of a decade of recession and stagnation.

In sum, I would submit that the lesson from populist experiments in Latin America is not that governments must be hard-hearted, but that they should be hard-headed and soft-hearted instead of soft-headed and soft-hearted (if populists were ever soft-hearted). The elements of a successful strategy for growth with equity in the region must include:

- overall fiscal balance;
- the avoidance of unrealistic wage increases;
- concentration of antipoverty action on government spending on low-end social services, especially in rural areas;
- an open-trade model for efficiency and greater labor intensity;
- and firm anti-inflation programs, because inflation is the biggest enemy of the poor.

II Country Experiences

4   Description of a Populist Experience: Argentina, 1973–1976

Federico A. Sturzenegger

4.1   Introduction

In a recent paper, Dornbusch and Edwards (1989) established a stylized outline of the macroeconomics of populism. They showed that the experiences of Chile under Allende and Peru under Alán García are very similar and consistent with features they consider characteristic of populist governments and policies. The purpose of my contribution is to reconsider that description to see if it also applies to the Argentine experience between 1973 and 1976 and to evaluate and understand both the possible motivations for such policies and their long-run implications.

During those years Argentina underwent an important economic policy experiment. At the same time the country was in the midst of strong political violence and social conflict. Violence had began around 1968 and had originated as the consequence of guerrilla activities. Among the guerrilla groups, the most prominent were the Montoneros, which initially worked from within the Peronist party, and the ERP (Ejército Revolucionario del Pueblo).[1] In the

Federico A. Sturzenegger is at the Department of Economics, Massachusetts Institute of Technology.

The author wants to especially thank Rudiger Dornbusch for encouragement and support. The author is also indebted to German Coloma for efficient research assistantship and to José De Gregorio, Guido Di Tella, Affonso Pastore, and Adolfo Sturzenegger for useful comments. The author claims responsibility for any remaining errors.

1. The sociology of the guerrilla movement is extremely complex. Montoneros belonged initially to intellectual groups educated in a violent nationalistic tradition. Afterward it combined a wide spectrum of ideological lines among which right-and left-wing nationalism, Marxism, Trotskyism, certain versions of Peronism, and the ideology embedded in the theory of dependency and liberation theology were all components. Montoneros had a strategy of selective attacks, murders, and kidnappings. It was predominantly an urban movement. The ERP, founded in 1971, had initially a Trostkyist and later a Guevarist orientation. They tried to carry on an open war against the government for which they made themselves strong in the north of the country. They were both an urban and rural movement (see, e.g., Floria and García Belsunce 1988; David Rock 1987).

early seventies, political violence escalated as extreme right-wing groups resorted to explicit violence as well. Among these, the most well known was the Triple A (AAA or Alianza Anticomunista Argentina), which was also later proved to have been commanded by chief Peronist party members. As violence gained the streets, the citizenry began to perceive the struggle not only as an ideological war but also as an internal struggle for power among the leaders of the ruling party. This, among other things, undermined the confidence in the democratic system and helped substantially in generating a consensus for the military coup of 1976.

Four different Presidents—Héctor Cámpora, Raúl Lastiri, Juan Domingo Perón, and Isabel Perón—held office between 1973 and 1976. The first, who came from the most left-wing groups of the party, had the support of guerrilla organizations and left-wing intellectuals. The second, Raúl Lastiri, belonged to the right-wing factions of the Peronist party. Perón supported a more ambiguous middle-of-the-road position, trying to maintain good relations with all the groups that constituted his movement. His strong personality and historical authority allowed him to control internal struggles or at least to keep them in a silent and hidden second place. Finally, Isabel Perón favored the right-wing factions, but her weak personality generated, while president, an open explosion of internal struggles of which she quickly lost control.

Surprisingly, especially considering the diversity of personalities that held the presidency between 1973 and 1976, the initial economic policy was maintained unchanged through all of them. Only during the government of Isabel Perón did the situation deteriorate to the point that corrections could not be avoided. The initial stability of the economic policies was due to the strong backstage influence of Perón, who imposed on Cámpora a minister of finance of his own choosing. During this period, José Ber Gelbard held office without interruption throughout the presidencies of Cámpora, Lastiri, Perón, and Isabel Perón.

But before reviewing the political events of the period and studying in more detail the implementation and evolution of economic policies, it is useful to briefly describe the main facts regarding populist policies and experiences as summarized in Dornbusch and Edwards (1989).

According to Dornbusch and Edwards (1989), the populist program arises as a reaction to a period of slow growth or recession, which has usually occurred under the patronage of the International Monetary Fund (IMF) and/or conservative governments at home.

The populist paradigm explicitly rejects conservative thought by dismissing the idea of resource constraints. Unemployed labor and idle capital capacity is seen as proof of lack of demand and the need of expansionary policies. Existing reserves provide room for a loosening of foreign restrictions, overvaluation of the exchange rate, and therefore for an increase in real wages. Demand expansion is not considered to be inflationary. Increasing returns to scale, declining average costs, and profit squeezing provide room for expansion with price stability. Higher real wages feed back by expanding demand and therefore generating efficiency gains, which allow reductions in prices, increased competitiveness, and efficiency. This improves the balance of payments, increases investment and output, which in turn initiates another round of the virtuous cycle.

Dornbusch and Edwards consider, then, that the policy prescription of populist programs is very simple: "reactivation with redistribution," which is to be achieved by wage increases, price controls, increased spending, overvaluation of the exchange rate, and the restructuring of production to generate higher savings and higher growth.

The macroeconomics of populism can be separated into two main topics. The first relates to the properties of the real equilibrium of the economy. In this respect it is assumed that the economy can do much better. The rhetoric has old-fashioned Keynesian tones and calls for strong expansion of government spending. Loose monetary policy is advocated on credit-rationing arguments. Even though these arguments may be outdated, the theoretical issue of multiple real equilibria remains an important one in the macro literature. Search models (Diamond 1982) and increasing-returns-to-scale models (Murphy, Vishny, and Shleifer 1989) support a similar view. The old price-rigidity arguments can be replaced by those of multiple equilibria, coordination failure, or thin and thick externalities, to give a neoclassical theoretical support to the possible long-run success of expansionary policies. It is necessary to note, nevertheless, that populist regimes were all but neoclassical. As will be shown below in the analysis of the Three Year Plan of the Peronist party it was accepted and believed that market forces should be strongly modified and reoriented in order to achieve improved social outcomes.

The second topic is that of macroeconomic adjustment. Here populist policies call for strongly heterodox programs: price and exchange controls with a freezing of wages and of public tariffs. Inflation is not viewed as a monetary phenomenon but as a consequence of income struggle. As noted previously, demand expansion is not consider inflationary, so that the basic strategy should concentrate on arranging an agreement between main economic interest groups so that income struggle stops. Theoretical work on this topic has been less developed.[2]

As will be seen below, the Argentine experience shows that heterodox stabilization policies, while by themselves insufficient to reduce inflation in the long run, may be extremely useful initially in the transition to a lower inflation rate. On the other hand, no support is given to the idea of multiple equilibria. The attempt to expand output was unsuccessful in the end.

According to Dornbusch and Edwards (1989), populist programs evolve in four phases. First, an initially successful stabilization is accompanied by

2. See Dornbusch and Simonsen (1987) for a review, or Bruno et al. (1988) for a review of recent experiences.

strong output expansion. In the second phase, problems begin to emerge as a result of the overheating of the economy and increased pressure on bottleneck sectors. Lack of foreign exchange begins to be a complication for the Central Bank. The third phase presents an acute worsening of problems, explosion of inflation, crisis in the balance of payments, capital flight, and an increase in the budget deficit. The government then tries to stabilize and adjust the economy, devalues the currency, reduces subsidies, and increases public tariffs. Real wages begin to fall. The end comes with an orthodox stabilization program, with wages falling below the initial level due to capital flight, a higher real exchange rate, and a shift of political power against labor unions and lower income classes.

As a brief summary it can be said that, for the Argentine experience between 1973 and 1976, it is not true that initial conditions featured a recession previous to the implementation of the program. In the postwar period and until the early eighties, Argentina's historic growth rate was of about 4% a year (Brodersohn 1973). The military had been in power since 1966 with GNP increasing by 0.6% in 1966, 2.7% in 1967, 4.3% in 1968, 8.5% in 1969, and 5.4% in 1970. In 1971 and 1972 growth of total GNP was 4.6% and 3.1%, respectively. The first half of 1973 was strongly expansionary with a growth rate of 6.1% in the first quarter and of 6.3% in the second.

The initial phase, implemented through the *Acta de Concertación* (Concertation Act) by Minister of Finance Ber Gelbard was extremely successful in achieving even higher growth, complete price stabilization, progressive redistribution of income, and an increase in the reserves held by the Central Bank. After a year, the results of the program had been so spectacular that even those most strongly opposed to the government had to give credit to the economic policy being implemented. Among these, Roberto Alemann, a well-known conservative said:[3]

> The economic policy implemented last May has in its favor the fact that it tries to stop inflation suddenly. In order to do that, it attacked simultaneously several factors: it froze and reduced prices, raised taxes, [and] fixed wages, markups, and other related measures. The immediate result was a halt in the increase of the cost of living. Annual inflation of 70% stopped, the stock market bounded upward, the black market exchange rate dropped, and tax collection increased. The country watches surprised [at] these results that nobody would have imagined before the twenty-fifth of May, maybe not even the authors of the policy. (*Clarín*, 12 August 1973)

After a year and a half problems began to emerge. The price freeze caught many producers with low real prices, and shortages appeared in different sectors. On the other hand, monetary and fiscal policies continued to be very permissive. The terms of trade began to move against the country, quickly worsening the external-sector situation. This eventually led to a shift in the

---

3. All of the following newspaper quotations were obtained from Di Tella (1977).

cabinet, which placed Gómez Morales, considered a more orthodox economist, as minister of finance. During his administration, problems went on accumulating, and even though some flexibility was introduced in the control of prices and wages, serious corrections of the economy's imbalances were avoided.

Following Dornbusch and Edwards (1989), the third phase arrives when problems become so intense that the government decides to make an adjustment of the economy. In June 1975, an acute crisis in the balance of payments precipitated that readjustment. It was carried on by the new minister of finance: Celestino Rodrigo, member of the right-wing faction of the Perónist party, which was now in control of the government. (Isabel Perón was already president and José López Rega, minister of social welfare and chief of AAA, had accumulated considerable power.) Real wages fell, inflation exploded, and a recession ensued. This lead to a quick discreditation of the right-wing group, which was therefore neutralized from the government.

After the Rodrigo experiment, center-left members of the party temporarily gained some power, and even occupied the office of the presidency for a short period. Isabel Perón, claiming medical reasons, asked for a temporary leave. Italo Luder, head of the senate and member of the center-left coalition, was provisionally sworn in as president. Antonio Cafiero, who had the confidence of the unions and the moderate groups of the Peronist party, became minister of finance. He implemented a gradualist strategy for reducing rampant inflation and maintained expansionary demand policies to avoid increasing unemployment.

In January 1976, President Isabel Perón engineered a comeback, displacing the more moderate groups and imposing tougher adjustment measures. By then though, the end of the regime was in clear sight. Phase 4 in Dornbusch and Edwards's characterization finally took place after March 1976 with a military coup and the implementation of strict orthodox policies.

After this brief summary it is clear that Dornbusch and Edwards's description of the evolution of populist programs fits reasonably well the Argentine experience between 1973 and 1976. If any differences should be distinguished, it would be that the adjustment phase appears to have been extremely long, alternating back and forth between shock and gradualist policies. The end was characterized by social unrest, political violence carried to its height, a fall in real wages, an increase in inflation, and a discreditation of the political parties and the democratic system in general.

As Guido Di Tella (1983) has put it: "The military coup met no opposition, and with it ended the two and a half years of Argentina's second populist experience. It had indeed been an unhappy one" (p. 83).

4.2   The Political Environment

The Peronist party came to existence and consolidation with the advent of Teniente Coronel Juan Domingo Perón's rise to power in 1946. In 1943 Perón had participated in a nationalist coup d'état, holding the office of Secretary of National Labor where he came to popularity and gained the love of Argentina's working class. Perón was elected president in 1946. His first six years in power were characterized by aggressive demand policies, industrial protection, import substitution, a hostile attitude toward foreign capital, progressive labor legislation, and a substantial increase in state intervention in the economy. After a constitutional reform, which enabled him to run for office for a second consecutive term, he was reelected by a landslide victory in 1952. That year the country experienced a balance of payment crisis, which forced a switch to an adjustment program that was sustained until the fall of Perón in 1955. Political totalitarianism, curtailment of the free press, open conflict with the church and with some sectors of the military created a wide coalition that eventually supported the coup of 1955, which ousted Perón and sent him to exile. From then until 1973 the Peronist party was forbidden to participate in any electoral contest.

The military called for elections in 1957, which led in 1958 to the election of President Frondizi, who, though not belonging to the Perionist party had the explicit support from exile of Perón. Frondizi implemented strong populist measures (basically granting substantial wage increases) during his first year of government, afterward switching to a different strategy (*El Desarrollismo*) which gave paramount importance to free enterprise, saving, and capital accumulation (see Mallon and Sourrouille 1975).

Another coup, in 1962, ousted Frondizi and new elections were called for in 1963. The election took a radical, Arturo Illia, to the office of the presidency. Illia won with 25% of the votes. Blank votes (which obviously corresponded to the proscribed Peronist party) totaled 19%. Three years later, in 1966, the military once again stepped in. The new president, General Onganía, declared then that "the system of pluralist democracy has been given its chance in Argentina and therefore something new should be tried now" (Ferns 1971).

This new military regime was completely discredited by 1972 and free elections were called. For the first time Peronism would not be banned, though Perón himself was. Elections were held 11 March 1973. Hector Cámpora, the Peronist presidential candidate, obtained 49.6% of all of votes. Cámpora had promised to give a kickoff to the Peronist program before resigning and calling for new elections in which Perón himself would be allowed to run for office. It is not surprising then that one of the campaign slogans was, "Cámpora to government, Perón to power."

Cámpora was sworn in as president 25 May 1973 and resigned 12 July 1973. The presidency was handed to Raúl Lastiri (head of the Chamber of Representatives). This designation was intended to prevent the head of the Senate, who was the legal successor but associated to the Cámpora ideology, from being sworn in.

New elections were to be held in September, and finally took place the twenty-third of that month. Perón was a candidate, with his wife Isabel running as vice president. The election resulted in a landslide victory for Perón. He obtained 57.3% of all votes followed by 26.3% for the formula of the Unión Cívica Radical (UCR).

Perón was sworn in 12 October 1973 and held office until his death on 1 July 1974. He represented the traditional constituency and policies of the Peronist movement, which were strongly based on labor unions and gave priority to state intervention, import substitution, and the redistribution of income. He always supported a moderate position, avoiding the extremes (both left and right) which had slowly, after so many years of proscription, made their way into the party. This orientation was the one he had already imposed on both Cámpora and Lastiri.

Isabel Perón, on the other hand, favored the right-wing groups (under the strong influence of her minister of social welfare, José López Rega). The right-wing program had five main goals: (*a*) moving toward market-oriented policies; (*b*) curtailing union power; (*c*) eliminating subversion and guerrilla activity; (*d*) gaining the support of the military; and, finally, (*e*) eliminating left-wing intellectuals from the University (Di Tella 1983).

The administration of Isabel Perón was therefore characterized by deep and violent struggle between the different groups and members of the Peronist party. Ideological differences, which had remained silent while Juan Perón was alive, became open and explicit during Isabel Perón's presidency. At the same time, economic problems appeared with a strength never before seen in Argentina, which, added to the open political fight, doomed from the start the possibilities of the vice president. Nevertheless it was still almost two years before the conflicts became so intense that the fall of the government finally took place, on 24 March 1976. Describing the economic evolution during this period is the purpose of the following pages.

4.3 The Three Year Plan

The Three Year Plan (Poder Ejecutivo 1973) was an extensive document intended to summarize objectives, instruments, and policies of the administration that took office in 1973. It is considered to represent the main lines of thought regarding economic policy held by the government or the people in the Peronist party at that moment. It is worth remembering that in 1973 there was a universal trend toward more state intervention in the economy. This trend was not unique to Latin America even though it was particularly forceful there, and it is clearly reflected in the Three Year Plan.

Among the objectives considered in the plan was that of social justice, which was defined as a fair distribution of income with special concern for eliminating extreme levels of poverty and unemployment. The plan endorsed (1) strong reactivation of the economy by means of developing specific industrial activities; (2) national unity, that is, correcting the economic and cultural differences between regions; (3) reorganization of the state, in order to fully realize its new activities as a guide for the economy as a whole, as a mechanism for income redistribution, and as a producer of goods and services; (4) economic independence, to be achieved by a strict control of capital flows, foreign investment, and international trade; and finally, (5) integration with Latin America.

The Three Year Plan considered that output growth would be led by basic industries (oil refineries, iron and steel) and state enterprises. Popular consumption would be the basis for massive production and therefore of an increase in efficiency. Prioritized among economic groups were state and local entrepreneurs (a reduction in the importance of foreign capital was also expected). Three basic conditions justified the feasibility of achieving higher growth rates. First, that the possibilities of growth had been jeopardized in the past by the action of special interest groups. Second, that political instability had also undermined the achievable levels of growth. And finally, that the present conditions in domestic and international markets were extremely favorable for the acceleration of the growth rate. The authors of the plan assumed that the strength of the new government would overcome the two first problems and that external and internal situations would continue to look good at least in the medium term. The quantitative goals were a 7.5% annual increase in GNP and a 12% annual increase of investment. Furthermore, it predicted a doubling of exports between 1973 and 1976.

Possible constraints were also taken into account. Among these the three considered most important were financial, energy, and external restrictions. These were to be overcome in the following way: the first through an increase in savings and tax collection, the second through a program of hydroelectric development, and the third through an aggressive program of export promotion. Nevertheless the main solution would be made through "an important effort in the organization and mobilization of resources which was going to be possible due to the political will to use them in favor of the popular majorities" (Poder Ejecutivo 1973).

The plan's backbone consisted of three instruments. The first was to obtain a compromise between the main economic interest groups and the state. The second was to pass a legislative package with laws oriented to changing the structure of the economy, and the third was to use direct economic policy measures. Among the latter, for example, a nationalization of deposits (i.e., a 100% of reserve requirement), an improvement in the quality of planning, and a tax reform. The plan previewed a strong increase in wage and price controls. Public enterprises would expand progressively, occupying those sectors in which the market had *already proven its failure* and redistributing income by charging higher rates to big consumers. A special law of industrial promotion would aim to develop small and medium-size firms.

For those measures concerning the external sector it is worthwhile to quote directly from the plan:

Regarding the external sector, the control of the state over commercial transactions will be increased and indirect mechanisms for obtaining equilibrium in the balance of payments will be avoided. Bilateral negotiations will be encouraged (especially with Latin America and Third World and Socialist countries). Traditional exports will be regulated by the Juntas Nacionales de Carnes y de Granos in order to maximize benefits for the country and to protect them from foreign interests. Industrial exports will receive fiscal incentives, easy credit and foreign exchange insurance. Imports will be planned regarding their level and characteristics meanwhile tariffs will protect national production, promote commerce and improve the allocation of resources.

In addition to the general policies the plan considered complementary instruments of economic regulation. I quote here again from the plan:

Such instruments would be principally the use of control enterprises [those in which the state is a producer in order to regulate a particular market] . . . production quotas for durables and semidurables [whose purpose is to achieve a quicker accommodation of supply to the changes in aggregate demand that will be produced as a consequence of income redistribution] . . . tariffs with a social and regional purpose [as an instrument of income redistribution] . . . subsidies in different categories [promotion of certain regions or sectors, modification of relative prices as compensation toward social necessary but inefficient firms] . . . import and export quotas [in order to rationalize the use of foreign exchange and to distribute the production of certain goods between internal demand and the international market].

The plan also contained a detailed description of all components of the national accounts, with predictions for all of them in the future.[4] It also contained a wide variety of different statements. It explained, for example, the need and advantages of increasing the consumption of fish, as well as arguing why the unemployment rate should be reduced from 6% to 2.5%.

The state was conceived as the moving force of development:

The state is conceived as a mechanism oriented by the political power who, in interpreting the needs and objectives of national popular majorities, has to establish the basic rules and orientations of its own behavior. Several are the tasks which the state will have under the spirit of the Trienal Plan. First, it will have to regulate the economy; this will take place by means of an open agreement with the main political, labor and business organizations, and will not have any technocratic or elitist connotations but will derive from a clear understanding of the interests of the people. Second it will take

4. For example, exports were expected to increase by 92% between 1972 and 1977. Agricultural exports were supposed to grow by 81%, cattle sector exports by 50%, and industrial exports by 381%. The service account was to improve by 30% due to an increase in insurance and freight made by Argentine ships and airline tickets sales. It is difficult to assess where these predictions came from.

over the production of goods and services, not only those related to social needs and traditional economic infrastructure but also those important in the process of development and which are characterized by having a big multiplier effect over all the economy and by being oriented by the concepts of sovereignty, national reconstruction and territorial integration. Third and final, the state will work on the important function of income redistribution, which will take place through social spending, wage increases and tax and credit policies to be implemented.

In order to achieve all these goals, the plan proposed, in addition to the basic agreement, several other instruments. Among these was the State Compromise Act, in which the national and provincial governments would agree to make public administration more efficient. Also included were the National Institute of Public Administration, an institution with the objective of teaching people how to run the state more efficiently, and the creation of the Corporation of National Enterprises, which would coordinate the functioning of state-owned enterprises.

As can be seen from the previous exposition, the plan was mainly voluntaristic, with changes to be achieved by means of agreements between the parties to improve things. It is difficult to determine whether the predictions it contained were anything more than numbers made up in order to fit consistently in the national accounts framework and to justify some of the basic objectives of the authors of the program. It is also hard to assess the final influence of the program on government policies. The National Pact was a key factor in the stabilization program, but the Corporation of National Enterprises, for example, never achieved anything of importance.

The Three Year Plan was a medium- and long-run program that was basically concerned with structural reforms. Many of these died out in Congress, and many of those that passed were never implemented. The program was in line with a common trend at that time—not only in Latin America but in the whole world—of increased intervention of the state in the economy, but it also fell short of socializing completely the economy. It therefore gained many critics from both the left and the right, and it eventually was only supported by the moderate group surrounding Perón. Later on it could be read, "With Perón in the Pink House the probability that this development plan will be implemented is high. This signals the strength of the plan but also shows its dependency on a particular source of constant and solid political power, such as the one that can be provided by the President" (*La Opinión*, 26 December 1973).

4.4   Initial Conditions

By June 1973 external and internal conditions for the Argentine economy guaranteed an optimistic forecast for the evolution of the economy in the near future. On the one hand, the economy was experiencing a period of high growth of GNP with growth rates in the two first quarters of 1973 of 6.1% and 6.3%.[5] The agricultural sector, which had done badly in 1972 (it finished with a drop of 7.9%), was experiencing a strong recovery due to high international prices and good weather conditions. (Agricultural output growth was 12.2% in the first quarter and 21.8% in the second.) The sector finished the year with a growth rate of 13.5%, which was not only important in itself but had a considerable positive impact on the availability of foreign exchange for the economy. The industrial sector had experienced a growth rate of 6% during 1972, increasing to 7.4% and 6.6% for the first two quarters of 1973. Investment at 21.6% of GNP in 1972 was slightly above historic levels, rising to 22.6% and 22.4% of GNP in the first two quarters of 1973. As much as investment is an intertemporal decision, these figures indicate that the expectations on the future evolution of the economy were optimistic.

Unemployment was considered to be at its natural rate. In April 1973 it had been 6.1% in greater Buenos Aires. Inflation was the biggest problem and was extremely high if compared with that experienced in the postwar period. The Consumer Price Index (CPI) in 1972 showed an increase of 64.2%, which almost doubled that experienced in any previous year of Argentine history (except for the strong inflationary peak of 1958). The importance of this number can be appreciated by repeating what was said at the moment the 1972 inflation rate was made public:

> The dramatic signification of the numbers reveals with absolute clarity that inflation is here a process apparently out of control. In the first place, it is by now proved that a reduction in the means of payment has been useless in the containment of inflation. That means that even though an increase in monetary circulation can be one of the factors which feed the inflationary process, this is a phenomenon which evolves through other channels. . . . Argentine inflation recognizes other causes. . . . They must be contained in the structural deficiencies of our economy. . . . The vicious circle of inflation threatens to become the image of frustration. (*Clarín*, 5 January 1973)

The Wholesale Price Index (WPI) had also had strong increases in the first three months of 1973. This was in part the consequence of the anticipation of the price freeze. If firms forecast a freeze but know that no restrictions will be applied to any possible rebates they may charge, then it is optimal for them to increase their price to the level expected to prevail at the end of the freeze while offering at the same time compensatory rebates. While nominal prices are fixed they can permanently adjust their real prices by changing the amount of the rebate. As firms were anticipating a freeze with the new government,

---

5. Growth rates considered in this paper arise from a comparison with the corresponding period of the previous year.

early in 1973 they tired to increase their relative price prior to its implementation. (See table 4.1 and fig. 4.1. Data provided in the statistical appendix of Di Tella 1983 was used.)

The fiscal deficit was high but not excessively so. Data from the Fundación Mediterránea shows a deficit of 3.7% of GNP in 1972. (Previous values had been 3.1% in 1971, 1.8% in 1970, and 0.9% in 1969.) It is true that the fiscal deficit was higher than that of the immediate previous years, but it was perfectly in line with the values observed in the 1950s and 1960s. Data from the Central Bank (which considers the central government's Treasury operations)

Table 4.1   Monthly Inflation Rates: The CPI and WPI

	CPI	WPI		CPI	WPI
1972:			1974:		
January	10.9	6.3	July	2.4	2.8
February	3.9	6.3	August	3.0	2.8
March	4.5	3.8	September	3.4	3.5
April	5.4	5.2	October	2.7	3.6
May	2.5	3.4	November	3.3	4.3
June	5.6	6.6	December	5.2	2.9
July	5.1	4.0	1975:		
August	1.0	2.3	January	2.9	5.7
September	2.6	4.7	February	4.6	12.5
October	3.8	3.2	March	8.1	5.6
November	4.0	1.8	April	9.7	3.5
December	1.6	3.3	May	3.9	5.2
1973:			June	21.3	42.5
January	10.3	4.9	July	34.9	32.2
February	7.9	6.9	August	23.8	15.3
March	2.9	6.5	September	10.9	13.1
April	5.0	.4	October	12.6	9.2
May	4.4	.6	November	8.1	9.7
June	− 2.8	− 1.4	December	11.5	9.5
July	.1	− .6	1976:		
August	1.9	1.2	January	14.8	19.5
September	.6	.4	February	19.3	28.6
October	.5	.1	March	38.0	54.1
November	.0	1.1	April	34.6	26.3
December	.9	1.3	May	13.1	4.8
1974:			June	28.0	4.7
January	− .6	.4	July	4.3	6.1
February	1.9	.4	August	6.7	8.0
March	1.5	.4	September	10.7	8.8
April	3.4	2.5	October	7.4	4.4
May	4.3	4.2	November	7.1	6.9
June	3.9	3.7	December	6.7	6.4

Source: Instituto Nacional de Estadisticas y Censos (INDEC).
Note: CPI = Consumer Price Index, seasonal; WPI = Wholesale Price Index.

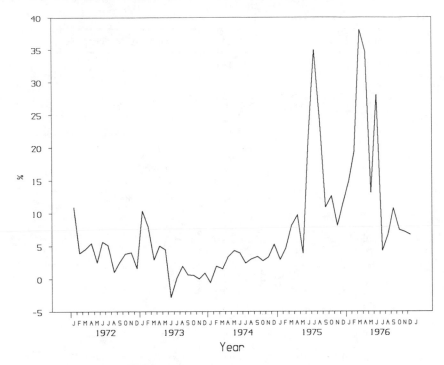

Fig. 4.1   Monthly CPI increases, 1972–76

shows in the first quarter of 1973 a positive but not very large increase in the
deficit (see table 4.2). Money creation was not only positive but was increasingly so. In 1972, M1 had increased by 44%.

In conclusion, on the internal side the economy was experiencing a period
of overheating induced by expansionary demand policies. At the moment the
same impression was supported as one could read, "There are indications that
the first quarter of 1973, which is half way through, keeps and even surpasses
the evolution which the economy exhibited at the end of 1972. . . . In summary it is possible to forecast for this first quarter of 1973 a rising level of
economic activity. This could vary substantially in the second quarter but not
enough to avoid making 1973 the tenth consecutive year of continued growth"
(*La Nación,* 18 February 1973).

On the external front, multiple exchange rates were in place. There was an
exchange rate for traditional exports, one for promoted exports, another for
imports, and one for financial transactions. All of these had been strongly
overvalued during the year, previous to May 1973. There was also a free parallel market. In May, trading in the parallel market was being done with a 32%
premium over the financial rate. (Part of this increase had been built up in the
weeks before the change in government.)

Export prices increased substantially in the period immediately before the

Table 4.2   **Public-Sector Deficit**

Year and Quarter	BCRA	Fundación Mediterránea
1972	2.43	3.70
I	2.10	
II	1.65	
III	2.56	
IV	3.12	
1973	5.43	7.60
I	3.86	
II	5.01	
III	5.58	
IV	6.93	
1974	6.54	8.10
I	5.43	
II	5.34	
III	6.35	
IV	8.24	
1975	11.71	16.10
I	7.12	
II	6.92	
III	9.75	
IV	16.38	
1976	8.01	13.60
I	12.94	
II	7.02	
III	7.79	
IV	7.18	

Note: BCRA (Banco Central de la República Argentina): Central government's treasury operations (as % of GNP); Fundación Mediterránea: Change in total public-sector indebtedness (as % of GNP).

beginning of the populist experience. This was the main cause in a substantial improvement of the terms of trade for Argentina. The export price index, which had a value of 100 in both 1970 and 1971, jumped to 121 in 1972 and 180 in 1973. The terms of trade, which had been around 100 in 1970 and 1971, jumped to 117 in 1972 and remained at that level until the third quarter of 1973. In 1974 they dropped to around 70 and stabilized there (see table 4.3). During the first half of 1973 the noninterest current account experienced a surplus of $400 million. Foreign exchange reserves increased from $300 million in the first quarter of 1972 to $900 million in the second quarter of 1973.

In summary, the situation in the external front in May 1973 was excellent: high international prices for Argentine exports plus abundant international reserves in the Central Bank.

4.5   Initial Phase of the Stabilization Program

On 25 May 1973, after being sworn as President, Hector Cámpora appointed José Ber Gelbard as minister of finance. Gelbard was a businessman and director of one of the main business lobbying groups, the Confederación General Económica (CGE), which basically represented national capital. The extreme left-wing groups that surrounded President Cámpora accepted this designation because it had been an imposition of General Perón.

Gelbard first attacked the most compelling problem of the economy, the extreme rate of inflation. The stabilization package consisted, as stated in the Three Year Plan, of an agreement among interest groups which was formalized in the Acta de Compromiso Nacional (National Compromise Act). This was in line with the inter-class cooperation approach usually put forward by the Peronist party but basically corresponded to the view that the inflationary process was a consequence of an income struggle which the Act intended to

Table 4.3   **Terms of Trade**

Year and Quarter	Terms of Trade	Export Prices	Import Prices
1972	117.4	121.5	103.5
I	105.0	106.0	104.0
II	114.0	117.0	102.0
III	120.0	126.0	105.0
IV	129.0	138.0	107.0
1973	108.9	180.3	165.5
I	112.0	151.0	121.0
II	120.0	168.0	140.0
III	114.0	205.0	181.0
IV	89.0	197.0	220.0
1974	71.9	195.7	272.3
I	83.0	214.0	258.0
II	65.0	113.0	283.0
III	69.0	196.0	239.0
IV	71.0	188.0	265.0
1975	71.2	170.2	239.0
I	66.0	166.0	265.0
II	71.0	171.0	240.0
III	76.0	175.0	230.0
IV	72.0	168.0	235.0
1976	69.3	179.0	256.0
I	72.0	179.0	248.0
II	73.0	187.0	260.0
III	69.0	177.0	264.0
IV	64.0	164.0	257.0

Source: Fundación de investigatiónes economicas latinoamericanas (FIEL).
Note: 1970 = 100.

stop. The explicit target was an inflation rate of zero, an objective too ambitious and which was afterwards to be sustained for too long.

Public tariffs were adjusted and prices of all goods were frozen until 1 June 1975.[6] The freeze involved the reduction in nominal terms of some prices. Medicine, clothes, and shoes prices, for example, were decreased by 15%. The price of meat was reduced 13.5% compared to that prior to the freeze. Regarding this measure it could be read on 3 June 1973 (*La Nación*), that "the most spectacular measure was the fixing of a maximum price for meat. This was a measure previously imposed by other governments and always generating wide resistance. Everything indicates in this case that there is a generalized will of cooperation among producers . . . In fact, these maximum prices generated a fall of approximately 15% in the price of cattle and even of 27% in some other minor categories."

Wages were raised by a fixed amount of $200. This had the double effect of increasing the real wage and of flattening the wage pyramid. Family subsidies were augmented by 40% and the minimum wage was raised to $1,000. After this, wages were to remain fixed until 1 June 1975, with an adjustment for productivity 1 June 1974. (This two-year freeze was a policy copied from Perón's 1952 stabilization program.) The increase in real wages had the double purpose of improving income distribution and of raising consumption demand, therefore reactivating the economy.

The exchange rates were fixed at the levels recorded 25 May, and nominal interest rates were reduced. Easy credit was issued, especially to finance the increase in wages. A 13% yearly nominal interest rate was set for these credits, in what was at most a suspicious policy that was to become almost a continuous practice in the subsequent years.[7] This expansion in money supply was of no concern to the authorities, which regarded inflation not as a monetary phenomenon but as related to structural characteristics of the economy such as income distribution and income struggle, which eventually generated a wage/price spiral. Concerning monetary policy it was stated that "the instrument of the fight against inflation in this popular government is not and cannot be exclusively monetary, said a top aide of the economic team. . . . We begin by accepting that the inflationary process in Argentina is related to a regressive income distribution, and it is that regressivity that we are committed to eliminate, and for that we will use stability as an instrument and not as an end in itself" (*La Opinión*, 15 August 1973).

Several important laws were also sent to and approved by Congress. Among these were a law regulating agricultural exports, the "Buy Argentine Act" (which forced public firms to have Argentine suppliers), and a foreign investment law, to restrict the remission of profits and the nationalization of

6. Petrol prices increased by 70%, natural gas by 30%, etc.
7. Recall that the CPI inflation rate had been 5% in April alone. It is true, nevertheless, that inflationary expectations are forward looking and, ex ante, the expected real interest rate may have been positive.

bank deposits. A tax reform, which included a moratorium on formerly undeclared taxes, introduced profit, capital, wealth, and value-added taxes. The
National Corporation of State Enterprises was created. The state was given
power to fix maximum prices. Professional work was regulated through the
Ley de Asociaciones Profesionales.

These reforms did not bear directly on the stabilization program but were
part of the government's policy that was not only oriented to stabilize the
economy but designed to change it in a permanent and distinguishable way.
Regarding income distribution, the final objective was an equal distribution
between labor and capital.

The announcement of this stabilization program and the structural reforms
just mentioned made clear that the government was implementing middle-of-
the-road policies, which corresponded to the traditional thought of General
Perón.

The program further alienated the extreme left, which considered it a sell-
out to interest groups and consequently increased its level of violence. The
businessmen, on the other hand, felt relief as they were expecting a much
more radical program. The conflict among left-wing intellectuals appears
clearly reflected in the following comment by M. Diamand, a strong supporter
of the government:

> The economic measures contained in the social pact . . . constitute an im-
> portant step toward the peaceful revolution announced by President Cám-
> pora. It is probable that many may be disappointed: a smaller than expected
> wage increase, followed by a rise in public sector tariffs and taxes and also
> accompanied by a suspension in wage negotiations which brings unpleasant
> memories. Nevertheless the price freeze, the structure of tax reforms, the
> allocation of public investment to social ends and an expansive monetary
> policy give to this package a completely different content, making it a pow-
> erful agent of income redistribution and increase in the level of activity. (*La
> Opinión*, 12 June 1973)

The results of the program were impressive. The inflation rate was negative
in June, with a decrease of 2.85% in the CPI and of 1.4% in the WPI. Inflation
remained extremely low afterward for almost a year. During the first 12
months of the plan, inflation was just 0.6% per month, and during the 17
months in which José Ber Gelbard was Minister of Finance it averaged only
1.4% per month (see table 4.1 and fig. 4.1).

Real wages increased, especially in July when they rose by 20.5% (see fig.
4.2 and table 4.4). Unemployment decreased from 6.1% in April of 1973 to
5.5% in July and 4.5% in October (De Pablo 1980a) (see fig. 4.3 and table
4.5).[8]

---

8. This trend continued in 1974 with unemployment rates of 4.2%, 3.4%, and 2.5% in April,
July, and October, respectively. De Pablo (1980a) considers that half the unemployment reduction
was due to an increase in public employees.

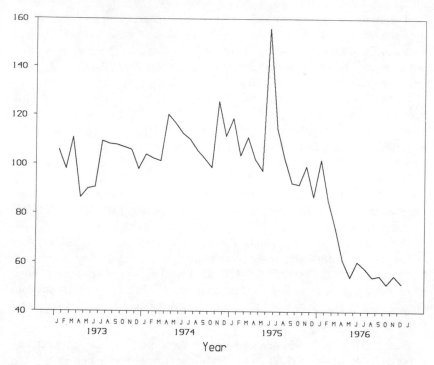

Fig. 4.2   Real wages, 1973 = 100

Output growth remained high: 5.8% in 1973 and 6.5% in 1974. The agricultural sector experienced the strongest increase, with a growth rate in 1973 of 13.5%, which fell but nevertheless remained high during 1974, at 6.2%. The industrial sector showed a more stable pattern, with growth rates of 6.4% in 1973 and 6.1% in 1974 (see table 4.6). Consumption also began to boom. As De Pablo (1980a) points out, it increased 7% in the last half of 1973, 7.3% in the last quarter of 1973 and 11% in the first three months of 1974. Most strikingly, the percentage of income accruing to wage earners increased by 4.2% of GNP in 1973 and stabilized at this new level in 1974. The wage increase implemented by the government had successfully achieved both an increase in consumption and a progressive redistribution of income. Already in September 1973, one could read: "Now almost at the end of the third quarter, the industrial sector shows consistent indications of a strong recovery. . . . The majority of firms considers, now, that the notorious deceleration of prices produced by the stabilization program will keep the change in inflationary expectations generating such a shift in increased productive behavior" (*La Opinión,* 13 September 1973).

Nominal money continued to expand. During 1973 the increase in the monetary aggregates doubled that of 1972. Nominal interest rates decreased and real interest rates became negative. Disinflation was at the same time quickly

Table 4.4   **Real Wage[a] Index**

Year and Month	Wages	Year and Month	Wages
1973	100.0	1975	105.6
January	105.7	January	118.6
February	97.8	February	103.4
March	110.7	March	111.0
April	86.3	April	101.7
May	89.9	May	97.2
June	90.6	June	155.9
July	109.2	July	114.3
August	108.0	August	102.1
September	107.7	September	92.2
October	106.7	October	91.6
November	105.7	November	99.1
December	97.8	December	86.6
1974	109.2	1976	63.3
January	103.8	January	101.8
February	102.1	February	85.3
March	101.1	March	74.1
April	120.2	April	60.9
May	116.6	May	54.0
June	112.3	June	60.3
July	110.0	July	57.6
August	105.4	August	54.0
September	102.1	September	54.7
October	98.5	October	51.1
November	125.5	November	54.7
December	111.3	December	51.4

Source: International Bank for Reconstruction and Development (IBRD).
[a]Unskilled married worker, 1973 = 100.

monetizing the economy. And M1 as a percentage of GNP was 9.2% during the first half of 1973, rising to 12.2% in the last quarter and to 14.4% in the first quarter of 1974. This represented for the government a revenue of 5.2% of GNP as seignorage in just nine months (see table 4.7). In those nine months, M2 increased by 9.5% of GNP.

The external sector was also improving substantially. Reserves began to increase, from $700 million in the first quarter of 1973, to $1,400 in the fourth and to its peak of $2,000 in the second quarter of 1974 (see fig. 4.4, and table 4.8 below). The free market exchange rate appreciated and fell to par. The noninterest current account experienced a surplus of $700 million in 1973, a sizable improvement compared to a deficit of $218 million in 1972. Exports increased 68% to $3,266 million. Imports being rationed increased by just 17%.

The economic team supported the idea that exports, and especially traditional exports, were not strongly responsive to prices. Therefore, a devalua-

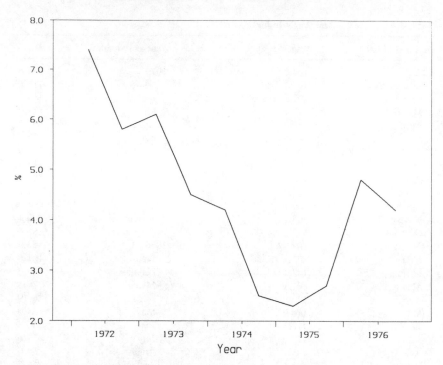

Fig. 4.3   Unemployment, April–October, 1972–76

Table 4.5   Unemployment Rate[a]

Period	Percentage
1972:	
April	7.4
October	5.8
1973:	
April	6.1
October	4.5
1974:	
April	4.2
October	2.5
1975:	
April	2.3
October	2.7
1976:	
April	4.8
October	4.2

Source: INDEC.
[a]Greater Buenos Aires.

Table 4.6   **Growth Rates of Output^a (%)**

Year and Quarter	GNP	Agriculture	Industry	Construction	Investment
1972	3.1	−7.9	6.0	4.9	5.2
I	4.7	−4.3	8.9	12.9	−.4
II	1.3	−13.2	7.6	8.0	−3.0
III	1.5	−3.7	5.2	1.6	−2.3
IV	3.3	4.0	2.9	−2.4	37.3
1973	5.8	13.5	6.4	−5.1	−1.3
I	6.1	12.2	7.4	−3.5	.7
II	6.3	21.8	6.6	−12.7	.5
III	4.1	12.1	4.6	−10.2	−14.8
IV	6.6	7.3	7.0	6.8	9.8
1974	6.5	6.2	6.1	12.2	3.9
I	4.3	8.8	3.2	6.9	−4.6
II	7.5	8.6	7.3	11.0	2.8
III	7.3	6.9	6.5	15.3	7.5
IV	6.8	−.6	7.0	15.8	9.5
1975	−1.3	−3.5	−2.8	−9.6	−7.2
I	3.3	−5.7	2.9	8.2	4.3
II	1.4	−5.9	1.4	−6.7	−2.2
III	−3.2	−3.6	−5.6	−11.3	−8.1
IV	−6.3	2.8	−8.9	−26.3	−20.2
1976	−2.9	3.5	−4.5	−14.1	−6.2
I	−4.4	7.9	−6.7	−26.7	−16.9
II	−5.2	−.1	−6.3	−15.0	−12.6
III	−1.7	.8	−2.9	−10.7	.5
IV	−.2	5.9	−2.0	−.3	5.4

Source: Banco Central de la República Argentina (BCRA).
^{a}Growth from same quarter of previous year.

Table 4.7   **Liquidity Coefficients**

Year and Quarter	M1/Y	Year and Quarter	M1/Y
1973	.1025	1975	.0902
I	.0933	I	.1416
II	.0910	II	.1119
III	.1078	III	.0791
IV	.1219	IV	.0875
1974	.1377	1976	.0621
I	.1440	I	.0793
II	.1339	II	.0551
III	.1416	III	.0666
IV	.1377	IV	.0674

Source: BCRA, (CEMYB).

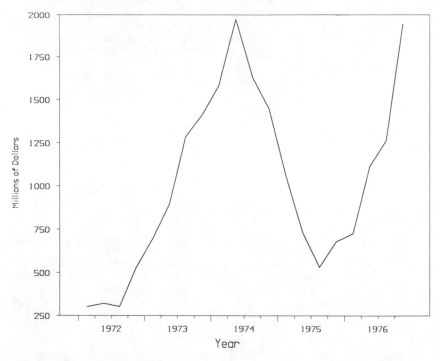

Fig. 4.4   Reserves in BCRA

tion of the currency was not considered a useful way of improving the trade balance.[9]

It is surprising that without a devaluation and in spite of strong growth in money supply and an expansion in domestic spending, both generated by an increase in the public-sector deficit and a strong increase in private consumption, the Central Bank was able to accumulate reserves for over a year. Several factors helped in achieving such a success. Among them the most important was the strong increase in the terms of trade during both 1972 and 1973. In the fourth quarter of 1973 the terms of trade began falling, but imports remained strictly controlled. This positive external shock gave open room for a loosening of the foreign restriction (see table 4.3 above).

4.6   Problems Begin to Appear

By the end of 1973 the stabilization effort was haunted by different circumstances: "The rigorous anti-inflationary policy of the government faces at the

9. The idea that traditional exports were unresponsive to prices was complemented with ideas about the contractionary effects of the devaluation that worked through the induced fall in real wages. Early work on this field had been done by Diaz Alejandro (1966) and Krugman and Taylor (1978).

beginning of 1974 three main threats. The first comes from the rest of the world and is expressed in the dramatic increase in prices of all the imported inputs needed by the country. The second enemy of stabilization policy is the wage increases pursued by some unions. . . . The stabilization faces a third problem, which is the lack of confidence by wide sectors about the sustainability of stability" (*La Opinión,* 25 January 1974).

Indeed, by December 1973 the program had been so successful that internal inflation was below international levels and pressure for revaluation of the currency began to arise. This pressure was generated by firms with fixed prices that were facing an ever higher price for their imported inputs. Two basic positions in the government were set forward, one supporting price flexibility and the other defending a revaluation of the currency. After approving an increase in the prices for those firms it considered were suffering from this problem, the government reversed its decision and revalued the currency for imports. This generated substantial losses (quasi-fiscal deficit) to the Central Bank, as it was paying exporters a higher exchange rate than the one it was charging to importers.

During the first quarter of 1974, inflation remained low and was about 3% during the whole quarter for the CPI and about 1.2% for the WPI. Finally the government gave in to union pressures and decided to adjust wages before the scheduled date in June 1974. As can be seen in figure 4.2, wages had slowly deteriorated since June 1973. A new National Compromise Act was signed 27 March 1974. It included an increase in wages of 13% from the first of April (but only if that increment was not less than $240, in which case it would equal $240). The minimum wage was raised by 30%. Easy credit at subsidized rates was issued to pay for these increases, and, in addition, nominal interests rates were reduced by 4 percentage points.

Tariffs were adjusted once again with the general index increasing by 53.4%, but with considerable dispersion between enterprises. At the beginning of April some 121 firms were allowed to change their prices from those they had had the previous year. (Special attention was given to the cases of negative profits.)

The decision to modify the adjustment scheme would prove a major cause in the subsequent collapse of the program. The agents realized that rules were really not that strict and that eventually the government was willing to give in. Unions intensified their pressures, firms became more aggressive, and confidence in the program immediately disappeared. The government gave up in this way one of its most valuable assets, which was its commitment to its own rules. Monetary and fiscal policies were also incompatible with complete nominal price rigidity. The combination of these with a fall in confidence and therefore demonetization made the situation explosive in the short run.

During the second quarter of 1974 signs of problems began to appear more clearly. Among these, illegal price increases and black markets began to proliferate. This had already been recognized by Ber Gelbard. When signing the new National Compromise Act, he said, "The CGT [Confederación General del Trabajo] has announced its decision of constituting sectorial commissions in order to control the adherence to the price and supply policy and therefore contribute to avoiding speculation and abuse, but this should not end with the work of the CGT. Each and every one of the Argentines must be an agent that should look after that policy, because the State, by itself or with its institutions, can't take care of the pockets of 25 million fools that don't do [this]" (*La Nación,* 28 March 1974.)

Other sources were also taking stock of the problem. M. Diamand had argued before the signing of the new act that:

> From the result of the negotiations underway between the CGE [Confederación General Económica] and the CGT over price and wage policies [hangs] the solution to the most difficult obstacle to the economic policy of the government, I refer to the shortages seen in the industrial sector, which every day are more serious.
>
> Every day we can hear of dozens of stories. Shortages of paper bags doesn't allow the provision of lime, sugar, etc. A TV factory stops due to lack of paint, . . .
>
> The complete freeze was very successful in the achievement of very difficult objectives. . . . Nevertheless, industrial firms in many cases could not compensate even variable costs. . . . In the present situation it is necessary to change from an income policy based on absolute stability to a policy based on price and wage flexibility. (*La Opinión,* 15 March 1974)

Gelbard later had to defend his own policy in this particular respect. In a conference given at the CGT on 22 May, he said: "We do not fool anybody in this or any other respect: there are shortages, there is a certain black market and a certain amount of speculation. But we hurry to say that, as we get notice of those responsible for these distortions we will fall on them with all the strength of law. . . . We think that these saboteurs of the process are the agents of counterrevolution" (*La Opinión,* 27 May 1974).

By 12 June, after knowing that the inflation of May was above 4% (both for CPI and WPI), the president himself decided to defend the economic policy of the government. In a message to the country, President Perón said, "Only months after the acceptance of that key agreement for the country [an allusion to the new National Compromise Act], it seems that some of those that signed it are decided in not obeying the agreement and want to make everybody believe the same way. . . . Those of us who have been for years in this job, know perfectly that about 80% or 90% of the things being said are invented by the professionals of the psychologic action" (De Pablo 1980, pp. 87–88).

But Perón himself was not making things easy. Five days later he announced the payment of a whole extra salary at the end of June.[10] Of course

---

10. Argentine labor legislation provides for the payment of an extra monthly wage each year, paid half at the end of June and half at the end of December.

this was to come from money creation, directly used by the government to pay the extra wages, or through easy credit to the private sector.

On the first of July a most dramatic event left the country shocked and stunned. At 1:15 P.M., President Juan Domingo Perón suddenly died. His wife, Maria Estela Martinez de Perón, was sworn in as president. With this, political expectations moved further against the government. The situation that Isabel Perón received was just about to become unmanageable.

The external sector was deteriorating very quickly. Terms of trade had fallen from 120 in the second quarter of 1973 to 65 in the second of 1974. The official exchange rates had become increasingly overvalued and furthermore, fiscal and monetary policies had continued to be strongly expansionary. Between July and October 1974, the Central Bank lost almost 25% of its reserves, and the noninterest current account surplus, which had been $704 million dollars in 1973, dropped to $127 million in 1974. But this number hides the real deterioration that the external sector was experiencing. Indeed, the economy had a surplus of $395 million in the first half of 1974 and a deficit of $268 million in the second.

Real interest rates, which had been about − 10% in the first half dropped to around − 20% in the second half of 1974, owing to the increase in the inflation rate.

It was by now clear that the price freeze would be removed any moment: "The reorientation of the process, to make it once again compatible with the social agreement, looks toward the implementation of a more flexible scheme. . . . The most difficult problem is that of eliminating the machinery of black markets and reduce to the legal level those prices which increased above [those limits]" (*La Opinión*, 22 June 1974). "Laws of this nature [the law on supply to markets], saturated with fines and terrific corporal punishments, is another negative result of an economic policy which has proven its failure" (*La Prensa*, 26 June 1974).

This became an open conflict within the government after Gómez Morales (president of the Central Bank) publicly declared that the whole price policy was in crisis. The president was already also suggesting that something had to be done; on 18 September, she declared: "Only a very significant change in the conditions that made Gral. Perón implement this economic policy would eventually suggest the need to implement changes in the road pursued" (*La Opinión*, 18 September 1974).

One month later it seemed that those significant changes in the conditions had arrived. On 21 October, as the situation worsened, the president reached a compromise with other sectors of the party and appointed Alfredo Gómez Morales, a respected traditional economist from Perón's first government, minister of finance.[11] The economic team of José Ber Gelbard had slowly

---

11. Gómez Morales had been president of the Central Bank since the presidency of Cámpora. Differences with Ber Gelbard resulted in his resignation shortly before Ber Gelbard left the office of minister of finance (De Pablo 1980b).

wasted away. "The difficulties of the economic team in the present reality must have taken it to this epilogue, in which it decides to retire. It must not [have] been prepared to assume the responsibility of the necessary fundamental rectifying measures" (Antonio Trocolli in *La Opinión,* 22 October 1974). "The economic program had arrived, under Minister Gelbard, at a situation of being completely worn out. Inflation was threatening to come back. . . . The previous team promoted the increase in public employees, reduced firms' profits and left the state 'to be' " (Mariano Grondona in *La Opinión,* 25 October 1974).

Gómez Morales was expected to bring more flexibility to the economic system and to make some adjustment in the increasingly disordered fiscal situation. For the president this postponed a full implementation of the right-wing program until later.

Gómez Morales once again gathered the main interest groups to agree on a new act. Signed 1 November 1974, it introduced a wage increase of 15% and an increase in equal amount of family subsidies. The minimum wage was raised to $1,600. Regarding price policy, Gómez Morales did not disappoint anybody and incorporated a new set of rules into the act that allowed firms experiencing increases in cost to raise prices. As Gómez Morales himself explained later, "The policy that we followed to stop inflation in 1973 was a 'shock' policy, prices and wages were frozen, but it was not adopted with enough flexibility. That shouldn't have lasted more than six months; afterward, facing imported inflation, we should have flexibilized the price market. As we didn't, a black market appeared for certain articles. . . . What should be done first is to flexibilize the price system to eliminate the black market" (as quoted in *La Opinión,* 12 November 1974).

These changes were received by the business community with relief. "The increases that the Executive Power has just authorized are a first positive and realistic step toward the organization of a market better prepared for productive activities" (*Clarín,* 11 November 1974). "The third stage begins with the return of the president of the Central Bank [Gómez Morales], now as minister of finance. In this final stage of the year—little more than 60 days—an increased realism seems to be the main characteristic, and old and forgotten worries reappear such as the fiscal deficit, the every-day-bigger black market, [and] the rise in the exchange rate, which the now relatively contractive money supply seems to have stopped momentarily" (*La Nación,* 29 December 1974).

In spite of the positive impression that Gómez Morales made in more orthodox circles, he did little to stop the increase in money supply and to reduce the fiscal deficit (see table 4.2). On the contrary, the fiscal deficit seems to have risen in the last quarter of 1974 and first of 1975. Money growth was strongly positive at the end of 1974. At the beginning of 1975 it declined substantially but remained high. Once again he declared, "The basic outline for the economic policy in 1975 will be to give more importance to savings and not to excessive consumption, and to fiscal discipline to drastically reduce the fiscal deficit" (quoted in *La Opinión,* 15 January 1975).

By 1 February 1975, prices of public enterprises were adjusted (the price of petrol was increased by 45%, electricity by 26%, railroad fares by 50%, etc.).

In February the CPI and WPI showed increases of 4.6% and 12.5%, respectively. As inflation accelerated real wages continued to decline, falling below the previous lower peak achieved before the November act. On 1 March 1975 a new adjustment had to be made. This time it was part of the so-called Great National Parity. Among the arrangements it contained was an increase in wages of $400 for all categories, further flattening the wage pyramid. A wage structure with wages at $100, $150, $200, and $300 by May 1973 was to be transformed at this moment, March 1975, to the following values: $100, $100, $125 and $168; that is, a wage difference of 200% was being reduced to one of just 68% (Arnaudo 1979). The minimum wage was increased to $2,000, an increase that "could not be shifted to prices."

Figure 4.2 shows the evolution of the real wage during this period. The real wage increased substantially after the signing of each agreement, meanwhile, in between agreements, it experienced a steady decline. What is perhaps most interesting are the dynamics implicit in the figure. The adjustments are made more and more frequently as the program evolves, with the initial adjustment being larger and larger. As inflation accelerates the decline in real wages also accelerates, generating the need to shorten the length of contracts and raise initial wages in order to compensate for the increased erosion. This was reflected in increased pressure on the government by labor unions to adjust the wages agreed on previously more often and by bigger amounts.[12]

At the end of February the black market exchange rate was trading with a 100% premium over the financial rate. Therefore, on 1 March, the economic team decided to devalue all the exchanges rates. The effective exchange rate devaluation (i.e., that obtained after eliminating trade policy changes) varied substantially across products. For export goods (and particularly for traditional export goods) the devaluation was almost completely compensated, with effective exchange rates moving between 0.6% and 1.4%. For imports the devaluation ranged from 11.5% to 51.3%. The tourist rate was devalued by 36.6% (De Pablo 1980a). The devaluation tried to stop a rage of speculative imports that were being carried out in anticipation of the devaluation. Gómez Morales, in a public communication, stated: "In contrast to what has been done in the past, this exchange reform doesn't include any preventive devaluation, nor has fiscal purposes, i.e., [it] has not been done to improve

---

12. This situation is analogous to that of nominal price setting, which has been extensively studied in macro literature. The price setter fixes a price and changes it only after the real price drops below a certain threshold value. If inflation increases, the price setter adjusts to a higher real price and does so more frequently. These dynamics are the same as those shown in fig. 4.2 (Blanchard and Fischer 1989, chap. 8).

the resources of the government. . . . Its purpose has been just economic" (*La Opinión*, 4 March 1975).

This contrasted strongly with his own opinions some months before:[13] "I reject even to consider modifying the exchange rate. A devaluation is useless, it is the last measure I will resort to" (Gómez Morales, press conference, 22 October 1974).

In April, Gómez Morales prepared an alternative emergency program, postulating the need for a contraction in demand basically through a reduction in the real wage. This, it was assumed, would worsen income distribution but would enhance the possibilities of achieving stabilization and increasing investment and efficiency. As he himself explained: "The fundamental problem is the lack of productivity of the society. . . . We have to stabilize an economy that has lost even a minimum of stability. It is not necessary to reach a stability of zero, but we cannot have the inflation that these first months are showing. . . . Without doubt, from May on, the freeze we have implemented will begin to show its effects" (statements made on the TV program "Tiempo Nuevo," 22 April 1975).

Even though monetary growth was almost cut in half in the first part of 1975, economic policy continued to be expansionary (M1 growth between October and March had been an average of 4.2% a month). The adjustment in public enterprise prices was being quickly eroded by inflation. Output growth slowed down substantially in the first two quarters of 1975 (quarterly GNP increased by 3.3% in the first quarter and 1.4% in the second). Nevertheless, unemployment continued to fall until April when it reached an all-time low of 2.3%. Private investment began to fall in the second quarter. Inflation accelerated, with the CPI increasing by 8.1% in March and 9.7% in April.

As inflation accelerated, real balances began to fall. As a percentage of GNP, M1 fell by 3% between the first and second quarters of 1975. The acceleration of the readjustments in the signing of the national acts was both a consequence and a cause of the increase in velocity. The fall in the terms of trade, the closing of the European market for Argentine beef exports, the overheating of the economy and the exchange rate, which continued to be overvalued, weakened substantially the external sector situation. Reserves were virtually disappearing, dropping between November and April from $1,573 million to $754 million. At this stage, a run on the Central Bank, as in Dornbusch (1987) or Flood and Garber (1984) was clearly under way.

The acceleration of inflation increased the fiscal deficit through the Olivera-Tanzi effect. The government therefore relied more heavily on money creation in order to finance its disequilibrium. Nevertheless, in the second quarter it was the private sector that accounted for the greatest share of money creation.

13. Of course it would be unwise for a Central Banker to anticipate the market on his planned devaluations. Nevertheless, Gómez Morales's statements reflected a standard position in the government at that time regarding the usefulness of a real devaluation in order to improve the external balance.

Too little had been done too late: the economy could not avoid a drastic readjustment. The public-sector deficit had already jumped from 3.7% of GNP in 1972 to 7.6% in 1973 and to 8.1% in 1974. During the first quarter of 1975 the situation appeared to stop worsening but the deficit remained incompatible with stability of nominal variables (see table 4.2).

4.7 The Readjustment

On 2 June 1975, Celestino Rodrigo, of the right-wing group of the party, was sworn in as minister of finance. He remained in office for 50 days, during which time a major readjustment took place in the economy. His economic measures would be thereafter remembered in popular memory as "El Rodrigazo."

Rodrigo considered that the balance of payments crisis was the consequence of overvalued exchange rates and expansionary fiscal and monetary policies. On 4 June he implemented a 100% devaluation of the financial exchange rate, of 80% for the tourist rate and of 160% for the commercial rate. In order to reduce the fiscal deficit he increased the price of oil by 181%, of gas by 40%–60%, electricity by 40%–50%, transportation by 75%, and so on. Wage negotiations were to be suspended. The government nevertheless allowed an increase of 65% in the minimum wage but left all other wages to be decided in collective bargaining between workers and firms.[14]

On 9 June the president announced that increases above 38% in nominal wages would not be accepted; three days later she had to increase this upper bound to 45% and 17 days later to 80%. Isabel Perón was feeling strong pressure from the unions, which were at this stage in open confrontation with the government. Strikes were proliferating everywhere and the discussion among union leaders was not if they should oppose the government but how far to go. During the month, wage negotiations became almost chaotic. On 18 June the construction union signed one of the first arrangements with a nominal wages increase of 45%, two days later textile workers negotiated an increase of 100% in their wages. The increases finally settled between 203% for the workers of leather and 78% for the (public) employees of water, electricity, and gas. Inflation jumped from 3.9% in May to 21.3% in June and 34.9% in July for the CPI. The WPI raised from 5.2% to 42.5% and 32.2%.

In an attempt to stop the price/wage spiral the government froze the prices of 30 products. On 30 June, Rodrigo addressed the country, explaining the evolution of the economic program:

> Also in prices we have advanced fundamentally a new policy that means the correction of real prices that the economy was paying, which were stimulating a black market more and more damaging to the interests of the coun-

---

14. It is worthwhile to remember that it was in June 1975 when the initial freeze was to end, and open negotiations between workers and firms were to take place.

try. We have defined a basket of basic food over which an efficient control will be imposed. . . . An important effort will be made to increase tax collection. . . . This wage policy is coherent with the economic plan implemented the first of June, and will allow [us] to avoid spectacular increases in the near future in the exchange rate and tariffs. . . . .It will avoid unemployment and will make more possible the solution of the external sector problems. (*La Nación,* 1 July 1975)

The real exchange rate recovered, and the external sector showed strong improvement in the third quarter. Nevertheless this seemed much more related to the recession than to the real devaluation; in the third quarter the agricultural-sector production experienced a decline of 3.6%. International reserves continued to decline, reaching a low of $529 million in the third quarter of 1975. At the values of the first half of 1975 this was not enough to pay for even two months of imports.

By the end of the month the president had lost a great part of her credibility and political support, and the right-wing faction had to step back as more moderate groups, especially those associated with the labor unions, were regaining positions. On 5 July, a long *solicitada* was published by union leaders in the main newspapers of Buenos Aires, which clearly shows the position of the labor sector regarding the economic policy. This *solicitada* contained the following six basic points:

1. Ratify the support of the organized labor movement to the president of the nation, Dona Maria Estela Martinez de Perón, and the unconditional defense of the *Doctrina Justicialista,* core of the National Movement.
2. Oblige firms to apply from the 1st of June the Law 14250 of Collective Bargaining, whose validity was accorded with the Minister of Labor, and therefore is of legal validity and of obligatory compliance.
3. Repudiate the discretionary use of power that is generating unprecedented confrontations in our Movement, between its chief and her workers, as well as [repudiate] the idea embedded in the measures that try to denationalize the economy, and worse than that, the national being; an economic policy that deteriorates the real wage and therefore is contradictory in facts with the *Justicialista* principles of a progressive redistribution of income in favor of the people and the liberation of the country.
4. Call for a general strike for 48 hours, from midnight of Monday, 7 July 1975, until midnight of Wednesday, 9 July, as support of what is explained in this resolution.
5. Give to the Directive Commission of the CGT the task of organizing this measure in essential public services.
6. Declare the Confederated Central Comity of the CGT in permanent session from today on.

It is difficult to determine the exact evolution of the real wage during the period because official statistics incorporate from 1 June retroactive increases that were obtained months later. Comparison is especially difficult because those increases differed substantially across sectors. The wage increases obtained in the June negotiation generated an important increase in the real wage for that month. Nevertheless the inflationary explosion eroded that increase very quickly (see table 4.4 and fig. 4.2). The fall in real wages induced by the adjustment is clearly perceived by looking at the figures for the following months. In September real wages fell to their lowest level since the beginning of the stabilization program.

As a consequence of the adjustment in the public sector, the strong devaluation, and the explosion of inflation, a strong recession ensued. In the third quarter total output was to fall at an annual rate of 3.2%. For the industrial sector the decline was even larger: 5.6%. Investment also began to decrease as firms were expecting hard times ahead. The third quarter showed an annualized decrease of 8.1% in total investment and of 11% in construction. In October the unemployment rate showed its first increase in almost two years.

The acceleration of inflation further deteriorated the fiscal deficit through the Tanzi-Olivera effect. The deficit increased in the third quarter by almost 3 percentag points. Money creation almost tripled in the third quarter, and monetization continued to drop significantly, falling by more than 3% of GNP between the second and third quarters.

A new devaluation (of about 8% for the commercial rate, 18% for the financial rate) was passed 16 July. On 20 July, Rodrigo's resignation was accepted.

4.8   The End

At this stage the government was strongly discredited and divided in its own ranks. The climate of political violence had intensified, and the military were quietly waiting for the reputation of the president to decline to the level at which they could safely stage a coup to regain power.

But the government of Isabel Perón still had eight months to go until on 24 March 1976, she was finally arrested and removed from power. Still, three ministers of finance were given the responsibility of handling the delicate postadjustment situation and trying to make it last.

The first of these was José Bonnani, a former minister of finance from Perón's first presidency, who had implemented the adjustment program of 1952. José Bonnani had an original idea: instead of gathering the main interest groups to sign a new agreement, as had been common practice with the first two ministers, he gave them the responsibility of formulating an economic program and raising it to the government for consideration. In a declaration on 22 July he said: "To those effects the ministry of which I'm in charge aims to convene all the sectors which represent the community as soon as possible, in order to design in agreement an Emergency Plan that the actual situation imperatively requires."

Several projects were presented to the government. Being the two most important those completed by the CGT, representing labor unions, and the CGE representing businessmen.

The document of the CGT included, among others, the following recommendations: to reconstitute the state's productive capacity with an efficient plan, to support the policy of workers' participation in management, to freeze and control prices, to reestablish subsidies to basic foods, and to support wage indexation, the nationalization of foreign trade, the reactivation of industrial promotion, special credit lines for private firms, and the creation of a National Council of Economic Emergency.

The document of the CGE was clearly more moderate and included, among others, the following suggestions: authorize the price increases that firms had demanded, allow the increase in costs to be reflected in higher prices, normalize the wage problems derived from the chaotic negotiations of the Rodrigo period, increase in credits, and pursue indexation of the exchange rate for exports after an initial devaluation, reactivation of public investment, establishment of a fiscal moratorium, and the creation of an Emergency Economic and Social Council.

In the meantime, Bonnani put forward a package of measures, among which were an increase of wages of 160% retroactive to 1 June (which Rodrigo had not signed). An increase in tariffs of between 60% and 80% and a 20% increase in the exchange rates.

The general outline of the policy was clear: "The strategy of the Bonnani team is to try to give the most importance to the execution of measures of extreme urgency, . . . but [to] avoid [any] decision that may become an obstacle for the concertation. In this sense Dr. Bonnani behaves as an anti-Rodrigo. At the same time, several enquires are made to establish coincidence points. . . . It has been known that the objective of Dr. Bonnani is to write a document that may function as a draft for a National Economic Program in a multisectoral meeting to be called soon" (*La Opinión*, 27 July 1975).

But the urgency in the execution, or the quickness in the convocation to the different sectors, may have been induced by the weak political support of the minister. No other measures were taken due to lack of time. Shortly after the publication of the "suggestions" and exactly 20 days after taking office, on 11 August, José Bonnani's resignation was accepted.

The next round went to Antonio Cafiero, a respected Peronist leader who had the confidence of the unions. Cafiero faced two serious problems: extremely high inflation, generated as a consequence of the drastic realignment in prices of previous months (inflation in July had been 34.9% for the CPI and 32.2% for the WPI), and a substantial increase in the rate of unemployment due to the recession.[15] The unemployment problem was considered a serious

---

15. De Pablo (1980a) quotes a survey in which the unemployment rate in greater Buenos Aires was about 6% in August. A consistent methodology produced twice a year by INDEC, shows an unemployment rate of 2.3% in April of 1975 and of 2.75% in October of the same year.

one by the government and was as such understood by the private sector: "FIEL [Fundación de investigatiónes economicas latinoamericanas], in a study on the Argentine economy in September 1975, that will be in print soon, emphasizes a fall in sales, production, employment, and predicts that it is not correct to expect that the government will remain insensible to the situation in this respect (basically the wage problem) or that it will assume responsibility of making the burden of price stabilization fall on the working class. To expect wage increases in the near future is basically correct" (*La Nación*, 5 October 1975).

In his first message, on 25 August, Cafiero gave the unemployment problem paramount importance. Regarding inflation, a gradualist strategy was to be implemented. But monetary growth was not restrained; M1 increased at a monthly rate of 15.3% while Cafiero was Minister.

In a public speech on 4 November, Cafiero said:

> The Argentines must remember that in August of this year we were confronted with the following situation: threat of massive unemployment in all sectors, a process of galloping inflation under way accompanied by acute illiquidity, and a virtual default on our external payments due to lack of foreign exchange.
>
> Of the three problems not one has been resolved completely. . . . Regarding unemployment . . . firms and even the public administration will be obliged to keep reducing, by direct or indirect procedures, the number of their employees. . . .
>
> In the first ten months of this year prices rose by 261%. . . . This proves that "inflationary pressures" still exist, but we have promised to reduce [them] gradually and we are indeed doing so.

Even days later one could still read:

> What are the basic things that Dr. Cafiero considers priorities? To begin a process of growth, he points out that it is necessary to reverse recessive tendencies, stop unemployment and generate expectations of recovery in the external sector. . . .
>
> The head of the Ministry of Finance leaves aside two issues: stopping inflation and achieving a redistribution of income.
>
> What makes Cafiero different from other ministers, especially from those who preceded him, is not the instruments he chooses to stop the crisis, but the "timing." Dr. Cafiero uses a "gradualist" approach. (Daniel Muchnick in *La Opinión*, 28 November 1975)

Regarding the exchange rate, Cafiero implemented a crawling peg in order to avoid an erosion of the real depreciation achieved by Rodrigo. An agreement was signed with the IMF and the World Bank in an important shift of strategy regarding multilateral organizations. International reserves began to recover, bouncing up to $680 million in the last quarter of 1975, and further to $725 million in the first of 1976.

It was decided that wages were to be adjusted every three months after an initial realignment on 1 November, which granted an increase of $1,500 for all categories and increased the minimum wage to $4,800. Family subsidies and retirement wages were also increased. Of course real wages were eroded significantly in the following months.

Tariffs were adjusted on 1 November (with an average increase of 25%) and were afterward to be indexed in an effort to protect fiscal revenues from inflationary erosion. Nevertheless the public-sector deficit deteriorated further in the fourth quarter. Data from the Central Bank puts the deficit at 16% of GNP for this period. Data from the Fundación Mediterránea puts it at 16.1% of GNP for the whole year, though it may well have been substantially higher for the last quarter (see table 4.2). The deficit was somewhat reduced in the first quarter of 1976 but at 12.9% of GNP remained too high to be compatible with a minimum of stability. Money growth continued unabated. During the whole year M1 had increased by almost 200%. Monetization remained at the low levels of the Rodrigo period.

Prices remained controlled. For basic wage goods, a maximum price was fixed. Twenty-four other important goods were also frozen, and prices of leading firms were supervised and could only be changed with the approval of the secretary of commerce. Inflation decelerated somewhat until November, but remained stubbornly above 10%. After that it began showing a clear positive trend. The CPI increased 8.1% in November, 11.5% in December, 14.8% in January, and 19.3% in February (see table 4.1).

In January the exchange rate market was further liberalized. All tourist transactions were shifted to a free market, and several goods were transferred from one exchange to another. These measures, in addition to the devaluations implemented through the crawling peg (between August and February they accumulated 71% for the financial rate), enhanced the trade balance, which went into surplus in the first half of 1976 (see Dornbusch 1986). This improvement was also a consequence of the strong recession the economy was undergoing. As a result, a deficit of $425 million in the second half of 1975 gave way to a surplus of $290 million during the first part of 1976 (table 4.8).

During the year, the GNP showed a strong contraction, which became extremely acute in the last quarter. The GNP fell by 1.3% during 1975. Output growth had been 3.3%, 1.4%, −3.2%, and −6.3% for the four quarters of the year. Construction dropped by 11.3% and 26% in the third and fourth quarters, respectively, while investment dropped by 8.1% and 20.2%. Unemployment also continued to worsen: from a 2.7% rate in October it jumped to 4.8% in April of 1976.

Overall, 1975 finished with a strong reversal in the income redistribution trend. Participation of wage earners in GNP fell by almost 2% (see table 4.9).

By January, criticism of the economic policy began to surface again: "In the absence of substantial changes in the political orientation, nothing makes it conceivable to assume that the bad economic situation of the beginning of the

Table 4.8   **Balance of Trade and International Reserves**

	Trade Balance (By Six-Month Period)		International Reserves (By Quarter)
1972:		1972:	
I	− 126.1	I	300.3
II	− 91.9	II	321.5
		III	300.7
		IV	529.0
1973:		1973:	
I	393.0	I	694.8
II	317.0	II	892.7
		III	1285.1
		IV	1412.4
1974:		1974:	
I	395.0	I	1582.9
II	− 268.0	II	1972.3
		III	1629.6
		IV	1446.4
1975:		1975:	
I	− 874.0	I	1057.6
II	− 426.0	II	732.7
		III	529.5
		IV	678.0
1976:		1976:	
I	289.0	I	725.7
II	361.0	II	1114.2
		III	1266.2
		IV	1943.9

Note: Both series are in millions of dollars.
Sources: BCRA and INDEC.

Table 4.9   **Percentage of Income Accruing to Wage Earners**

Year	Percentage
1950	49.7
1965	40.6
1966	43.8
1967	45.5
1968	44.9
1969	44.6
1970	45.8
1971	46.6
1972	42.7
1973	46.9
1974	46.7
1975	44.8

Source: Ministry of Finance.

year may change during 1976" (*La Nación*, 4 January 1976). And after Cafiero's resignation:

> The administration of the tandem Cafiero–Di Tella, that initially generated positive expectations in some sectors, finished without any of the problems being resolved. Their action seemed marked by a complete lack of mobility that limited them to some financial arrangements abroad of little result, late adjustments regarding wages, a frustrated tax reform and finally in what most was done, successive and [ever-larger] adjustments in the exchange rate.
>
> The image that he provided was, summarizing, that of someone who thought [he] knew how to "administer the crises" but finally just made it "survive." (*Clarín*, 8 February 1976)

In January, the president, who had been on leave for a month and a half while Italo Luder held the presidency, tried to regain some of her power: the right-wing program was to be given a last chance. Mondelli was named minister of finance on 3 February 1976.

The expectations of his administration are well described below:

> It is accepted that the real wage cannot be defended but through an increase in the total product of the economy, which now is stagnant or declining. . . . A realistic readjustment of tariffs, or the cost of public services and the price of energy products [must be expected]. The public administration spending, especially those on employees will be strictly constrained. . . . It is believed that with the help of the IMF and complementary help, the situation in the external sector could be solved. (*La Nación*, 26 February 1976)

Or, as Mondelli himself put it some years later:

> At the moment of my arrival there were very serious problems. . . . Let's give an example: Argentina, at that time, had a spectacular balance of payments crisis. . . . That balance of payments crisis had to be dealt [with] as one would handle such a crisis, not more, not less. . . . There was no other remedy than repeating, perhaps not to such a great extent, the measures that Minister Rodrigo had taken. It's very easy to say that such a medicine is sour, but there is no other choice if one has to take it in order not to die. (as quoted in De Pablo 1980b)

In the two remaining months real wages fell even though a nominal adjustment of 12%, which afterward became 20%, was granted. Tariffs were increased: on oil by 77%, on some derivatives by 300%, phone services 70%, transportation 150%, postal services 100%, and so on. The exchange rate market was partially unified in an official market, which unified the previous financial and special financial exchange rates with a devaluation for both of them of 82% and 28%, respectively. (Nevertheless, part of this devaluation was, once again, compensated.) Prices were to be strictly controlled, and

a new arrangement was signed with the IMF. In March the CPI increased
by 38%.

The plan once again gained criticism from the labor unions: "To the judg-
ment of the committee gathered in La Plata, the Mondelli Plan will only provoke a fall in the real wage, a fall in consumption, a fall in investment, an
increase in unemployment, shortages, and the disappearance of the State as
investor" (*La Opinión*, 12 March 1976).

But by this stage the government had no credibility and inflation was clearly
accelerating. By mid-March the political events took over, as everybody was
expecting from one moment to the other the fall of the president.

The coup finally took place on 24 March 1976. An even sadder period of
Argentine history was about to begin.

4.9 Conclusions

As an experiment in economic policy, the Argentine experience between
1973 and 1976 has to be considered a failure. In the end all its initial objectives: stability, redistribution of income, growth, investment and increased
standard of living were not only not achieved, but seemed even more distant
in 1976 than they were in 1973.

During 1973 the heterodox approach to fighting inflation implemented by
Gelbard was extremely successful; it shows that wage and price freezes can be
a very useful (and perhaps unavoidable) mechanisms for achieving disinflation without recession. By coordinating expectations, a painful learning process can be avoided if the government is able to convince the public that a
new equilibrium has been achieved. In the case of Argentina, the stabilization
program was strongly supported by the increase in the terms of trade, which
avoided exchange rate problems until well into 1974. The strong increase in
money demand gave the government an extended span of time during which
it could have tackled the fiscal deficit problem at the root of the inflationary
process. Unfortunately, this did not happen; on the contrary, the fiscal deficit
increased during 1973, setting the economy on an unstable path toward higher
inflation.

If the basics of inflation are not controlled, the heterodox approach is
doomed to failure from the start because the expansionary fiscal and monetary
policies finally induce wage increases and price pressures that generate,
sooner or later, either shortages with a corresponding monetary overhang or
black markets and illegal wage rises. Eventually the economy has to be readjusted, prices are freed, and the economy reverts to an equilibrium compatible with fiscal and monetary policies.

The obvious question to ask is why, then, do governments follow such inconsistent policies? Given that failure seems to be guaranteed and that such
failure entails big costs to the government (as this and other chapters of this

volume document),[16] how can one rationalize, from the perspective of the policymaker, the implementation of these policies?

The first hypothesis that comes to mind is that policymakers are irrational or ignorant. Populist policymakers may not understand or know the basics of macroeconomic theory and therefore may engage in policies that prove to be unsustainable, a fact they would have realized ex ante had they known better. Even though this may seem plausible, it basically states that there is no explanation for the emergence of populist policies. The basic problem with this hypothesis is that it cannot explain either the pervasiveness of this phenomena in Latin America or the fact that no learning takes place even when similar experiences failed in the past. Furthermore, a government is a set of individuals who necessarily have *personal objective functions* that they try to maximize. Recognition of this fact implies the need for explanations not based on the irrationality hypothesis.

A more stylized version of the irrationality hypothesis is that policymakers are ideologues whose behavior is constrained by the bounds imposed by their beliefs. Even though ideological elements seem very important in the claims and announcements of government policies (see section 4.3 above on the Three Year Plan), an understanding of the origins and of the social role of an ideology is necessary if any learning is to be obtained from this explanation.

A third possibility is that stabilizations are aborted because of "bad luck." When the government decides to undertake a stabilization program it balances benefits and costs. Costs are an increasing function of the outcome of a certain random variable (e.g., the costs of sustaining a fixed exchange rate system may increase with decreases in the terms of trade). The government decides to begin a stabilization program because it expects benefits will be larger than costs. For a range of realizations of the random variable it may reverse its policy because the ex post costs exceed the benefits (Dornbusch 1988b). The problem with this approach is that it seems to work the other way around. The government never did a serious fiscal reform in the first year and a half when external and internal conditions were extremely favorable. On the other hand, it seemed more committed to assume the costs of adjustment with Rodrigo and afterward, that is, after a serious balance of payments crisis.

A fourth explanation is that governments have extremely high discount rates. If they think they may not be around when the stabilization program collapses, then policymakers may try to induce short-run gains even though they know the program is unsustainable in the long run. This interpretation is also not convincing because usually it is the same government that implements these policies and then suffers their consequences. This is not only true

16. In some cases the costs are so high that they cast doubt on the existence of an explanation based on rational behavior. In the case of Chile the populist experience led to the death of the president. After 1976 the leaders of the Argentine government eventually ended up in prison or abroad.

of the Peronist administration discussed in this paper, but of almost all the other experiences discussed in this volume.

A fifth possible explanation is the "interest groups" hypothesis. The government represents a subset of the population and therefore does not care about the implications of its policy for other groups. This hypothesis includes several possible interpretations. Corruption, for example, is the special case in which the subset of the population represented by the government is the government itself. More generally the policymakers may represent either a certain factor of production, a particular region, or specific industries. This thesis is appealing for the experience studied in this paper because all the national agreements signed by the Peronist government included only entrepreneurs and industrial workers and basically consisted of transfers from the government to these two groups. If the government cared only about them, then it may have been willing to incur the inflationary costs of its own policies as the necessary outcome of transferring real resources to those two groups. The problem with this hypothesis is that the policies implemented eventually harmed even these groups, an outcome documented in sections 4.6 and 4.7 above. Nevertheless, this explanation must contain much of the truth.

A sixth explanation relies on the nature of the political environment. In a politically unstable society, and particularly where the policymaker's horizon is subject to unanticipated changes, it is very difficult for the voter to assign responsibilities. If there is a principal/agent problem in the relation between voters and policymakers we know, from the theory of optimal contracts, that this imperfect monitoring effect leads to a contract that relaxes the agent's incentives to run an efficient administration as compared to a situation where it is easier to observe directly his actions. (For example, in Argentina it is usually believed that many policymakers or political parties would have never been reelected had they been allowed to complete their constitutional terms without being overthrown by the military.) This explanation has the implausible characteristic that, in reality the consequences of an economic policy are clearly observable, but has the advantage of explaining why almost every government, independent of its ideological position, has been unable to reduce the fiscal deficit in a sustainable way in recent Argentine history. The same argument works for many other Latin American countries, particularly those in which populism has been recurrent.

Another related explanation that also captures the fact that no government has been able to reduce the fiscal deficit in a sustainable way relies on the nature of the budgetary process in Argentina (this being true for many other Latin American countries as well). The fact that spending and taxing decisions are taken arbitrarily by the executive power (when Congress approves the budget it usually does so months after the beginning of the economic period) weakens the position of the government in its relations with different economic interest groups. Instead of deciding fiscal policy in a single process during which all interest groups have to confront each other, the government has to bargain individually and separately with each one. This decision process generates a bias toward deficits and inflation because when a certain group deals with the government part of the costs of transferring resources to this group will be borne by the other sectors. This externality, which is internalized by everybody, induces a pattern of transfers far greater than the one that would result from a simultaneous bargaining process. If on top of the sequentiality of the spending process one adds the weak position of the government generated by the unstable political process, the bias toward deficits is strongly enhanced.

Finally, Alesina and Drazen (1990) suggest that stabilization may not take place or may not be fully implemented because conflict between interest groups may paralyze the government. Finally one group dominates and imposes the costs of stabilization on the other. This explanation looks particularly attractive in order to analyze the period after Rodrigo and to understand why a strong fiscal adjustment was only possible after the 1976 coup. It nevertheless leaves unanswered the question of why the government engaged itself in an unstable process when initially it commanded overwhelming support and power derived from the electoral outcomes of 1973.

The previous explanations are just partial solutions to the difficult question of understanding why the government engages in unsustainable policies. A complete theory of this phenomena is yet to be found.

The price freeze was a basic instrument in the stabilization program. What sometimes has been overlooked is that it generates optimal responses from price setters in the economy. If a price freeze is anticipated, there is an increase in the rate of inflation in the months before its implementation; firms prepare a price cushion, which they can optimally use by proper adjustment of rebates while the freeze lasts. This explains why, in the months before the change in government, there was a substantial increase in the price level. If the freeze is not anticipated or lasts more than initially expected, then either black markets develop in which commodities are sold above the official prices or, if the price freeze is strictly enforced, shortages and a monetary overhang will begin building up. In both cases an adjustment of official nominal prices takes place when the policy is finally abandoned. This may also have happened and might explain why the adjustment that Rodrigo implemented generated such a strong outburst of inflation. The Peronist government set itself too high standards. Trying to achieve a zero inflation rate, it attached itself for too long to a strict freeze that, soon after its implementation, was already generating strong distortions, shortages, and black markets.

The experience also shows what happens when the authorities consciously or unconsciously forget the need to sustain external balance. As soon as the exceptional price situation of 1973 began to reverse, the economy immediately fell into a deep balance of payments crisis. This made an adjustment unavoidable and generated a strong decline in the real wage, therefore leading to a reduction in the standard of living of the low- and middle-income classes.

In the introduction I remarked that the possibility of expansion was basically justified with old-fashioned Keynesian ideas. I also showed that the idea of increasing returns to scale, multiple equilibria, coordination failure, and externalities in general were also consistent with this idea. Both the Argentine experience and other populist regimes discussed in this volume show that these contentions are dubious. It was not possible to sustain the equilibrium with high levels of activity, which generated in the end a balance of payments crisis and increasing inflation.

Recent contributions by Dornbusch (1988a) and Sturzenegger (1990), study the relations between populist policies and real wages in a general equilibrium context. According to Dornbusch, the increase in real wages, by reducing the profitability of capital, initially generates a process of capital decumulation (this fact is not supported by the data for 1973). This decumulation makes the adjustment even more difficult because real wages have to fall below their initial level in order to make sufficiently profitable the levels of investment that will allow the stock of lost capital to reaccumulate. Dornbusch and Edwards (1989) consider this to be one of the main mechanisms that explains why, when the readjustment takes place, real wages fall below their initial level. Sturzenegger bases his explanation of the fall in real wages on the real depreciation that endogenously takes place with the readjustment of the economy. In the case of Argentina, this can clearly be seen in table 4.2. Real wages eventually declined in 1976 to half the value they had at the beginning of the program.[17]

Unfortunately, the strong procyclical spending policy implemented by the government eventually required a substantial readjustment of the economy, which contributed to the discredit and fall of the president and led to a dictatorship that lowered real wages even further. In addition to the capital flight and the fall in real wages (Dornbusch and Reynoso 1989) that accompanies the readjustment process, the military substantially weakens the bargaining power of unions. Finally the working class is made much worse off than it would have been had more moderate and sustainable policies been implemented.

References

Alesina, A., and A. Drazen. 1990. Why Are Stabilizations Delayed? Harvard University. Mimeograph.

Arnaudo, A. 1979. El Programa Antiinflacionario de 1973. *Desarrollo Economico.* Buenos Aires: IDES.

17. In a neoclassical framework with intertemporal optimization in an open economy, Sturzenegger (1990) shows that it is possible to replicate the basic macro facts outlined for this experience as an optimal response to a small set of fiscal policies.

Blanchard, O., and S. Fischer. 1989. *Macroeconomic Theory.* Cambridge, Mass.: MIT Press.
Brodersohn, M. 1974. Política económica de Corto Plazo, Crecimiento e Inflación en la Argentina, 1950–1972. *Jornadas de económia, problemas economicos Argentina, diagnosticos y politicas.* Buenos Aires: Ediciones Macchi.
Bruno, M., G. Di Tella, R. Dornbusch, and S. Fischer. 1988. *Inflación y Estabilización, la Experiencia de Israel, Argentina, Brasil, Bolivia y Mexico.* Mexico City: El Trimestre Economico.
De Pablo, J. C. 1980a. *Economia Politica del Peronismo.* Buenos Aires: El Cid.
———. 1980b. *La Económia que yo hice.* Buenos Aires: El Cronista Comercial.
Diamond, P. 1982. Aggregate Demand Management in Search Equilibrium. *Journal of Political Economy* 90.
Diaz Alejandro, C. 1966. *Devaluacion de la Tasa de Cambio en un Pais Semi-Industrializado: La Experiencia de Argentina, 1955/61.* Buenos Aires: Editorial del Instituto.
Di Tella, G. 1983. *Argentina's Experience under a Labour Based Government.* New York: Macmillan Press.
———. 1977. *Los Diarios.* Buenos Aires: Instituto Torcuato Di Tella.
Dornbusch, R. 1988a. Real Exchange Rates and Macroeconomics: A Selective Survey. NBER Working Paper no. 2775.
———. 1988b. Notes on Credibility and Stabilization. NBER Working Paper no. 2790.
———. 1987. Collapsing Exchange Rate Regimes. *Journal of Economic Development* 27: 71–83.
———. 1986. Special Exchange Rates for Capital Account Transactions. *World Bank Economic Review,* vol. 1.
Dornbusch, R., and S. Edwards. 1989. Economic Crises and the Macroeconomics of Populism in Latin America: Lessons from Chile and Peru. Mimeograph.
Dornbusch, R., and A. Reynoso. 1989. Financial Factors in Economic Development. NBER Working Paper no. 2815.
Dornbusch, R., and M. Simonsen. 1987. *Inflation Stabilization with Incomes Policy Support.* New York: Group of Thirty.
Ferns, H. S. 1971. *La Argentina.* Buenos Aires: Sudamericana.
FIEL. 1973–76 (various issues). *Indicadores de Coyuntura.*
Flood, R., and P. Garber. 1984. Collapsing Exchange Rate Regimes: Some Linear Examples. *Journal of International Economics* 17: 1–13.
Floria, C., and C. García Belsunce. 1988. *Historia Politica de la Argentina Contemporanea.* Buenos Aires: Alianza Editorial.
Krugman, P., and L. Taylor. 1978. The Contractionary Effects of Devaluations. *Journal of International Economics* 8 (September): 445–56.
Mallon, R., and J. V. Sourrouille. 1975. *Politica Economica en una Sociedad Conflictiva.* Buenos Aires: Amorrortu Editorial.
Murphy, K., R. Vishny, and A. Shleifer. 1989. Industrialization and the Big Push. *Journal of Political Economy* 97 (5): 1003–26.
Poder Ejecutivo. 1973. *El Plan Trienal.* Buenos Aires.
Rock, D. 1987. *Argentina, from Colonization to Alfonsín.* Santa Barbara, Calif.: Santa Barbara University Press.
Sturzenegger, F. 1990. Fiscal Policies in an Open Economy: An General Equilibrium Approach. Massachusetts Institute of Technology. Mimeograph, February.

Comment   Guido Di Tella

Until not so long ago it was not easy to explain the pervasiveness of populist policies in Latin America. Sturzenegger finds unsatisfactory six common interpretations, ranging from those that assume irrationality to others that assume optimal behavior of the various actors.

However, if not irrationality, at least ignorance of basic economic criteria is a necessary ingredient of any valid explanation. A case in point is the alleged irrelevance of the fiscal deficit, justified quite wrongly on pseudo-Keynesian arguments. Another more complex case has been the role attributed to the state which, at least until the 1960s, was believed to exemplify a benevolent and visible hand that allowed the attainment of public good in a better and quicker way than the market. This, in the real Latin American world of the last three decades, has proven to be erroneous. Whether it was inherent or just a special case is beside the point, but it is clear that this belief is behind the quick adoption of quantitative and price controls instead of (and not in addition to) serious fiscal policies.

If one wants to go behind the reasons for those attitudes and "mistakes," one can see that the desire to postpone harsh measures was a common denominator.

Populism, as defined in this discussion, is dead in Latin America; a more subtle survival can be detected in the heterodox-orthodox stabilization debate. Despite the efforts of serious heterodox economists to explain their policies, which should be taken over and above fiscal measures, they were interpreted as if they could be taken *instead* of the fiscal ones, repeating—mutatis mutandis—the populist propositions of the previous decades. No doubt, many heterodox stabilizers are cousins to yesterday's populists.

If one should ask, as Sturzenegger does, What are the strong reasons behind the prevalence of populist policies which have been so predominant in Latin America? one has to go back to two basic causes, economic and social. The first is that Argentina, as many other Latin American countries, started its development based on staples. Argentina, and most of the other countries, showed at a later stage the Dutch-disease kind of syndrome, particularly the post-boom sort of problems. When the bounty of nature has to be replaced by the bounty of human diligence, when new nonresource based activities have to be found, it is not unlikely that their productivity will be no match to those of the resource-related activities of the previous stage.

At this juncture, it is not uncommon to see protectionism and state intervention appear so as to create quasi rents as high as the previous rents. What is strange in the case of Argentina is the extent, intensity, and length of time of the protective policies characteristic of the post-boom stage. But one has to

Guido Di Tella is minister of foreign affairs, Argentina, professor of economics at the University of Buenos Aires, Argentina, and associate fellow at St. Anthony's College, Oxford, England.

accept that the post-boom redress will not be an easy one, as all Dutch-diseased economies know well.

The other cause for the populist pervasiveness of times past, is indeed the revulsion against extremely unfair distributive patterns and the existence of large sectors below the poverty level. "Direct action" seemed to be the only answer, while confidence on a market "solution" seemed excessively remote and diffuse and because of that, even irrelevant and immoral. But it is obvious that we must add, to these two main causes, an extraordinary degree of ignorance and naiveté about the ways in which these problems had to be tackled. Inevitably, we have to go back to the view that ignorance is one of the more deeply seated roots of this very counterproductive course.

But fortunately a learning process has taken place, as can be seen in the new turn imposed by the popularly based governments of Meném in Argentina, Collor de Mello in Brazil, Aylwin in Chile, and Paz Zamora in Bolivia. They are supported by the same social sectors as the "populists" of previous times; and although they have basically the same social "Weltanschauung," their policies are very different.

We have learned the hard way, and we know the appropriate means, even if we are still stuck with the same problems. But new knowledge and new attitudes mean that the future, populist or not, will fortunately not be the same.

5   What Have Populists Learned from Hyperinflation?

Roque B. Fernández

5.1 Introduction

We define populism as an approach that emphasizes income redistribution by government expenditures and income policies and deemphasizes the problems of deficit financing and inflation. The question analyzed here is whether populist governments can stop high inflation. If they can, developing nations like Argentina might be able to grow again. If they cannot, stagnation and the risk of hyperinflation seem the natural outcome.

Argentina's efforts to stop high inflation are almost permanent, and the last decades are full of attempts to stabilize prices. Attempts were made by populists, liberals, and conservative governments, by military dictatorships and democratic governments. Analyzing some major economic policies of the last decade, this paper will try to explain why stabilization has not been successful. It also will explain why a change in the populist stance is necessary but not the only condition needed to achieve stabilization.

An important attempt by a populist government started in 1985. Known by the name "Austral Plan," because of the new legal currency introduced, it tried to put an abrupt end to inflation. The plan failed, and it could not be rescued in spite of a variety of policy measures implemented by the government.

Another attempt was the Primavera Plan, which also failed. It started in 1988 and was the prelude to the hyperinflation of 1989 and 1990. Section 5.2 of this paper deals with these two experiences.

Section 5.3 explains the process of hyperinflation and the measures undertaken to control it. Section 5.4 describes the first plan of the new administra-

Roque B. Fernández is president of Banco Central de la República Argentina and professor of macroeconomics and international finance at Centro de Estudios Macroeconómicos de Argentina.
The views expressed in this paper are those of the author and do not necessarily reflect those of colleagues or institutions.

121

tion that took power after the resignation of President Alfonsín, who felt himself unable to manage the economic crisis.

Section 5.5 discusses two major items of monetary theory related to high inflation that I believe to be highly relevant for Argentina. One of these items is the phenomenon known as "unpleasant monetarist arithmetic" (Sargent and Wallace 1981) and refers to the policy dilemma of the government that must decide how to finance the deficit and has no other choices than printing money or bonds.

The other issue is the problem known as the "time consistency of the optimal plans"; in Argentina this is related to the policy dilemma of debt repudiation through hyperinflation or forced debt restructuring. Auernheimer (1974) was the first to notice the impact on government finance of repudiation of money with price jumps. Kydland and Prescott (1977) and Calvo (1978) formalized and extended the discussion, and Lucas and Stokey (1983) raised the issue of debt term structure and time consistency. Finally, section 5.6 contains concluding remarks.

5.2 Stabilization Attempts

5.2.1 The Austral Plan

The Austral Plan was organized around three basic measures. First, prices of public sector enterprises were increased to reduce their cash flow deficit. Second, all prices, public and private, were frozen at the level prevailing on 14 June 1985. For some sectors, however, prices were frozen at the level they had held some weeks before 14 June. This occurred because there had been some anticipation of price controls, and several firms (if not all) increased prices accordingly. Third, the president promised in a public speech that, from 14 June on, the Central Bank would not print any money to finance public-sector operations.

A few days after this announcement the plan was accepted by the International Monetary Fund (IMF). It essentially respected the monetary and fiscal targets of the standby agreement reached in the previous week; even more, it was said that the plan set more ambitious targets than those agreed upon with the IMF.

Besides freezing prices and salaries, as well as public service prices (after upward adjustments), the Austral Plan included exchange control and banking system control with a regulating scheme of the main financial activities. Foreign trade regulations and the general level of protection were left without major modifications.

Before the Austral Plan, the economic conditions were very worrying, with an accelerating rate of inflation that reached levels of 30% a month and with big fears that the process should turn into a hyperinflation. Although this was foreseen by the community as a serious hyperinflation risk, price increases were more the result of private agents' anticipation of price control than the result of a fiscal and monetary overflow.

The prevailing high inflation rates and the anticipation of changing government policies affected expectations. High expected inflation spread all across the economy in high nominal interest rates, indexation schemes, and in all types of contracts with deferred payments. If a sudden stabilization would occur, unanticipated lower inflation would cause a problem to all nonindexed contracts.

To take account of unanticipated lower inflation, the Austral Plan took the legal provisions of adjusting contracts by means of a schedule contemplating the difference between the old expected inflation and the new expected inflation supposedly generated by the stabilization plan. This measure did not have any direct implication for the working or dynamics of the stabilization program by itself. The measure just tended to avoid unexpected wealth transfers under the assumption that the plan would be successful.

Although high real interest rates and concentration on short-term maturities reflected a lack of credibility, the Austral Plan started with favorable public opinion, at a popular level at least. The popular support of the plan can be interpreted in one of two ways. First, the public may have accepted the stabilization plan as a reasonable approach to stop inflation. Or, second, the public did not know what a reasonable approach was, but accepted the plan anyway because it approved of the government's decision to give serious consideration to the problem of inflation. (Before the Austral Plan, the monthly rate of inflation had more than doubled from December 1983 to June 1985, reaching 42% in the latter month.)

The mass media (much of which was directly controlled by the state) advertised the Austral Plan and produced a favorable effect on general expectations; an abrupt fall in prices and free interest rates followed.

The favorable impact created by the government's advertising did not last, nor did the favorable public opinion. The lack of fiscal discipline—in conjunction with unsound monetary management—accelerated inflation in 1986–87 to an average level of nearly 10% per month. Interest rates for loans denominated in australs increased to reflect expected inflation, and domestic interest rates for operations in U.S. dollars reflected an important element of country risk.

Interest rates for operations in U.S. dollars were about four times the London Interbank Offer Rate (LIBOR). This high rate reflected the poor credit assessment by foreign creditors, who, unable to collect any payments, lacked alternatives other than restructuring most of Argentina's external debt. For the first time in the twentieth century Argentina decided to ignore the reputation effect of debt restructuring.

The consequences of the Austral Plan lasted for several years. The credibility of the government's announcements was low and became even lower. There grew in the mind of the citizenry the idea that populist democracy had

Table 5.1   Argentina: Per-capita GNP and Real Wages

	Per-capita GNP		Real Wages	
Year	Real Australs (1970 = 100)	Real U.S. Dollars	Minimum Wage	General Average
1984	96.0	2,883.5	89.4	95.2
1985	90.3	2,710.6	64.6	81.7
1986	93.8	2,815.7	78.2	83.5
1987	94.3	2,829.8	72.9	76.9
1988	90.0	2,701.9	48.7	66.3
1989	84.7	2,542.5	46.3	60.0

Source: Carta Economica.
Note: GNP is measured with real U.S. dollars from the third quarter of 1989. Real Wage is an index with the base January 1984 = 100.

failed again. Most important, the economic standard of living of low-income people—the group to whom populist governments are said to pay special attention—deteriorated or remained at the same level of the previous decade. Table 5.1 illustrates this last point for the six-year period corresponding to Alfonsín's presidency.

Although the Austral Plan was presented and discussed in the media as a "new" approach to stabilization, it contained hardly anything new. It followed the traditional income-policy approach. The only exception was the public commitment of a populist president to stop the monetary emission to finance public-sector operations. For the first time in Argentina's history a populist president sounded like his archenemies, the monetarists.

The traditional approach to stabilization in Argentina was to announce a program of fiscal discipline plus price controls; the traditional result was increasing inflation after a short period of stabilization. The Austral Plan confirmed this tradition, since, after a few months, inflation accelerated again, this time reaching a two-digit monthly rate by the beginning of 1988.

Those who elaborated the plan, and were in charge of managing it, believed that stabilization was a necessary precondition to discussing the reform of the public sector that would lead to a sound and permanent monetary and fiscal policy.

Those who did not share the heterodox view of stabilization were doubtful about the real possibility of this approach and believed that the transformation of public-sector enterprises and the institutional behavior of local and provincial governments were both prerequisites to stabilization. The failure of Argentina's Austral Plan seemed to confirm this last interpretation. President Alfonsín—who resigned five months before the constitutional date for the change of governments—acknowledged his failure to take the necessary actions to reform the public sector.

President Alfonsín's promise to stop monetary emission to finance public-sector operations was not honored. The Banco Hipotecario Naciónal (Mortgage National Bank) spent almost $5 billion (U.S. dollars) in concessional loans presumably related to the political campaign. Another $2 billion were granted to countries with poor credit ratings like Cuba, Nicaragua, and some African countries, presumably to support the Argentine chancellor as Secretary to the U.N. General Assembly. The loans were granted in domestic currency to be used in purchasing domestic goods. These two operations alone meant more than doubling the monetary base.

As fiscal discipline was not achieved with the Austral Plan, deficits forced the government to borrow from different sources to close the budget. One source of financing was monetary creation by the Central Bank. To sterilize part of the monetary emission, the Central Bank increased reserve requirements, paying competitive interest rates on them.

This disguised borrowing eventually resulted in a dominant force that drove the hyperinflation of mid-1989, a subject I will discuss later. First, I will discuss some complementary policy actions that attempted to rescue the Austral Plan from total failure.

Mazzorin's Chickens and Other Heterodox Measures
Complementing the Austral Plan

During 1987 the government undertook some policy actions to complement the Austral Plan. Some policies were a repetition of previous policies, but another was new.

The repeated policies were a new price freeze plus discretionary authorizations to increase prices up to 10% for some items. Authorizations were granted to those items that did not violate special price schedules elaborated by Secretary of Commerce Mazzorin.

Price controls did not work, and the economic authorities decided to take more direct actions to stop inflation. Somehow they imagined that increasing the supply of foodstuffs would stop inflation. One way of increasing it was importing chicken. So Mazzorin—spending additional government money in a deficit-ridden country—imported several tons of chicken. Unfortunately, he imported the wrong kind of chicken. Argentineans refused to consume imported chickens fed with anything except corn from the pampas.

Even with a gradual decrease in chicken prices, consumers did not want them. Especially when the chickens started to smell bad. Rotten chickens were the final outcome of Mazzorin's stabilization strategy. He imported too many chickens in proportion to the taste and freezing capacity of the consumers in Argentina.

Inflation did not fall, neither, in the long run, did the relative price of chicken. In the short run, the demand for chicken fell because people reduced their consumption of chicken in restaurants and other places where they might have purchased "elaborated" chickens. They were afraid of consuming a rotten chicken disguised as a special dish or delicacy. Many domestic producers went into bankruptcy, which in turn reduced the supply of the right kind of chickens that people would like to consume.

The government also determined a wage policy in an attempt to control salaries according to price inflation. In October 1987 the economic authorities increased the minimum wage by 75% (from 200 to 300 australs per month) and increased general wages, in both the private and public sectors as well as in pensions by 12%. Yet the average real wage decreased, which raised angry complaints by labor union leaders who called several labor strikes. Toward the middle of 1988 a general strike by public-sector utilities workers ended with a severe disorder in the Plaza de Mayo and several acts of vandalism in downtown Buenos Aires. Then labor union leaders asked for the resignation of the economic minister.

As in previous stabilization plans, the government did not reduce public spending and tried to close the fiscal budget by borrowing and increasing the tax burden. But, borrowing in the capital market meant severe crowding out and high real interest rates, therefore, the government opted to use "forced borrowing."

This measure implied that the government obtained from tax payers a mandatory loan equivalent to 40% of last period revenue from income tax and net assets tax. First introduced in 1985/86 as an emergency measure, forced borrowing was reintroduced in 1987, affecting again government credibility and reputation.

The government increased the fiscal burden by raising the tax on imports, cigarettes, and checking accounts. This last particular tax—a true innovation in fiscal policy—charged current accounts each time the account was debited. To avoid tax evasion check endorsements were restricted. The tax was paid by current account holders, and commercial banks acted as a withholding agent for the government.

Fiscal experts cannot figure out the rationale for a checking account tax, but the secretary of the treasury, who proposed this tax, claimed to have a good explanation: "It was well known that neutral taxes are very high in Argentina, therefore, there is much evasion and [many] tax exemptions. So, tax revenue is low in relation to the level of taxes. But, black market operations, exempted operations, and evaders, all use checks; therefore, taxing checks increases revenues and improves the neutrality of the system." The flaw in this explanation is that all checks are taxed, and people who do pay taxes do use checks. The explanation would be right only if eluders and evaders were more intensive users of checks than regular taxpayers.

A new element in the economic policy undertaken during 1987 was the liberalization of the exchange market. This was not a full liberalization because there were two markets: the official market for commercial operations and the financial market for everything else. But the recognition of this last market ended with several years of ineffective restrictions to stop capital flight.

Jointly with the liberalization of exchange markets came an announcement of new commercial policy. Import restrictions would gradually be eliminated: the intention was to improve resource allocation, not to engage in arm-twisting measures designed to force entrepreneurs to keep prices low.

The commercial policy measures were two. First, nontariff restrictions were substituted by a system based upon indifference tariffs, which, supposedly, would eliminate redundant protection. Second, temporary admission was granted to all kinds of inputs. These measures were very weak in relation to the level of effective protection but they were in the right direction.

Another favorable event was an improvement in Argentina's terms of trade, which was used to launch another economic plan known as the Primavera Plan.

5.2.2   From the Primavera Plan to the Hyperinflation

"Primavera" means "spring season" in Spanish, and that was the name given by the press to the economic plan introduced months before the spring of 1988.

Argentina's favorable terms of trade were mostly due to the drought in the northern hemisphere that increased the international price of some agricultural commodities. Table 5.2 presents the monthly evolution of nominal and real exchange rates, which in July 1988—when the Primavera Plan started—was at 113.3. This was a figure lower than the levels of the previous months, but it was a profitable level for soybeans and other crops of the season.

The Primavera Plan allowed the government to realize a profit in the exchange operations. The proceeds from exports were obtained at a lower commercial exchange rate and were sold at a higher rate in the financial market. Table 5.2 shows that, during several months, the spread between the financial rate and the commercial rate exceeded 20%. To sell dollars in the financial market the Central Bank fixed a minimum value about which it would sell foreign exchange, although not in unlimited amounts. The amount announced was large enough to affect the price of the dollar in the short run.

Although not explicitly stated, a second intention of the government was to influence inflationary expectations affecting the path of the dollar in the free market. Other measures attempting to affect inflation were the following: first, a price agreement with trade unions to keep the rate of inflation in the order of 3%-4% per month in September and following months. On the other hand, and as a part of the agreement, the government offered to decrease the value added tax by 3%.

Second, government and trade union representatives created a Price Commission to follow up prices and costs as well as public-sector finances. At the beginning of August there was a 30% increase in prices of public-sector utilities. This increase was thought to be large enough to guarantee the balancing of the budget of public enterprises.

Third, collective agreements with labor unions would set the path for nom-

Table 5.2   Argentina: Nominal and Real Exchange Rates

	Real Exchange Rate	Nominal Commercial Exchange Rate	Nominal Free Exchange Rate		Real Exchange Rate	Nominal Commercial Exchange Rate	Nominal Free Exchange Rate
1984:				**1987:**			
January	110.5	24.89	30.77	January	108.8	1,292.76	1,713.55
February	107.4	27.77	40.51	February	110.0	1,383.22	1,712.22
March	100.4	30.86	50.05	March	113.8	1,541.00	1,879.86
April	95.7	35.08	54.62	April	111.3	1,541.00	2,039.47
May	94.4	40.84	64.90	May	110.7	1,590.79	2,066.84
June	94.2	47.62	69.28	June	110.8	1,706.19	2,076.40
July	93.9	56.17	75.55	July	110.9	1,894.18	2,384.50
August	94.1	68.40	98.19	August	110.0	2,115.17	2,926.50
September	92.0	83.39	113.25	September	109.9	2,457.34	3,451.40
October	98.6	105.42	122.23	October	120.3	3,243.29	3,955.79
November	109.6	133.38	166.91	November	120.9	3,510.00	4,068.50
December	108.4	160.84	180.79	December	121.6	3,535.00	4,572.00
1985:				**1988:**			
January	110.2	201.07	240.00	January	122.2	3,892.00	5,454.00
February	111.6	242.49	317.25	February	121.7	4,334.20	5,781.90
March	110.5	306.39	402.93	March	119.9	4,922.70	6,329.50
April	109.4	396.46	527.38	April	119.8	5,772.00	6,923.00
May	112.4	525.44	619.14	May	117.9	6,736.60	8,226.20
June	115.5	736.60	797.47	June	118.0	8,702.00	10,243.50

[handwritten annotation: "Overvalue"]

July	124.2	801.00	942.73
August	122.7	801.00	952.05
September	122.0	801.00	939.52
October	121.0	801.00	924.57
November	120.0	801.00	898.01
December	118.4	801.00	855.24
1986:			
January	117.1	801.00	899.43
February	115.6	801.00	860.88
March	111.9	801.00	908.68
April	111.1	827.82	921.82
May	110.9	849.57	900.12
June	109.9	873.63	895.11
July	107.0	903.73	914.91
August	105.9	965.05	1,086.48
September	109.0	1,050.36	1,222.27
October	107.8	1,093.59	1,198.26
November	107.6	1,150.85	1,349.75
December	108.2	1,212.90	1,564.75

July	113.3	9,653.30	12,176.70
August	108.9	12,000.00	14,115.30
September	101.3	12,000.00	14,321.80
October	97.3	12,223.50	14,943.00
November	95.9	12,674.10	15,389.10
December	93.6	13,138.60	15,772.40
1989:			
January	91.0	13,665.50	16,808.60
February	94.8	15,378.80	24,998.90
March	107.7	20,325.30	40,476.20
April	214.3	57,411.70	64,387.00
May	246.7	124,493.3	135,000.0
June	183.3	208,333.0	416,429.0
July	157.7	563,238.0	660,714.0
August	148.3	650,000.0	673,727.0
September	140.5	650,000.0	653,430.0
October	137.3	650,000.0	703,000.0
November	131.1	650,000.0	887,770.0
December	117.0	875,807.0	1,350,000.0

Source: Carta Economica.

inal wages, and employees of the central government administration received a salary increase of 25%.

Fourth, commercial policy measures included the intention to reduce tax on exports for 500 products and to eliminate nontariff restrictions on 3,000 products. Nontariff restrictions were introduced during the Malvinas War (1982) and later with a special provision (Annex II, 1983) and were never removed during the Alfonsín administration.

Fifth, all reserve requirements for different kinds of deposits were substituted by two special government obligations denoted "A-1241" and "A-1242," according to the Central Bank resolutions that created them. Although I have liberally used the denomination of "reserve requirements" to give a first approximation to the idea, a word of caution is necessary. A large part of reserve requirements were not "reserves," as banks could not cash them. They were special bonds (or nondisposable deposits in the Central Bank) that substituted for reserve requirements.

The government obligations A-1241 and A-1242 were remunerated with the average deposit rate of commercial banks plus 0.5% monthly. This meant that a large part of commercial banks assets were a particular bond that, on average, would pay whatever average interest rate the commercial banks were willing to pay depositors.

For example, if depositors were afraid of a devaluation they would try to cash deposits to buy dollars. Bankers, to avoid a decrease in deposits, would increase the deposit rate, which in turn would imply a higher interest in A-1241 and A-1242. If expectations of a fiscal deficit were what generated the expectation of a devaluation, then a devaluation would occur even with fiscal surplus. An overall deficit would always occur as interest accruals on most of the domestic debt were indexed to panics.

Although some measures implemented with the Primavera Plan were in the right direction—especially the exchange rate liberalization and the commercial policy—the plan did not succeed. Fiscal reform was not realized, and the perverse dynamics of the remuneration of most of the domestic debt drove the system to accelerating inflation. Table 5.3 shows that inflation decreased from 27.6% in August to 5.7% in November 1988. In February 1989—the turning point to hyperinflation—the monthly inflation rate was 9.6% and kept increasing to reach a peak of 196.6% in July.

In a general evaluation of the period 1984–88, Fernández and Mantel (1985, 1988) concluded that price controls—of the sort introduced with income policies and heterodox polices—delayed the adjustment path to steady-state equilibrium. Firms, anticipating price controls in oligopolistic markets, set prices higher than they normally would in order to protect themselves from the government's political incentive to fix prices lower than long-run marginal costs. With a positive probability of a stabilization failure, firms may be temporarily better off with "nonoptimal" higher prices. It may perfectly be the case that, if stabilization fails the higher price will cushion the firm, for a while at least, from "authorized-prices" lower than long-run marginal costs.

Table 5.3   **Argentina: Inflation and Nominal Interest Rates**

	Inflation in Consumer Prices	Average Depositors Interest Rate		Inflation in Consumer Prices	Average Depositors Interest Rate
1984:			1987:		
January	12.5	12.9	January	7.6	8.3
February	17.0	12.5	February	6.5	7.5
March	20.3	13.4	March	8.2	4.0
April	18.5	17.5	April	3.4	7.1
May	17.1	20.8	May	4.2	7.7
June	17.9	20.3	June	8.0	8.3
July	18.3	19.3	July	10.1	10.6
August	22.8	18.5	August	13.7	12.3
September	27.5	22.1	September	11.7	15.4
October	19.3	24.2	October	19.5	12.4
November	15.0	20.0	November	10.3	8.9
December	19.7	30.9	December	3.4	12.3
1985:			1988:		
January	25.1	24.9	January	9.1	13.2
February	20.7	20.9	February	10.4	13.3
March	26.5	23.5	March	14.7	15.7
April	29.5	27.4	April	17.2	16.2
May	25.1	31.1	May	15.7	17.2
June	30.5	16.8	June	18.0	19.5
July	6.2	5.2	July	25.6	22.7
August	3.1	5.7	August	27.6	10.6
September	2.0	5.3	September	11.7	9.1
October	1.9	4.3	October	9.0	9.3
November	2.4	4.4	November	5.7	10.2
December	3.2	4.4	December	6.8	12.2
1986:			1989:		
January	3.0	4.4	January	8.9	12.1
February	1.7	4.5	February	9.6	18.9
March	4.6	4.9	March	17.0	21.7
April	4.7	4.4	April	33.4	44.5
May	4.0	4.4	May	78.5	127.8
June	4.5	4.3	June	114.5	135.1
July	6.8	4.6	July	196.6	40.1
August	8.8	6.5	August	37.9	12.8
September	7.2	6.9	September	9.4	7.4
October	6.1	7.9	October	5.6	6.1
November	5.3	7.7	November	6.5	9.6
December	4.7	8.3	December	40.1	30.0

Source: INDEC and BCRA. Average interest rate for December 1989 is preliminary.

A similar argument can be elaborated for nominal and real interest rates. These conclusions had three important implications. First, given that delaying the adjustment might imply that the real interest rate can remain for a longer period at higher values than the long-run natural rate, it is doubtful—at the least—that price controls can help to avoid the recessionary effects usually associated with stabilization. Second, higher real rates introduced by a particular stabilization plan with price controls suggest the existence of short-run economic wealth transfers across sectors that should be carefully evaluated before justifying the "social advantage" of price controls. Third, price controls with fiscal lags imply an important delay in the adjustment of the global deficit, since its size depends on the magnitude of the real rate of interest and of the rate of inflation.

Although the economic plan failed, the authorities insisted on price controls even after the monthly rates of inflation were well above 10%. Of course, price controls were totally ineffective, and a high inflation accelerated even more. When the authorities abandoned the idea of "heterodox" economic policy-making, and gradually moved to more orthodox measures such as reduction of public-sector deficit and sound monetary management, it was too late. The strong credibility available at the beginning of the Austral Plan was gone, and the side effects of orthodox measures in the absence of credibility was taking a significant political toll. The lack of credibility and the fear of repudiation of the government debt increased interest rates to levels never seen before in Argentina. Government borrowing in the domestic financial system, at the beginning of 1988, took place at annual effective rates of more than 30% for operations adjusted to the U.S. dollar; that is, at four times the LIBOR rate.

Structural reform of the public sector was never given serious consideration by the political authorities. There were timid attempts at deregulation and privatization, and when they wanted to be more effective on structural reform it was too late; they awoke in the middle of the hyperinflation.

5.3   The Administration of Hyperinflation

During the second half of 1988 inflation was kept under control with the Central Bank auctioning dollars in the free market. But a growing debt and the political campaign for the presidential elections, which would be held in May 1989, were the dominant forces driving the economy.

Advertising during a political campaign may have different forms, and many of these forms can be inconsequential for economic developments. But the form chosen by the ruling party had severe consequences for the administration of the economic crisis.

Toward the end of 1988 the polls showed a clear advantage for the opposition candidate. The political advertisement of the ruling party characterized the opposition candidate as representing "chaos." Therefore, the situation in Argentina at the beginning of 1989 was a ruling party driving the economy to increasing inflation and an opposition party that represented future chaos.

The chaos exploded for the ruling party as soon as 6 February 1989, when the exchange rate policy became unsustainable and the economic authorities introduced the following modifications. First, they devalued the commercial exchange rate by 2.5% to 14.45 australs per U.S. dollar and announced an additional devaluation of 6% for the rest of the month. Second, they created a new differential exchange rate 25% higher than the commercial rate to trade special goods and services. Third, the Central Bank ceased to intervene in the free market by auctioning foreign exchange. Fourth, the Central Bank released 6,500 million australs worth (about 11% of the monetary base) of reserve requirements in the form of nondisposable deposits (previously created by Central Bank Resolution A-1324).

The run against the austral continued, and the economic authorities were forced to introduce new measures almost every week. Some important measures include the following. The two official commercial exchange rates were unified in a single official rate. Imports and exports of goods, and also interest corresponding to the financing of commercial operations, were exchanged 50% at the official rate and 50% at the free market rate. Services were allowed 100% at the free market rate.

The financial problems caused by the run against the austral induced the monetary authorities to create every financial asset that could possibly be imagined. Irrespective of its cost, the government issued anything the public would be willing to hold. Therefore, the Central Bank, by means of Resolution A-1388, created five new bonds indexed to: the free exchange rate, the stock market quotation of BONEX (a Treasury bond in U.S. dollars), the exchange rate for imports, the greater of either the consumer price index or the nominal interest rate, the greater of either the free exchange rate or the nominal interest rate. A special deposit indexed to the price of crops, was also created for producers and exporters (Central Bank Resolution A-1391).

Several people and financial institutions took "advantage" of these options; but later, such advantages could not be realized, as the government was unable to honor them. Other people, understanding the nature of the Ponzi scheme in which the government was involved, decided to buy U.S. dollars in the free market, driving up their price and forcing the government to take new actions.

On 13 April 1989, the government decided that all transactions in the official exchange rate market were transferred to the free market. Exports were taxed at a floating rate computed as the difference between the free market exchange rate and a reference price of 36 australs per U.S. dollar. Reference prices would be modified periodically. The government also decided to increase by 14% the price of public utilities and by 16% the price of gasoline. Income policy remained unchanged.

Inflation, which in March 1989 was 17% monthly, could not be mitigated. It doubled to 33.4% in April and more than doubled to 78.5% in May. This was the month when general elections were held, elections that the ruling party lost.

From May to 10 December—the constitutional date to transfer the power—the ruling party was supposed to manage the Argentine economy. A very difficult task if the official pronouncement was right in characterizing the next government as representing "chaos." The ruling party tried at all costs to transfer the government immediately, something that the opposition party did not want. Therefore, the ruling party lacked alternatives other than to manage the hyperinflation.

There is an abundant literature explaining the failure of heterodox plans designed to try to stop inflation in Argentina, but there is no literature analyzing heterodox measures to manage hyperinflation. From May to July 1989 I have the empirical evidence of a populist government using heterodox measures to stop hyperinflation. Of course, hyperinflation accelerated.

In May the government introduced the following measures. First, the economic authorities announced new taxes on durable goods (real estate and automobiles) and increases in prices of public utilities and gasoline. Second, the payment of forced savings and other fiscal obligations were claimed in advance. Third, the minimum wage was increased to 4,000 australs (the equivalent to $23 monthly in U.S. currency at the official exchange rate at the end of May). Prices were frozen for almost all goods except fruits, vegetables, meats, and fish and other seafood.

Plain figures perhaps are not the best indicators of the nature of the difficulties during the period April–July 1989. To illustrate the drama of hyperinflation the following paragraphs give a special timetable of financial restrictions affecting depositors, financial institutions, exchange houses, and the stock market.

April 3 and 4 were mandatory banking and exchange holidays; April 17, an exchange holiday but a working day for financial transactions. April 28 was a mandatory banking and exchange holiday.

May 2 was a mandatory exchange holiday. May 22, 23, and 24 were mandatory banking and exchange holidays. Bank withdrawals were restricted to 20,000 australs in each bank account. May 26 and 29 were mandatory exchange and banking holidays. May 30, withdrawals from time deposits and acceptances were restricted to 40,000 australs. Balances in excess of withdrawals were restructured to become due seven days later.

June 6: bank withdrawals were restricted to up to 50,000 australs for any type of operation. On June 9, the withdrawal restriction was increased to 100,000 australs.

Exchange controls were reintroduced, fixing the exchange rate toward the end of May. The Central Bank would buy each U.S. dollar at 175 australs and would sell it at 177 australs. Buying or selling foreign exchange outside the official regulated market was considered a misdemeanor, and, according to legislation, it would be punished through a special criminal law for exchange operations.

Yet there was another law that authorized the exchange of BONEXs by foreign exchange and BONEXs by australs. Triangulation through BONEXs replicated a free market for foreign exchange, and that was how the most important transactions were made. In fact, and independently of what the monetary authorities decided, Argentina was operating in an unrestricted market for financial operation in foreign exchange at least since 1978 when the BONEXs were introduced for the first time.

The hyperinflation measured as the rate of devaluation of the austral in the free market reached its peak of 186.4% per month in June. If measured with the consumer price index the peak is in July with 196.6% monthly.

The severity of hyperinflation and the danger of social unrest forced the elected government to accept an immediate transfer of power. A new populist administration took power on 9 July and insisted on price controls, although not everything was heterodoxy in the BB Plan.

5.4   The Meném Administration and the BB Plan

The announcements of the new administration were a mix of heterodox and orthodox doctrines. On the one hand, the heterodox idea of having an income policy was always present from the very beginning. But on the other hand, the rhetoric and the appointment of high ranking officials tended to be orthodox. As I construct this discussion, I have doubts about how to classify the policy-making of the period July–December 1989. I would not call it heterodox because the problems of the budget constraint of the public sector were given serious attention even though they were not provided serious solutions. Neither would I call the policy-making orthodox because policymakers firmly believed that price "agreements" were effective to deal with inflation.

The first plan of the Meném administration was the BB Plan. Here, "BB" means Bunge Born Corporation, the multinational firm that provided the government with a high-ranking executive to take the post of economic minister.

The political rhetoric was very impressive and unexpected from a populist leader. President Meném announced a program of privatization of almost everything that could be transferred to private hands. The Argentine Telephone Company, ENTEL, was scheduled for privatization during 1990. Two TV channels owned by the state were privatized toward the end of 1989. Oil exploration and exploitation was subject to privatization and, in less than 90 days, Argentina signed a standby agreement with the IMF. Table 5.4 summarizes the projection of public finance of the BB Plan and its relation with previous years.

The preliminary figures for 1989 indicated that the overall deficit decreased 1.6% of GDP from 1988 to 1989. A further reduction was expected for 1990 according to budgetary projections.

The BB Plan was effective at stopping the hyperinflation of the moment and reaching inflation levels of one digit per month during September, October, and November. But in December the Argentine economy was again heading for hyperinflation with the monthly rate of 40.1% in the consumer price index.

The evidence available so far does not support the hypothesis of a fiscally driven high inflation process toward the end of 1989. During the months fol-

Table 5.4   Argentina: Public Finances as a Percentage of GDP

	1984	1985	1986	1987	1988	1989	1990
Public-sector operational deficit	8.0	4.8	2.4	4.8	5.0	6.2	−.1
Central Bank quasi-fiscal deficit	2.5	2.8	1.1	.9	1.4	1.4	1.5
Overall public-sector deficit	10.5	7.7	3.5	5.7	6.4	4.8	1.4

Source: Ministerio de Economia and BCRA.
Note: All figures measured on cash basis. The table reflects preliminary figures for 1989 and budget estimates for 1990.

lowing the hyperinflation, the Central Bank did not issue any significant amount of money to cover the operating expenses of the public sector. Most of the monetary emission of the period was generated by the purchases of foreign exchange by part of the Central Bank (some of it was used to pay international organizations). Part of the monetary emission was sterilized issuing CEDEPS or short-term Central Bank debt.

This new debt was issued at very high nominal rates. Given that it was announced to keep a fixed exchange rate of 650 australs per U.S. dollar up to the end of 1990, in the period from July to October the average yield of financial assets was more than 15% monthly in U.S. dollars. This seemed not to be a serious problem for bankers or depositors because most of the money was lent to the government, which remunerated average reserve requirements of about 80% of private bank deposits.

All indexed debt created by Resolution A-1388 (see sec. 5.3) that became due in the second half of 1989 was compulsorily reprogrammed with a new bond called BOCON.

Even the most naive of depositors knew that the situation could not last long, and, at a given point in time, he or she would consider it reasonable to convert austral deposits to U.S. dollars. In a few months a few smart depositors could realize in Argentina a gain that would take almost a decade to obtain in the world financial market. Of course, not all could realize such a gain. It was the attempt of many to capitalize on such a gain that promoted the run on the financial system and led to hyperinflation.

I believe that, more than fiscal disarray, debt dynamics is the simpler and more powerful explanation of the hyperinflations of 1989, with one episode beginning in February and the other starting in October, but being aborted in January 1990. Hyperinflation was aborted by a compulsive conversion of most of the short-term domestic debt to a long-term debt in the form of a new series of BONEX.

Table 5.5 shows the evolution of monetary and debt aggregates. Notice that the last column of the table correctly predicts the demonetization process of

Table 5.5   **Argentina: Monetary and Domestic Debt Aggregates**

	M1	M5	Debt	BCRA Debt in U.S. Dollars	Total of Austral Debt in U.S. Dollars	Share Debt (%)
1987						
January	6.4	19.6	13.2	4,550	5,387	84.5
February	6.3	19.8	13.5	4,765	5,669	84.1
March	6.5	19.4	12.9	4,729	5,838	81.0
April	6.6	19.6	13.0	4,646	5,755	80.7
May	6.5	19.5	13.0	4,629	5,740	80.6
June	6.1	18.6	12.5	4,964	6,246	79.5
July	5.8	17.8	12.0	4,545	5,762	78.9
August	5.2	16.8	11.6	4,040	5,537	73.0
September	4.8	16.2	11.4	3,671	5,162	71.1
October	4.4	14.7	10.3	3,390	5,192	65.3
November	4.4	15.3	10.9	3,634	5,370	67.7
December	4.7	16.8	12.1	3,508	5,303	66.1
1988						
January	4.7	16.4	11.7	2,973	4,687	63.4
February	4.5	16.6	12.1	3,187	5,139	62.0
March	4.3	16.6	12.3	3,792	5,371	70.6
April	4.2	16.4	12.2	3,798	5,506	69.0
May	3.8	15.3	11.5	3,829	5,392	71.0
June	3.5	14.0	10.5	3,801	5,294	71.8
July	3.2	13.3	10.1	3,877	5,439	71.3
August	3.0	12.9	9.9	4,471	5,956	75.1
September	3.3	14.2	10.9	6,117	7,322	83.5
October	3.6	14.8	11.2	6,357	7,617	83.5
November	3.5	15.8	12.3	6,750	7,955	84.9
December	3.9	17.2	13.3	6,972	8,187	85.2
1989						
January	4.1	18.9	14.8	7,967	9,222	86.4
February	4.3	19.3	15.0	5,692	7,125	79.9
March	4.1	18.4	14.3	3,909	5,456	71.7
April	3.7	17.8	14.1	3,120	4,905	63.6
May	3.0	13.8	10.8	2,388	3,760	63.5
June	2.6	12.4	9.8	1,857	2,989	62.1
July	1.6	7.9	6.3	2,594	3,984	65.1
August	2.1	10.0	7.9	4,158	5,547	75.0
September	2.8	12.2	9.4	5,176	6,658	77.7
October	3.6	13.9	10.3	5,133	6,763	75.9
November	4.3	14.7	10.4	3,584	5,183	69.1
December	. . .	. . .	. . .	1,866	3,639	51.3

Source: Carta Economica.

Note: Monetary aggregates in proportion to GDP, debt aggregates in millions of U.S. dollars.

hyperinflations. The last column measures the share of nonindexed debt denominated in australs but earning a substantial nominal interest rate. As government's debts are private-sector assets, and as the private sector decided to shift from australs to dollars, a run began leading to hyperinflation. Notice the turning points in February and October 1989 where the share of the austral debt leads any of the monetary aggregates.

Sometimes in the standard financial programming exercises an increase in M1 suggests credibility and monetization of the economy. The empirical evidence for 1989 does not confirm this interpretation, and there may be some instances—as will be explained in the next section—where monetization is achieved by increasing the real interest rates.

5.5   Economic Policy and High Inflation

There are two topics in monetary theory that deserve special attention in high inflation environments. One is the case of "unpleasant monetarist arithmetic" that deals with the policy dilemma of financing deficits by printing money or by printing bonds. The other is the problem of time inconsistency and the existence of nominal bonds in private hands.

5.5.1   Unpleasant Monetarist Arithmetic

Sargent and Wallace (1981) ask what would happen if the government decided to decrease the share of the deficit financed with money creation. By itself this would tend to decrease inflation. But if the government is expected to shift to full money creation later, lower money creation means faster transitory accumulation of debt and higher money creation in the future. Anticipations of higher money creation in the future imply higher inflation today.

With a positive constant real interest rate, a higher debt means higher interest payments in the steady state. If the economy is on the left side of the Laffer curve, an increase in the stock of debt implies a higher inflation tax in the steady state. However, if the economy is on the right side of the Laffer curve, a higher debt will require a lower inflation and the Sargent and Wallace proposition would not hold.

When the assumption of a constant interest rate for different levels of government debt is replaced by the assumption that higher debt is associated with higher real interest rates, higher inflation is obtained on both sides of the Laffer curve. This can be verified with the following set of relationships (see Fernández 1990, for an optimization model with a liquidity constraint providing the micro-foundations for this subject).

The government financial policy dilemma is represented by the following steady-state relationships:

(1) $$\alpha \cdot b \cdot r = m \cdot \pi,$$

(2) $$(1 - \alpha) \cdot b \cdot r = s.$$

The first relationship is the share (α) of the quasi-fiscal deficit (that is, the deficit generated just by the real interest on government debt) that is financed by inflation. The second relationship is the share $(1 - \alpha)$ of the quasi-fiscal deficit that is paid with the primary surplus s.

Let $\phi(\pi) = m/b$ be the proportion of real money yielding no interest to the stock of real government debt with $d(\phi)/d\pi < 0$. In the particular case of Argentina, m corresponds to the definition of real M1 and b can be considered bonds and deposits yielding interest. Deposits are government obligations because of the high reserve requirements remunerated at competitive rates by the Central Bank. Let $b = b(r, \pi)$ with $db/dr > 0$ and $db/d\pi < 0$. Substitute this relationship in (1) and (2) to obtain

(3) $$r = (1/\alpha) \cdot \phi(\pi) \cdot \pi,$$

(4) $$b(r, \pi) \cdot r = s/(1 - \alpha).$$

Assume that $\pi \cdot \phi(\pi)$ is increasing in $\pi < \pi'$ and decreasing in π for $\pi > \pi'$. This implies that, if the stock of bonds $b(\cdot)$ were a constant or independent of π and r (as in most of the literature on inflation tax), the graph of seigniorage revenue against the inflation rate would have the usual Laffer curve property.

Figure 5.1 illustrates relationships (3) and (4). Fernández (1990) shows, in a model where the dynamics are explicitly specified, that the line representing

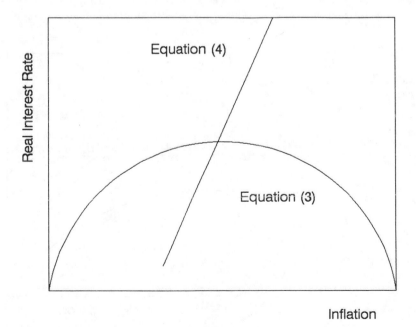

Fig. 5.1   Determination of inflation and real interest rate

(4) must cut from below the line representing (3) to obtain a saddle-point equilibrium; otherwise the system is unstable.

A decrease in α implies an upward shift in (3) and a rightward shift in (4) and, as shown by figure 5.2, I obtain a solution with higher inflation irrespective of whether the economy is on the left side or on the right side of the Laffer curve (see points A' and B').

What this analysis tells us is that the crowding-out effect on the service of government debt by increasing borrowing produces higher inflation. The impact of higher borrowing on the stock of debt and on real interest requires more inflation to pay for it than the alternative of not borrowing. The alternative of just printing money to pay for debt services produces less inflation than the alternative of paying a lower share but of a higher total debt service increased by borrowing.

Notice that the old remedy to stop inflation, that is, by reducing deficits or by increasing primary surplus, works nicely on either side of the Laffer curve. This result constrasts with previous literature, where this inflation remedy would work only on the left side of the Laffer curve.

5.5.2   The Problem of Time Consistency of Optimal Plans

A textbook risk-free government bond paying low interest is a concept found in textbooks but not in Argentina's financial markets. Governments with poor reputations cannot issue risk-free bonds. So, we wonder, when a government loses its reputation how can it be regained? Starting from a positive debt, the real interest cost to build up one's reputation might be too high

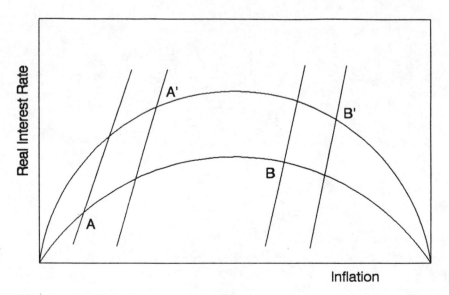

Fig. 5.2   The effect of increasing borrowing

to afford. Perhaps if debt is canceled or substantially reduced through hyperinflation, repudiation, or reprogramming, the social cost is lower than collecting distorting taxes to pay for debt services. Perhaps it is higher. These are topics that should be carefully analyzed, and I have not been able to find definite answers to all these questions. Below, however, I will venture some answers.

In policy discussions in Argentina, Ricardo Arriazu (Arriazu, Leone, and Murphy 1988) emphasized the necessity of a careful analysis of government financial wealth before considering a change in the stabilization policy of the late seventies. That policy consisted of a preannouncement of future devaluations in an attempt to reduce inflationary expectations.

Eventually that policy produced a revaluation of the peso. To correct the revaluation, a series of devaluations were introduced in 1981 that accelerated inflation and caused a deterioration of the financial wealth of the government. Those results tend to confirm Arriazu's conjectures and suggest that before changing policy the government should pay special attention to the composition and the time structure of claims and liabilities.

The failure to understand this point may imply that to correct a real distortion—a real appreciation of the peso—a greater distortion is introduced. In other words, if inflation must increase, the government should first try to restructure the debt toward long-term nominal claims at fixed interest rates. Unfortunately, as time consistency analysis emphasizes, it would be very hard to find private agents willing to accept such unhedged restructuring, as Resolutions A-1241, A-1242, and A-1388 and the general experience of 1988 and 1989 confirmed in Argentina. Those resolutions were issued to provide fully hedged positions to financial investors.

The success of time consistency analysis to explain some important issues of stabilization is not because populists are inconsistent, either because they do not know economic theory or because they commit obvious policy mistakes. If neutral taxes are unavailable governments would tend to maximize social benefits, repudiating debt either through taxes, inflation, reprogramming, or the like. Yet, if this were the case, why would rational people in populist countries hold nominal debt?

It could be the case that nominal bonds yield liquidity services (as assumed in Fernández 1990) or that people hold nominal debt if they can fully hedge it. Hedging a nominal bond could be implicit; for example, tax deferrals or fiscal lags are good hedges against jumps in the price level. Also it could be the case that in countries like Argentina, where the stock of nonindexed domestic debt is substantially less than 10% of GDP, tax deferrals and the Olivera-Tanzi effect of fiscal lags might imply a zero-net-present-value nominal debt.

I have tried to analyze this topic elsewhere (e.g., Fernández 1989a, 1989b). Working with the original Lucas-Stokey cash-in-advance framework, the proof of the time inconsistency of government nominal debt is straightforward. But is a zero-net-present-value nominal debt time inconsistent? In a model with money in the utility function as used by Persson, Persson, and Svensson (1987), Calvo and Obstfeld (1988) show that zero-net-present-value for nominal debt does not solve the time inconsistency problem (see references for other results on time inconsistency). I obtained the same results for a cash-in-advance model.

However, another result follows. For example, a policy able to produce a shift from a government net-positive-nominal debt to a net-negative-nominal debt can be made time consistent. Also, time consistency might be achieved in several cases where individual agents are not deprived of volition at the stage of nominal assets restructuring.

A very important underlying assumption in the time inconsistency results is that governments may restructure, at will, all real and nominal obligations at market prices, and economic agents will passively accept such restructuring. If this is not so, as some available evidence on private-sector behavior incurring in fiscal lags and tax deferrals suggests, the problem under discussion becomes a true differential game where time inconsistent solutions are more difficult to obtain.

The compulsive reprogramming of the domestic debt at the beginning of January 1990 as an alternative way to avoid hyperinflation in Argentina is perhaps the most interesting case to analyze this type of problem. Obviously, if people would have willingly accepted restructuring, compulsion would have not been necessary. This occurred in January 1990, and it is too soon to evaluate the results and the future consequences of such policy action. But it will certainly be the subject of my future research.

5.6   Conclusions

The question we raised at the outset was, Can populist governments stop high inflation? If the answer were yes, developing nations like Argentina might be able to grow again. If the answer is no, stagnation and the risk of hyperinflation seem the natural outcome.

Populist governments used to approach economics by emphasizing income redistribution and paying little attention to deficit finance and the risk of hyperinflation. The experience I have analyzed seems to suggest that the populist approach to economic policy has failed to achieve even a minimum improvement in the well-being of low-income people. Traditional political parties have not disappeared from electoral competition, but they are in a process of aggiornamento and rationalization of their later experiences.

Populist leaders learned that they were wrong when they believed that transitory stabilization through price controls was a necessary condition to carry out the reform of the public sector. They thought of transitory stabilization as buying time for a structural reform that, in the future, would result in a sound and permanent monetary and fiscal policy. But they never had the time to reach the future. They also learned that the transformation of public-sector enterprises and institutional behavior of local and provincial governments were prerequisites to stabilization. The failure of Argentina's Austral Plan, Primavera Plan, and BB Plan were the learning experiences.

After decades of failures, governments of any type lose their credibility, and transitory stabilization with heterodox measures increases real interest rates and the burden of the domestic debt which, in turn, builds up pressures for a new inflation burst. The problem of high inflation is usually the problem of an oversized public sector and fiscal disarray. Any program that does not immediately attack these two problems will almost surely fail. It remains to be seen, at least in Argentina, whether a successful heterodox plan is possible. Heterodoxy has failed, not because all heterodox plans are wrong or illogical, but because those that were employed were used to postpone reforms of the public sector that had been badly needed for several decades.

What populist leaders have also learned is that not all the problems facing a country like Argentina are the result of naive income policies or the government spending too much. Domestic debt, credibility, financial runs, and policy mistakes are almost as important as naive populism.

The change in the populist approach of basing stabilization on deficit-ridden income policies is a necessary condition for price stability. It is also necessary to start the stabilization with well-known fundamental reforms in the public sector. Any delay in taking these measures is seen as a lack of political will and deteriorates even more the low credibility of the government. Finally, careful attention must be paid to domestic debt dynamics that can easily jeopardize any serious attempt at stabilization. It may be the case that domestic debt restructuring is necessary to assure the stability in financial markets.

References

Arriazu, Ricardo, Alfredo Leone, and Ricardo Lopez Murphy. 1988. Politicas Macro-economicas y Endeudamiento Privado: Aspectos Empiricos. In *Deuda Interna y Estabilidad Financiera*, vol. 2, ed. Carlos Massad and Roberto Zahler. Buenos Aires: Grupo Editor Latinoamericaco.

Auernheimer, Leonardo. 1974. The Honest Government's Guide to the Revenue from Creation of Money. *Journal of Political Economy* 82:598–606.

Calvo, Guillermo A. 1978. On the Time Consistency of Optimal Policy in a Monetary Economy. *Econometrica* 46:1211–1428.

Calvo, Guillermo A., and Maurice Obstfeld. 1988. Time Consistency of Fiscal and Monetary Policy: A Comment. University of Pennsylvania. Mimeograph.

Fernández, Roque B. 1990. Real Interest Rate and the Dynamics of Hyperinflation.

The Case of Argentina. International Monetary Fund, Research Department, Washington, D.C. Mimeograph.

————. 1989a. Hiperinflación, Repudio y Confiscación: Los Límites del Financiamiento Inflacionario. Documentos de Trabajo CEMA, no 65.

————. 1989b. Time Consistency and Inflationary Finance. International Monetary Fund, Fiscal Affairs Department, Washington, D.C., April. Mimeograph.

Fernández, Roque B., and Rolf R. Mantel. 1988. Fiscal Lags and the Problem of Stabilization: Argentina's Austral Plan. In *Latin American Debt and Adjustment*, ed. P. Brock, M. Connolly, and C. Gonzalez. New York: Praeger Publishers.

————. 1985. Estabilización Económica con controles de precios. *Ensayos Economicos*. Banco Central de la Republica Argentina, December.

Kydland, Finn E., and Edward C. Prescott. 1977. Rules Rather than Discretion: The Inconsistency of Optimal Plans. *Journal of Political Economy* 85:473–92.

Lucas, Robert E., and Nancy L. Stokey. 1983. Optimal Fiscal and Monetary Policy in an Economy Without Capital. *Journal of Monetary Economics* 12:55–93.

Persson, Mats, Torsten Persson, and Lars E. O. Svensson. 1987. Time Consistency of Fiscal and Monetary Policy. *Econometrica* 55:1419–31.

Sargent, Thomas, and Neil Wallace. 1981. Some Unpleasant Monetarist Arithmetic. *Federal Reserve Bank of Minneapolis Quarterly Review* 5:1–17.

Additional Sources

Barro, Robert, and David Gordon. 1983. Rules, Discretion and Reputation in a Model of Monetary Policy. *Journal of Monetary Economics* 12 (July): 102–21.

Baxter, Marianne. 1988. Toward an Empirical Assessment of Game-Theoretic Models of Policymaking. A Comment. *Carnegie-Rochester Conference Series on Public Policy* 28:141–52.

Blejer, Mario I., and Adrienne Cheasty. 1988. High Inflation, Heterodox Stabilization, and Fiscal Policy. *World Development* 16a (8):867–81.

Bruno, Michael, and Stanley Fischer. 1987. Seignorage, Operating Rules and the High Inflation Trap. NBER Working Paper no. 2413. Cambridge, Mass., October.

Canzoneri, Matthew B. 1985. Monetary Policy Games and the Role of Private Information. *American Economic Review* 75:1056–70.

Chamley, Christophe. 1985. On a Simple Rule for the Optimal Inflation Rate in Second Best Taxation. *Journal of Public Economics* 26:35–50.

Olivera, Julio H. 1967. Money, Prices and Fiscal Lags: A Note on the Dynamics of Inflation. Banca Nazionale del Laboro *Quarterly Review* 20 (September): 258–67.

Phelps, Edmund S. Inflation in the Theory of Public Finance. *Swedish Journal of Economics* 75:67–82.

Rogers, Carol Ann. 1988. A Simple Rule for Managing the Maturity Structure of Government Debt. *Economics Letters* 28:163–68.

Tanzi, Vito. 1978. Inflation, Real Tax Revenue, and the Case for Inflationary Finance: Theory with an Application to Argentina. *IMF Staff Papers* 25, no. 3 (September):417–51.

————. 1977. Inflation, Lags in Collection and the Real Value of Tax Revenue. *IMF Staff Papers* 24 (1):154–67.

Turnovsky, Stephen J., and William A. Brock. 1980. Time Consistency and Optimal Government Policies in Perfect Foresight Equilibrium. *Journal of Public Economics* 13:183–212.

Comment   José De Gregorio

In my remarks I want to focus on the following issues: First, there are two kinds of policy failures, those where the announced plan does not work and those where the plan is aborted before all the measures are implemented. The former case is the most relevant, and I want to stress that the key issue is not *what* the missing component was rather than *why* it was actually missing. Second, I will concentrate on the timing of a disinflation. There is tension between the stabilization shock, which may include monetary reform, incomes policies, and so on, and the long-run transformation required to live with lower inflation. Then I will refer to the relevance of incomes policies as a component of a stabilization program. This is an old discussion but in this case important to address in light of Fernández's claims.

Why Are Stabilizations Abandoned?

It is not puzzling to see that many stabilization programs end up failing. In Argentina this is the case in all three programs analyzed in the paper. The disturbing issue is not what were the measures not undertaken during the stabilization but rather why they were not implemented in spite of the fact that they may have been announced.

On the reasons for the program's failure there is enough evidence showing that the lack of fiscal adjustment was the main reason. However, there is little work on why the fiscal adjustment was not carried out. I want to discuss some of the possible explanations.

We could argue that the policymakers are "ignorant populists." This may be true not only for this vaguely defined species called "populist." This seems the explanation underlying Fernández paper. Unfortunately the answer is not as simple as to send policymakers to study macroeconomics. Especially in Argentina, where most economists had the chance to stop inflation, they certainly are not ignorant. At a deeper level it is not an attractive assumption to consider that private agents make rational decisions while governments are completely irrational. In the particular case of the Austral Plan, Fernández mentions that Alfonsín promised not to create money to finance the budget. Hence, we can discard the "ignorance hypothesis."

An alternative hypothesis is that the program had bad luck (bad terms of trade) or a lack of credibility (reforms that were not believable). The problem with these explanations is that programs fail without being completely implemented. Governments abandon stabilization plans before they are able to see

José De Gregorio is an economist at the Research Department of the International Monetary Fund.

The author is very grateful to Rudiger Dornbusch and Federico Sturzenegger for valuable comments. The usual caveat applies.

whether they will be successful. The Austral Plan started with a large degree of support, so the lack of credibility is also not a serious issue.[1]

Finally, I think the most plausible reason for program failure is that some institutional and political factors impose severe constraints on the completion of the program. The costs that the government has to bear, if they stick to the original plan, are so high that they prefer to abort it. I will develop an example that looks consistent with the Argentinean experience.[2]

Let us consider the Austral Plan. It has everything needed for success, especially unprecedented popular support. Despite the fact that the plan worked for some period, the deep roots of inflation were not eliminated.

Why was Alfonsín's economic team unable, although they may have been willing, to make the fiscal correction? It is possible that they did not know how difficult it would be to implement a fiscal reform. After the first stages of the plan were implemented, they realized that the required adjustment was more substantive than they had originally expected. They could not find enough political willingness, in the Congress or in the political parties, to support the adjustment needed to carry forward the required reforms.[3] The cost that the government would have to bear alone would have been too high to make continuing worth the effort. Hence they prefer to administer the crisis in the hope of better luck in the future.

All further attempts to stop inflation are condemned to fail unless there exists a broad consensus among the main interest groups to support fundamental economic reform. The costs the country has to pay in order to reach this stage are enormous. Meném's first attempt to incorporate radicals into the government shows that the search for an agreement is considered important.

What Should Come First: The Fiscal Reform or the Short-Run Shock?

An interesting discussion raised by Fernández is the question of the fiscal reform and its timing. A summary of his point is that proponents of the Aus-

---

1. The evolution of interest rates also shows that successful programs are not necessarily those that had the most credibility. In some sense, credibility came later. On a recent failed stabilization in Ireland and its contrast with Poincaré in France in 1926, see R. Dornbusch, "Credibility, Debt, and Unemployment: Ireland's Failed Stabilization" (*Economic Policy* 8 [1989]: 174–201). For a discussion of the Bolivian hyperinflation, see J. Sachs, "The Bolivian Hyperinflation" (NBER Working Paper no. 2073, Cambridge, Mass., 1986). In the Argentinean case the large drop of nominal interest rates in the months following the Austral Plan shows that the plan did not lack credibility.

2. In "Why Stabilizations Are Delayed" (Mimeograph, 1989), A. Alesina and A. Drazen model the delay of stabilization as a concession game among different interest groups. Nevertheless, my example will suggest that the stabilization will come when everybody agrees to share the burden of stabilization rather than when a particular group concedes and bears the entire cost of stabilization. Another related model is discussed by R. Fernández and D. Rodrik, "Why Is Trade Reform So Unpopular?" (CEPR Discussion Paper Series, No. 391, March 1990).

3. A simple formalization of this point is that there is uncertainty about the Olivera-Tanzi effect. Therefore, when inflation is reduced they realized that the fiscal adjustment has to be greater than the expectation they had before starting the program.

tral Plan would argue that the plan was a necessary condition for a serious discussion on the budget issue. The opponents of the plan thought that a precondition of implementation should have been a transformation of the public sector.

There are at least two reasons why the stabilization should start with the anti-inflationary shock. It is necessary to know how the economy will look like with low inflation to have a good sense of the magnitude of the reform. Also, the recovery of seignorage after the remonetization generates enough revenues while better taxation is designed.

These seem the reasons why Daniel Heymann and Stanley Fischer, in their analysis of the Austral Plan and the Israeli stabilization of 1985, support this timing. The last paragraphs of their respective discussions are:

> Still high inflation and stagnation are more than occasional problems in Argentina. Longer-run changes . . . seem necessary to overcome them. The stabilization program has stimulated a debate within the country that may, hopefully, produce some agreement on such reforms.

> Second, the economy needs major structural reforms. The ending of inflation was a necessary precondition for dealing with the economy's real problem.[4]

However there are also reasons why starting with a structural reform may be preferred. It can help to avoid time consistency problems of the fiscal reform. The increase in seignorage has the disadvantage in that it reduces the incentive to undertake the "deep reform," then the reform may be time inconsistent. It is also possible that after many failed attempts to stop inflation the effectiveness of new short-run programs is diminished. The endogenous accommodation of the economy to high inflation will make stabilization very difficult.

It seems that in Argentina today to reduce inflation it is first necessary to press for a deep reform of the public sector. Short-run attempts have all failed, and it is unlikely that a new one will succeed.

However, before classifying the Austral Plan as a useless program we have to ask: Would it have been possible to implement a deep fiscal reform before the Austral Plan? If Alfonsín's team did not succeed with the high level of support he had when the plan started, it is extremely unlikely that they would have succeeded in bringing public-sector reform without the anti-inflationary shock. If they did not have the incentive and/or the support to carry out that enormous and risky operation at the peak of their popularity, they surely would have not been able to do it without the Austral Plan.

Today there is consensus that fiscal reform is essential, and this is the result of the failure of previous attempts. It seems that disinflation is like "experi-

---

4. See D. Heymann, "The Austral Plan" (Papers and Proceedings of the *American Economic Review* [1987]: 284–87) and S. Fischer, "The Israeli Stabilization Program" (Ibid., pp. 275–78).

ence goods" in industrial organization: you have to try them to know their quality. You have to try to stabilize to know how difficult it is.

Incomes Policy Support to Stabilization[5]

Fernández also raises the question of whether incomes policies are an important component of a stabilization program. He argues that they were a mistake and elsewhere he shows that they only delayed the "adjustment to the steady state."

In Argentina, only incomes policies have been implemented. It is obvious that they alone are not enough to control inflation. The idea that high inflation comes purely as an indexation phenomenon is generally false. There is always an ultimate macroeconomic imbalance that triggers this process. It is not a surprise to find that incomes policies introduce an additional disequilibrium when the problem is not entirely resolved. Incomes policies are justified only as a complement of a stabilization program that helps to reduce the recessive costs of disinflation. Their failure in Argentina is not a case against incomes policies, but a case in favor of a complete program. Otherwise it should be necessary to question why stabilization programs that included incomes policies have been successful in Israel and Mexico.

Incomes policies are not a panacea, and they involve some risks that are worth mentioning. Relative price distortions are always a problem; however, in high inflation they may be a second-order cost. Their most pervasive effect is in the pricing strategies of firms that are expecting a price freeze. The expectation of price controls may lead to an overreaction in the magnitude of price adjustment; this introduces an additional friction into the price dynamics. New pricing practices will emerge in order to avoid being caught with prices too low when the price freeze occurs. A typical example is the existence of rebates. Firms can have permanently high quoted prices and then adjust them through discounts. Although this pricing mechanism may allow for relative price adjustments during a disinflation, it also jeopardizes the effectiveness of a price freeze since firms will be effectively increasing prices. This may suggest that incomes policies should only focus on the control of few key prices and allow the rest to adjust during the disinflation.

Some Concluding Remarks

The more a stabilization program is delayed the higher are its recessionary costs. The reason for this is that, as inflation remains high, the macroeco-

5. I will not repeat studies on incomes policies instead of focusing on Fernández's remarks. For extensive discussion of the subject, see R. Dornbusch and M. Simonsen, *Inflation Stabilization with Income Policy Support* (New York: Group of Thirty, 1987); E. Helpman and L. Leiderman, "Stabilization in High Inflation Countries: Analytical Foundations and Recent Experience" (*Carnegie Rochester Conference Series on Public Policy* 28 [1988]: 9–84); M. Kiguel and N. Liviatan "Inflationary Rigidities and Orthodox Stabilization Policies" (*World Bank Economic Review* 2 [1988]:273–98).

nomic fragility is increasing. Sophisticated pricing practices and other ways to circumvent price controls emerge. The monetary and financial system also become very unstable, which makes it too costly to raise seignorage.[6]

The fundamental cause of inflation is still the budget deficit. The fact that the government is following an unsustainable policy weakens the contemporaneous correlation between inflation and the budget, which of course can make even more obscure the design of a coherent disinflation program.[7] Fernández discusses other problems, such as the monetarist arithmetic of Sargent and Wallace and the time consistency of public debt. All these considerations reduce the degrees of freedom for sound macroeconomic policy and the economy accumulates significant losses. Unfortunately these may be the costs that trigger the necessary willingness to undertake a serious disinflation effort.

6. See J. De Gregorio, "Welfare Costs of Inflation, Seignorage, and Financial Innovation" (MIT, Cambridge, Mass., Mimeograph, 1990).
7. See A. Drazen and E. Helpman, "Inflationary Consequences of Anticipated Macroeconomic Policies" (*Review of Economic Studies* 57 [1990]: 147–66).

6 Sixty Years of Populism in Brazil

Paulo Rabello de Castro and Marcio Ronci

6.1 Introduction

Populism is a form of political conduct, adopted by a person or a group of people, that may be identified by the use of economic tools and other means designed to produce favorable results quickly, regardless of how short-lived they may be, in so much as these actions are instrumental to acquire and maintain authoritarian power.

Under this definition it can be said that, while populism is less than a political system proper, it nevertheless represents more than mere demagoguery. Populism is in fact more than just political promises; the populist leader will actually try to deliver them. There are two words key to understanding populism: *instability* and *discontent*. Let us begin with the former. When the political system qualifies as a stable one, there is hardly any room for populism. Whether democratic or autocratic, a stable political system will tend to restrict populist behavior. That is why one cannot rightly refer to occasional demagogic actions of a politician in a consolidated democracy as populism. These activities would lack the systematic character of populist conduct.

It might also be confusing to refer to socialist dictatorships as populist, not only because the ruling party is firmly entrenched in power but also because most of their social and economic policies are not designed for immediate results but, on the contrary, only envisage an "officially determined long run."

It is political (and economic) instability that creates the right momentum for the populist appeal. The political system must be vulnerable and fragile to provide a basis for the growth and expansion of populism.

Paulo Rabello de Castro is professor of economics at the Fundação Getulio Vargas. Marcio Ronci is senior economist at RC Consultores.

The authors are grateful to Uriel de Magalhaes and Lauro Flavio Vieira de Faria for helpful comments and to Aloisio Campelo, Jr., who efficiently and tirelessly collected and prepared the data used in this essay. Any opinions expressed are those of the authors.

The other element is discontent. Very quick social transformations are a sure source of discontent, as is a fairly long period of stagnation. Furthermore, unequal wealth and income distribution also play an important role, especially if accumulation is understood to have taken place at the expense of the majority of the people.

One may argue, however, that if discontent could be channeled through a democratic representation there would be hardly any room left for populism. Discontent without representation tends to generate disenchantment, and people become more vulnerable to a solution in the realm of magic. Populism is a way of bringing back hope for those who feel misrepresented in society. Thus populism is fostered with more ingredients than just the manipulation of economic tools.

There is clearly a political relationship between the populist ruler, his group, and their represented sectors, thereby establishing an alternative legitimacy to his (or their) authoritarian deeds. So populism is not just demagoguery. It is rather political activism in search of power. This is precisely the ultimate characteristic of populism—the struggle on the part of the activist group to acquire and maintain more power. Given political instability as a prerequisite, populism is not compatible with democracy; every political blank must be filled by the populist in search of consolidating his own authority (or that of his group) and not the authority of the democratic regime itself. In essence, every populist draws on authoritarianism. Nevertheless, in its current practice, populism may show itself in the form of numerous middle-of-the-road situations that defy the analytical spirit of an attentive observer.

Despite the obvious difficulties of determining a more generic or universal definition for the phenomenon, a case-by-case study of populism only becomes meaningful if the theoretical concept of populism is previously established. In that sense, the mere detection of the wrong economic policies does not qualify those policies as a story of populism; on the other hand, there are quite a few experiences of populism that have achieved fairly good success for quite some time before their structural misdoings finally showed up.

The political elements of discontent and instability are the key factors that seem to be at the core of populism, for which reason the aspects of power struggle and domination tend to offset the contours of an "economic" populism so defined. Otherwise the economist's view of an essentially political phenomenon may end up dragging him to the extreme of labeling every failed growth policy or distributive action as populist. In other words, not every dictator is a populist and, surely, not every populist is a dictator; however, every authoritarian ruler does *lean toward* populism whenever challenged by political instability. On the other hand, not every distributive or income policy has to be a populist one, although there is no populism without actions designed to placate discontent.

This paper holds a view that objects to the argument that politicians only undertake populist actions because of social pressures. According to the prevailing approach, unequal income distribution and widespread poverty press politicians toward emphasizing growth and income distribution with no regard to other restrictions, such as inflation, deficit finance, and balance of payments equilibrium (see e.g., Sachs 1989 and Dornbusch and Edwards 1989). Accordingly, politicians are basically naive in their purposes or, worse yet, they are "victims" of circumstance. The opposite view argues that the populist leader carries out careful political calculations for each of his actions and uses economic policies as a means to reach his objectives. Besides, depending on the brand of populism, populist policies do not necessarily end up thorough failures.

In the remaining sections of this paper we will go over the contemporary history of Brazil for the past 60 years and try to frame populism as a form of political conduct. Economic tools used in those periods will be pointed out, and their economic consequences will be briefly discussed. In so doing, our main task will be to try to validate our tentative definition of the term "populism" in light of the recent Brazilian experience.

6.2   Revisiting Vargas: Classic Populism, 1930–54

The contribution of Getúlio Dornelles Vargas to the consolidation of a populist tradition in Brazilian politics cannot by any means be underestimated. Vargas's political conduct represents what one would call a classic approach to the use of economic and noneconomic tools to produce the best results for the acquisition and maintenance of authoritarian power. Vargas was a dictator for eight years (1937–45) but that is not what makes him a classic populist. It is rather the manipulation of power mechanisms in order to influence public opinion in favor of his centralizing authority that qualifies his entire period as a populist one.

Vargas had been a discreet and rather orthodox minister of finance in the late 1920s, serving dutifully under the man he eventually overthrew from power at the turn of the decade. The 1930 revolution brings the voice of the people into the political scene for the first time in contemporary Brazil. There was enough discontent among the emerging proletariat by 1930 to create a demand for a popular leader. People were tired of the Republican aristocrats from the states of Minas Gerais and São Paulo who had been alternating power since the overthrow of the emperor in 1889. Political instability completed the scene. The 1930 revolution had broken up the old regime and brought forward a group of "young lieutenants"—mostly military—that lined up in favor of a new protectionist rule to promote domestic industries and to foster the urbanization of a then vastly rural Brazil (70% of the people in the fields as compared to 30% in the cities by 1930).

The Vargas era and the relationship of the ruling man with politics and economics clearly demonstrates that *classic populism* does not go overboard in terms of short-run economic policy. In other words, the classic populist is the one who indeed knows that the economy has to be run under a budget constraint and that it has a hard currency reserve limit to compel it back toward its own boundaries. That was absolutely perceived by Vargas, he himself having once been a finance minister.

During his first period in power (1930–45), Vargas had to cope with huge political and economic pressures. After a brief period as provisional president, Vargas was elected for a 1934–38 term. He had to fight a counterrevolution in 1932, beating the *paulistas* but placating them with a protectionist industrial policy. Worldwide, the Great Depression incubated fascism and Nazism. Meanwhile, communism was on its way up. Inside Brazilian borders, the new regime made its first attempts to crack up the political bones of the coffee-growing aristocracy—a task made easy by the collapse of coffee prices—and, at the same time, the new regime stretched itself to manage the unmanageable by standing in the middle of *integralistas* (the domestic version of fascism) and *comunistas*.

Vargas led a coup on 10 November 1937, closing the Congress and imposing himself as ruler. He dressed up his actions with a lot of grandiose designs that were summarized by the expression "Estado Nôvo," or "the new state." A new constitution was written under the influence of the powerful Francisco Campos, who promoted a totalitarian and nationalistic philosophy for Brazil. According to him, "centuries of experience have demonstrated that the principle of liberty did not improve the lot of the average citizen or keep the strong from taking advantage of the weak. Only a strong state can guarantee to the individual the rights he ought to have" (Dulles 1967, pp. 174–75). Under the 1937 constitution, the nationalization of mines, sources of energy, banks, insurance companies, and basic and essential industries were to be regulated by law.

On the external front, the Great Depression (1929) hit the country hard, as the price of coffee, the main export, fell sharply. Vargas's government reacted buying part of the coffee production and so avoiding the reduction of domestic demand (see Skidmore 1976, p. 66, and Furtado 1976). All servicing of foreign debts was suspended. With regard to the exchange policy, official devaluations more than offset the rate of increase of prices in Brazil until 1939, while it did not change much during the Second World War, even though inflation in Brazil was greater than in North America. The overvaluation of the exchange during the war made up for the real devaluation of the previous decade (Goldsmith 1986, pp. 186–89).

The monetary policy was, in general, loose in 1932–37 (with a brief contraction in 1933), which pushed the recovery of the economy after 1932. The inflation rate was relatively low, around 10% a year. After 1941, the money expansion became very loose to finance the war effort, so inflation stepped up.

The war experience showed the need for an active monetary policy, which resulted in the creation of SUMOC in 1945, an embryo of the Central Bank.[1]

In his first period in power, Vargas also laid down the foundations of the interventionist model. In 1933, the Brazilian Coffee Institute (IBC) was created and would dominate all the coffee matters in Brazil for the next 55 years. A similar organization—Instituto do Acucar e do Alcool (IAA)—was set to prevail over the sugar industry, from production to final marketing. The Ministry of Finance, under Artur de Souza Costa began to articulate the centralization of policy-making in Brazil. In the early 1930s, the Social Security Institutes were created to offer medical assistance and welfare protection (old-age retirement and pensions) to the working classes. All were under federal control. The government also gave incentives to the formation of workers' unions, provided that they were approved under the newly installed Ministry of Labor, headed by the articulate and dynamic Lindolpho Collor, grandfather of Fernando Collor de Melo, now president of Brazil.

Vargas stood in power until 1945 when World War II was over. By then, the foundations of a strong and pervasive state had already been laid down. After an interim presidency (by Vargas's former Minister Eurico Dutra) between 1946 and 1949, the former dictator came back to power as a democratically elected president in 1950. It goes to show that a classical populist's political platform is often long-lasting.

During his second period in power (1951–54), Vargas tried to achieve an impossible balance between the external restriction, inflation, and his investment strategy. He sought to work under the rules of the international system and accepted foreign collaboration to finance his investment plan (e.g., the Brazil-USA commission of 1951–53). In 1953, he adopted a more flexible exchange rate policy. These gestures helped to convince foreign investors and international institutions that he was prepared to keep a policy of external balance.[2] On the other hand, Vargas appealed frequently to the people's nationalistic and xenophobic sentiments and channeled investments through state companies in order to satisfy the opposition (Skidmore 1976, p. 128). At the end of 1952, the balance of payments situation and inflation had become critical. Vargas again showed understanding of the limits of his populism. In August 1954, he reshuffled his cabinet and adopted a quite orthodox stabilization program under the supervision of one of his most competent collaborators, Oswaldo Aranha.[3] The plan was not carried out by Aranha himself because of a political crisis that came to an end with Vargas's suicide.

1. For an account of the monetary policy in the period 1930–45, see Neuhaus (1975, pp. 128–29).
2. See Skidmore (1976, p. 124). For an account of the exchange rate policy, see Goldsmith (1986, p. 251).
3. See Skidmore (1976, p. 151). The Aranha stabilization program would be put into effect by Eugenio Gudin, who mentioned it in his speech when he took office at the Ministry of Finance.

Vargas committed suicide in the midst of a sea of accusations against his government's moral conduct. That last gesture was to give him a political afterlife for another 10 years. Vargas's farewell message, written right before he put a bullet through his heart, contains all the vital elements of classic populism in Brazil:

Domination and plunder on the part of international and financial groups, . . . The excess-profits law was held up by Congress, . . . Hatreds . . . against the just revision of minimum wages. . . . National freedom . . . by means of Petrobrás, . . . Electrobrás was obstructed; . . . They do not want the worker to be free; . . . Profits of foreign companies were reaching as much as 500 percent per annum; . . . Came the coffee crisis . . . we tried to defend its price and the reply was such violent pressure. . . . I fought against the spoliation of Brazil. . . . Now I offer my death. (Dulles 1967, pp. 334–35)

For the entire 15-year period of his first term—as provisional and constitutional president and then as a dictator, from 1930 to 1945—and again during the short period of his second and last term as elected president from 1950 to 1954, Vargas never disregarded the aspect of short-run macroeconomic equilibrium as it can be shown by the average data related to those periods. As we can see in the table 6.1, real gross domestic product (GDP) grew an average of 4.4% a year in the first of Vargas's periods and 6% in his second period; these are good records, particularly if we bear in mind that during his first period he had to maneuver the economy through a world recession, a civil war, and, then, a world war. As regard to inflation, the average price increase was 6.7% a year in Vargas's first period and 17% a year in his second period. External accounts were in surplus in his first period and experienced a deterio-

Table 6.1   Main Macroeconomic Indicators of the Brazilian Economy (Average Values of the Period)

Stages of Populism	Real GDP (1)	Nominal Wages (2)	Inflation (3)	Money M1 (4)	Money M2 (5)	Trade Balance (6)	Current Account (7)
Vargas's first term (1931–45)	4.41	—	6.75	14.46	13.39	7.18	2.47
Vargas's second term (1951–54)	6.18	18.09	17.15	20.56	18.04	.97	−3.43
Kubitschek (1956–60)	8.23	26.15	20.13	25.61	23.72	1.45	−1.36
Goulart (1961–63)	5.27	46.36	54.40	48.85	47.34	.24	−1.22
Castelo Branco (1964–67)	4.18	56.27	53.13	62.61	61.95	1.82	.41
Médici/Geisel (1968–78)	9.14	29.62	29.58	40.56	45.06	−.96	−3.54
Figueiredo (1979–84)	2.38	107.23	119.25	84.94	105.90	.94	−4.22
Sarney (1985–89)	4.64	528.00	515.62	435.62	412.44	4.14	−0.16

Sources: See appendix A.
Note: Cols. 1–5 are annual percentage growth rates; cols. 6–7 are percentage shares of GDP.

ration in his second term in office. Vargas had been trying to cope with infla-tion and external imbalances in 1954 when he was cut off by a political crisis which ended in tragedy. Nevertheless, he was a downright populist in the sense of using *noneconomic* tools to his best advantage and in order to achieve and maintain some kind of authoritarian power. Such tools would finally in-clude his own death as a last resort.

The lessons to be drawn from the Vargas period help to clarify the intersec-tion between populism and economics. First of all, the populist's mind has the unavoidable tendency to promote *the centralization of economic power.* That, in turn, leads the economy toward nationalization and excessive regulation of private activities. In fact, it was Vargas who laid down the foundations for all the subsequent expansion of the state as an entrepreneur: Petrobrás, Elec-trobrás, the steel corporations (several of them, starting with Companhia Siderurgica Nacional), the mining company Vale do Rio Doce—all these giants, that would later reproduce themselves into many other companies, were created under Vargas's inspiration.[4]

Those huge corporations implied the establishment of a complex network of private interests that permeated the whole economy. The private sector under the public corporations' umbrella would incorporate their motto in fa-vor of permanent government control. That, in turn, would determine the of-ficial manipulation of the so-called strategic prices, thus persuading the public to believe the fallacy that "important" prices, like those of gas, oil, steel, sugar and wheat, could not be set up under market conditions.

Such a heritage of economic interventionism is absolutely more relevant in explaining the Brazilian populist experience than the occasional propensity toward inflationary policies or the balance of payments crises. The structural distortions generated by outright intervention and excessive regulation would eventually provoke stagflation in the late 1970s and throughout the 1980s. Nevertheless, that only came along after a fairly long period of time. In the meantime, the apparent results seemed to be quite favorable because of the effects of centralized economic decision making.

The second important heritage of populism that comes with nationalization and regulation is what we may call *institutional underdevelopment.* It may sound like a paradox that such extensive centralization of decision making and the multiplication of government agencies to control the economy would not entail the development of sound institutions that are characteristic of liberal democratic countries. The explanation for that apparent paradox can be found in the authoritarian nature of populism, and that is precisely why there is no such a thing as democratic populism. The search for power and the struggle to keep it under a populist rule produces the disruption of traditions that is so important in forming the nature of public institutions and agencies. In other

4. For an account of Vargas's interventionist policies during the period 1930–45, see Skidmore (1976, pp. 66–67) and Baer (1983, pp. 16–28).

words, under populism such institutions and agencies exist to serve the ruler's intentions and not the other way around.

Take, for instance, the Central Bank. The idea of creating an independent Central Bank in Brazil dates back to the 1920s. In the late 1930s, the U.S. government tried to influence Brazil in the same direction, by conditioning certain refinancing clauses of the country's external debts to such institutional developments sought by the Brazilian negotiator, Oswaldo Aranha. It was a useless attempt. The Brazilian Central Reserve Bank was never established (see Dulles 1967, pp. 203–4). At the end of the Second World War, as the inflationary pressures increased, a governmental agency, SUMOC, was set up to control the monetary policy; however, it had limited powers. Vargas understood well the need for an independent Central Bank to fight inflation, but he could not go so far as to create one because it would limit his powers. A third attempt was to be carried out in the 1960s, but the result was another failure.

Summing up, Brazil owes to populism much of its best and worst moments when we look into the subsequent acts of its recent history. Classic populism was pretty abiding to the limits of fiscal and external budgets, and one can even praise its first movements in terms of centralizing economic power, which did fulfil a vacuum of decision making in a historical period when every nation was fighting the Depression, then coping with a world war, and finally recovering from the war effects under the prevailing academic tutorship of Lord Keynes and his followers, who, by all means, advocated a widening of government's intervention in the economy. In that sense, populism in the 1930s, all the way through the 1950s, was a very clever political adaptation of some less-developed countries to the current tides of that time. The sequels thereof have to be understood in that perspective.

6.3   Three Decades between Conservatives and Populists: 1954–84

In the 30 years' time that elapsed from Vargas's death (24 August 1954) to the return of a civilian rule (15 November 1984), Brazil has oscillated between populism and conservatism, and has sometimes experienced an inextricable mix of both. The main trend, however, can be said to have remained a populist one, basically faithful to the foundations that Vargas laid down. The role of conservatives can be identified as being rather transitory *reformist intermezzos,* which were nonetheless powerful enough to reform and strengthen the interventionist model without being able to transform it into a free market one. This is where the controversy about the role of those reformist intermezzos is centered. There is still much confusion between the liberal intentions of the so-called reformists and the effective results of their policies, which were not able to revert the main structure of state interventionism inherited from the Vargas period.[5]

5. *Liberal* is employed in this essay in the radical sense of political liberalism in the European tradition, not in the rather opposite American use of the term.

It is through those episodes of economic rationality that the old regime managed to survive until the 1980s, showing a fairly good economic performance, although increasingly inflationary, for most of those three decades. The first reformist intermezzo took place in the short period of eight months between August 1954 and April 1955, when Eugenio Gudin, a lonely liberal, took office at the Ministry of Finance. The second intermezzo lasted longer: that was between April 1964 and March 1967, when the team Roberto Campos-Octavio Bulhões conducted the Brazilian economy under the first military period after Vargas. General Castelo Branco was the President. Despite every reasonable doubt, we may refer to a third intermezzo between February 1983 and November 1984, when the team led by Delfim Netto finally gave in to the international evidence and adjusted the country's balance of payments following the 1983 exchange devaluation.

During the first reformist intermezzo, Gudin brought about a tightening of monetary controls during the short period he stayed in office: the average monthly expansion of M1, in Gudin's period, was 1.44%, as compared to the 2.86% monthly growth in the preceding period, while the monthly inflation rates dropped from an average of 1.95% to 0.94%.[6] His intentions, however, were actually centered on a free exchange market that he envisaged for the country. Whether or not he realized it, he attacked the interventionist model at its most important pillar: the official control of the exchange rate. Of course, he was never able to accomplish his goal. He did, however, manage to pass Instruction no. 113, which permitted the import of investment goods without exchange coverage. That amounted, in other words, to enable importers of industrial equipment—Brazilians and foreign firms—to update their plants and even install new ones at an effective exchange rate that was neither the official nor the black market one.[7]

What followed Gudin's brief stay as Minister of Finance was a very interesting experience in terms of our definition of populism: the Juscelino Kubitschek administration (1956–60). Kubitschek's concern with development was explicitly embodied in his Targets Program. This was not a global planning of the economy. It did not cover all basic industries. Investments in infrastructure were directed to eliminate bottlenecks, and, in many cases, projects that had been prepared by the earlier Brazil-USA Commission (1951–53) were then used. In terms of basic industries, the objective was to give incentives to sectors such as metallurgy, cement, chemicals, heavy mechanics, shipbuilding, and the automobile industry. He built a new capital—Brasília—as a symbol of his government.[8] He wisely took advantage of Gudin's Instruction no. 113, which gave an incentive for foreign companies to invest in Brazil. In the 1956–60 period the Brazilian economy achieved high growth rates. The country's GDP expanded 8% a year, on average. This was the result of a policy of

6. For an account of Gudin as a finance minister, see Bulhões (1979, pp. 79–89).
7. On Gudin's views on exchange rate policy, see Gudin (1978a, pp. 84–87, 107–8).
8. For an examination of Kubitschek's Target Plan, see Lessa (1983, pp. 27–91) and Benevides (1979, pp. 224–33).

industrialization at any cost, protected by heavy custom duties and currency exchange incentives and large public investments. However, in 1958, the inflationary pressures were evident, and the government made an attempt to stabilize the economy under the command of Lucas Lopes and Roberto Campos. The government, however, soon abandoned the program and had to break up with the IMF (see Skidmore 1976, 218–19).

Kubitschek's economic policies were certainly expansionary. His political target was to make Brazil's "50 years in five." He drove close to a balance of payments crisis and publicly rejected the IMF's recipe when the international community tried to make him swallow it. Was he a populist? If so it was not because of those actions. Although the economic repercussions of his period may have led to some public discontent and political instability, Kubitschek's performance was clearly democratic. His mandate was a regular one, and he handed over the presidency to the man who had opposed him fiercely during the 1960 campaign. His economic targets were set in the long run and certainly provoked short-run imbalances, which horrified some conservatives. But they were never placed in the direction of acquiring or maintaining some form of authoritarian power.[9]

The same cannot be said with such assurance about the two presidents who came into power after Kubitschek. Jânio Quadros, the first of the two, was a champion of popularity at the time he was elected. He could deal with the passion of the masses in a way that had not been seen in Brazilian politics since Vargas.

However, following a very short period of eight months in office, Quadros abruptly handed his resignation to Congress. Historians argue that his actual intention was to be reinstated "in the arms of the people" with enough power to carry out the "reforms" that had been constantly obstructed by a reactionary Congress. But the people remained apathetic. The elements of discontent and of political instability were right there. What ensued can be traced back to the old Vargas style of populism and was enacted by none other than his closest political heir, who happened to be right on the scene: incumbent vice president João Goulart.

For the first time, the populist group that stepped in did not know enough about the limits of the fiscal budget and the exchange reserves. The political attitudes were "revolutionary"—which shook the conservative minds that were already used to populist manipulations—enough to placate the people's discontent but not to the point of letting the government believe in them. That single experience of populism under a leftist influence in Brazil clearly shows us the central difference between classic populism and the variant form carried out by "well-intentioned" leftists. The difference is that the latter does not know the limits of the balance of payments.[10] The features of Goulart's popu-

---

9. This view is shared by Benevides (1979).

10. For an account of the economic policies undertaken in this period, see Skidmore (1976, pp. 285–97, 325–31).

lism fit nicely into the description of a conventional mishandling of economic tools.

The most important lesson to be drawn from the Goulart period is that his populism did not have to be the way it came out. There is no evidence of any particularly serious deterioration of the Brazilian terms of trade, as often alleged by "structuralists" during that time, or any domestic setback such as that brought about by a bad crop.[11] It is also quite worth observing that *leftist populism* is infinitely less efficient than the classic one in terms of overtaking and keeping authoritarian power. Eventually, João Goulart and his group were all overthrown by a military coup supported by the conservative elite, an act easily accepted by the public opinion. Thus the economic heritage of that period is rather poor in the sense that leftist populism was not able to project its impact into the future by means of lasting institutions.

After Goulart's departure, in April 1964, the Castelo Branco administration (1964–67) formulated a short-run policy program (Government Economic Operation Program, or PAEG), whose main goals were to control inflation and correct the distortions inherited from state intervention in the economy. Severe measures were adopted, such as cuts in government expenditures, the elimination of subsidies, a squeeze in private credit, and wage controls. The new administration also carried out a successful tax reform, which greatly increased tax revenues.[12]

The crucial aspect of this period is the objectives that were not achieved rather than the ones that were eventually reached. The frustration of certain goals represents the dividing line between conservatism and liberalism in Brazil. The latter was never experienced at any time. Conservatism, on the other hand, is a form of political conduct that will not reject certain means employed by populists. In that sense, although it cannot be said that classic populism ensued from the second reformist intermezzo, it is certainly not wrong to say that conservatism inherited from populism some important characteristics, namely, the official doctrine of "security and development," according to which the maintenance of authoritarian power is justified to the extent that the government's economic performance is successful. This aspect would become very clear later, under the Medici period, when the interventionist model reached its "golden age."

During Castelo Branco's administration, there were a number of liberal ideas that unfortunately were not carried out. The first was that of an independent Central Bank. The legislation was actually produced, but the facts overrode the ink on the paper. Soon after Castelo Branco left in 1967, the Central Bank had a confrontation with General Costa e Silva who had succeeded Castelo Branco; the final result goes without saying.

11. On CEPAL's structuralist view, see Campos (1979, pp. 142–48).

12. A summary of Castelo Branco's economic policies can be found in Simonsen (1974, pp. 39–40). For a more detailed account, see Skidmore (1988, pp. 68–77, 116–17) and Viana Filho (1975, pp. 128–79, 208–38).

The second important point relates to the exchange rate liberalization. Roberto Campos, the planning minister, tried to free it, but again the "national interests" prevented the continuation of that experiment. A third area of conflict relates to the procedure used to set the prices of public utilities and of oil by-products, in particular. The price-setting process has never been made flexible. Despite Campos' firm attempts to break those monopolies, the bureaucracy would not renounce the right to intervene to equalize regional differences and impose an income policy through strategic prices.

That second intermezzo, however successful it was in protracting the life of the interventionist structure, could never achieve its reversal toward the free market as long as it remained under conservative influence, to the silent frustration of the liberal architects, Campos and Bulhões, who would have liked to reverse that model entirely. In hindsight, the times were not ripe for that change. Another three decades would have to pass in order to achieve that transformation.

Right after the Campos-Bulhões team, the *paulistas* took over under the firm leadership of Antônio Delfim Netto during Costa e Silva's and Médici's governments (1968–73). Delfim's greatest merits lie in the fact that he managed to neutralize the exchange rate deadlock by introducing crawling peg devaluations. In so doing, during a period of continuous expansion of world trade, he managed to ride the wave of progress by driving the Brazilian industry toward exports as a complement to the growing domestic market. The 1968–73 period contrasts with the years of economic slowdown, 1962–67. The Brazilian GDP grew at an average of 10% a year.

On the sinful side, Delfim Netto must take the blame for the legislation that erased the servicing of internal debt from the Treasury's budget, thus letting the rollover of domestic debt fall under the responsibility of the Central Bank. That was the beginning of endogenous money creation in Brazil, which, coupled to indexation, finally led to the hyperinflationary bias that is borne by the economy today. Another negative outcome of this period was the expansion of the productive activities of the public sector.[13] Despite the investment of state companies being one big source of growth in the 1968–73 period, the majority of state corporations were not operated under efficiency criteria, and, as a consequence, their investments resulted in low capital productivity, which would negatively affect the potential growth of the economy later on.[14]

In 1973, when the oil crisis broke out, Delfim avoided an exchange devaluation. After he stepped down, the economy came into the hands of Mario Henrique Simonsen, whose elbow room for reform was quite narrow given the political style of the new president, Ernesto Geisel. After 1973, the Geisel

13. For an account of Delfim Netto's policies, see Skidmore (1988, pp. 181–89, 274–86) and Baer (1983, pp. 242–45).
14. The various negative effects of the state's intervention in the economy during this period are discussed in Martone (1985) and Suzigan (1988). The expansion of state companies is also well documented and criticized in Gudin (1978a, pp. 405–37; 1978b, pp. 261–82).

administration (1974–79) sought a policy of accommodation in order to pre-serve real GNP at the expense of a rise in inflation. The government undertook an ambitious investment program with its state companies after 1975, which reached its peak in 1979. This program was mainly directed toward the pro-duction of energy (the building of power plants, oil mining, and the produc-tion of alcohol as an alternative fuel) and a second round of import substitu-tion (heavy engineering, fertilizers, and metallurgy of nonferrous metals). In order to finance this program it was necessary to borrow heavily both from abroad and in the domestic market. The government's deficit as a percentage of GDP grew from 1.4% in 1974 to 13.1% in 1979 (see Marques 1985, p. 361). Inflation rose from 15% a year in 1973 to 40% in 1979. In spite of the visible effects of the oil crisis, the Geisel administration simply did every-thing to avoid a real devaluation.[15]

This period of a "stepped-up march" revived old aspects of classic popu-lism.[16] The main figure of the popular ruler was not there, but the interven-tionist policies to secure the dominance of the state certainly were. Geisel had been close to Vargas since the beginning. His presence in the Brazilian politics dates back to the lieutenants' time in the 1920s. He had been one of them. His policies could not be much different. So, it has to be reckoned that a mix of conservatism and populism were again present in that period. The military, as a whole, acted as a searching authoritarian power, although not any one of them in particular.

In 1979, the Figueiredo administration (1979–84) was faced with: a huge external debt, the servicing of which consumed 67% of export revenues; the second oil crisis, as a consequence of the Iranian situation; and the impact of rising interest rates. In December 1979 the government adopted the following measures to cope with the increasing disorder in the economy: it put in place a 30% devaluation; it eliminated many tax exemptions; it increased tariffs of public services; it reduced the tax on interest sent abroad from 12.5% to 1.5% to stimulate borrowing from abroad; and it introduced a new wage bill, which reduced the period of adjusting wages from one year to six months. However, right after announcing these measures, early in 1980 the government made the fatal mistake of fixing beforehand the exchange rate devaluation for the whole year at 40% and indexing contracts at a limit of 45%. It also strengthened price controls. The government also planned to limit credit expansion to 45% for that year (see Baer 1983, pp. 414–15). However, actual credit expansion was a great deal above the target (79%), the wage bill contributed to increased industrial costs, and price controls were not effective. As a consequence of this boost of aggregate real demand, GDP grew 7.9% and inflation rose from 77% in the previous year to 110% in 1980. The improvement in export com-

15. Alternatives to devaluation were a 100% compulsory deposit on imports, and fiscal and credit subsidies to exports.

16. The expression, "stepped-up march," was coined by Antônio Barros de Castro (1985) in his book on that period.

petitiveness due to the devaluation that had occurred in December 1979 was completely lost, because the prefixed devaluation fell short of inflation during 1980 (Baer 1983, p. 417).

After the disastrous experience of 1980, a third reforming intermezzo began. Figueiredo changed course toward more orthodox policies. Monetary policy was tightened in 1981, and, after the outbreak of the international debt crisis in 1982, the exchange rate was devalued again by 30% in February 1983 while a new wage bill was passed in order to control wage increases. Agreements with the IMF were signed, but all too often the targets for public deficits and monetary expansion were missed. Figueiredo succeeded in balancing the external accounts, raising international reserves, and cutting subsidies and government expenditures, and inflation nevertheless leveled off at 200% a year.

The third intermezzo only started making sense in 1983, through the exchange devaluation carried out by Delfim Netto, the same man who would not do it 10 years before, at the beginning of the first oil crisis. This third intermezzo, under a very clear conservative influence, was just enough to keep the country's finances afloat until the November presidential elections of 1984.

Summing up, the macroeconomic indicators (see table 6.1) show that there were two periods of fast growth, namely the Kubitschek and Médici-Geisel periods after 1954, when the average growth rates of real GDP were 8% and 9% a year, respectively. These two periods were preceded by reforming intermezzos—Gudin's and Campos-Bulhões's—which checked inflation and external imbalances. After 1978, however, the growth and inflation performance became increasingly poorer. In Figueiredo's period, the GDP average growth fell to 2% a year and inflation rose to 120% a year on average. The picture we get from the whole 1954–84 period is clearly one of an economy under increasing strain, with growing inflation, external imbalances, and falling growth rates. The interventionist model inherited from Vargas gradually shows all its damaging effects on the economy. The reforming intermezzos stretched the model's life without managing to alter its regulatory nature.

6.4   Notes on Aging Populism: 1985–90

Both conservatives and populists have taken advantage of the interventionist model created and developed by Vargas's heritage. Both of them have used the means of an authoritarian power to control the economy and affect the market forces to the benefit of their distributive purposes. Through different policies, conservatives and populists have showed evidence of their disbelief in market forces as a correct way to achieve higher productivity, better wages, and fairer distribution of income and wealth. We cannot seriously deny the fact that they have almost operated together during the last three decades of Brazilian politics.

This apparently contradictory picture became clear after the *abertura*.[17] By 1984, the opposition was ready to take over the power from the army. So they acted with Tancredo Neves—an aging moderate politician—who died before his inauguration. José Sarney, an odd vice president of a last-minute political coalition, took over in Tancredo's place.

Through his five years in office, Sarney was a political hostage of the groups from which he had borrowed support. His team was not settled; he had to negotiate it. A new constitution (1988) was to be written up. Such a political set up, permeated by discontent and instability provided fertile soil for the resurgence of populism.

In what sense does populism in the 1980s differ from classic populism? The answer is that classic populism in Brazil was so well absorbed by the ruling elite that it could be identified, through the 1960s and 1970s, with the conservatives rather than with the so-called leftists or "progressivists." In fact, the conservatives have tried to preserve (i.e., to conserve) the existing structure of the interventionist model laid out by Vargas. That model had been a "miracle worker" for Brazil for so many years that the ruling elite developed all sorts of vested interests around it. Even when the model began to falter, they clung to it, through an authoritarian coup (1964), which led to 20 years of military rule.

Therefore, the opposition to the conservatives was concentrated in the political sector, that is, against the military in power, but not against the interventionist model that both conservatives and populists actually upheld. This is precisely the reason why very little was turned upside down when the "progressivists" took over after 1984. Under a representative regime—democracy in political terms—the interventionist model was not denounced but reinforced.

Throughout his mandate, President Sarney let *aging populism* prevail and dominate economic policies. The difference between classic and aging populism lies in the degree of proficiency in manipulating economic tools. The former is much more efficient than the latter. Aging populism tends to resort to extensive controls of the economy that eventually produce very few permanent effects but do create dramatic consequences in terms of macroeconomic imbalances (see table 6.1).

Sarney attempted three stabilization programs without any success because these programs tried to cope with the symptoms of the collapsing interventionist model rather than to focus on structural reform. One aspect common to all these policy experiments was their overinterventionism, in complete disregard of the markets.

17. *Abertura*, the Brazilian equivalent to *glasnost*, took place after 1979 and culminated with elections on 15 November 1984, when the opposition candidate, Tancredo Neves, was the winner. He had been minister of justice in Getúlio Vargas's last cabinet. As a young politician then, he inherited part of Vargas's political legacy.

All programs were based on two main ideas borrowed from a wide spectrum of academic economists, ranging from the left to the right: the "inertial inflation" and the "external debt-stagnation" hypothesis. The former argues that tight fiscal and monetary policies would have little effect upon inflation, leading only to a protracted recession.[18] The latter says that, in order to service the external debt, the debtor country is forced to transfer resources abroad that otherwise could be used to foster domestic investment and growth. On the other hand, as the country must run a trade surplus to finance its external debt service, it is necessary to restrain domestic demand and accelerate real devaluations of the exchange rate, actions that cause both stagnation and inflation. Both hypotheses proved to be thoroughly wrong.[19]

Nevertheless, these "theories" gave good excuses for a weak government not to control its public deficit and the money supply and deregulate the economy. It is not surprising, therefore, that the political coalition of conservatives and leftists eagerly carried out the policy recommendations of those "theories": wage and price controls to break the price inertia and nonpayment of interest on external debt. They were both popular and both bypassed painful structural adjustments.

The first stabilization attempt, the Cruzado Plan (28 February 1986), led by the messianic Dilson Funaro, the late finance minister who froze wages and prices and declared there would be no public deficit. There was a massive monetary expansion to cover the public deficit and buy back domestic public debt. Six months later, despite all of Funaro's patriotic efforts, the inflation rate showed its nasty face again and the external balance deteriorated. Nevertheless, the political gains, in the short run, were huge: the governing coalition managed to elect most of the state governors and a large number of seats in the Congress in the November 1986 elections. By early 1987, all popular support for the Sarney government had faded away. Then, the government blamed the "external debt" for all its problems and declared a moratorium without any results. The default of external debt received no popular support.

Bresser Pereira was then called in to substitute for Funaro. He carried out the second stabilization program, the so-called Bresser Plan (12 June 1987). Again wages and prices were frozen, and external debt was blamed for all problems. Bresser, a pragmatic economist, attempted both to control the public-sector deficit and to reach an agreement with external creditors. However meritorious his efforts were, he lacked the political support necessary to carry out his plan. More important, his mistaken assessment of the Brazilian

18. For an explanation of the inertial hypothesis of inflation, see Lopes (1984) and Simonsen (1986). The inertial hypothesis of Brazilian inflation has been challenged by various authors (e.g., Ronci 1988).

19. For a more detailed argument on the debt-stagnation hypothesis, see Bacha (1988), Cardoso and Dornbusch (1989), and Sachs (1987). For a critical examination of the external-debt hypothesis, see Castro and Ronci (1989).

economic crisis led to more intervention in the markets without addressing the more fundamental issue of structural reform.

In 1988, Mailson da Nobrega, a career civil servant, took over the Ministry of Finance. Initially, da Nobrega tried to control the public deficit, without success, on a day-by-day basis ("rice and beans policy") and then yielded to political pressure by freezing wages and prices once more as well as delaying the interest payments on external debt (the Summer Plan, January 1989). The effects of this plan were again short-lived: inflation rates went down the first three months and then rose to a 30% level and then moved upward.

All three attempts were basically flawed in both their diagnosis of the economic crisis and their solutions for it. The crisis stemmed from the inherited interventionist model. First, the excessive intervention in the markets was the true cause of growth stagnation rather than the burden of external debt in the 1980s. Government intervention through subsidizing certain activities, excessive regulation, subsidized interest rates to certain sectors, and the protection of domestic industry from foreign competition has stimulated a large number of low productive investments. The private sector in Brazil has received distorted signals from interest rates and relative prices, investing in sectors or regions where the return on capital was low. On the other hand, from the mid-seventies onward the government has substantially expanded its role as a producer of goods and services. As the majority of state corporations were inefficient, a good deal of their investments also resulted in low capital productivity. Finally the growth of the so-called entrepreneurial state also led to a decline of investments in health and education. The low quality of health and education has resulted in low productivity of labor and has sustained a perverse income distribution (see Martone 1985 and Suzigan 1988).

Second, institutional underdevelopment has led the Central Bank to cover the public-sector deficit by printing money and restricting its freedom to pursue an independent monetary policy to fight inflation.[20] Without a stable currency, the Tanzi effect operates against budget equilibrium. Internal debt piling sets in. As public finances deteriorates, credibility is affected and capital flight increases.

6.5 Concluding Remarks

The main points of this present essay are:

1. Politicians do not undertake populist actions simply in response to social pressures. The populist leader carries out careful political calculations of his actions and uses economic and noneconomic tools as a means to reach his objectives, which are to seize and keep power in an authoritarian fashion.

2. We cannot identify economic failures as always associated with populist

20. For a detailed examination of the Brazilian Central Bank, see Brandao (1989).

policies. Therefore, the concept of *economic populism* becomes meaningless for policy identification.

3. The main feature of populism is the institutional underdevelopment it provokes. Populism hates limits to the ruler's power that sound institutions would otherwise bring about. As a consequence, the countries that experience populism do not have strong institutions, like an independent Central Bank, an active Supreme Court, or a democratically elected Congress.

4. Regarding Brazilian history, Vargas's classic populism understood that the economy had to be run within the limits of financial constraints. In general, classic populism managed the economy quite well in the short run. However, it laid down the foundations of an interventionist model—excessive regulation of the economy and the expansion of the state as an entrepreneur—which distorted the allocation of resources and negatively affected Brazil's potential output.

5. All the events of the three decades after 1954 can be interpreted as a sequential attempt to cope with the long-run problems generated by the interventionist model inherited from Vargas. Brief intervals of conservative economic policies—indeed, reformist intermezzos—extended the life span of the model, but could not avoid its degeneration. Economic performance eventually collapsed regardless of the strengthening of controls over the economy.

6. Populism is an aging phenomenon in Brazil.

Is there an alternative to populism? We hold the view that liberalism can offer a way out of the predicament of most Latin American countries. But how can liberal formulas become "popular"? Maybe they do not have to. What has to become popular is the idea of democracy. This is the basic prerequisite for the growth of liberalism as a form of economic policy-making. From an evolutionary viewpoint, the time seems ripe for liberalization in Brazil. It will not come, however, through any rational decision of the elite but through various pressure elements stemming from the basis of the economic system.

Appendix A
Sources of Data for Table 6.1

Column 1.—Real gross domestic product (GDP) growth for the 1930–70 period was obtained from *Estatística Históricas do Brasil* (1987, p. 94) published by the Brazilian Institute of Geography and Statistics (IBGE). Real GDP growth for the 1980–89 period was obtained from the National Account Department of the IBGE.

Column 2.—The nominal wage index for the urban sector of the center-south region during the 1945–77 period was obtained from Goldsmith (1986, pp. 239 and 347). The nominal wage index for the manufacturing sector of

São Paulo State in the 1977–89 period was obtained from the FIESP index reported in *Conjuntura Econômica,* various issues.

Column 3.—Inflation was measured by the annual variation of the GDP deflator. For the 1930–80 period, it was found in *Estatisticas Históricas do Brasil* (1987, pp. 11–112, 159). For the 1980–89 period, it was obtained from the National Account Department of the IBGE.

Columns 4 and 5.—Here, M1 is defined as currency plus deposit accounts, and M2 is defined as M1 plus time deposits. Money figures are annual average balance variations. Data for the 1930–80 period was obtained from *Estatísticas Históricas do Brasil* (1987, p. 492–93, 503–5). For the 1980–89 period, it was obtained from the Central Bank of Brazil.

Columns 6 and 7.—Trade and current accounts in million of dollars for the 1930–80 period were obtained from *Estatística Históricas Brasileiras* (1987, p. 535–39) and for the 1980–89 period from *Conjuntura Econômica,* various issues. In order to calculate their shares of GDP, it was necessary to generate a series of GDP in dollars. First, we calculated the real GDP in billion of U.S. dollars using the IBGE estimate of GDP in 1988—$350 billion—and the real growth rates of GDP. Having done that, we inflated the real GDP series using the producer price index for the United States as reported in *Main Economic Indicators* of OECD, various issues.

Appendix B

Table 6B.1   Macroeconomic Data of the Brazilian Economy

Year	Real GDP (% Variation)	Nominal Wages (% Variation)	Inflation, GDP Deflator (annual %)	Money		Trade Balance (% GDP)	Current Account (% GDP)	Exchange Rate (annual %)
				M1 (annual %)	M2 (annual %)			
1930	-2.1	...	-12.36	...	...	7.5	-6.3	...
1931	-3.3	...	-10.87	-.83	.03	12.4	.4	46.1
1932	4.3	...	1.56	12.68	3.95	9.0	2.5	-.7
1933	8.9	...	-2.04	15.20	6.88	6.4	1.3	-6.0
1934	9.2	...	6.26	7.24	2.59	8.1	2.3	17.5
1935	2.9	...	4.79	6.17	8.08	5.0	-2.2	16.9
1936	12.1	...	1.64	7.79	9.21	7.4	.6	-1.2
1937	4.6	...	9.45	7.02	9.16	3.6	-3.4	-5.9
1938	4.5	...	3.16	14.73	10.29	2.7	.2	9.4
1939	2.5	...	2.04	17.72	15.39	4.5	1.6	9.5
1940	-1.1	...	6.70	-4.13	5.04	2.8	-.7	2.1
1941	5.0	...	10.22	3.92	8.12	6.8	4.3	1.5
1942	-2.7	...	16.24	23.66	22.41	9.9	8.6	.0
1943	8.5	...	16.61	28.68	25.76	9.1	7.4	.0
1944	7.6	...	20.64	41.82	39.56	9.2	6.3	.0
1945	3.2	...	14.92	35.16	34.32	10.8	7.8	.0
1946	11.8	...	14.57	13.90	15.70	9.8	4.7	.0
1947	2.3	...	9.04	13.57	10.04	2.6	-3.0	14.7
1948	9.7	...	5.90	-.63	-.85	4.6	0.0	18.4

Year								
1949	7.7	14.93	8.10	4.90	5.54	2.5	-1.3	8.5
1950	6.8	7.36	9.20	16.36	15.39	6.1	2.0	9.6
1951	4.9	8.47	18.4	27.56	24.83	.8	-5.0	-6.5
1952	7.3	14.13	9.3	19.50	16.84	-3.4	-7.3	13.7
1953	4.7	2.93	13.8	15.29	12.72	4.8	.6	31.0
1954	7.8	46.84	27.1	19.87	17.76	1.6	-2.1	39.2
1955	8.8	31.90	11.8	22.58	21.02	3.1	.0	18.5
1956	2.9	17.65	22.6	18.91	16.01	3.9	.5	0.1
1957	7.7	27.64	12.7	20.49	18.75	.9	-2.1	3.6
1958	10.8	14.58	12.4	28.13	26.64	.5	-1.8	71.6
1959	9.8	38.65	35.9	28.42	27.16	.5	-2.0	21.0
1960	9.4	26.51	25.4	35.15	32.77	-.1	-2.8	19.2
1961	8.6	29.62	34.7	40.88	41.09	.6	-1.2	52.8
1962	6.6	47.79	50.1	45.80	44.32	-.4	-1.9	80.0
1963	.6	61.67	78.4	59.87	56.61	.6	-.6	67.9
1964	3.4	74.83	89.9	65.52	64.23	1.6	.7	93.3
1965	2.4	67.60	58.2	85.70	84.97	3.0	1.7	11.5
1966	6.7	39.08	37.9	74.80	73.79	1.8	.2	17.3
1967	4.2	43.59	26.5	24.40	24.80	.8	-.9	22.3
1968	9.8	8.87	26.7	44.80	46.65	.1	-1.8	41.1
1969	9.5	25.58	20.1	38.04	38.81	1.0	-.8	6.6

References

Bacha, Edmar L. 1988. Latin America's economic stagnation: domestic and external factors. Discussion Paper no. 199. Catholic University, Department of Economics, Rio de Janeiro.

Baer, Werner. 1983. *A industrialização e o desenvolvimento econômico do Brasil*. Rio de Janeiro: Editora de Fundação Getúlio Vargas.

Benevides, Maria Victoria de Mesquita. 1979. *O governo Kubitschek: desenvolvimento econômico e estabilidade política*. Rio de Janeiro: Editora Paz e Terra.

Brandao, Carlos. 1989. A divida pública interna: Seus problemas e soluções. *Conjuntura Econômica*, 43, nos. 10, 11 (October/November).

Bulhões, Octavio Gouvea. 1979. O Ministro Eugênio Gudin. In *Eugênio Gudin visto por seus contemporâneos*, ed. Alexandre Kafka, et al. Rio de Janeiro: Editora de Fundação Getúlio Vargas.

Campos, Roberto. 1979. O fraturador de mitos e profeta incômodo. In *Eugênio Gudin visto por seus contemporâneos*, ed. Alexandre Kafka et al. Rio de Janeiro: Editora da Fundação Getúlio Vargas.

Cardoso, Eliana C., and Rudiger Dornbusch. 1989. Crises da divida brasileira: passado e presente. In *Divida externa: crise e soluções*, ed. Luiz Bresser. São Paulo: Editora Brasiliense.

Castro, Antônio Barros de. 1985. *A economia brasileira em marcha forçada*. Rio de Janeiro: Paz e Terra.

Castro, Paulo Rabello de, and Ronci, Marcio. 1989. Is the Brazilian external debt an obstacle to growth? Typescript. Rio de Janeiro, August.

Dornbusch, R., and S. Edwards. 1989. The macroeconomics of populism in Latin America. NBER Working Paper no. 2986. Cambridge, Mass.

Dulles, W. F. 1967. *Vargas of Brazil: A political biography*. Austin: University of Texas Press.

Estatísticas históricas do Brasil: Séries econômicas, demográficas e sociais de 1550 a 1985. Rio de Janeiro: Brazilian Institute of Geography and Statistics.

Furtado, Celso. 1976. *Formação econômica do a Brasil*. São Paulo: Compania Editora Nacional.

Goldsmith, Raymond W. 1986. *Brasil, 1850–1984: Desenvolvimento financeiro sob um século de inflação*. São Paulo: Editora Harper & Row do Brasil.

Gudin, Eugênio. 1978a. *O pensamento de Eugênio Gudin*. Rio de Janeiro: Editora Fundação Getúlio Vargas.

———. 1978b. *Reflexões e comentários: 1970–1978*. Rio de Janeiro: Nova Fronteira.

Lessa, Carlos. 1983. *Quinze anos de política econômica*. São Paulo: Editora Brasiliense.

Lopes, Francisco. 1984. Inflação inercial, hiperinflação e desinflação: Notas e conjecturas. Discussion Paper no. 77. Catholic University, Department of Economics, Rio de Janeiro.

Marques, Maria Silvia Bastos. 1985. Aceleração inflacionária no Brasil: 1978–83. *Revista Brasileira de Economia* 39, no. 4.

Martone, Celso Luiz. 1985. A espansão do estado empresário no Brasil. In *A crise do bom patrão*, ed. Paulo Rabello de Castro. Rio de Janeiro: CEDES/ANPEC.

Neuhaus, Paulo. 1975. *Historia monetaria do Brasil: 1900–1945*. Rio de Janeiro: Instituto Brasileiro de Mercado de Capitais.

Ronci, Marcio. 1988. Credibilidade de política monetária e Banco Central independente. *Conjuntura Econômica*, 42, no. 12 (December).

Sachs, J. D. 1987. Trade and exchange rate policies in growth-oriented adjustment programs. NBER Working Paper no. 2226. Cambridge, Mass.

————. 1989. Social conflict and populist policies in Latin America. NBER Working Paper no. 2897. Cambridge, Mass.

Simonsen, Mario Henrique. 1974. *Brasil 2002*. Rio de Janeiro: APEC Editora.

————. 1986. Rational expectations, income policies and game theory. *Revista de Econometria*.

Skidmore, Thomas. 1976. *Brasil de Getulio a Castelo*. Rio de Janeiro: Editora Paz e Terra.

————. 1988. *Brasil de Castelo a Tancredo*. Rio de Janeiro: Paz e Terra.

Suzigan, Wilson, 1988. Estado e industrialização no Brasil. *Revista de Economia Política* 8, no. 4 (October/December).

Viana Filho, Luiz. 1975. *O Governo Castelo Branco*. Rio de Janeiro: José Olympio Editora.

7　The Socialist-Populist Chilean Experience, 1970–1973

Felipe Larraín and Patricio Meller

7.1　Introduction

Chile's experience under the Unidad Popular government of President Salvador Allende is a unique blend of socialism and populism that has not been present in other Latin American populist experiences. It was not merely an unsustainable expansion of aggregate demand to achieve distributive goals. Marxist ideology played a key role in the Unidad Popular economic program, as the ultimate goal was to replace the capitalist system with socialism.

Most of the economic discussion during the initial period of the Allende government was focused on the massive and deep structural changes that were being implemented in the Chilean economy. These involved a substantial transfer of assets and resources from the private sector to the state. Even though income redistribution was a high-priority goal for the Unidad Popular, the sharp and fast increases in real wages had an additional purpose: they were intended to increase the workers' political support for the program so that the government could advance with the structural changes from a strong base.

Macroeconomic policies initially played a highly supportive role for the implementation of the structural changes that the Unidad Popular promoted. But, as point out by Dornbusch and Edwards (1989), a sharp expansionary macroeconomic program is implemented by populists without any regard for internal or external constraints. Therefore, eventually, the initial success ends in complete failure.

The second section of this paper provides a short overview of the Chilean economy before 1970. It also includes the Unidad Popular's particular diag-

Felipe Larraín is associate professor of Economics at Pontificia Universidad Católica de Chile. Patricio Meller is executive director of CIEPLAN (Santiago, Chile).

The authors would like to thank Vittorio Corbo, Rudiger Dornbusch, Sebastian Edwards, and Simón Teitel for their comments.

nosis and perceptions of the Chilean economy and its economic proposals. As will become clear later on, populism is only one aspect of a more complex picture. Section 7.3 studies the deep structural reforms with a special discussion for each one of the main sectors: copper nationalization, land reform, bank statization, and industry takeover. Various effects of these reforms, including the uncertainty that they generated over property rights, are discussed at the end of the section. Section 7.4 provides an overview of the macroeconomic policies and their results. There it becomes clear that, after a seemingly successful beginning, the Unidad Popular experiment ended in a full collapse. Section 7.5 provides the conclusions.

7.2 The Chilean Economy before 1970 and the
Unidad Popular Perspective

7.2.1 Selected Aspects of the Chilean Economy before 1970

During the 1950–70 period, Chilean economic performance was characterized by chronic and high inflation, moderate growth, and frequent balance of payments crises. In fact, the country's economy constituted one of the prototype cases used on the old structuralist-monetarist controversy. On the other hand, Chile had for a long time a very stable democratic political system that constituted a hallmark among Latin American countries.

A highly schematic description of the two administrations prior to 1970 highlights the elements that follow.[1] The government of President Jorge Alessandri (1958–64) was elected with the support of conservative and center-right parties, obtaining 34% of the votes. Initially, its main economic focus was inflation stabilization. Over the longer term, its perspective included two main elements: (1) After the success of the anti-inflation program it was considered that the improved economic conditions would automatically stimulate growth. (2) The distributive problems would mainly be solved by the trickling down of the economic expansion. The Christian Democrat administration of President Eduardo Frei (1964–70) came to power with an absolute majority of 56% of the popular vote. It was supported by a spectrum of political parties spanning from right to center. The government's main economic focus was the implementation of basic structural changes such as the land reform process and the Chilean participation in the ownership of the Big Copper Mines (owned by American companies at that time). The Christian Democrats' long-run perspective could by synthetized as an attempt to redistribute with growth, in a scenario of changes to the ownership structure of some economic sectors (copper, agriculture).

The Frei government, which preceded the Unidad Popular period, at-

1. For a detailed analysis and review of the economic policies of these two governments see Ffrench-Davis (1973).

tempted some basic structural reforms that were slowly implemented in order not to impair macro stability. In this respect, there was a certain perception that structural reforms could generate short-run disequilibriums. Thus, when there was an accumulation of inflationary pressures, priority was to be given to the restoration of macro stability. The agrarian reform process was implemented to change the existing skewed pattern of land tenure and to incorporate the peasants to the political and economic structure. "Chileanization" of the Big Copper Mines implied that Chile acquired a 51% share of the ownerships of the big mines through bargaining. Government expenditures on social areas were increased and oriented mainly toward middle- and low-income groups. At the same time, the government provided guidelines for wage readjustments, which included a 100% backward CPI indexation.

During the 1960s there was a sharp increase in political and social activity. The number of registered voters grew from 1.5 million people in 1958 to more than 3.5 million people in 1970; the percentage of voters with respect to total population, which had been around 15% prior to 1960, went up to almost 30% by 1970 (Bitar 1979). Furthermore, the number of people affiliated with unions doubled during the Frei government. In a six-year span, blue-collar union membership increased by 38%, white-collar union membership increased by 90%, and peasant union membership grew from less than 2,000 people (1964) to more than 114,000 people (1970); (see table 7.1).

A synthesis of the evolution of the main macroeconomic variables during the Frei government, using annual averages for the 1965–70 period, is provided in table 7.2. The growth rate (GDP) was 3.9%, while inflation reached 26%; the national unemployment rate was 5.6%; the increase of real wages was 9.7% per year; and the level of the fiscal deficit (as a percentage of GDP) was 2.1%. Table 7.2 also provides the evolution of these variables for each year between 1968 and 1970. It is clear from these figures that the first part of the Frei government had, in general, a better performance with respect to growth and inflation than that corresponding to the latter part.

Table 7.3 provides the evolution of external-sector variables for the 1968–70 period. Total exports were more than $1.1 billion (in U.S. dollars), of which copper had a share larger than 75%. The 1968–70 period was positively influenced by the high world price of copper, which reached its all-time high

Table 7.1   **Number of People Affiliated with Unions in Chile (Number of Affiliates)**

	Blue-Collar Workers	White-Collar Workers	Peasants	Total
1958	154,650	119,666	2,030	276,346
1964	142,958	125,926	1,658	270,542
1970	197,651	239,323	114,112	551,086

Source: Bitar (1979).

Table 7.2   Selected Macroeconomic Variables in Chile, 1965–70

	Economic Growth (GDP) (1)	Annual Inflation Rate (CPI) (2)	National Unemploy- ment Rate (3)	Annual Increase of Real Wages (4)	Fiscal Deficit (5)
1968	2.9	27.9	4.9	−2.0	1.5
1969	2.9	29.3	5.5	4.3	0.4
1970	3.6	34.9	5.7	8.5	2.7
Average, 1965–70	3.9	26.0	5.6	9.7	2.1

Sources: Col. 1, 2, 3, and 5: ODEPLAN and Central Bank.
Note: All figures are percentages; col. 5 is % of GDP.

Table 7.3   External Sector Variables for the Period Prior to 1970 (in Millions of U.S. Dollars)

	Exports FOB	Imports CIF	Current Account Balance	Balance of Payments	Level of International Reserves
1968	911	802	−135	118	125
1969	1,173	927	−6	175	285
1970	1,112	956	−81	114	394

Source: Central Bank.

in real terms during these years. Regarding international reserves, it had always been at the two-digit level before 1968. The relatively large level of foreign reserves achieved in 1970 ($394 million; i.e., almost five months of imports) was considered by the Frei government as an indicator of responsible economic performance.

Popular perceptions about the Frei government in 1970 were mixed. On the one hand, there had been a good initial performance during the first three years, when growth increased and inflation was reduced. But on the other hand, at the end, there was a sense of frustrated expectations between the increased political and social participation and the expected economic outcome. In this respect it is interesting to note that in spite of a sustained and relatively important increase of real wages during the Frei government, the number of strikes increased considerably (see table 7.4). Moreover, the macroeconomic responsibility to contain inflationary pressures, which prevailed from 1967 on, was neither supported by nor understood by most of the workers, even though there was no deterioration of real wages and no significant increase of unemployment.

Perceptions about the evolution of the economy during the Frei government (i.e., a good performance at the beginning and a sharp slowdown later) hurt

Table 7.4   **Number of Strikes and Evolution of Real Wages**

	1960–64[a]	1965	1966	1967	1968	1969	1970
Number of strikes	98	142	586	693	648	1,127	1,580
Annual increase of real wages (%)	.0	13.9	10.8	13.5	−2.0	4.3	8.5

Sources: Number of strikes: Martner (1988); real wages: Ffrench-Davis (1973).
[a]Figures provided correspond to the total for the period, i.e., the total number of strikes was 98 during 1960–64; 0 was the annual average and the total change of real wages in the 1960–64 period.

the Christian Democrats' presidential candidate in 1970, who finished third in the election. Salvador Allende, as head of a coalition of left and center-left parties (the Unidad Popular), was elected President with 36% percent of the vote.[2]

7.2.2   The Unidad Popular Diagnosis of the Chilean Economy

According to the Unidad Popular (UP), the Chilean economy presented four major characteristics by 1970 that had to be corrected. According to them, the economy was monopolistic, (externally) dependent, oligarchic, and capitalistic.[3] In what follows, we provide the diagnosis of these problems from the UP's perspective.

The following indicators for the 1960s provided the evidence on the alleged monopolistic nature of the economy (i.e., its degree of concentration): (*a*) 248 firms controlled all of the economic sectors, and 17% of all enterprises concentrated 78% of total assets (Alaluf 1971). (*b*) In industry, 3% of the firms controlled more than 50% of value added and almost 60% of capital. (*c*) In agriculture, 2% of the farms owned 55% of the land. (*d*) In mining, three foreign (U.S.) companies controlled "large mining" copper production, which represented 60% of Chilean exports by 1970. (*e*) In wholesale trade, 12 enterprises (which represented 0.5% of the total) accounted for 44% of all sales. (*f*) In banking, the state bank (Banco del Estado) controlled close to 50% of all deposits and credits. However, it was pointed out that 3 banks (of a total of 26 private banks) controlled more than half of the remaining 50% (Bitar 1979).

These big monopolists had allegedly increased their share and their profits thanks to special state measures, like preferential credit lines, subsidies, special tax incentives, tariff differentials, and special access to foreign exchange

---

2. The candidate who finished second (former President Jorge Alessandri) got 35% of the vote, while the candidate of the Christian Democrats (Radomiro Tomic) got 28%. The total number of voters was 3 million, and the difference between Allende and Alessandri was less than 40,000 votes.

3. For a deeper discussion of these issues see Aranda and Martínez (1970), Caputo and Pizarro (1970), Ramos (1972), and Bitar (1979).

(Alaluf 1971). In short, and according to a UP analyst, "the role of the state has always been to favor large monopolistic capital and its fundamental interests" (Ramos 1972).

Different aspects were pointed out on the issue of Chile's external dependence, including (a) the mono-export nature of the country, where copper (large, medium, and small mines) represented more than 75% of total exports. This implied that fluctuations of the copper price in world markets would have a major impact upon the Chilean balance of payments and upon government revenues. Also of note was (b) the relatively high profit remittances by foreigners, which represented around 20% of exports, and (c) the high share of multinationals in Chilean industry. Of the largest 100 industrial firms at the end of the 1960s, 61 had foreign participation.

According to Vuskovic (1970), the significant presence of foreign firms led to high dependence because of two main reasons. (1) Imported technology determined that Chile's production methods were copied from the outside. (2) Chile also acquired the developed countries consumption pattern, that is, the "demonstration effect." In synthesis, foreign forces imposed what to consume and what to produce. These issues highlighted the increasing importance and presence of foreign capital. And, moreover, the Chilean bourgeoisie had begun to acquire a pattern of preferences and interests that were more identified with international capital than with national interests.

The oligarchic feature was justified on the highly skewed income distribution of the 1960s. While the poorest 10% of the population had a 1.5% share of total income, the highest 10% income group had a 40.2% share of income. The ratio between the income of both groups was 1 to 27.[4]

Given the above characteristics, and from the UP viewpoint, the fruits of Chilean economic development were highly concentrated on a small privileged elite, thereby excluding low-income groups from the benefits. According to Vuskovic (1970), this process was self-perpetuating and worked in the following way: (1) The inequitable income distribution generated a given pattern of consumption and demand, and thus the market was dominated by the goods in demand from the high-income groups. Accordingly, modern firms' production was designed only to satisfy this type of demand. (2) There existed a dual productive system, with a modern high-technology sector and a backward one. Only the modern sector incorporated technological progress in their production of goods for the high-income groups, while the backward sector remained stagnant. The increasing participation of foreign investment reinforced the prevailing dual structure of the economy. (3) Due to the relatively reduced volume of goods demanded by the high-income groups, and given its wide spectrum, modern firms produced a low level of output; therefore, they were operating at an inadequately low scale with a poor efficiency level. In

4. At the end of the 1960s the Chilean Gini coefficient was 0.51, lower than Brazil (0.58) and Mexico (0.58) but higher than Argentina (0.44) (Bitar 1979).

short, the production structure was inefficient, as it produced mostly non-essential goods for high-income groups. The small output scale led to a higher monopolistic concentration level, which reinforced the skewed initial income distribution pattern.

To summarize the UP perspective, Chile was characterized by a vicious circle, where the unequal original income distribution pattern generated a highly monopolistic productive structure, which reinforced the existing skewed income pattern. The structure of the economy got more and more oriented toward the satisfaction of consumption patterns of the high-income groups, while there existed stagnation of productive sectors producing (essential or basic) wage goods for the majority. The income and wealth inequalities led to a high degree of concentration of power, that is, only a few had control upon the main decisions. Thus, the interrelationship between political and economic power reinforced the prevailing structure of the country. In order to change the economic conditions it was required to alter substantially the property structure. This would generate a different demand pattern that would stimulate the production of basic goods consumed by the big majority. Then, economic resources would not be wasted in the production of nonessential goods (Vuscovic 1970; Bitar 1979).

7.2.3   The Unidad Popular Economic Proposals

The UP program made an explicit statement about its anti-imperialist, anti-oligarchist, and anti-monopolist nature, which set the tone for the deep structural changes that it proposed to follow. As a counterpart, the program stated that it would benefit workers in general (blue collar and white collar), peasants, and small entrepreneurs, that is, the big national majority. The UP government was going to be a historical experiment where the implementation of the transition toward socialism would be carried out using the existing institutional structure. Two elements were required to facilitate this transition: statization of the means of production and increased popular participation.

The political objectives of the UP were stated very clearly (Martner 1988). The alleged purpose was the establishment of the most democratic regime in Chilean history through the transfer of power from the dominant groups to the workers and the peasants. To achieve this, Chilean workers would have to acquire *real* power and use it effectively. The purpose of the structural changes was to "overcome capitalism." What was at stake was the replacement of the then-current economic structure for the construction of socialism.

The UP structural reforms had a wide and deep coverage, including (*a*) the nationalization of Chile's main basic resources—copper (the Big Copper Mines), coal, nitrate, iron and steel—which would imply a sharp confrontation with U.S. companies, (*b*) the expansion of the Social Property Area, which implied the statization of the largest industrial enterprises, (*c*) the intensification of agrarian reform, (*d*) statization of the banking system, and (*e*) state control of the main wholesale trade and distribution firms.

In short, the structural reforms aimed to put the control of the means of production in the hands of the state. The advantages of and the rationale for this objective were given as follows (Romeo 1971). (1) If the state achieved the control of the means of production, it would be in a better position to make economic decisions using a social criteria that would consider the welfare preferences of the large national majority (i.e., the workers). (2) This control would produce an increase of the economic surplus controlled by the state. With the additional resources obtained, the state would be able to plan and to guide economic development in a direction that would benefit the large majority. (3) In fact, "The main problem is not efficiency, but power; that is, who controls the economy and for whom? . . . What is at stake is the property of the means of production by a small minority; then, the real economic issues are: Who has the power to set prices, and therefore profits, and who captures the economic surplus and decides how to re-invest it. . . . To focus the discussion on efficiency avoids discussing who really has the economic power, and why a small minority who owns the means of production is able to subjugate the majority". In synthesis, as Minister of Economics Pedro Vuskovic declared, soon after Allende took office, "State control is designed to destroy the economic basis of imperialism and the ruling class by putting an end to the private ownership of the means of production" (as quoted in Moss 1973, p. 59).

One view inside the Unidad Popular stated that short-run macroeconomic policies were complementary and supportive of structural reforms, showing in this way that "it is possible to make deep structural reforms and at the same time achieve important positive results in income redistribution, growth, inflation, and employment" (García 1971). This, it has been explained, was due to the fact that even traditional macroeconomic policies have implicitly a class element: "short-run policies are, by definition, a tool to maintain the status quo," that is, these tools are not only the expression of a given institutional environment, but they are also oriented toward its consolidation. In this respect, UP macroeconomic policies cannot be analyzed separately; "this would be a serious analytical mistake. . . . They should be examined in the prevailing environment which would provide the rational of why was done what was done" (García 1971).

In a distinct perspective, it is argued that the control of inflation was really a key UP objective due to political and economic reasons (Bianchi 1975). At the political level, the UP had pointed out during the campaign that it would get rid of inflation, and it criticized previous governments for their incapacity to control this problem. Moreover, due to the proximity of municipal elections (March 1971), the UP government wanted to show quickly an indicator of success. At the economic level, given the fact that the goal of income redistribution was going to be implemented through increases in nominal wages, it was important to slow down inflation to ensure an increase in real wages.

The key elements that provided the basis of the UP macro policy were the following: (*a*) The Chilean economy presented a large level of unused capacity and high unemployment. (*b*) There existed a high level of international reserves and industrial stocks. As has been pointed out (Griffith-Jones 1980), UP economists made no comments with respect to the limitations related to the following elements: (1) Specific sectoral capacity levels may be very different from global figures. (2) The utilization of available unused capacity is an element of the "once and for all" nature, that is, you can use it only once. (3) There was the mechanistic perception that structural transformations would very quickly help solve macro problems.

The main economic tools for short-run macroeconomic policy were the following (García 1971): (*a*) Nominal wage readjustment and price control. This would lead to increased real wages, which would then constitute the main redistributive mechanism. Moreover, higher real wages would increase the demand for basic goods leading to higher levels of production and employment. This process would reactivate and expand the economy using the existing unused capacity. (*b*) Increased public expenditures would complement the higher real wages in reactivating the economy. (*c*) Passive monetary and credit policy would provide the required liquidity for the expansion of the economy; monetary policy should not act as a brake to stop reactivation. (*d*) There would be a fixed nominal exchange rate, which would help to avoid cost pressures upon domestic production. (*e*) The nationalization of basic resources (copper) would expand exports and therefore provide additional foreign exchange. (*f*) The existence of a relatively high initial level of international reserves would provide the adjustment valve through imports, for eventual disequilibrium problems.

The UP view of anti-inflation policy was based on the following elements (Griffith-Jones 1980): (*a*) Inflation is really a structural phenomenon. Price control, elimination of the crawling peg system, and the implementation of the new economic structure would stop inflation. (*b*) State control of the greater part of the productive and marketing apparatus would lay the foundations to stop inflation. (*c*) Given price controls and wage readjustments, wages would increase more than prices, leading to a reduction in the unit profit rate. However, given the existence of unused capacity, the augmentation of output and sales would compensate the decline of unit profit while maintaining the overall level of profits.

According to a high UP authority, the effects of the previous measures will imply that very shortly "price increases will disappear and in the future inflation will be remembered as a nightmare of previous Governments which were the servants of big capital" (Millas as quoted in Bianchi 1975). A more moderate view was stated in the UP program where, as the outcome of structural transformations, inflation would disappear due to anti-monopolist measures and due to the support of the majority of the people.

7.3 Structural Reforms

7.3.1 Redistribution of Real Assets

As we discussed in section 7.2, structural transformations of the economy were the fundamental element of the Unidad Popular program. These changes were centered around the redistribution of real assets in four main sectors of the economy: the big-mining sector, agriculture, banking, and industry. The government resorted to a vast array of methods in order to transfer private property—both Chilean and foreign—to the state, and the redistribution of real assets was massive. As a result, the public sector experienced substantial growth during the 1970–73 period, as we analyze below.

Nationalization of Copper and Other Mining

Nationalization of the big copper companies had been in the agenda of both the Unidad Popular and the Christian Democratic candidates for president in the 1970 election. In fact, the process had already started during the preceding Frei administration, as mentioned before. The so-called "Chileanization" of copper had begun in 1967, when the State Copper Corporation (CODELCO) bought 51% of the El Teniente mine from Kennecott for $80 million and acquired a 25% stake in the Andina and Exotica mines. When a dramatic surge in the world price of copper followed these agreements and increased the companies' profits, the pressure mounted on the Frei government to expand the state's ownership of the big copper mines. In 1969, the administration bought 51% of the Chuquicamata and El Salvador mines for $180 million, to be paid for at an annual interest rate of 6% over the next 12 years. The terms of these agreements were criticized by some UP analysts as being overly generous with the foreign companies.[5]

The UP came to power and decided to complete the process of nationalization of the copper mines in the shortest possible time. This action had strong legislative and popular support, and the government decided to pursue the nationalization through a constitutional amendment rather than through a regular law. The project was approved unanimously in July 1971 by the opposition-controlled national Congress. The nationalization decree explicitly stated that the state of Chile had absolute and exclusive control over all Chilean mines. Nonetheless, as the goal was to nationalize only the big mining properties, a temporary provision allowed the private sector to continue operating small and medium-sized mines, although their legal status was not totally clear. All the big copper companies (Chuquicamata, El Salvador, El Teniente, and Exotica) however, came to be owned 100% by the state.

The most important problem that the government encountered as a result of the copper nationalization was not inside Chile. Rather, it was related to the

---

5. For a statement of this argument see De Vylder (1974, chap. 4).

issue of compensating the previous foreign owners, that is, the U.S. companies Anaconda and Kennecott. The indemnification was to be determined by the Comptroller General according to the book value of the companies as of December 1970. However, the president of the republic was authorized to deduct from this value the excess profits obtained by the foreigners since 1965. Allende used this provision to deduct some $800 million from the total indemnification.[6] In practice, this meant that the owners of the three biggest mines got nothing.

This aggressive stance regarding compensation has been criticized by insiders of the Allende regime for opening a significant source of trouble in Chile's international relations on a matter that was negotiable. Bitar (1986, pp. 71–72) states that:

> From a strategic point of view, what was essential was not the compensation paid but the control of basic wealth. . . . Winning this control was vital, and its importance rendered quarrels about the exact amount of compensation relatively insignificant. Furthermore, it seems clear that internal political support stemmed chiefly from the nationalization itself and did not depend on the amount given in compensation. Thus the decision to refuse compensation did not produce any new favorable political dividends. From the international point of view, the no-compensation decision and the principle of deduction for excessive profits were unacceptable to the U.S. government, both because of the loss they represented in themselves and because of the precedents they set. There was little advantage in thus linking the nationalization of copper with a larger problem, one with international implications and consequences beyond Chile's control. Our own conclusion is that the decision to deny compensation, even though juridically unobjectionable, robbed the Allende government of flexibility at a critical moment.

The government also took over the large coal, iron, and nitrate mines during the first half of 1971. Comparatively much less important than copper, this process had neither the drama nor the publicity that surrounded the copper nationalization. The foreign owners reached an agreement with the government and sold their property. Thus by the end of 1971 the UP program had already been completed in mining, as the government controlled all large mining operations in the country.

Intensification of the Land Reform Process

Land reform had been initiated before the Allende government came to power, bringing about major changes in agriculture beginning in the early sixties. A law of agrarian reform had been preceded by a modification of the constitution that permitted deferred payment for expropriated land.[7] Subse-

---

6. A detailed analysis of these nationalizations can be found in Vargas (1973).

7. The Agrarian Reform Law, law 15.020, was passed in 1962 under the administration of President Alessandri and was subsequently amended under the government of President Frei.

quent legislation made it increasingly difficult for landowners to oppose actions against property (i.e., it prohibited the division of farms to avoid expropriation).

The Allende government drastically intensified the process of land reform using the existing legislation. Clearly, the UP wanted to amend the law so as to increase the scope of the process, in particular extending it to farms below the legal limit of 80 basic hectares. But, lacking a legislative majority, this was not possible. In the words of Jacques Chonchol, the minister of agriculture,

> The government decided, for two reasons, to use the Agrarian Reform Law which was approved during the Frei administration even though, in many aspects, it does not coincide with the U.P. Government's agrarian policy. We are using this law because, as a Government, we are obliged to act within the legal framework, and secondly, because any changes in such a complex and controversial law . . . would certainly have required many months of discussion, which would paralyze the agrarian reform process resulting in great frustration among the peasantry who are pressing for the acceleration of the process. Also it was felt that, given the political willingness to use the existing law much more thoroughly, it would be possible to accelerate the agrarian reform process. (quoted in Zammit 1973, p. 107)

In spite of the legislative constraint, the Unidad Popular took to the task with remarkable speed. By mid-1972, practically all privately owned farms of over 80 basic hectares had been eliminated. Not only were increasing numbers of farms expropriated under existing laws, but the occupation of agricultural land by peasants (*tomas*) also became a very popular way of de facto expropriation. For example, over 500 farms were illegally occupied in 1971.

By 1973 the land reform program had implied the expropriation of close to 10 million hectares from almost 6,000 farms, or 60% of Chile's agricultural land (Larraín 1988, table 10). About two-thirds of these estates were expropriated during the tenure of the UP government. In fact, the Allende administration expropriated more than twice as many farms in less than half the time than had the preceding Christian Democrat Government.[8] This major intensification of the land reform program from 1970 to 1973 required vast growth in the state's administrative apparatus responsible for its implementation. For example, the corporation of land reform (CORA), the most important government institution in this sector, saw its work force increase by 70% in this period.

A major challenge for the government was how to organize the reformed sector. The previous administration had favored the *asentamiento*, whereby each expropriated farm was transformed into a cooperative settlement of the former peasants. The Allende government introduced land reform centers

---

8. During 1971, the first year of application of the program, the UP expropriated almost as many estates as the Christian Democrats had in the whole period 1964–70.

(Centros de Reforma Agraria, or CERAs), which were formed from the merger of geographically close previously private farms. However, this new form of organization met with resistance from the peasants. In the end of the land reform process, only a rather small fraction of the expropriated land was distributed to peasants through individual property or cooperatives, most of it during the Frei period. Almost all the estates expropriated or taken over during the UP government remained in the hands of the state.

Overall, the agrarian reform program had a significant wealth redistribution effect. Recent estimates indicate that former landowners had a capital loss of between $1.2 and $1.6 billion as of 1973, considering all expropriations of the 1965–73 period and the present value of the compensations they received. This amounts to between 100% and 130% percent of Chile's GDP in 1973. If we consider the restitutions of land effected during the military government, the capital loss of the previous owners is in the range of $800 million and $1.1 billion.[9]

The Statization of Banking

The Unidad Popular initiated at the outset an organized attempt to obtain absolute control of the banking sector, as President Allende had publicly declared one month after taking office. During the first months of 1971, the government was able to acquire all foreign banks. This was achieved in a negotiation process that established the compensation to be paid in each case. But foreign banks represented just a tiny fraction of financial activity in the country. The big challenge was to attain control of the local private banks.

Lacking a legal basis to expropriate the banks, and feeling the impossibility of passing such a law through Congress, the government resorted to a simpler method. It opened a purchasing power for bank stocks at very attractive prices. At the same time, it started to intervene in banks based on two causes: the detection of some financial wrongdoing or the existence of labor problems that prevented normal operation. Faced with the option of selling shares at good prices or eventually ending with stocks of dubious value in troubled banks, stockholders in large numbers decided to sell.

This process was, as in mining and agriculture, extraordinarily fast. By the end of 1971, state control over the banking system was almost total. As Finance Minister Americo Zorrilla proudly announced in November 1971, "The nationalization of the banking system is practically completed. The state now controls sixteen banks which together provide ninety percent of all credit. . . . This process of nationalization has signified that the links between financial and industrial monopoly capital have been broken." [10]

Thus, in about one year, CORFO acquired majority participation in 14 commercial banks and less than 30% participation in five other banking insti-

9. From Larraín (1991, table 10), on the basis of figures provided by the Department of Agriculture Economics, Universidad Católica de Chile.
10. Quoted in De Vylder (1974, p. 161), from Zorrilla's *Second Exposition*.

tutions. Ultimately, the state came to control the most important private banks (among them Banco de Chile, the largest one) and an overwhelming part of credit. Of the 17 commercial banks in existence in September 1973, 14 were in the banks of the public sector and only three were left under private administration.

Participation by the state in financial operations was even greater than the banking situation suggests. Several other public institutions provided medium- and long-term credit, the most important of them being CORFO, the Agrarian Reform Corporation (CORA), the National Mining Corporation (ENAMI), and the National System of Savings Loans (SINAP). Overall, 85% of Chile's financial sector came into the hands of the state.

The Takeover of Industry

Between 1970 and 1973, the UP government engaged in a major expansion of the "area of social property" (the state-owned sector). This program involved a massive takeover of firms, a step viewed as necessary to achieve official allocative and distributive goals. The profits of the expropriated companies were considered monopoly rents, which needed to be given to the companies' workers and the poor sectors of society, and resources needed for investment.

It was precisely in this part of its program that the UP encountered the bigger obstacles. Firm owners themselves constituted a stiff resistance to nationalization, much more so than in mining and banking and comparable to that of farmers in the south of Chile. For example, the method of purchasing shares in the open market, which had worked so well to acquire the banks, produced disappointing results among nonfinancial companies. Resistance of firm owners included the initiation of legal actions against the government, which generally had favorable reception in the courts, and even the outright physical defense of the properties.

The government lacked solid legislation for the nationalization of local industries, and so it resorted to an obscure law passed in the 1930s during the short period of the socialist republic.[11] This law, which had never been used before, stated several causes that could lead to a company's expropriation: price speculation, stockpiling, interruption of production, or the existence of unused productive capacity in times of shortages. The definition of these concepts was vague enough so that most companies could eventually qualify for expropriation. There was a caveat, however. Expropriation required full cash compensation, as determined by an independent court. In short, the law was there, but its use was expensive.

An alternative to expropriation was soon found to attain government control of private companies. Another little-known law of the 1940s established that companies could be subjected to intervention, and thus placed under state

11. Decree Law (DFL) no. 520 of 1932.

administration, whenever labor disputes occurred. Clearly, this procedure could not be used directly to transfer the ownership of the company. But in practice, this was many times the outcome. Labor disputes were often instigated by the authorities or carried out spontaneously in order to trigger government intervention. At that time, a firm's financial position had already deteriorated. Subsequent administration by a state-nominated director, and a growing scarcity of raw materials, further weakened the company. After a while, many owners were ready to sell their firms to the government.

The authorities also counted on an administrative procedure to weaken the resolve of company owners. A state agency, DIRINCO (Dirección Nacional de Industria y Comercio), was empowered to approve price increases for goods and services throughout the economy. By the simple expedient of denying the price adjustment at a time of rapidly rising wages, DIRINCO could jeopardize substantially the financial health of a company. This was another procedure used to convince entrepreneurs to sell.

By September 1973, CORFO controlled or had significant participation in 507 firms. Of these, 259 had been taken over through intervention with no actual transfer of property (see table 7.5). In spite of these impressive numbers, the UP was unable to sweep the industrial sector as it had done with mining, banking, and agriculture. This was, in fact, the only sector where the original program of the government went unfulfilled, as some major firms were still in private hands by September 1973. The most prominent case was that of the Compañía Manufacturera de Papeles y Cartones ("Papelera"), the top Chilean producer of pulp and paper and the major supplier of local newspapers.

What accounts for this partial outcome? On one hand was the private sector's substantial resistance to the nationalization of industry. On the other hand was the lack of adequate legislation to accomplish this task. As Eduardo Novoa, the most prominent legal expert of the UP government, put it in March 1972, "In order to be able to operate, this government has had to resort to a series of legal dispositions which lay almost forgotten. But once having used these to their maximum the moment has arrived when there is no legal mechanism with which to proceed any further" (quoted in Zammit 1973, p. 29).

7.3.2   Consequences of the Asset Redistribution Program

The Expansion of the Public Sector

As can be expected, the growth of the public sector was spectacular during this period. The "social area" of the economy increased its share of productive activities to unprecedented levels, as table 7.6 shows for six different sectors of the economy.

Having 1965 as a base year, public enterprises increased their share of output in utilities from 25% to 100% in 1973. In addition, by the end of the UP experiment the government came to control 85% of banking and mining, 70%

Table 7.5 Public Sector's Stake in Productive Activities, 1970–73 (Number of Firms)

Industrial Sector	Participation in Equity Capital												Total
	Over 50%		10%–50%		Less than 10%		Majority Participation with Other Public Entities		Other Subsidiaries		No Participation in Equity Capital but Intervened		
	1970	September 1973	1970	September 1973	1970	September 1973	1970	September 1973	1970	September 1973	1970	September 1973	
Forestry	5	9	0	1	0	5	0	0	0	0	0	7	27
Fishing	4	7	0	0	0	1	0	4	0	1	0	8	22
Construction	1	5	0	0	0	4	0	1	0	2	0	10	25
Textiles	0	4	0	2	0	3	0	0	0	0	0	36	45
Chemicals	4	0	1	1	0	2	2	1	0	2	0	17	31
Energy	3	2	0	0	0	5	0	2	2	2	0	2	14
Electronics	2	2	0	0	0	0	0	0	0	1	0	16	21
Agriculture	1	5	0	0	0	0	0	0	0	0	0	0	16
Agro-industry	3	8	0	4	0	8	5	0	0	1	0	42	71
Metallurgy	2	5	0	2	0	0	1	1	0	23	0	49	83
Automotive	1	7	0	0	0	0	0	0	0	0	0	3	11
Pharmaceutical	0	1	0	0	0	1	0	0	0	0	0	3	6
Mining	0	6	1	2	0	1	2	1	0	1	0	13	27
Metals	0	1	0	0	0	4	0	0	0	0	0	0	5
Various industries	5	11	0	3	0	15	0	3	0	5	0	26	68
Services	0	0	0	0	0	0	0	0	0	0	0	27	27
Subtotal firms	31	72	2	16	0	49	11	10	2	36	0	259	488
Subtotal banks	0	14	0	2	0	3	0	0	0	0	0	0	19
Total	31	86	2	18	0	52	11	10	2	36	0	259	507

Source: Larraín (1988).

Table 7.6   Public Enterprises' Share in Sectoral and Total Output (%)

Sectors	1965	1973
Mining	13.0	85.0
Industry	3.0	40.0
Utilities	25.0	100.0
Transport	24.3	70.0
Communications	11.1	70.0
Financial	n.a.	85.0
Output in all sectors[a]	14.2	39.0

[a]The estimates do not include agriculture.

of both transportation and communications, and 40% of industry. Overall, the public sector achieved direct control over 39% of the country's output (excluding agriculture).

The Difference between Mining and the Other Sectors

The UP program represented the most radical economic transformation since Chile's independence. But clearly, some aspects of the program were more controversial than others. The nationalization of the foreign-owned mining sector, especially of the big copper mines, had already started during the previous government and enjoyed the support of a vast majority of the country. In no other way would the UP have been able to pass the required legislation through Constitutional amendment, approved unanimously by Congress. And, to place it in perspective, this trend toward the nationalization of foreign companies' controlling natural resources was a general phenomenon throughout Latin America during the 1970s (e.g., Peru under Juan Velasco, and Venezuela under Carlos Andrés Pérez).

However, the situation in the other sectors was substantially different. The difficulties and controversies of the other elements of the program were evident in that the government was not able to pass through Congress one other significant piece of legislation that would expedite nationalizations. The land reform program was carried out using the laws that existed in 1970, and also through the use of some extralegal means (the *tomas*). Since occupations of farms and expropriations often occurred in estates below the legal minimum of 80 basic hectares, the government alienated basically all landowners, regardless of their size.

In banking, the procedures used were the simple purchase of shares for domestic banks and direct negotiations with private banks; in spite of major apprehensions about the implications of the government's near-total control of credit, opposition to the measures could not prevent the change of ownership from taking place.

Nonfinancial firms were, however, the toughest test of the program and the scene of greater confrontations. The government could not agree with the congressional opposition on a list of enterprises to be nationalized, and no new legislation was passed for this purpose. To pursue their program, the authorities relied on obscure legislation of the 1930s and 1940s and on administrative means. These procedures, and the way they were applied, alienated not only the big entrepreneurs (the original targets of the program) but also medium and small company owners.

The Uncertainty over Property Rights

One of the most fundamental effects of the UP program on the private economy was to spread general uncertainty over property rights. The economic effects of such an environment are clear. Private investments are scaled down dramatically, even to the point where they fail to cover the maintenance of existing capital. As the pace of expropriation accelerates, the horizons of asset owners are reduced to a few months, even weeks, and investment ceases altogether. The incentives are given to extract as much as possible from the asset with the available capital stock, while one is still the owner.

Uncertainty over property rights derived first from the Unidad Popular program, which stated:

> *As a first step* [emphasis added], we shall nationalize those basic resources like large scale copper, iron and nitrate mines, and others which are controlled by foreign capital and national monopolies. These nationalized sectors will thus be comprised of the following:
> 1. Large scale copper, nitrate, iodine and coal mines.
> 2. The country's financial system, especially private banks and insurance companies.
> 3. Foreign trade.
> 4. Large distribution firms and monopolies.
> 5. Strategic industrial monopolies.
> 6. As a rule, all those activities which have a strong influence over the nation's social and economic development, such as the production and distribution of electric power, rail, air and sea transport, communications, the production, refining and distribution of petroleum and its by-products, including liquid gas, the iron and steel industry, cement, petrochemicals and heavy chemical, cellulose and paper. (Quoted in Zammit 1973, p. 266)

The scope of the nationalization program is striking, as it encompasses all firms of significance. And the wording of point 6 is sufficiently broad that it leaves room for nationalization of just about any economic activity. Furthermore, the program explicitly states that this is just "a first step." Thus, it was reasonable to presume that nationalization would go beyond large companies.

This presumption proved to be correct. Industry and agriculture were the sectors most affected by property uncertainty. In industry, the government failed to specify the exact criteria that would lead to a firm's expropriation during the whole first year of application of the program. Late in 1971, it attempted to reach a congressional agreement based on the nationalization of

Chile's largest 254 firms, as measured by the size of their capital. But no accord was reached. Later on, the government pushed for a legislative agreement to nationalize a reduced group of 90 strategic firms, but to no avail. However, while the government was declaring its intentions to limit its program to the biggest firms, interventions occurred in a large number of medium- and small-sized firms. This spread uncertainty to the whole industrial sector.

A similar problem happened in agriculture. The law established that only farms over 80 basic hectares—or those badly exploited or abandoned— would be subject to expropriation. However, many occupations occurred in smaller and well-exploited estates. In practice, all landowners worked under the threat of either expropriation or occupation, which ultimately had similar effects.

In banking, the uncertainty was quickly cleared. The nationalization was so fast and widespread that by the end of the first year about 90% of the sector was controlled by the state. The few—and small—remaining private banks may have still feared some form of state intervention, but they were not in a position to affect the results of the financial system in any significant way. In mining, the aim was to nationalize the large mines, whose property remained in foreign hands. As opposed to industry and agriculture, here the government stuck to its program, and no attempt was made to take over the medium- and small-sized mines owned by nationals. What may have affected private domestic miners was the general climate of uncertainty spilling over from the other sectors of the economy.

Could the uncertainty over property rights have been avoided? Bitar (1986) has argued that the publication of companies to be nationalized should have been made at the very outset and expropriation should have been carried out right away. This, in his view, would have precluded the negative effects over the medium- and small-sized entrepreneurs and, to the economy in general. In our view, however, uncertainty over property rights would not have been reduced significantly by such an action. First, the program of the UP stated that nationalization of large companies was only a first step. Second, the government would have had to publish the list and stick to it strictly; the problem was then how to control the pressure from labor unions, which in several cases pursued long disputes with company owners to trigger intervention. And finally, there was the experience of agriculture, where many medium and small properties not qualifying for expropriation were occupied indefinitely. To make a significant dent in the uncertainty, the government would have had to be prepared to enforce property laws, even if this implied the use of public force in illegal occupations. And this was quite unlikely.

Management Problems in the Nationalized and Reformed Sectors

It is widely recognized, even by insiders of the Allende regime, that the performance of the nationalized and intervened sectors was far from optimal. The main problems were to be found in the administration of properties that came into the hands of the state, especially in industry. Bitar (1986), for example, recognizes that the emphasis on transferring ownership was not parallel to an interest in the administration of the nationalized companies. Others put it more bluntly. Alberto Baltra (a respected university professor and the leader of the Left Radical party, which left the government in April 1972), in judging the performance of UP management, stated: "Although it seems incredible, the social area did not work in a planned way during the UP Government. There was planning and planners, but plans stayed on paper. Companies under state control did not submit to an authentic social decision, but functioned according to the will of interventors (state designated managers), who lacked knowledge and experience" (1973, p. 56).

Neither were management problems in the state-owned mining sector insignificant, as many of the top managers and technicians of the mines left the country after the nationalization. For example, over 150 top professionals working at Chuquicamata left Chile in 1971.[12] An analogous exodus occurred in the other big mines. And the government did not have the qualified personnel or the organizational structure to handle the task.

Similarly, there were many difficulties in organizing production in the reformed sector of agriculture. Most prominent among them were the problems of incentives inherent to collective farming. Member workers of an agrarian unit continued to work for a fixed wage and received a given share of profits at the end of the year. Thus, there was little link between work effort and compensation.

Bitar (1986, p. 188) summarizes some of these problems with great clarity: "[In industry,] as in the agrarian reform and the nationalization of copper, there was also a delay here between state takeover and organization. This lapse is a consequence of the secondary importance attached to organization per se in the UP strategy. It was argued, of course, that the change in form of property ownership would allow the introduction of a new form of economic rationality, but how this rationality was to be attained was never specified."

7.4   Macroeconomic Policies and Results

In the first part of this section we will examine the evolution of macroeconomic variables during 1970–73. Later on, we will conduct a more detailed analysis of the expansionary public-sector policies, centered on their most important aspect: the fiscal side.

7.4.1   The Year 1971: A Successful Beginning

The Chilean economy experienced an unprecedented boom in 1971, the result of highly expansionary government policies. This generated a widespread improvement in the standard of living of the population, and a sense of

12. As reported in De Vylder (1974, p. 137).

total success among UP leaders. Yet a cool analysis of the economic situation
could already perceive a mounting disequilibrium, as we analyze below.

The Measure of Success

Looking at the traditional macroeconomic variables, the first year of the UP
Government achieved relatively spectacular results for the Chilean economy
(see tables 7.7 and 7.8). The annual growth rate of GDP reached 8.0% in
1971, much higher than the 3.6% of the previous year (1970), and the highest
since 1950. Table 7.9 provides a sectoral breakdown for GDP growth. Industry and commerce were the top performers among all sectors during 1971 and
showed a remarkable expansion compared to 1970. Between 1970 and 1971,

Table 7.7   **Macroeconomic Indicators for 1970–71 (%)**

	1970	1971
Economic growth rate (GDP)	3.6	8.0
Inflation rate	36.1	22.1
National unemployment rate	5.7	3.8
Average increase in real wages	8.5	22.3

Sources: Central Bank, INE, and ODEPLAN.

Table 7.8   **Quarterly Data for Inflation and Unemployment, Chile, 1970–71 (%)**

	Inflation Rate (CPI) Accumulated During Year		Gran Santiago Unemployment Rate	
	1970	1971	1970	1971
March	16.2	3.4	6.8	8.2
June	23.9	11.1	7.0	5.2
September	32.9	13.9	6.4	4.8
December	34.9	22.1	8.3	3.8

Sources: INE and University of Chile.

Table 7.9   **Main Sectoral Growth Rates, 1970–71 (%)**

	1970	1971
Agriculture	3.6	−1.8
Mining	−3.0	6.0
Industry	2.0	13.6
Commerce	−1.5	15.8
Services	4.8	7.0

Source: Central Bank.

Table 7.10   Indices of Minimum and Real Wages for Blue-Collar and White-
                    Collar Workers, 1970–71

	Minimum Real Wages (1970 = 100)		Real Wages (April 1970 = 100)		Differential between Blue-Collar and White-Collar Minimum Wages
	Blue-Collar Wages	White-Collar Wages	Blue-Collar Wages	White-Collar Wages	
1970	100	100	100	100	49
Quarter in 1971:					
1	156	123	112	107	35
2	146	116	123	127	35
3	134	105	125	124	35
4	120	95	121	117	35

Source: World Bank.

the rate of growth of industrial output increased from 2.0% to 13.6%, while in commerce in 1971, the rate of expansion went from -1.5% to 15.8%.

Inflation decreased from 36.1% in 1970 to 22.1% in 1971. It is interesting that during the first half of 1971 the rate of price increase had been reduced to very low levels by Chilean standards. In the first quarter of 1971 inflation was 3.4% at an accumulated annual rate, compared to 16.2% in the equivalent period of 1970. During the second quarter of 1971, inflation reached 11.1% (also on an accumulated annual basis) compared to 23.9% a year earlier.

National unemployment registered a remarkable drop, from 5.7% in 1970 to 3.8% in 1971. Incidentally, this 3.8% figure was by far the lowest unemployment rate registered in Chilean statistics.[13] Quarterly unemployment data for Gran Santiago shows a reduction of joblessness from 8.3% in the fourth quarter of 1970 to 3.8% in the fourth quarter of 1971. At the same time, average real wages increased a remarkable 22.3% during 1971.

Another interesting outcome corresponds to the improvement of income distribution and to the reduction of income inequality even among workers, that is, low wage workers had higher real wage increases than relatively high wage workers (see table 7.10). The labor share in GDP increased from 52.2% (1970) to 61.7% (1971), whereas the average value of this variable during the 1960–69 period was 48.4%. Minimum real wages for blue-collar workers were increased by 56% during the first quarter of 1971, while in the same period real minimum wages for white-collar workers were increased "only" 23%. In this way, the differential ratio between blue- and white-collar workers' minimum wage decreased from 49% (1970) to 35% (1971). The closing of the gap between white- and blue-collar workers was less pronounced if one looks at the evolution of the average real wage during 1971: while the average

13. National unemployment rates are available in Chile on an annual basis since 1961.

real wage of blue-collar workers increased by 20.3%, that for white-collar workers increased by 18.8%.

These results were obtained by a combination of policies oriented mainly toward obtaining an increase of aggregate demand. Wage policy implied increases of annual real wages which ranged between 39% (minimum blue-collar wages) and 10% (minimum white-collar wages), with an overall average of 22.3%. Central government expenditures increased by 36% in real terms, raising the share of fiscal spending in GDP from 21% (1970) to 27% (1971). As part of this expansion, the public sector engaged in a huge housing program, starting to build 76,000 houses in 1971, compared to 24,000 for 1970. Finally, monetary policy was accommodating, so as not to impair the expansion of demand and output: M1 increased by 119% during 1971. A more detailed examination of the public-sector expansion and its financing is provided in the third part of this section.

These policy measures were supported by widespread price controls. With nominal wage readjustments of over 40%–50%, nominal government expenditures increasing by more than 60%, and money supply augmenting by more than 100%, the annual inflation rate of 1971 (22.1%) seems surprisingly low. The single most important explanation of this phenomenon is related to price controls on the private sector and a freeze of tariffs and prices in the public sector. Two factors explain the relative success of price controls (World Bank 1979; Bianchi 1975). First, the government gained direct and indirect control of the different links in the chain between production and consumption through many institutional changes. The authorities increased the commercial functions of existing public marketing and control agencies and created several new ones; moreover, major private wholesaling and importing firms were nationalized. Furthermore, through Government intervention, credit lines facilities were related to pricing agreements. Finally, vigilant consumer committees were created at the neighborhood level (Junta de Abastecimiento y Precios, or JAPs), which had to watch that local stores obeyed official prices and maintained goods in supply. Second, the overall environment of structural reforms, where so many firms had been expropriated or taken over by the government, induced most entrepreneurs to follow official price guidelines. It was too risky not to do it, so, "entrepreneurs had to think twice before violating official prices, because this (UP) Government was not like the previous ones" (N. García as quoted in Bianchi 1975).

Thus, the overexpansion of real wages in 1971 was significantly related to the effectiveness of price controls. However, workers' wage adjustments in bargaining surpassed the limits set up by the UP government-CUT (Central Unica de Trabajadores, the principal national union organization). This happened in spite of the fact that CUT was controlled by the UP political parties. Two principal elements explain this behavior: (1) the long tradition of unions to maximize wage readjustments, and (2) the competition from Christian

Democrat union leaders, who tried to outbid their UP rivals to gain popularity among workers (Griffith-Jones 1980).

Early Warnings of Disequilibria

Despite the overall bright picture that emerged in 1971, there were several indicators that suggested the presence of increasing disequilibrium throughout the year. (1) The budget deficit of the general government increased from 3.5% of GDP in 1970 to 9.8% in 1971. At a broader level, the consolidated nonfinancial public deficit increased from 6.7% (1970) to 15.3% (1971). (2) The credit to the public sector alone increased by 124%; more than 90% of the credit provided by the Central Bank to the public sector was in the form of high-powered money. This was one of the factors behind the 119% increase of M1. In short, monetary policy was totally out of control. (3) The level of international reserves dropped from $394 million (1970) to $163 million (1971), a 59% reduction. The loss of reserves could have been higher, but on November 1971 the UP government suspended external debt service and entered into rescheduling negotiations. (4) The trade balance changed from a $95 million surplus (1970) to a $90 million deficit (1971). The sharp drop of the world copper price from 64.1¢ a pound in 1970 to 49.3¢ a pound in 1971 is the main factor behind the trade balance deterioration. Drastic import controls, in the presence of an exchange rate appreciation, avoided a larger external trade deficit on 1971. Besides exchange controls, the main tool for import controls was the use of a 10.000% prior deposit requirement, an existing regulation that the UP government used intensively by significantly increasing the number of goods included in it. (5) While the overall consumption level increased by 12.4% during 1971, gross investment dropped by 2.3%; that is, gross investment reduced its share of GDP from 23.4% (1970) to 20.8% (1971). (6) Given the sharp increase of real wages and the tight price controls, there was a squeeze of corporate profits. (7) The first signals of shortages began to appear during the second half of 1971. These shortages were not considered by UP economists to be a serious problem. Rather, they were thought to be the natural outcome of income redistribution policies and a symptom of a past disequilibrium problem. The major increase of meat consumption in 1971 (+18%), for example, was related to redistribution. In the past, a high-income family consumed 180 kilograms a year while a low-income family consumed only 20 kilograms a year. Thus, a redistribution of income toward low-income families had necessarily to increase overall meat consumption (García 1971).

Answering the criticism that the economy was becoming overheated, some UP officials reacted as follows: "If the income redistribution policy would have failed, if the anti-inflationary policy would have failed, there is no doubt that there would have been enough unused capacity, international reserves, and stocks of goods, because that would have been a repetition of the traditional adjustment mechanism of the previous years. The success of the [UP] economic policy is precisely related to the disappearance of slack variables" (Garretón 1975, p. 218).

At the end of 1971 there were many signals suggesting that inflation would significantly accelerate in 1972: the large increase of money supply, the large fiscal deficit, the new wage readjustment of January 1972, the practical impossibility of further contracting corporate profits, the depletion of stocks and inventories, the sharp contraction of international reserves, and the appearance of shortages and black markets in many different goods. However, the reaction of UP authorities was practically null. While in the official speeches of 1970 inflation was considered to be a key variable, in the finance minister's November 1971 message to the nation not much was said with respect to inflation. The only mention made in this respect stated that the same anti-inflationary policy of 1971 would be maintained during 1972.

7.4.2   Decline and Full Collapse, 1972–73

The decline and full collapse of the UP experiment during the years 1972–73 is a clear consequence of the "successful" overexpansive policies implemented in 1971. The favorable initial outcome increased the UP government's popularity. In this context, criticism related to the presence of distinct types of disequilibria were disregarded as mere technical observations.[14] Moreover, the UP government had a difficult dilemma; a cut of real wages was a necessary step in order to reduce the existing disequilibria, but this solution would hurt its progressive and revolutionary image (Dornbusch and Edwards 1989). Ideology prevailed, that is, maintenance of the progressive and revolutionary image was more important than reduction of the disequilibria.

Macroeconomic Disequilibria

Up to 1972, nominal wage readjustments were provided at the beginning of the year. In this respect, the wage readjustment policy of 1972 followed the same pattern of the previous year; that is, the official policy specified increases of nominal wages fully indexed to the 1971 CPI (22.1%), with (nominal) minimum wages increasing more (32%). But again, during the first quarter of 1972, wages increased more than the amount specified by the official policy. Even the government did not follow its own wage policy, and public-sector (employment-weighted) average wages increased by 48% (see Bianchi 1975 for disaggregated data information). This was not a useful way to reduce the 1971 public deficit of 15.3% (of GDP).

The increase of the public-sector wage bill, the large expansion of subsidies to the state-owned enterprises (4.6% and 9.5% of GDP in 1972 and in 1973, respectively), and the deterioration of tax collection (revenues dropped 3% of

14. The seems to be a general pattern with Governments implementing populist policies; Governments think that "Deux et machina" type of solutions will appear in the future which will solve the technical disequilibria (Sachs 1990). In the UP case, it was thought that the structural transformations carried on in the present would solve future problems.

GDP in 1972, and a further 3% of GDP in 1973) generated an impressively large and increasing public deficit of 24.5% in 1972 and 30.5% in 1973. (This subject is examined in more detail in the next section). Given the rudimentary characteristics of the prevailing capital market, a significant part of the public-sector deficit (60% in 1972 and 73% in 1973) was financed by money issued by the Central Bank. The final outcome was an increase in the total quantity of money by 173% in 1972 and 413% in 1973; between 1970 and 1973 the total quantity of money was augmented almost 30 times.

The large increase in the quantity of money clearly had destabilizing effects upon repressed inflation, shortages, and the external disequilibrium. Black markets spread for most goods, and the gap between official and black market prices increased. On the external front, the overvalued exchange rate led to export smuggling.

Table 7.11 provides a perspective about the evolution of the years 1972–73 within the overall period. The following elements can be observed: (1) The drop of GDP was relatively not so spectacular in light of the paralyzed market environment of the economy. Growth rates of 1972 and 1973 were -0.1% and -4.3%, respectively. (Table 7.12 provides the growth rates for the main GDP sectors. See fig. 7.1 for the evolution of industry's annual growth rate.) (2) Inflation (as measured by the CPI) exploded, reaching the highest consecutive levels in the long history of Chilean inflation: 260.5% in 1972 and 605.1% in 1973. (See fig. 7.2 for the evolution of inflation by quarters.) Note, however, that the wholesale price index (WPI) provides an inflation figure larger than 1,000% for 1973. (3) The national unemployment rate had a small increase,

Table 7.11   Evolution of Main Macroeconomic Variables, 1970–73 (%)

	1970	1971	1972	1973
Economic growth rate (GDP)	3.6	8.0	−.1	−4.3
Annual inflation rate (CPI)	36.1	22.1	260.5	605.1
National unemployment rate	5.7	3.8	3.1	4.8
Annual increase of real wages	8.5	22.3	−11.3	−38.6

Sources: Central Bank, CIEPLAN, and ODEPLAN.

Table 7.12   Main GDP Sectoral Growth Rates, 1970–73 (%)

	1970	1971	1972	1973
Agriculture	3.6	−1.8	−7.4	−10.3
Mining	−3.0	6.0	−3.8	−2.3
Industry	2.0	13.6	2.2	−7.7
Commerce	−1.5	15.8	3.8	−6.4
Services	4.8	7.0	−.2	−.6

Source: Central Bank.

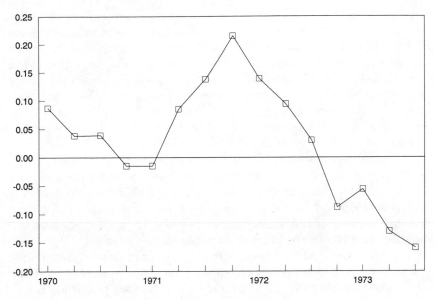

Fig. 7.1   Industry annual growth (in percentages)

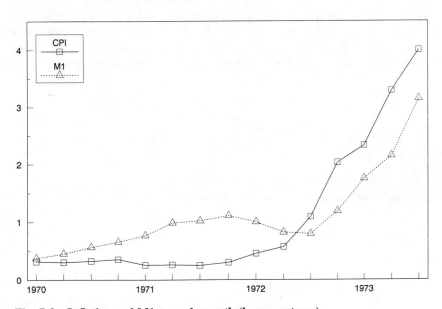

Fig. 7.2   Inflation and M1 annual growth (in percentages)

from 3.1% in 1972 to 4.8% in 1973. (4) Real wages dropped spectacularly, by -11.3% in 1972 and -38.6% in 1973. This last figure includes a 30% cut induced in the fourth quarter of 1973, after the military coup. (See fig. 7.3 for the quarterly evolution of real blue-collar wages.) In any case, it should be remarked that the mechanism of using nominal wage readjustments to increase real wages and to improve Chilean income distribution failed completely. It took eight years, up to 1981 (during the "peak of the boom") for real wages to recover the level they had held in 1970 before the UP government.

A disaggregated evolution of real wages tends to present a very dramatic situation, even if the exact figures depend upon the type of deflator used, in a context where black markets and barter prevailed. Table 7.13 shows that, even within the UP period, blue- and white-collar minimum wages had half the real purchasing power of 1970 by the third quarter of 1973; it is also observed that white-collar real wages had a larger drop than blue-collar wages.

When shortages and bottlenecks spread, the external sector constitutes the escape valve; a restricted supply of imports is visualized by most agents as the main economic constraint. However, the drop of domestic production constituted in many cases the principal factor related to internal food shortages, as in the agricultural sector. Table 7.14 shows the sharp increase of 51.4% of total imports (in current dollars) between 1970 and 1973; while food imports increased 2.3 times between 1970 and 1972 and 3.8 times between 1970 and 1973, imports of capital goods dropped (in current dollar terms) during the same period. Table 7.15 shows the large surge of wheat imports from 200,000

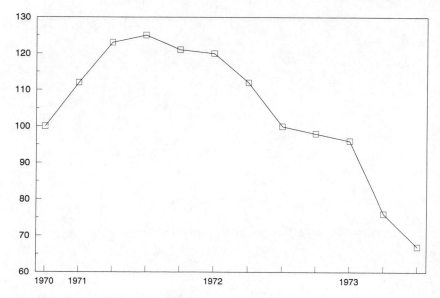

Fig. 7.3   Index of blue-collar real wages (April 1970 = 100)

Table 7.13   Minimum Real Wages and Average Real Wages of Blue-Collar
Workers and White-Collar Workers, 1970–73

	Minimum Real Wages (1970 = 100)		Average Real Wages (April 1970 = 100)	
	Blue-Collar	White-Collar	Blue-Collar	White-Collar
1970	100	100	100	100
Quarter in 1971:				
1	156	123	112	107
2	146	116	123	127
3	134	105	125	124
4	120	95	121	117
Quarter in 1972:				
1	151	106	120	111
2	125	88	112	101
3	94	66	100	93
4	121	82	98	92
Quarter in 1973:				
1	96	64	96	118
2	81	49	76	62
3	50	32	67	54

Source: World Bank.

Table 7.14   Selected Components of the Balance of Payments, 1970–73
(Millions of U.S. Dollars)

	1970	1971	1972	1973
Total exports (FOB)	1,112	999	849	1,309
Copper exports	839	701	618	1,049
Total imports (CIF)	956	1,015	1,103	1,447
Food imports	136	192	318	512
Imports of capital goods	276	248	186	243
Trade account	156	−16	−253	−138
Current account	−81	−189	−387	−295
Overall balance of payments	114	−300	−231	−112

Source: Central Bank.

tons (1970) to 951,000 tons (1973) while domestic production decreased by
43% during that same period.[15]

Central Bank net (short-run) international reserves were reduced to $62
million in 1972, which represented a decline of 62% with respect to the 1971
level; that is, the UP government lost 84% of its initial stock of international

15. A similar situation is observed with many other food products.

Table 7.15   Domestic Production and Imports of Wheat, 1970–73
(Thousands of Tons)

	1970	1971	1972	1973
Domestic production	1,307	1,368	1,195	747
Imports	200	367	745	951

Sources: INE and ODEPA.

reserves in a mere two years. By 1973, the level of available net (short-run) international reserves were equivalent to 22 days of imports.

Shortages, Black Markets, and Rationing

During the second half of 1972 there was a coexistence of high and accelerating inflation (at the three-digit level on an annual basis), widespread shortages, and proliferation of black markets. Two segmented goods markets with two different price systems prevailed in the economy: the official market and the black market. The differential between them went as high as five to ten times for a wide range of goods.

The official explanation given by UP economic authorities for the large increase of shortages and black markets was the following: Shortages and black markets were due to the counterrevolutionary action of reactionary groups and enemies of the people ("enemigos del Pueblo"); "the black market is the synthesis of the antipatriotic action of the Conservatives. . . . It is a lie to impute present consumption problems to bad Government policies" (see Banco Central, *Boletín Mensual,* January 1973).

Within a context of shortages and black markets, the use of nominal wage readjustments to maintain the real purchasing power of low-income groups becomes ineffective. The official CPI underestimates the real inflation rate, and the access to goods offered at official prices becomes crucial. Then, UP economists argued that direct government control over the distribution of goods and rationing became the necessary and efficient mechanisms to combat black markets and to guarantee the maintenance of real consumption of low-income groups.

On December 1972, the minister of finance announced that the following measures would be implemented in order to deal with shortages and black markets (see Banco Central, *Boletín Mensual,* January 1973): (1) The creation of a national state agency (Secretaría Nacional de Distribución) would centralize the wholesale trade in order to avoid the flow of goods to the black markets. The state-owned enterprises would send all their production there, and they would stop payments in goods to its workers. Special sale agreements "which will be difficult to reject" would be offered to private firms. (2) At the retail level there would be direct control over distribution of goods so that "all families would receive a basket of goods according to their real needs"; for this purpose the agency "established a quota of goods per family like oil, sugar, rice, coffee, meat, up to a total of 30 goods which would be distributed by the JAP. . . . The JAP would define the real requirements per family".

The impact of an official speech announcing that "rationing is coming" was the following: (*a*) There was a sharp increase of demand, especially for non-perishable consumption goods. Everyone tried to get, first, all those goods specifically listed by the minister of finance and second, all the types of consumption goods that were assumed to be included in the "basket of 30 goods." In short, the official announcement of measures to solve the problems of shortages and black markets increased considerably the prevailing shortages; most families tried to keep home stocks of every consumption good that was found on the market. (*b*) The political opposition to the UP government became stiffer. There was a perception that the Chilean economy would end up having the state institute widespread comprehensive rationing under the JAPs' control (where money would be displaced by party credentials and connections). (*c*) Moreover, there did not exist at that time the infrastructure to implement the rationing scheme; there were only scattered "popular food baskets" (*canastas populares*) distributed by some state agencies to their political clientele and to JAPs located in low-income communities.[16]

In spite of the dramatic and chaotic situation, the UP government obtained 45% of the vote in the March 1973 parliamentary elections. Several distinct factors were at play. There was an important increase in the number of "popular food baskets" distributed in the period prior to the election. Rhetorics and ideology also played an important role, that is, the low-income groups perceived that the "UP government was their government," and that they had to support it in the good and bad times. However, after the March elections, the situation deteriorated considerably more, and the economy started on the path to a full collapse. The end of the story is well known.

7.4.3   The Fiscal Explosion

The UP government pursued from the outset an aggressive policy of fiscal stimulation. Spending by the general government increased markedly,[17] and was mostly concentrated on current items. As table 7.16 shows, the bulk of the fiscal expansion involved wages and social security payments, which rose by more than 7 percentage points of GDP from 1970 to 1972, and transfers to the rest of the public sector (included in the item "other" of the table). The growth in investment by the general government during the same period was

16. It is estimated that in 1973 there were between 2,000 and 2,500 JAPs in the whole country, with 50% of them located in Santiago.

17. The general government includes both centralized institutions whose financing depends on the Treasury, and decentralized institutions, which generally have their own sources of funds to complement the Treasury's contributions. The latter enjoy greater independence in the use of their funds; they include, e.g., the state-run social security system.

of a second order of importance—only 1% of GDP—as compared with current spending.

Public enterprises were another important cause of the expansion in public expenditures during this period. As shown in table 7.16, the bulk of the increase in their current expenditures came from purchases of goods and services other than labor, which rose by almost 5% of GDP between 1972 and 1973. The rise in their wage bills was more moderate than was true for those in the government, mostly because of a smaller increase in real wages. Quite remarkably, during 1973 the total sales of goods and services were insufficient to cover purchases of intermediate inputs.

However, we have not yet mentioned what became the most substantial source of increased public spending during 1972 and 1973: the subsidies necessary for the continued operations of medium- and large-sized private industrial firms taken over by the government. The authorities had expected to benefit from surpluses in those companies, but in practice they proved a major drain on public resources. The disruption in production provoked by this process necessitated government contributions of almost 9% of GDP in the form of subsidies during 1973 (table 7.16 and fig. 7.4a).

These expansionary policies became unsustainable in 1973, and general government spending fell abruptly. This drop was accelerated after the coup of September 1973, which clearly influenced the figures for that year. Most of the contraction occurred in the same items that had experienced the unprecedented growth in the previous two years; the wage bill and social security contributions fell to even lower levels as a proportion of GDP than they had been in 1970. Judging from the evidence presented in the previous section, it is clear that most of the crash was borne by real wages. The decline in investment was also pronounced (1.6% of GDP), even if softer than that of current spending. The decrease in the real values of current and capital expenditures was even more pronounced than the ratios to GDP shown in table 7.16, however, given that GDP collapsed by over 4% in 1973.

The contraction in government spending during 1973 was not attributable to a change in the economic strategy pursued by the UP administration. Instead, it was the result of both an unsustainable policy of demand expansion, which ran into bottlenecks on the supply-side and gave rise to very high inflation, and to changes in the last quarter of 1973 following the military takeover.

Inflation, Increased Subsidization, and the Revenue Side

The mounting fiscal deficits of 1970–73 were not only due to an expenditure surge, as public revenues also dropped significantly during this period. Part of this drop had its origins in the substantial decline of copper prices in 1971, coupled with the fixing of the copper exchange rate at an artificially overvalued level. The combination of these effects drastically reduced the revenues of copper companies and thus the taxes those companies paid to the government.

Table 7.16a Public-Sector Operations (% GDP): General Government Compared to Public Enterprises

General Government

	1970	1971	1972	1973
Current revenues	31.58	32.81	29.14	23.55
Taxes	25.50	26.35	23.60	20.37
Direct taxes	7.73	6.19	4.28	5.68
Personal and business income	3.82	4.80	3.52	4.76
Copper companies	3.10	.38	.05	.55
Property	.81	1.01	.71	.37
Indirect taxes	10.82	11.66	11.13	10.12
Goods and services	9.11	9.82	9.52	9.69
International trade	1.71	1.84	1.61	.44
Other, net of VAT rebates	.00	.00	.00	.00
Social Security contributions	6.96	8.51	8.19	4.58
Nontax revenues	6.07	6.46	5.53	3.17
Sales of goods and services	1.76	1.57	1.09	1.21
Profit transfers and other revenues	4.31	4.89	4.45	1.96
Current expenditures	25.27	32.21	33.01	26.02
Wages and salaries	9.81	11.82	12.92	9.41
Purchases of goods and services	2.58	3.23	2.77	4.17
Social Security payments	8.60	11.87	11.86	6.03
Transfers and subsidies to private sector	3.43	1.82	2.26	1.73
Interest on public debt	.73	.72	.62	.68
Internal	.20	.16	.40	.04
External	.53	.56	.22	.64
Other	.13	2.75	2.58	3.99
Savings	6.31	.60	-3.87	-2.47
Net capital revenue:	-3.56	-2.99	-2.86	-2.21
Revenue	1.66	3.15	.94	2.16
Revenues less financial investment and other transfers	-5.23	-6.14	-3.80	-4.38
Capital formation	6.26	7.38	7.38	5.84
Total expenditures	31.53	39.58	40.39	31.86
Overall surplus	-3.51	-9.76	-14.12	-10.52
Financing	3.50	9.76	14.12	12.27
External (net)	-.07	-.59	-.09	.95
Drawings	1.12	.71	.25	2.11
Amortization	-1.19	-1.29	-.34	-1.16
Internal (net)	3.58	10.35	14.20	11.32
Banking system	3.14	12.45	14.42	10.23
Other and statistical discrepancies	.43	-2.10	-.22	-.65

Public Enterprises (Excluding CODELCO)

	1970	1971	1972	1973
Current revenues	9.14	9.29	9.90	11.43
Sales of goods and services	6.64	6.64	8.04	7.83
Transfers from general government	.71	1.12	1.38	2.51
Transfers from private sector	1.68	1.47	.26	.75
Other	.11	.06	.22	.33
Current expenditures	9.28	11.12	12.54	19.40
Wages and salaries	3.63	4.67	5.30	4.72
Purchases of goods and services	4.84	4.40	5.83	10.34
Taxes and transfers	.14	.20	.06	1.62
Interest on public debt	.40	1.03	.63	1.88
Internal	.18	.30	.29	1.57
External	.22	.73	.34	.31
Other	.27	.82	.72	.84
Savings	-.14	-1.83	-2.64	-7.97
Net capital revenue	-.01	-.01	-.09	-.13
Revenues	.03	.01	.01	.01
Revenues less financial investment and other transfers	-.04	-.02	-.11	-.14
Capital formation	2.23	2.32	1.97	2.27
Total expenditures	11.51	13.44	14.51	21.67
Overall surplus	-2.38	-4.16	-4.70	-10.37
Financing	.16	4.16	4.70	10.37
External (net)	.99	2.25	1.87	-.46
Drawings		2.81	2.41	.30
Amortizations	-.83	-.57	-.54	-.75
Internal (net)	2.22	1.91	2.83	10.83
Banking system	1.02	2.11	3.80	N.A.
Other and statistical discrepancies	1.20	-.20	-.97	N.A.

Source: Larraín (1988), tables 4, 6, and 8.

Table 7.16b   Public-Sector Operations (% GDP): Consolidated Nonfinancial
                     Public Sector

	Consolidated Nonfinancial Public Sector			
	1970	1971	1972	1973
Current revenues	38.14	37.65	34.48	21.26
Taxes	25.50	26.35	23.60	20.37
Direct taxes	7.73	6.19	4.28	5.68
Indirect taxes	10.82	11.66	11.13	10.12
Social security contribution	.96	8.51	8.19	4.58
Nontax revenues	12.63	11.30	10.88	.88
Net sales of goods and services	6.33	4.87	5.82	−2.22
Profit transfers and other revenues	6.31	6.43	5.06	3.10
Current expenditures	30.86	39.45	46.41	41.05
Wages and salaries	15.83	19.54	20.50	15.76
Social security payments	8.60	11.87	11.86	6.03
Transfers and subsidies to private sector	3.43	1.82	2.26	1.73
Interest on public debt	1.13	1.75	1.55	2.67
Other	1.86	4.47	5.63	5.36
Subsidies to social area	.00	.00	4.60	9.49
Savings	7.28	−1.79	−11.93	−19.79
Net capital revenue	−3.57	−3.00	−2.96	−2.35
Capital formation	10.41	10.48	9.64	8.35
Total expenditures	41.27	49.93	56.05	49.39
Overall surplus	−6.69	−15.28	−24.53	−30.48
Financing	6.68	15.27	24.53	30.48
External (net)	.09	1.66	1.82	.08
Internal (net)	6.60	13.61	22.71	30.40

Another important player in the evolution of public revenue was inflation, which rose from almost 35% in 1970 to over 600% in 1973. Prices started to increase in 1972 at a faster pace as a consequence of the money-financed fiscal expansion. In the presence of significant lags in tax collections, rising inflation depressed fiscal revenues and thus fed back into the fiscal deficit (the Olivera-Tanzi effect).

The Olivera-Tanzi effect was clearly at work in Chile and helps explain the low levels of tax revenues in the period 1970–73. Indeed, a regression (for the 1950–82 period) with the public-sector deficit as the dependent variable shows that a 10% rise in inflation increases the deficit by 1.2 percentage points of GDP. This result shows that inflation has a bigger effect in depressing the revenues of the public sector than on reducing expenditures. A simple look at

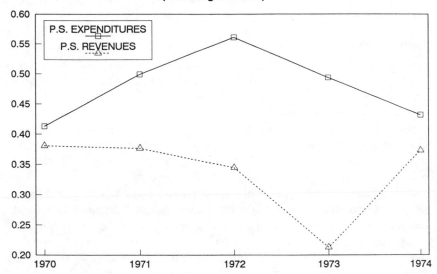

a. **Public Sector Expenditures and Revenues**
(Percentages of GDP)

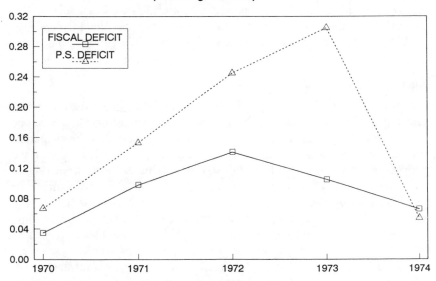

b. **Fiscal and Public Sector Deficits 70-74**
(Percentages of GDP)

Fig. 7.4 **Public and fiscal sector information**

the numbers suggests that this story fits well the Chilean situation in the period 1970–73. In every year in which inflation increased, tax revenues fell, reaching their lowest level as a proportion of GDP in 1973.

The Tax System

Certain tax systems are better equipped to cope with inflation than others, and thus the relationship between inflation and fiscal revenue is neither stable across countries nor over time within a country. The tax legislation in Chile in the early seventies was not suited to an inflationary environment, even if a partial indexation of income taxes was introduced in the late sixties. With lags in collections estimated to be around one year, the rise in inflation to levels well above 100% in 1972 and 1973 accounted for a sizable part of the decline in tax revenues during those years.

Another aspect of the tax system that conspired against higher revenues was significant evasion,[18] the result of many factors, among them: insufficient and inefficient policing by the Internal Revenue Service (SII); the proliferation of groups receiving special treatment, which helped to produce a highly complicated tax system that encouraged taxpayers to disguise one source of income as another in order to qualify for a lower tax rate; and the existence of an indirect sales tax applied to the total value of every transaction (rather than a value-added tax), a provision that significantly encouraged evasion. In the words of Ffrench-Davis, by the end of the sixties "big scale evasion persisted, as well as a number of special tax treatments which benefited a minority" (1973, p. 185). This process was intensified during the UP government, as Cheyre (1986) has documented.

Increased Subsidization

It is interesting to look at the revenue side of public enterprises when attempting to explain their deficit. Even if inefficient management had been one cause of the decline in real revenues by the end of the period, it is only part of the picture. It is clear that the prices charged for almost all the goods and services produced by public firms fell significantly in real terms from 1970 to 1973 (table 7.17). Perhaps the most dramatic case was that of electricity; its price declined by over 85% in the period. A similar trend was apparent in gasoline sales and telephone services. In the case of other fuels (gasoline, kerosene, diesel oil, and fuel oil), the downward trend was clearly present in 1970–72, when their prices decreased by an average of 40% in real terms, while world prices were steadily rising. In 1973 there was a substantial adjustment in the cost of oil in the international markets.[19] Thus, income trans-

18. The real value of tax revenues almost doubled in the second half of the sixties after the rates were raised and new taxes were introduced. However, revenues seemed to be far from their potential.

19. The world price of oil increased by approximately 100% between 1970 and 1973, even before the first oil shock of 1974. After adjustments in 1973, the domestic prices of fuels remained only 40% higher, on average, than their levels in 1970.

Table 7.17   Real Prices of Selected Public Enterprise Output (1970 = 100)

					Fuels			
Year	Electricity	Postal Services	Telephone Services	L.P. Gas	Gasoline	Kerosene	Diesel Oil	Fuel Oil
1970	100.0	100.0	N.A.	100.0	100.0	100.0	100.0	100.0
1971	87.6	169.0	N.A.	102.6	79.5	83.6	90.0	84.6
1972	67.7	177.0	100.0	67.7	69.4	61.1	68.1	57.8
1973	13.5	67.0	76.7	80.6	141.6	140.4	146.5	181.8

Source: Larraín (1988), table 9.

fers to the private sector in the form of increasingly higher subsidies through controlled prices for goods and services sold by public enterprises contributed some points to the growth of the public deficit during the Allende government.

As a result of the spending pressures and the decline in revenues, the consolidated public-sector deficit soared from 6.7% of GDP in 1970 to 30.5% in 1973, a level unprecedented in Chilean history (fig. 7.4b). One-third of the deficit can be attributed to subsidies for the "social area"; the rest was divided almost evenly between the general government and public enterprises. As table 7.14 shows, in 1973 all the financing came from internal sources, the overwhelming part of which was monetary emission. This pattern is not surprising, given that the executive branch of the government traditionally controlled the Central Bank.

A different interpretation of the deficit than ours is provided by Vuskovic (1975, pp. 18–19), who claims that "behind the fiscal deficit lie the open and covered resistance of the bourgeosie against contributing the resources to sustain the basic public services and to improve the income of public sector workers; the refusals of Congress to approve new taxes, and the budgetary cuts that it imposes; and even an active campaign of resistance against the payment of existing taxes."

7.5 Conclusions

The Chilean UP experience does not fit into Paul Drake's definition of a "reformist set of policies tailored to promote development without explosive class conflict" (as quoted in Dornbusch and Edwards 1989). Sharp structural reforms and open conflict were major elements in Chile during 1970–73. It fits several but not all of the elements of the so-called populist paradigm (Dornbusch and Edwards 1989). The main discrepancy lies in the initial conditions of Chile's experience. The previous government, helped by rising copper prices, had improved income distribution and the standard of living of the population and had introduced significant structural changes (agrarian reform and copper Chileanization). The UP government did not receive a stagnant economy, but one that had decelerated from a strong showing in the initial three years of the previous administration. Rather than stagnation or outright depression, Chile's case at the time was better characterized as one of pent-up expectations that went unfulfilled.

The policy prescription was indeed reactivation, redistribution, and restructuring, but the relative weights were very different when compared to the other populist experiments of the subcontinent (with the exception, perhaps, of Juan Velasco's populist authoritarianism in Peru). The weight of structural changes was overwhelming, while reactivation and redistribution were in an important way subordinated to it. As we have pointed out, expansionary policies were deemed necessary by the UP leaders to provide a strong base of support for the radical changes that were being implemented in the Chilean economy and society. There is no doubt that the fundamental goal of the whole experiment was this radical transformation and not a mere improvement of income distribution and a higher growth rate. The UP was talking of nothing less than substituting a capitalist system with a socialist model, and they really meant it.

Notwithstanding these caveats, the other elements of the populist paradigm were basically present in the Chilean case. The UP government inherited an important stock of international reserves—equivalent to around five months of imports—which provided a substantial cushion for its expansive policies. Yet UP authorities emphasized (understandably) that the cushion was really provided by the existence of major unutilized capacity in the industrial sector. But the key for a populist government to be able to hold an expansionary party, is the existence of foreign exchange cash (in either reserves or loans). Whatever the source of the initial cushion, the Unidad Popular acted with no regard for macroeconomic constraints.

The phases of populist experiments (as identified in Dornbusch and Edwards 1989 and Sachs 1990) are indeed present in the Unidad Popular experiment. The initial expansion of 1971 drives output and real wages upward and reduces unemployment; remarkably, it goes with reduced inflation. But by the end of 1971 the signals of disequilibrium were clear for a dispassionate observer. Bottlenecks appeared in strength during 1972, and 1973 witnessed the collapse of the whole experiment. Political instability mounted, and a coup ultimately replaced the UP Government with a military junta.

In the end, ideology proved to be a bad substitute for macroeconomic realism. When shortages are either considered to be a good symptom of the performance of the economy or deemed to be the "fault of the Chilean bourgeoisie and the international system" (Vuskovic 1975), when the fiscal deficit is blamed on the noncooperative bourgeoisie, and when JAPs are considered a good mechanism to increase people's participation, then ideology obscures the perception of reality to the limit. In light of Chile's experience of 1970–73, the problem of the Unidad Popular economic policies was deeper than trying "a rapid attack on all fronts at the same time" (Bitar 1979, p. 193). It was the failure of ideology.

References

Alaluf, D. 1971. La coyuntura económica y las transformaciones estructurales en 1971. In *La Economía Chilena en 1971*, ed. Instituto de Economía. Santiago: Universidad de Chile.

Alexander, R. 1978. *The Tragedy of Chile*. Westport, Conn.: Greenwood Press.

Aranda, S. and A. Martínez. 1970. Estructura económica: algunas características fundamentales. In *Chile, hoy*, ed. A. Pinto et al., pp. 55–172. México City: Siglo XXI.

Baltra, A. 1973. *Gestión económica del Gobierno de la Unidad Popular*. Santiago: Editorial Orbe.

Bianchi, A. 1975. La política económica de corto plazo de la Unidad Popular, 1970–1973. Woodrow Wilson School, Princeton University, May. Mimeograph.

Bitar, S. 1986. *Chile: Experiments in Democracy*. Institute for the Study of Human Issues.

———. 1979. *Transición, socialismo y democracia*. México City: Siglo XXI.

Boorstein, E. 1977. *Allende's Chile: An Inside View*. New York: International Publishers.

Caputo, O. and R. Pizarro. 1970. Dependencia e inversión extranjera. In *Chile, hoy*, ed. A. Pinto et al., pp. 173–212. Mexico City: Siglo XXI.

Cheyre, H. 1986. Análisis de las reformas tributarias en la década 1974–83. *Estudios Públicos* (Summer). Santiago.

Choncol, J. 1973. The Agrarian Policy of the Popular Government. In *The Chilean Road to Socialism*. ed. J. A. Zammit. Austin: University of Austin Press.

De Vylder, S. 1974. *Chile 1970–73: The Political Economy of the Rise and Fall of the Unidad Popular*. Stockholm: Unga Filosofers Forlag.

Dornbusch, R., and S. Edwards. 1989. Macroeconomic Populism in Latin America. NBER Working Paper no. 2986. Cambridge, Mass.

Ffrench-Davis, R. 1973. *Políticas económicas en Chile, 1952–1970*. Santiago: Editorial Nueva Universidad.

García, N. 1971. Algunos aspectos de la política de corto plazo de 1971. In *La Economía Chilena en 1971*, ed. Instituto de Economía, pp. 47–270. Santiago: Universidad de Chile.

Garretón, M. A., ed. 1975. *Economía política de la Unidad Popular*. Barcelona: Editorial Fontanella.

Griffith-Jones, S. 1980. *The Role of Finance in the Transition to Socialism*. London: Frances Pinter.

Larraín, F. 1991. Public Sector Behavior in a Highly Indebted Country: The Contrasting Chilean Experience 1970–85. In *The Public Sector and the Latin American Crisis*, ed. F. Larraín and M. Selowsky. San Francisco: ICS Press.

Martner, G. 1988. *El Gobierno del Presidente Salvador Allende, 1970–1973. Una evaluación*. Concepción: Ed. Literatura Americana Reunida.

Moss, R. 1973. *Chile's Marxist Experiment*. New York: John Wiley.

Novoa, E. 1973. The Constitutional and Legal Aspects of the Popular Unity Government's Policy. In *The Chilean Road to Socialism*, ed. J. A. Zammit. Austin: University of Texas Press.

O'Brien, P. 1976. *Allende's Chile*. Praeger.

Ramos, S. 1972. *Chile: ¿Una economía en transición?* Santiago: CESO, Editorial Universitaria.

Romeo, C. 1971. El carácter clasista y el contenido ideológico de la política económica del Gobierno de la Unidad Popular. In *La Economía Chilena en 1971*, ed. Instituto de Economía, pp. 23–46. Santiago: Universidad de Chile.

Sachs, J. 1990. Social conflict and populist policies in Latin America. In *Labour Re-*

lations and Economic Performance, ed. R. Brunetta and C. Dell'Aringa. London: Macmillan.

Sideri, S., ed. 1979. *Chile 1970–73: Economic Development and Its International Setting.* The Hague: Martinus Nijhoff.

Sigmund, P. 1977. *The Overthrow of Allende and the Politics of Chile.* Pittsburg: University of Pittsburg Press.

Vargas, E. 1973. *La Nacionalización del Cobre y el Derecho Internacional.* Santiago: CIEPLAN, Universidad Católica de Chile.

Vuskovic, P. 1975. Dos años de política económica del Gobierno popular. In *El golpe de Estado en Chile,* ed. P. Vuskovic. México City: Fondo de Cultura Económica.

———. 1973. The Economic Policy of the Popular Unity Government. In *The Chilean Road to Socialism,* ed. J. A. Zammit. Austin: University of Texas Press.

———. 1970. Distribución del ingreso y opciones de desarrollo. *Cuardernos de la Realidad Nacional* no. 5 (September): 41–60. Universidad Católica de Chile.

World Bank. 1979. *Chile: An Economy in Transition.* World Bank, Report no. 2390-Ch. Washington, D.C., June.

Zammit, J. A. 1973. *The Chilean Road to Socialism.* Austin: University of Texas Press.

Comment   Simón Teitel

The Larraín-Meller paper describes very well what happened in Chile during the Allende government and what led to the failure of its economic program. However, one might argue that the experiment that the authors analyze went well beyond populism; it was really an attempt to bring about socialism without a revolution or foreign invasion—an international first! Moreover, the analysis of this particular case cannot be restricted just to *macro*economics, but should include, as the authors do, some of the important *micro*economic preconditions and consequences of the reforms that were undertaken.

These comments are organized as follows: (1) background and nature of the program, (2) macroeconomic features and constraints, (3) microeconomic diagnosis and performance, and (4) lessons for the future.

Background and Nature of the Program

The Unidad Popular (UP) program was not based on an effort to recover from an IMF adjustment program or from an otherwise recessionary economy. Chile had experienced low to moderate economic growth, as well as favorable terms of trade (due to high copper prices) during the two preceding years. Substantial foreign reserves,[1] sizable unused industrial capacity, and probably

Simón Teitel is Senior Research Advisor, Inter-American Development Bank.

Comments by S. Payson are appreciated. The points of view expressed in this paper are those of the author and do not purport to represent the official position of the Inter-American Development Bank.

1. Since the estimates of foreign exchange amounts vary from an equivalent of four months to an equivalent of six months of imports, by no means can these be considered as very large re-

also inventories, made possible an initially noninflationary expansion in demand fueled by the increases in real wages and public expenditures engineered by the government. By reducing real prices and squeezing profits, price controls further contributed to the stimulation of demand.

Although several of the changes resulted in an improvement in the distribution of income, the redistribution objective was superseded by a major attempt to alter, drastically, the structure of ownership in all major economic sectors. The extent of the reforms undertaken is particularly striking in view of Allende's rather narrow base of political power. The UP only received approximately one-third of the electoral vote. (In comparison, Frei, the previous president, had been elected by a clear majority.) Although the UP claimed to carry out its reforms legally, and within the existing institutional structure, it is unclear how it could be argued that the fundamental changes in property rights they tried to implement did not entail major institutional changes.

In all fairness, and as the authors do not fail to note, nationalization of the mining sector, and agrarian reform in agriculture, had already been initiated before the Allende government and had received substantial support—especially in the case of mining. However, similar attempts in industry and banking were more controversial.

Nevertheless, with the exception of the manufacturing sector, Allende's government nationalization failures can mostly be traced to implementation errors, including a lack of control of the processes and management inefficiencies, rather than to strong opposition.

Macroeconomic Features and Constraints

An initial shift in demand was attained by increasing wages and public expenditures. Still, given the increases in nominal wages (40–50%), in central government expenditures (more than 60%), and in the money supply (more than 100%), the 22% annual inflation rate of 1971 seems quite low. The authors attribute this low rate to effective price controls in the private sector and a freeze on the prices of public services. Nevertheless, real wages increased beyond the established limits due to a lack of restraint by unions.

Although all the initial measures clearly were one-time instruments, the first year increases in output, employment, and investment, while also reducing inflation, were impressive. However, as well described by the authors, symptoms of macroeconomic instability were already present after the first successful year of the program—particularly, the increase in the fiscal deficit. Other indications of macroeconomic incoherence appeared later on.

Early warnings (1971) of macroeconomic disequilibria were: (*i*) the in-

---

serves, especially when compared, for example, to the level of reserves with which Perón started his first presidency, which was equivalent to four *years* of imports. See Carlos F. Díaz Alejandro, *Essays on the Economic History of the Argentine Republic* (New Haven, Conn.: Yale University Press, 1970), table 73, statistical appendix.

crease in the government budget deficit from 3.5% of GDP in 1970 to almost 10% in 1971; (*ii*) a 124% increase in credit to the public sector; (*iii*) a drop in international reserves from almost $400 million in 1970 to $163 million in 1971; (*iv*) a trade balance shift from a $95 million surplus in 1970 to a $90 million deficit in 1971 (the fall in the price of copper from $0.64 per lb. in 1970 to $0.49 in 1971 was a key factor in this deterioration); and (*v*) an increase in consumption accompanied by a drop in investment.

The first shortages appeared during the second half of 1971, and by the end of 1971 there were also indications that inflation would accelerate in 1972. These indications included: an increase in the money supply, new wage adjustments, a depletion of inventories, further contraction of international reserves, and the emergence of black markets for many products. Still, the government did not react by emphasizing the fight against inflation, as it had done at the beginning.

The collapse took place in 1972–73. Expansionary policies became unsustainable, and government spending fell sharply. The areas most affected were those that had been increased substantially before. As an example, the share of wages in GDP fell to a value that was even lower than it had been before 1970.

The fiscal deficits of the period were aggravated by the fall in copper prices and by the maintenance of an overvalued exchange rate. The overvalued exchange rate was maintained for fear of the inflationary impact of devaluations, but it resulted in lower export revenues for the mining companies and thus in lower government tax revenues. Rising inflation also contributed to a fall in revenues due to the lag in tax collections. Public enterprises' prices had not kept up with inflation, thus substantial subsidies were required that also contributed to the expansion of the fiscal deficit. For example, the price of electricity declined in real terms by 85% in the period 1970–73. As a result of all these factors, the consolidated public-sector deficit increased from 6.7% of GDP in 1970 to 30.5% in 1973.

Thus the misalignment of the basic prices in the economy (wages, exchange rate, and the interest rate), which favored the initial expansion in domestic demand and absorption, when maintained for a longer period of time eventually led to macroeconomic instability.

Microeconomic Diagnosis and Performance

The diagnosis of UP economists included some interesting microeconomic ideas. They assumed that a deficit in consumption (and consequently in production) existed because of the skewed distribution of income that favored consumption by the few. They maintained that this pattern of consumption led to diseconomies of scale in production and reflected the demand for luxury goods by the rich. These luxury goods were more capital intensive than the "simple" consumer goods demanded by the majority of the population, and thus, led to a less than desirable employment level. In addition, it was argued, the structure of production reflected oligopolistic concentration resulting in monopoly rents that could be returned to the general population if the producers were forced to increase their output and to lower their prices.

Undoubtedly, the increase in purchasing power of the population, via the increase in salaries and price controls, gave rise to a substantial shift in demand that resulted in a reactivation of industrial production with all its attending benefits: larger runs, economies of scale, and lower production costs. As for the composition effect of this shift in demand, admittedly, there might have been not only significant differences in the propensities to consume among different socioeconomic classes, but also in their tastes and preferences. On the other hand, the claim regarding changes in factor intensity due to changes in the product mix seems more questionable. Some luxuries, like jewelry, cosmetics, and furs, may be more labor intensive than other goods favored by the working class—such as processed foods or consumer durables. Moreover, the employment effect of the shift in demand that took place, by the sheer size of the income effect, would be likely to dominate any factor-substitution effect due to differences in the factor intensity of the new product mix. Still, this interesting proposition remains to be tested by careful empirical studies.

The same could be said for the issue of the existence of monopoly rents in the manufacturing sector as a justification for leeway to reduce prices while still maintaining feasible enterprises. It was assumed that while the unit profit rate of industrial firms would be reduced, the increase in output and sales would compensate for it and maintain the overall level of profits. However, among the reasons for the increase in public spending were the large subsidies required for the continued operation of the industrial firms taken over by the government. Instead of sharing the monopoly rents with the population, these enterprises become a major drain on public resources (about 9% of GDP in subsidies during 1973 due to the disruption in production generated by the socialization process).

The cancellation of the indemnification to the foreign owners of mines, via the allegation of "excessive profits," was probably the most egregious mistake made by the Allende government. Perhaps even a partial payment would have sufficed to temper the foreign opposition. Instead, foreign owners of mines had a very strong argument against the government, while support for the nationalization of the large mines had indeed been unanimous (This support was particularly striking taking into account that the Congress was controlled by the opposition.)

A failure of the agrarian reform was that the expropriated estates largely remained in the hands of the state rather than being distributed among the farmers. Similarly objectionable was the illegal occupation of farms (or *tomas*) in the face of an otherwise very rapid expropriation program. Because of the occupations of farms, irrespective of their size, the government managed to alienate all types of landowners.

In order to assume control of the industrial sector, the government had to find excuses. The unions obliged with labor disputes, which at times were also instigated by the government itself. It was also possible for the government to refuse price increases, which were tantamount to the survival of firms, in an effort to convince owners to sell their enterprises. These methods alienated not only large entrepreneurs (the original targets of the program), but also medium and small-size proprietors. Owners of industrial firms put up a much stronger resistance than those in other sectors, and, consequently, the takeover of industry could not be completed.

In spite of all the difficulties in carrying out the changes in asset ownership, in 1973 the government had control of 100% of utilities, 85% of banking and mining, 70% of transportation and communications, and 40% of industry.

One standard critique of expropriations concerns the negative impact of so-called uncertainty over property rights. However, the general influence of this effect may have been overstated. In Chile, the main effect probably resulted from the "certainty" that substantial changes in property rights would indeed be forthcoming. Seeing that the prices set by larger firms were being controlled, and their profits squeezed, entrepreneurs recognized that the rules of the game were changing unfavorably for all of them. This provoked opposition and surely had negative effects on planned investment. Even small firms, which could originally have counted on not being expropriated, could not ignore the existence of an antiprivate economic environment. Moreover, in a dynamic context, such firms could not expect to thrive and succeed because if they were to grow rapidly, they would soon become an expropriation target.

Thus many undesirable effects were generated by the "certainty" of the changes in ownership which were to be expected from a Socialist government, even for those who might have expected to be personally exempted from them. This argument is, to some extent, recognized by the authors in connection with mining, a sector in which the government kept the original targets and did not try to take over small and medium-size mines.

Lessons for the Future

The Allende program had three of the expected phases—initial success, signs of macroeconomic disequilibria, and bottlenecks and collapse—but, as noted, was not preceded by a depression or an IMF adjustment program. It was also very different from other populist experiments in the extraordinary weight it placed on structural changes rather than on reactivation and redistribution. The objective was a change in the economic system from capitalism to socialism, with perhaps a brief populist "prelude" to broaden the support of the government before undertaking major structural reforms.

The question initially posed by the organizers of this conference remains unanswered. Are redistribution policies cum growth possible without running into macroeconomic instability? Clearly, in the long run, the only source of real income increases is via productivity growth. Other means to change incomes are one-shot affairs based on using up existing unutilized resources or temporarily squeezing profits by means of price controls. They do not entail long-term solutions.

One assumption underlying the question appears to be that domestic demand should remain preeminent and that it must be increased via redistribution. The disregard for the need to complement domestic demand with foreign demand for industrial exports is particularly troubling because, while it is true that domestic demand will generally remain dominant, exports of manufactures are needed to break the dependence on erratic revenues from exporting raw materials, and to serve as a catalyst for productivity enhancement in the industrial sector, which could raise overall productivity.

In this respect, Ranis has argued that Latin America may have "missed the boat" because of its failure to develop labor-intensive exports earlier in its industrialization process (in contrast to the East Asian exporting countries).[2] However, this argument disregards the substantial differences in natural resource endowments that have existed between the two regions. Exports of manufactures from Latin America have been shown to include products based on natural resource processing as well as those originally manufactured for the internal market under protected import substitution.[3] Further expansion of such exports is possible without creating a major disruption in industrialized countries because the extent of penetration of Latin American products in those markets is generally limited. Chile has been quite successful in expanding nontraditional exports: some are manufactures, others natural resource products such as fruit and wood products. Brazil and Argentina are successful exporters of food products, as well as chemicals, metal products, and machinery. Venezuela is expanding its exports of metallurgical and metal products together with those of petrochemicals. Colombia has successful exports of leather goods and textiles, together with flowers and other natural resource products.

As a corollary, given the critical importance of these exports, there could be little tolerance for overvaluation of the currency or for wage increases not based on real productivity growth. Moreover, the incentives initially required by industrial exporters should be kept in a sustained fashion and made very clear to perceive.

Another point involves the definition of populism. Evidently, some people follow Lewis Carroll's dictum and call things by the names they wish to call them. However, it must be recognized that substantial differences exist between "classical" populism, based on the existence of populist movements (e.g., with charismatic leaders such as Perón and Vargas), socialist experi-

---

2. See the discussion of Simón Teitel, "Industrialization, Primary Commodities and Exports of Manufactures," in *The Balance between Industry and Agriculture in Economic Development,* ed. N. Islam (New York: International Economic Association, Macmillan Press), pp. 315–41.

3. See Teitel (n. 2 above).

ments, (like Allende in Chile or the "Sandinistas" in Nicaragua), and incomes-policy-based non-orthodox stabilization programs (such as the Austral and Cruzado plans in Argentina and Brazil, respectively), all of which are at times also labeled as populist programs. Obviously, not all bad economic policies are populist policies, and not all wage and price controls imply populism.

In recent years we have witnessed the failure, in Chile and other countries, of extreme reform-minded programs from both the right and left. We have also seen that these programs may end up having opposite effects to those originally intended—Chile is a prime example.[4] The question then becomes, Can such mistakes be avoided in the future?

The recent political constellation in Latin America includes a new phenomenon that goes beyond the previous seesaw of rightist and leftist experiments. It is the popular election of charismatic leaders, who, although running on a populist platform, choose, once elected, to carry out pragmatic programs. Presidents Carlos Meném and Carlos A. Pérez are good examples of this new development. Is this the wave of the future? The new Chilean government has issued reassurances that the macroeconomic stability and equilibrium attained during the latter part of the Pinochet regime will be preserved as a matter of high priority. The message seems to be that whether one comes from the right or the left, macroeconomic equilibrium must be respected. We know, however, that this, by itself, will not be enough to guarantee democratic socioeconomic development—Colombia represents the most relevant counterfactual example.[5]

These days, structural reforms are also proposed as a necessary element in all economic programs. These reforms are quite dissimilar to populist or socialist prescriptions, and proceed from very different diagnoses.[6] A major problem arises, however, from the divorce between the reforms that are proposed, and often carried out, and the means to reactivate the economy. Re-

4. Interestingly enough, the stabilization cum reforms programs attempted later on in the Southern Cone countries, including Chile, while obviously not sharing at all the basic motivation of the Allende program, all resulted in similar overvaluation phenomena. See Vittorio Corbo, Jaime de Melo, and James Tybout, "What Went Wrong with the Recent Reforms in the Southern Cone," in *Growth, Reform and Adjustment: Latin America's Trade and Macroeconomic Policies in the 1970s and 1980s*, ed. S. Edwards and S. Teitel. Special issue of *Economic Development and Cultural Change*, vol. 34, no. 3, (April).

5. This country not only has a record of relative macroeconomic stability but also has had one of the longest stretches of elected governments. Yet, it could be argued that today no other country in Latin America stands closer to a violent institutional breakdown than Colombia. R. Albert Berry and Francisco E. Thoumi, "Post-War and Post National Front Economic Development of Colombia," in *Democracy in Latin America,* ed. D. L. Herman (New York: Praeger, 1988), pp. 63–85.

6. An interesting twist in the argument has been proposed by Sachs and others who argue that a more egalitarian distribution of income is a prerequisite for gaining support from the general population for the deep structural reforms now being attempted in many countries in the region. See John Sheahan, "Development Dichotomies and Economic Strategy," in *Hirschman's Thinking and a New Development Strategy for Latin America*, ed. S. Teitel (forthcoming).

duced government size, price stability, and income redistribution have not been shown to be sufficient to induce investment, and, without investment, no further economic growth or productivity increase that permits real wages to rise will be forthcoming.

One of the puzzles raised by the failure of populist programs concerns the reason for a government to continue carrying out policies that lead to its own demise. Is it due to irrationality, that is, the pursuit of extreme ideological agendas in the presence of adequate knowledge? Or is it due to a lack of information, thus reflecting honest mistakes, which, had the government known better, would have been avoided so that the government could continue to stay in power?

To better understand this problem we may have to cease considering the government as a monolithic entity. Recently I had occasion to converse with an eminent member of Alfonsín's economic team, and I was impressed by the reverence that the technician still held for the politician, even after fully experiencing the consequences of the *caudillo*'s failure. This led me to think about asymmetries in the access to technical information and political power. While the government may pursue a program with strong political objectives (Allende), or constraints (Alfonsín), either of which may render it a failure because of its economic implications, the technical imperatives of the situation may not become clear to the politicians until it is too late. If they were able to share more of their political power (or share it earlier) with economic technicians, and if the latter were able to share more of their knowledge (or share it earlier) with the politicians, such *fracasos*, as recently experienced in Latin America, could perhaps be avoided.

In addition, it must be recognized that, due to limitations in our knowledge, many of the interactions and macroeconomic effects of such programs are not always easy to foresee, in particular those related to how people form expectations and react to certain economic measures.

8 Populism and Economic Policy in Mexico, 1970–1982

Carlos Bazdresch and Santiago Levy

8.1 Introduction

Economic historians will probably look back at the 1970s in Mexico as a puzzling period during which the "miracle" of the 1950s and 1960s was slowly transformed into the "debt crisis" of the 1980s. The figures are quite dramatic. From 1954 to 1970, average annual GDP growth was 6.8%; the corresponding figure for inflation 3.5%. By the end of 1970 the ratio of foreign debt to GDP stood at 16.2.[1] The period was also marked by improving real wages: urban (rural) wages grew by 4.6% (4.7%). The next 18 years witnessed a dramatic reversal of these events: from 1971 to 1988 GDP growth averaged 4.1%, inflation 43%, urban (rural) wages 0.1% (2.0%);[2] the foreign debt/GDP ratio stood at 77.5. Equally important, the standard deviations of the growth and inflation rates during the former period are 0.019 and 0.04; the corresponding figures for the latter period are 0.03 and 0.39. Macroeconomic performance was not only less satisfactory during the latter period, it was also more erratic.

This paper centers its attention on the period 1970–82, which we label one of "populist macroeconomic policies." These macro policies stand in contrast to those implemented during the "stabilizing development" of the 1960s and the attempts at macroeconomic stabilization that followed since 1983. Our purpose is not to provide yet another critique of the policies followed during that time. Rather, our aims are two: one, to understand the origins of these

Carlos Bazdresch is president of the Centro de Investigacion y Docencia Economicas. Santiago Levy is associate professor of economics at Boston University.

The authors thank Enrique Cardenas, Sebastian Edwards, and Shane Hunt for comments on an earlier draft, as well as Dorothy Avery for her able work as research assistant. The usual disclaimers apply.

1. The figure relates to long-term debt only.
2. The data for wages refers only to the period 1970–82; see table 8.1 below.

policies in Mexico and, two, to explain their economic effects. As the rest of the papers in this volume attest, the history of Latin America—and Mexico is no exception—is full of "populist episodes," and so we wish to ask not only what these episodes consist of, but why they occur and what their short- and medium-term effects are.

The term "populist" is used to refer to different regimes. Thus, the Cárdenas presidency in Mexico is termed populist, but so is the Peronist regime in Argentina and the Vargas regime in Brazil. More recently, and despite substantial differences with past experiences, the term populist is also applied to Allende's regime in Chile, Echeverría's and López Portillo's presidencies in Mexico, and García's in Peru. The ideological differences among these regimes are large, as is the international context in which they take place. Perón is considered to originate in the "military right," while Allende was "on the left." Cárdenas was consolidating the postrevolutionary regime in Mexico; Allende intended to build socialism in Chile.

If the term "populist" had a precise meaning it could clearly not be used to account for such diverse historical circumstances. Thus, its use as an analytical category is both risky and dangerous; it may generate more heat than light. And yet, language may not betray us completely: there are some similarities in these experiences.[3] In economic policy they relate to the profligate use of public expenditures, the intensive use of price controls, systematic overvaluation of the exchange rate, and uncertain policy signals with depressing effects on private investment. In politics they relate to the regime's reliance on the support of workers' and peasants' organizations, which generally puts the regime in conflict with the country's private sector. But, with the exception of Allende's Chile, these conflicts are rarely absolute; moreover, the private sector seems to survive them more often than the governments that provoke them. These similarities, nevertheless, are insufficient to distinguish populist from nonpopulist regimes. Many other governments share the characteristics just mentioned. And the distinction, surely, cannot be made ex post on the basis of which regimes succeeded and which did not; populism should not be a portmanteau category to describe any set of inconsistent policies. The question remains, Why does the adoption of a set of policies that many governments use sometimes lead to the populist label? What is really meant by such label?

3. Sheahan (1987, p. 316) writes that: "Populism is not merely the name for a disorder, but instead a fairly systematic manifestation of widely shared popular objectives. . . . But some features are certainly common: dislike of the traditional elite dominance, of foreign investment and influence, of erratic and unfair market-determined prices for necessities, and of any appeal to the need for overall restraints on spending on social programs. In the Latin American version they have all favored activist governments committed, at least verbally, to protection of workers and of wages, to industrialization, to nationalism, to policies of cheap food for urban consumers, and to favors for worthy groups as the norm and goal of good government. Rejection of efficiency criteria and of concern for macroeconomic balance became *principles,* not accidental byproducts" (emphasis in the original).

We organize the paper in four sections. Section 8.2 analyzes the origins of populist policies in Mexico. Section 8.3 looks at the period of stabilizing development. While it has been extensively analyzed before, we nonetheless review it briefly, as it provides the background for the period under study. Section 8.4 describes the populist episodes of 1970–82, dividing them, as seems natural in the Mexican context, into the six-year presidential terms (or *sexenios*) of Echeverría (1970–76) and López Portillo (1977–1982). Section 8.5 provides an assessment of populist policies along with concluding remarks.

8.2 Populist Economic Policies

After 1910 Mexico experienced a long and violent revolution with strong nationalistic and popular overtones. The revolution took some time to consolidate into a stable government, but by the end of the 1930s this task was accomplished by President Cárdenas through pacts with various popular organizations, chief among them the peasants' confederation (Confederacion Nacional Campesina, or CNC) and the workers' central trade union (Central de Trabajadores de Mexico, or CTM).[4] Through these pacts the government traded protection for the social interests represented by these organizations in exchange for political support. This network of alliances, coupled with the previous emergence of a single political party (Partido Revolucionario Institucional, or PRI), maintained social peace for a long time, while at the same time keeping political power firmly in control of the government.

Naturally, the leaders of the revolution were very critical of the previous regime. Among many criticisms, two stood out: (*i*) the extreme misery in which the majority of the population lived and (*ii*) the unwillingness or inability of the government to remedy this situation.[5] Two ideas derived from these criticisms were to play a major and persistent role in the emerging system. First is the idea that the country's growth should not occur at the expense of basic popular rights. In practice, this was interpreted to mean that bounds should be imposed on the operation of markets; limits to land ownership, protection of workers from the vagaries of the labor market, and preclusion of foreign participation in the exploitation of natural resources. The second idea is that the government should be responsible for, and have the power to, impose the desired outcome.

Thus, far from having only to "regulate trade and commerce and provide social peace," the government born out of the Mexican Revolution had to be activist, "protecting" the lower-income classes and, more generally, pursuing distributive justice. Economic growth became one of the central raisons d'être

4. See Meyer (1974), Ianni (1983), and Cordoba (1974) for further analysis of the Mexican political system and the Cardenist period.
5. Some argued, in addition, that the prior constitution—that of 1857—imposed too many restrictions on the government to act in economic matters.

of the government, as its political legitimacy derived from its ability to raise the standard of living of the population. To insure that growth had the desired characteristics, the government had an explicit mandate, enshrined in the constitution,[6] to intervene in the economy. This was manifested in various forms—first through land redistribution, and second in the control of fiscal and monetary policy.[7] Among other manifestations are, third, through the creation of public enterprises in manufacturing, transportation, banking, and other areas; fourth, through price controls for selected commodities; and fifth, through interventions in foreign trade and investment, labor legislation, credit policy, and the like. All this, in turn, had two key implications: first, the government would be the central actor or protagonist in the economic life of the country. Second, the government would take the role of referee or mediating agent, balancing the conflicting demands of workers, peasants, and entrepreneurs. And government, in the Mexican context, meant the executive branch, as a strong presidential regime was another key characteristic of the political arrangements set by the 1917 Constitution.

With growth as a priority, the government had to develop a special alliance with entrepreneurs (or the private sector), as the latter controlled the supply of capital and entrepreneurial ability. And, while the private sector was formally out of the PRI, the government nonetheless created the conditions for it to flourish: fiscal policy, labor laws,[8] trade protection, and other instruments were chosen to enhance the profitability of private investment. In exchange, the private sector would not directly challenge the government's monopoly on political power. Still, the private sectors' support for the government was less forthcoming than that of workers' or peasants' organizations. At the root of the arrangement lay a fundamental asymmetry: while workers and peasants were not, on the whole, internationally mobile, the opposite was true of capital. Hence the greater bargaining power of the latter group vis-à-vis the government.

A necessary condition for the government to perform effectively its role as leading agent of growth and referee of social conflict is that it be powerful. Economic policy, broadly defined, would be a pillar of this power. Thus, the principle emerged that economic policy could—and, when necessary, should—be used in the pursuit of the government's political goals. These goals could be distributive, though this was not always the case. But regard-

6. See in particular Article 27 of the Mexican Constitution, where reference is made to the "Rectorship of the State" in economic affairs.

7. The Central Bank—Banco de Mexico—was founded in 1925, but was not designed to function as a truly autonomous institution. The director of the bank is either confirmed or appointed by the president, who has the power to renew his term in office. The director is responsible to the Board of Governors headed by the minister of finance.

8. We note, however, that there were at times important differences between the formal labor laws and their implementation. Although the letter of the law placed great emphasis on workers' rights, these were at times suppressed by a combination of trade union corruption and outright repression.

less of whether government interventions had distributional intentions, they always had a parallel goal: to strengthen the political power of the government through its control of economic activities. Many forms of government action therefore had this double role. The *ejido,* for example, was a mechanism to distribute land to peasants and impose bounds on land ownership, but it was also an institution that tied the loyalties of *ejidatarios* to the government.[9]

The large role given to the government in the economy, as well as the limits imposed on the free operation of markets, created an inherent conflict between the government and markets; this conflict reflected a deep-seated distrust in market operation.[10] We see two reasons that account for it. First, we know that, for given preferences and technology, income distribution is strongly determined by the size and distribution of productive assets.[11] In Mexico's case the distribution of productive assets has been highly concentrated. Thus, the undiluted action of market forces, barring any government action, would probably generate a very skewed distribution of income. This outcome would be incompatible with the ideals of the revolution: too much economic power would be concentrated in few social groups.

Second, distributional problems aside, the requirements for market forces to produce efficient outcomes are very strong; incomplete markets for risk, costs, and asymmetries in the availability of information, increasing returns, and other nonconvexities imply that market equilibrium are Pareto-suboptimal.[12] Although not articulated in this language, it is probably the case that these factors played a large role in the thinking of some revolutionaries, who felt the need for mechanisms to achieve more equitable and efficient outcomes than what the markets of that time delivered; it was believed that the government could do better.[13] Thus, the set of laws and regulations that gave

9. For example, neither *ejidos* as a whole nor individual *ejidatarios* are allowed to offer land as collateral, thus limiting any access to credit from private sources; credit is offered to the *ejido* as a whole by public-sector institutions.

10. Sheahan (1987, p. 319) has put the matter aptly: "The low popularity of free-market economics in Latin America is not evidence that radicals have misled the people: the majority of the public is probably no more confused about what they want and why than the rest of us are. It is rather that the conviction runs deep that market-oriented economic strategies are likely to maintain special privilege, work adversely for the poor, impede industrialization, and strengthen foreign influence."

11. This point has generated some misunderstandings. For instance, Cordera and Tello (1989, p. 82) think neoclassical theorists claim that "the free interplay of market forces . . . would insure the *best and fairest* distribution of income between the various classes that participate in the production of goods and services" (our translation and emphasis). In fact, no such claim is made.

12. A long tradition in development economics—associated with the names of Rosenstein-Rodan, Hirschman, Scitovsky and others—can be interpreted as dealing with these issues. See Stiglitz (1988) for a modern rendition of the arguments and Bardhan (1988) for a particularly illuminating discussion of alternative approaches to development economics. We note, as Bardhan does, that "the differences between the more sophisticated versions of alternative approaches, even though substantial, are narrower than is generally perceived" (Bardhan 1988, p. 40).

13. From a welfare-theoretic point of view, of course, the presence of market failures is a necessary but not sufficient condition to justify government intervention. For the latter, it is necessary to show that, given the government's information and administrative capacity, such inter-

power to the government to intervene in the economy had, aside from the political considerations mentioned above, a separate origin.

As many historians have pointed out, not all revolutionaries were in favor of this role for the government. A subset of them argued that Mexico's growth should be based on the development of markets and free enterprise. Hence, the Constitution of 1917 embodies these two visions. From this difficult cohabitation inconsistent laws and policies have emerged on more than a few occasions. For our purposes, however, the key point is this: given Pareto suboptimal equilibriums and skewed distributions of productive assets, the issue is not whether the government will intervene, but with what policies. Risking oversimplification, we distinguish two types of interventions. On the one hand are those that try to alleviate market failures or improve the distribution of income by means that do not interfere with price signals but pay attention to the resulting incentive structure.[14] On the other are those—which we label *populist*—that implicitly or explicitly disregard resource constraints, the informational content of prices, and the reaction of agents to the incentive structure and attempt to replace markets by direct government allocations.

The combination of three conditions creates the background for populist policies in Mexico: (1) an activist government born out of a revolution with a mandate to intervene and a desire to do so to pursue its political goals; (2) market failures and distributional considerations that create a need for government intervention; and (3) the appeal associated with interventions that suppress markets or try to allocate by other means. Thus, the potential for populist interventions is a phenomenon rooted in the political institutions dominant in Mexico since 1917.

It should be clear from this description that populist interventions should not always be seen as the response of "the constrained referee of social conflict" to inconsistent demands by various social groups. This view ignores the second objective of government's intervention in the economy: that is, to remain in political control. Even when distributional conflict is not at center stage, governments may engage in populist policies if they believe that by doing so they can diminish the political power of certain groups. In contrast to what Dornbusch and Edwards (1989) and Sachs (1989) argue is the case for Latin America, in Mexico the primary cause for populist policies has not always been social pressures arising from inequality.

Of course, interventions by governments never take a pure form: in almost every regime there is a mix of market-oriented and populist policies. This creates a need to make a distinction between populist policies and populist

---

vention will increase welfare. Put differently, it is necessary to show that those responsible for designing and implementing government policy have the ability (and incentives) to make credible and consistent (social) welfare improving interventions.

14. By incentive structure we mean here the set of current and expected future relative prices (and possibly quantity constraints) that agents, given the information at their disposal, use to make their economic decisions.

episodes. We argue that populist economic episodes occur when populist policies come to the fore and, more particularly, when the mix of macroeconomic policies tilts strongly in the populist direction. Thus, all regimes have "populist features" in the sense that to some extent they all engage in populist policies. A combination of political circumstances, external shocks, and individual personalities determines when populist policies cease to be *pecata minutia* and instead dominate the bulk of macroeconomic policies taken by the government, that is, when populist episodes occur. Of these three, political circumstances occupy a central role: the government might find it expedient to resort to populist policies to accommodate the demands of certain groups, to increase its legitimacy, to solve a political crisis, or to bypass or postpone structural reforms. Alternatively, the government may implement a particular populist policy in an attempt to reassert political control. External conditions also matter, however, as access to external borrowing, and/or terms of trade shocks, and/or swings in the rate of growth of the world economy have important domestic repercussions. An elastic supply of foreign credit is a precondition for a large buildup of debt. A government tempted to populist actions might find them irresistible in the event of a positive terms of trade shock. Conversely, a negative terms of trade shock coupled, say, with an inelastic supply of foreign credit might preclude a government from engaging in populist policies, even if it was predisposed to do so. The government in Mexico plays the leading role in the economy; it does not control external events. Finally, personalities also matter, particularly in the short run, given the strong concentration of political power in the executive branch.

Thus, given the potential for populist policies that is always present, populist episodes result from the interaction of a complex set of events. Because these policies can yield short-run benefits, there is always a temptation to engage in them. Because they do favor certain groups (although not necessarily, nor always, the poor), they create political constituencies that support and encourage them. Because their implementation may at times be easier or politically more viable (e.g., raising revenues through the inflation tax or foreign borrowing rather than through a tax reform), governments may opt for them. And because there might be a belief that they can alter the distribution of power in the society, governments may at times feel that they have no other option than to resort to them.

In Mexico's postrevolutionary history there have been two main populist episodes. The first occurred during the Cárdenas administration (1934–40), a period during which (*i*) land redistribution was extensive, (*ii*) the corporatist nature of the political system was consolidated, (*iii*) large numbers of public enterprises were formed, and (*iv*) oil resources were nationalized. The second populist episode occurred during the presidencies of Echeverría and López Portillo. These two episodes are very different, and it is probably misleading to use the same adjective to refer to both. In any case, we emphasize that, in this paper, we deal only with the second one. Before we turn there, however, one additional remark is necessary.

While governments in Mexico have great leeway to intervene in the economy, they are all bound to follow, at least in principle, the ideology of the Mexican Revolution. This ideology emphasizes, among other things, the notions of economic nationalism and a mixed economy (Cordoba 1973). But these notions are sufficiently vague to allow for various interpretations, giving governments enough space to stress this or that particular interpretation of the mixed economy, or of economic nationalism, as the conditions of the time require. Nevertheless, specific economic policies cannot be implemented without recourse to some economic justification. When governments follow orthodox macroeconomic policies, their rhetoric emphasizes fiscal prudence. In these circumstances governments borrow freely, but selectively, from orthodox economic theory. Conversely, when populist policies are implemented, the rhetoric emphasizes nonorthodox approaches. Governments in Mexico are not committed to (nor do they strictly follow) a narrowly defined economic philosophy. In our view, it is misleading to identify populist economic policies with a specific school of economic thought, whether Marxist, structuralist, or otherwise. Rather, these ideas are pragmatically invoked when it is necessary to justify a particular action taken by the government in pursuit of its political interests. To the extent that structuralist ideas do not emphasize the relationship between budget deficits and inflation, for instance, these ideas are welcomed, nay solicited, by the government to justify its use of deficit finance. (Whether budget deficits do or do not cause inflation is a separate matter.) And while Marxist and/or structuralist ideas can be invoked and incorporated into the populist rhetoric, they are rarely applied in a pure form. It is futile to look for consistency between, say, structuralism and the economic policy of a particular regime. This implies, in turn, that the analysis of populist economic policies is not synonymous with the analysis of a particular school of thought. Economists might place great emphasis on purity of thought, consistency, and rigor. Mexican governments have been historically less inclined to do so and have consumed theories and ideas from a wider menu.

8.3 A Glimpse at Stabilizing Development

Stabilizing development—the period running from the mid-1950s to 1970—was characterized by very low inflation and nominal exchange rate stability. After an initial interlude of mildly falling real wages in the mid-1950s, the next decade experienced the opposite phenomenon: real urban (rural) wages rose, on average, 6.6% (6.7%).[15] In addition, real per capita

---

15. Data on real wages in Mexico should be interpreted with caution, as different sources give different results; see Gregory (1986) for further discussion.

growth was positive and steady. Such a simultaneous occurrence of events had never been experienced before, nor has it been observed since.

The core element of macroeconomic policy was the control of inflation, a sine qua non for exchange rate stability in an economy with full capital mobility. Low inflation was basically produced by tight control of public finances; small budget deficits were financed with moderate growth of external borrowing (cf. tables 8.1 and 8.2). Small budget deficits, in turn, were the outcome of tight fiscal expenditures, not high taxes.[16] Tax policy was instead used to promote private investment and grant subsidies to selected sectors and commodities (energy, food, transportation) via the pricing policies of public enterprises. Low inflation and low inflationary expectations along with credible exchange rate policies induced asset holders to invest in domestic assets, both physical and financial. A savings rate growing jointly with positive domestic real interest rates increased substantially the degree of financial intermediation during the period.[17] The same was true of private investment in real capital. Capital flight—a phenomenon that would plague the economy in later years—was mostly absent. In addition, the international environment was also conducive to growth.

The orthodox management of aggregate public finances, the exchange rate, and interest rates contrasts with the nonorthodox management of many other aspects of economic policy. First, protective trade policies associated with import substitution industrialization resulted in a strong "domestic bias" of the trade regime. Industry grew behind a combination of import permits, quotas, and tariffs. The trade regime did increase the share of industry in GDP, but also induced tariff-jumping direct foreign investment and inefficiencies in industries where the domestic market was insufficient to exploit economies of scale. It also created opportunities for rent-seeking activities, and it was a major factor (together with tax and credit regulations) in the creation of oligopolistic industrial structures; the resulting increases in price-cost margins probably had a regressive effect on income distribution.

Second, agricultural growth slowed considerably as the extensive margin was reached and the easy irrigation projects completed (Yates 1981). This, together with price controls on key agricultural goods, food, housing and transport subsidies for the urban workers, and protective tariffs on industrial products, altered the terms of trade in favor of the urban-industrial areas.[18] Growth had, in the language of Lipton (1977), a strong "urban-bias." Third, the pricing policies of public enterprises in key areas of oil, electricity, trans-

16. Hansen (1974, p. 114) argues that, when account is taken of all sources of government revenue (including social security taxes), Mexico's tax effort in 1965 ranked among the lowest of Latin American countries, with a total tax coefficient of 10.4%, compared to Brazil's 30.4%, Chile's 25.8%, and Argentina's 18.9%.

17. The ratio M3/GDP increased from 0.28 in 1960 to 0.51 in 1970.

18. For example, the real price of corn and wheat fell by 6.4% and 22.8% between 1960 and 1970; see Secretaria de Agricultura y Recursos Hidralicos (1983).

Table 8.1   Basic Macroeconomic Indicators

Year	GDP Growth Rate[a] (%)	Per Capita Growth Rate[a] (%)	Inflation Rates		Total Foreign Debt[b]	Real Wage Indices[c]		
			WPI for Mexico City (%)	CPI for Nation (%)		Rural[d]	Urban[d]	Minimum
1955	8.5	5.2	13.4	...	...	37.8	39.5	...
1956	6.8	3.6	5.1	...	...	37.0	39.0	...
1957	7.6	4.3	3.9	...	...	...	...	...
1958	5.3	2.0	4.7	...	...	36.4	37.7	...
1959	3.0	−.2	.9	...	...	...	...	...
1960	8.1	4.7	4.9	...	...	43.8	42.8	...
1961	4.9	1.6	1.3	...	...	...	...	...
1962	4.7	1.4	1.7	...	...	52.9	52.6	...
1963	8.0	4.6	.4	...	...	...	...	...
1964	11.7	8.2	4.5	...	...	62.6	54.9	...
1965	6.5	3.1	1.6	...	...	...	...	...
1966	6.9	3.5	1.5	...	...	67.7	70.3	...
1967	6.3	2.9	2.7	...	...	...	...	...
1968	8.1	4.7	2.2	...	...	75.4	77.5	...
1969	6.3	2.9	2.5	...	...	...	...	...
1970	6.9	3.5	6.0	5.2	8.63	79.1	81.1	83.6
1971	4.2	.8	3.7	5.3	9.22	...	...	79.2
1972	8.5	5.0	2.6	5.0	10.08	81.6	83.6	89.8
1973	8.4	4.9	16.0	12.0	12.74	...[e]	...	84.3
1974	6.1	2.8	22.4	23.8	16.68	90.2[f]	92.5	92.3

1975	5.6	2.4	10.4	15.2	22.71	95.1[g]	98.9	93.7
1976	4.2	1.2	22.4	15.8	29.45	99.8	102.5	104.2
1977	3.4	.5	41.2	28.9	32.34	100.0	100.0	103.5
1978	8.2	5.2	15.7	17.5	36.40	103.5	99.2	100.0
1979	9.2	6.1	18.3	18.2	41.12	103.1	92.3	97.9
1980	8.3	5.4	24.4	26.3	49.03	101.7	95.1	91.0
1981	8.8	6.3	24.5	28.0	74.35	100.1[h]	87.3	92.5
1982	-.6	-2.9	56.1	58.9	92.41	89.7[i]	78.2	88.6
1983	-4.2	-6.3	107.3	101.9	93.78			67.9
1984	3.6	1.4	70.3	65.5	96.65	...	...	63.3
1985	2.5	.4	53.6	57.7	96.57	...	...	62.5
1986	-3.7	-5.9	88.4	86.2	100.99	...	...	57.2
1987	1.5	-.6	135.6	131.8	107.47	...	...	53.6
1988	1.1	-.8	103.3	114.2	100.38	...	...	47.1

Sources: GDP and inflation rates: Indicatores Economicos, Banco de Mexico; for rural and urban real wage indices, 1955–83, Gregory (1986); for minimum real wage index, 1970–88; CIDE, Economia Mexicana; for total foreign debt: Macroasesoria, Inc.

[a] In 1970 prices; 1980–88 in 1980 prices.

[b] In billions of U.S. dollars.

[c] 1978 = 100.

[d] 1954–75 data are two-year averages.

[e] In the period between 17 September and 31 December 1973, the index for rural and urban minimum wages is 86.2 and 88.3, respectively. In the period between 1 January and 7 October 1974, the index for rural and urban minimum wages is 87.3 and 89.4, respectively.

[f] Effective 8 October 1974 to 31 December 1975.

[g] In the period between 1 October and 31 December 1976, the index for rural and urban minimum wages is 104.5 and 107.3, respectively.

[h] In the period between 1 November and 31 December 1982, the index for rural and urban minimum wages is 92.8 and 80.9, respectively.

[i] In the period between June 1st and December 31st, 1983, the index for rural and urban minimum wages is 77.0 and 67.2, respectively.

Table 8.2   Indicators for Public Finance (% of GDP): Consolidated Public Sector

Year	Revenues		Expenditures				Financial[b] Deficit
	Total	Oil	Total	Current[a]	Capital	Interest	
1965	18.0	. . .	18.8	. . .	. . .	. . .	.9
1966	17.3	. . .	18.4	. . .	. . .	. . .	1.2
1967	17.5	. . .	19.7	. . .	. . .	. . .	2.4
1968	17.7	. . .	19.6	. . .	. . .	. . .	2.2
1969	18.1	. . .	20.0	. . .	. . .	. . .	2.2
1970	18.9	. . .	22.4	. . .	. . .	. . .	3.8
1971	18.4	3.0	20.5	14.6	4.3	1.6	2.5
1972	18.7	2.8	22.9	15.4	5.7	1.8	4.9
1973	20.2	2.6	25.8	17.0	7.0	1.8	6.9
1974	21.1	3.4	27.0	17.9	7.2	1.9	7.2
1975	23.2	3.3	31.9	21.0	8.6	2.3	10.0
1976	23.8	3.3	32.0	20.7	8.0	3.3	9.9
1977	24.6	3.8	30.0	19.3	7.6	3.1	6.7
1978	25.9	4.5	31.4	19.5	8.7	3.2	6.7
1979	26.7	5.6	33.0	19.5	9.8	3.7	7.6
1980	26.9	7.3	33.5	19.8	9.6	4.1	7.5
1981	26.7	7.3	39.7	21.4	12.9	5.4	14.1
1982	28.9	9.9	44.5	25.1	10.2	9.2	16.9
1983	32.9	14.2	41.0	20.7	7.5	12.8	8.6
1984	32.2	13.0	38.8	20.7	6.7	11.4	8.5
1985	31.2	11.5	39.2	21.1	6.1	12.0	9.6
1986	30.3	9.0	44.8	21.5	6.0	17.3	16.0
1987	30.6	9.8	45.0	19.5	5.6	19.9	16.1
1988	29.8	7.5	39.0	17.9	4.4	16.7	12.3

Sources: Data for 1977–88; Indicadores Economicos, Banco de Mexico; data for 1965–76; Direccion General de Planeacion Hacendaria, SHCP; Financial deficit, 1965–70: Gil Diaz and Ramos (1988).

[a]Excluding interest payments.

[b]The financial deficit includes also "financial intermediation" expenditures, so that it is not equal to the difference between total revenues and total expenditures.

portation, and food were used not only as mechanisms to promote private investment and turn the terms of trade against rural Mexico, but also as signaling devices for inflation control: insofar as these prices were nominally constant inflationary expectations would be reduced and the credibility of the exchange rate enhanced. Nevertheless, the resulting structure of relative prices induced distortions in the use of intermediate inputs and indirectly channeled subsidies to high income groups.[19] Fourth, price controls were also

19. Levy (1988) develops a model to trace through the effects of public-sector prices on the distribution of income, showing that generalized price subsidies are a very expensive way of helping the poor, as these subsidies spill over into higher income groups that consume a significant share of the subsidized products.

applied to important commodities produced by the private sector. Thus, the nominal prices of wheat, corn, tortillas, bread, and sugar, as well as of urban transport, electricity, and other services were left unchanged throughout the sixties. This aimed at reinforcing the nominal stability of prices, but produced a rigid structure of relative prices and, at times, squeezed profit margins in some private firms.[20] Stability of nominal prices, particularly the exchange rate, were almost an end in itself. Yet a fifth characteristic is associated with public expenditures. A low tax coefficient made little room for social expenditures (see table 8.3). Serious deficiencies in the provision of health and education ensued precisely at a time when the rate of growth of population was accelerating. This phenomenon, together with a highly skewed distribution of income,[21] was an important ingredient of the political crisis that was under gestation toward the end of the 1960s.

In sum, stabilizing development brought about sustained growth, but a gamut of structural problems lurked behind the screen of price and exchange rate stability: agricultural stagnation, inward-biased industrialization, regional disparities and urban bias, and insufficient attention to income distribution and poverty. The strategy generated growth, but at increasingly higher costs. As the period came to an end, trade and exchange rate policy were turning more incompatible, real wage increases in excess of productivity growth threatened price stability, while restrictive government expenditures generated social problems. Even those responsible for economic policy during the period emphasized the fragility of the macroeconomic balance, and the difficulties of recuperating it if it was ever lost.[22] Thus, it is fair to say that, in 1970 the economy was in need of reform, although the reforms required were mostly microeconomic in nature. And while this can be said with the benefit of hindsight, a clear awareness of the difficulties inherited did not exist at that time.

20. A side effect of this policy would be the need to 'nationalize' private firms that could no longer produce profitably at the given prices. This was, for example, the case for sugar mills.

21. It is difficult to make comparisons in the pattern of income distribution overtime, as the Lorenz curves for the years for which income-expenditure surveys are available cross. After making various corrections and using alternative measures of inequality, Aspe and Beristain (1984b, p. 54) conclude that: "Whatever measure of inequality is observed and whatever indicator of relative position is used, whether income or expenditure, the main conclusion . . . is that the income distribution structure of the country remained basically unaltered between 1950 and 1977." Note that while income shares have been mostly time invariant, at any point in time the distribution is highly unequal. For 1977 we find that the poorest decile of the population earned 1.2% of all income, while the richest received 42% (Aspe and Beristain 1984b, p. 38). On the other hand, during stabilizing development: (i) the absolute income levels of the lowest deciles increased and (ii) grew faster than during any other period. Thus, while income inequality was pronounced, there were substantial improvements in the welfare levels of the poor; poverty and inequality are distinct phenomenons.

22. Ortiz Mena, finance minister during the period 1958–70, and generally recognized as the chief architect of stabilizing development, pointed out the need for policy changes in his classic article published at the end of the period (see Ortiz Mena 1970).

Table 8.3   Indicators for Public Finance (in Constant Prices)[a]

Year	Total Revenues	Growth Rate (%)	Oil[b]	Growth Rate (%)	Total Expenditures[c]	Growth Rate (%)	Current	Growth Rate (%)	Capital	Growth Rate (%)
1965	57,236				57,236					
1966	58,827	2.8			59,847	4.6				
1967	63,270	7.6			66,523	11.2				
1968	69,158	9.3			72,284	8.7				
1969	75,236	8.8			78,148	.1				
1970	83,967	11.6			90,631	16.0				
1971	85,093	1.3	13,789		87,314	-3.7	67,463		19,850	
1972	93,920	10.4	14,005	1.6	105,867	21.2	77,506	14.9	28,362	42.9
1973	109,759	16.9	14,264	1.8	130,393	23.2	92,337	19.1	38,056	34.2
1974	121,674	10.9	19,403	36.0	144,773	11.0	103,195	11.8	41,578	9.3
1975	141,243	16.1	20,134	3.8	180,901	25.0	128,187	24.4	52,715	26.8
1976	151,086	7.0	21,111	4.9	182,435	.8	131,883	2.9	50,553	-4.1
1977	161,926	7.2	24,724	17.1	177,225	-2.9	127,138	-3.6	49,874	-1.3
1978	184,657	14.0	32,134	30.0	201,423	13.7	138,935	9.3	61,879	24.1
1979	207,575	12.4	43,577	35.6	229,854	14.1	151,692	9.2	75,932	22.7
1980	236,835	14.1	64,384	47.7	263,445	14.6	174,115	14.8	84,487	11.3
1981	252,968	6.8	69,392	7.8	329,119	24.9	202,711	16.4	122,124	44.5
1982	272,178	7.6	92,936	33.9	341,249	3.7	236,558	16.7	95,609	-21.7
1983	293,771	7.9	127,055	36.7	256,029	25.0	184,531	-22.0	66,824	-30.1
1984	292,864	-.3	118,687	-6.6	373,035	45.7	183,521	-.5	61,284	-8.3
1985	295,932	1.0	109,343	-7.9	263,231	-29.1	199,990	9.0	57,384	6.4
1986	279,066	-5.7	82,669	-24.4	260,157	-1.2	197,689	-1.2	55,319	-3.6
1987	277,729	-.5	89,270	8.0	228,822	-12.0	176,696	-10.6	50,419	-8.9
1988	270,738	-2.5	68,400	-23.4	202,748	-11.4	162,764	-7.9	39,522	-21.6

Sources: Data for 1977–88: Indicadores Economicos, Banco de Mexico; Data for 1965–76: Direccion de Estadisticas Hacendarias, SHCP.

[a]Current price data is deflated by the GDP implicit price index (1970 = 100).

[b]Does not include tax revenue from PEMEX.

[c]Does not include interest payments.

8.4 Populist Economic Episodes

8.4.1 The Echeverría Regime

Change was the distinctive feature of Echeverría's presidency. Foreign policy took a more active role and tilted in favor of Third World interests (Green 1977). The political management of the country changed: political reforms, which continue to this day, were initiated (Middlebrook 1986). Political style and rhetoric were different.[23] Economic policy also changed. The cautious approach to macroeconomic management was abandoned as the government began to use public expenditures and other instruments more aggressively. Why did economic policy change paths? What objectives were being pursued? What was accomplished by the change?

To understand Echeverría's motives we must begin by recalling the political crisis that characterized Mexico in 1970 and its connection to the 1968 student-led protests and subsequent repression. Two factors were dominant: (1) the erosion of the government's political legitimacy and (2) the possibility of a guerrilla movement developing at a time when leftist ideology was significantly more important in Latin America than it is today. These two factors placed the need for political action at the top of the agenda; economic problems took a secondary role. Echeverría signaled throughout his election campaign his wish for a negotiated solution to the political crisis; his desire for eschewing repression stemming, at least in part, from a desire to avoid increasing the role played by the military.

A politically moderate government like the Mexican one sought a negotiated solution to the political crisis. This was difficult since a new element was present: to incorporate the left into the political system real concessions had to be made, yet at the same time it was important that the actions taken by the government not give the impression that the country would turn socialist, given fears of alienating the right. These factors reduced the government's space for finding a solution. Yet, barring some members of the private sector, a consensus appeared that the political crisis should be tackled by more "state activism." This "return to the state" was strongly advocated by the leftist-leaning intellectuals whom Echeverría had recruited from the national university (UNAM), and other places, into his circle of advisers. These intellectuals had long criticized the government for "betraying" its popular and revolutionary origins and surrendering to capitalism for the sake of rapid growth. More state activism, however, was also advocated by other economists not identified with leftist ideologies.[24] These economists coincided with those on the

23. The rhetoric was different not only in its emphasis, but also in its amount: observers hesitated between labeling the president a demagogue or a preacher (Cosio Villegas 1973).
24. For example, D. Ibarra, L. Solis, V. Urquidi, and even Ortiz Mena recommended an increase in public expenditures in order to most effectively meet the various social needs. And while they also advocated the simultaneous need for increasing government revenues, the general message was for more state intervention (see Ibarra et al. 1972). One should also recall that the

left in signaling unequal income distribution, or at least widespread poverty, as a central problem.

In short, at the beginning of the Echeverría regime, informed opinion favored stronger use of the government's capacity to intervene in the economy to reduce poverty, increase public investment in areas where private investment was not forthcoming, and reduce the importance of foreign firms. Among the many promises that Echeverría made in his inaugural speech two stood out: political reform and changes in economic policy to reduce poverty. The announcement of political reform was accompanied by a clear message: the government would lean in the direction of those who advocated a more democratic and open system; the "apertura democratica" signaled substantial change. The same was not true of economic policy; while reducing poverty and income inequality were announced as objectives, the *means* by which this would be attained were not clearly specified. Thus it was announced that low inflation and nominal exchange rate stability remained as targets along with real wage increases. The mixed economy and the "nationalist" businessman were praised, but stern criticisms were made of the business community. And while affirming that "free enterprise can only render fruit if the government has sufficient resources to coordinate the fulfillment of the great national objectives," Echeverría's inaugural address made no references to taxes.

The promise of reduced income inequality, therefore, was and was not an important goal of the unspecified changes in economic policy. It was important to the extent that it was obviously desired. It was unimportant to the extent that there was a simultaneous promise that everything, or almost everything, would remain the same. The abundance of promises suggests that the government intended to neither commit itself to a particular policy, nor waive its right to any policy. Today, with the benefit of hindsight, what Echeverría had in mind appears clear: that economic policy should henceforth obey the needs of the government, not those of the private sector. Put differently, Echeverría had a new attitude to economic policy, not a new solution to the problems of policy. So we find here tinges of populism or, if you will, evidence of a "voluntaristic" attitude toward the economy: willing change without providing solid means for it. In any event, after more than a decade of stabilizing development, the government's leading role in the economy took a new turn in 1971: shared development had arrived.

The world economy also changed in important ways in the early 1970s. Two such changes were important for Mexico. One, higher world inflation contributed, through import prices, to increase domestic inflationary pressures. Two, the 1973 oil shock enlarged substantially the country's access to international finance, as the world capital markets sought outlets for the large

---

substantial economic literature criticizing import substitution industrialization appeared later on (e.g., the influential OECD study by Little, Scitovsky, and Scott 1975). The benefit of hindsight makes many things obvious now, not then.

petrodollar deposits. Private capital flows became a more important source of external savings.[25]

Shared development inherited a stable macroeconomic environment with unstable microeconomic foundations. Microeconomic reforms, however, were not on the agenda. Although 1971 experienced a deceleration in growth, it was more the result of the standard slowdown in spending associated with a change in administration than of tight fiscal policy aimed at holding back inflation and reducing a growing trade deficit. The stated aims of policymakers were to preserve price stability and the fixed exchange rate, while at the same time augmenting social spending and accelerating growth to increase employment.[26] The government took the lead in promoting such growth, and in 1972 substantially increased both public expenditures and domestic credit: the former increased by 21.2% in real terms in that year, the latter by 7.9%. Yet the key fact about the expansion of government spending was that it occurred in the absence of a significant tax reform.[27] While at the beginning of the administration the sales tax rate was increased by 1%, this was insufficient to cover the added spending. (Later on, at the end of 1972, serious consideration was given to a fiscal reform that would increase income taxes. But the private sector threatened with large capital flight. This, in turn, could threaten the constancy of the nominal exchange rate, something that Echeverría thought he had to defend as a sign of continuing stability and continuity with stabilizing development.) In addition, public enterprise prices—which in Mexico must be thought of as an integral part of fiscal policy—were not changed until 1973, and only increased in nominal terms. And while real public enterprise prices lagged behind, an ambitious program of expansion in public enterprises was begun.[28] The deterioration in public finances followed soon (see table 8.2).

Strong aggregate demand expansion continued in 1973 and 1974, triggered again by deficit spending. With little slack after strong growth in 1972, part of this expansion began to be reflected in prices: the inflation rate increased from 5% in 1972 to 12% in 1973 and to 23.8% in 1974, significantly in excess of world inflation.[29] Two effects followed immediately. One, as figure 8.1

25. As opposed to the past, however, these flows took the form of commercial bank lending rather than bonds or equity investments. Thus, the distribution of risk changed.

26. An influential report that appeared at that time (Grupo de Estudio del Problema del Empleo [GEPE], n.d.) argued the existence of a substantial problem of unemployment and underemployment in the country, of the order of 40% of the labor force. See Levy (1979) for a discussion of the employment figures in Mexico and Gregory (1986) for a critique of the GEPE figures and an alternative view of the functioning of the labor market.

27. Tax policy was an issue of contention between Echeverría and the private sector from the very beginning. In December of 1970 Echeverría sent a small tax reform to Congress (a 1% increase in the sales tax rate). The then leader of COPARMEX, an association of private-sector businessmen, called on the president to say that this was not the way policy was done, and that tax matters had to be negotiated directly with the private sector.

28. For example, between 1970 and 1972 the real price index for transportation fell by 3%, while that of gasoline and oil by 8%.

29. As measured by the United States WPI. The relevant inflation figures for that country were 3.1%, 9.1%, and 15.3% for 1972, 1973, and 1974, respectively.

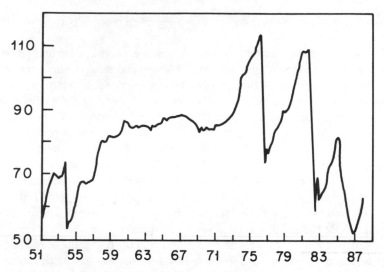

Fig. 8.1   Real exchange rate index (1980 = 100)
Source: Dornbusch (1988).

shows, the real exchange rate started to appreciate as the policy of fixing the nominal exchange rate was maintained. Two, as inflation rates exceeded domestic nominal interest rates, the growth of financial intermediation observed during the 1960s began to reverse itself.[30]

The expansion of aggregate demand also had an impact on the current account. This deficit increased from 0.2% of GDP in 1971 to 3.7% of GDP in 1974 due to the excess of domestic expenditure over income and the progressive overvaluation of the exchange rate that began to erode the service component of the current account. These two elements could be tied directly to the government's fiscal stance. A third element, in addition, reflected the long-term structural stagnation of agriculture, which began to exert its toll as significant imports of foodstuffs and grains appeared in 1971. The changed world environment, however, modified the nature of foreign borrowing obtained to cover the current account deficits. Now resources came mostly from private banks rather than multilateral institutions, with shorter maturities and variable interest rates.

As of 1972 the government exercised its leading role with a set of macroeconomic policies that departed from those of the past 15 years. As macroeconomic policies changed, so did the government's rhetoric, which had to respond to a private sector witnessing negative domestic real interest rates and a progressive overvaluation of the exchange rate. The notions of fiscal prudence

---

30. The ratio M3/GNP reached a peak of 0.53 in 1972 and then steadily declined to 0.46 by 1976. Real interest rates for the last four years of the Echeverría *sexenio* were: −5.5, −12.3, −2.0 and −33.4; see Solis (1981).

Table 8.4   **Allocation of Public Social Spending**

| | % of Public Expenditure | | % of Public Investment | | | |
Dates and Administration	Education	Health	Social Welfare	Education	Health	Agricultural Development
1934–40, Lazaro Cárdenas	12.5	2.9	9.6	1.0	1.2	17.6
1940–46, M. Avila Camacho	9.9	3.6	11.1	.2	2.4	17.3
1946–52, Miguel Aleman	7.8	3.2	13.5	3.0	3.1	19.8
1952–58, A. Ruiz Cortines	8.7	3.1	14.6	2.6	1.5	13.6
1958–64, A. Lopez Mateos	11.4	3.6	24.1	2.7	7.3	9.9
1964–70, G. Diaz Ordaz	13.2	3.1	24.7	4.8	4.9	11.0
1970–76, L. Echeverría	19.4	4.5	22.2	6.6	4.3	17.3
1976–82, J. Lopez Portillo	7.7	1.1	9.5	2.6	3.1	18.5

Source: Aspe and Beristain (1984a, p. 26).

and financial orthodoxy no longer served, so official rhetoric began to rely more on "nonorthodox economics."[31]

On the other hand, other aspects of economic policy remained much the same as during the stabilizing development. Three merit special attention. One, trade policy: the anti-export bias of the trade regime was maintained despite the fact that fiscal incentives for exports were introduced. No attempt was made to liberalize imports. In fact, as the current account deteriorated, the government responded with more stringent import controls, further strengthening the anti-export bias of the trade regime. Two, regional policy: to the credit of the administration, an effort was made to channel more resources to the rural areas (see table 8.4). But while the share of agriculture in total public investment increased from 13.4% in 1970 to 17% in 1974, policies that increased the attractiveness of urban areas continued. Services like water and transportation in Mexico City continued to be highly subsidized, transferring resources from the rest of the country into the relatively richer capital city. In addition, the administration launched an ambitious housing program for urban workers (INFONAVIT). All in all, the urban bias of the prior regime continued (Moore 1984). Three, the exchange rate: although there were strong disagreements in this regard, it was finally decided that the policy of keeping a fixed nominal rate would continue, despite expansive fiscal policy and its effects on the trade deficit. It is important to point out that the Central Bank supported the fixed exchange rate policy, though perhaps for different reasons than those held by the government.

Negative domestic real interest rates, progressive overvaluation of the real

31. At the beginning of 1973 the minister of finance (Margain) resigned as a result of differences of opinion with regards to economic policy.

exchange rate, and growing foreign indebtedness were clear signs of the un-sustainability of the policy stance. As expectations of an eventual change in policy amplified, capital flight began. And although this could be construed as a political response to the changed rhetoric, it was perhaps more simply the natural response of asset holders who realized that the option value of liquid capital abroad, corrected by the expected devaluation, would exceed the profitability of new investments in domestic physical capital or in peso-denominated deposits. In consequence, despite the fact that the economy was growing relatively fast and bottlenecks appeared, and that fiscal incentives for private investment were granted,[32] the latter did not respond as expected. The incentive structure had changed, and even if the government was unwilling to see its deleterious effects, the same was not true of other agents.

At the same time, public investment increased (cf. tables 8.5 and 8.6) and, along with it, the degree of public intervention in the economy: while a total of 83 major public enterprises were created between 1952 and 1970, the equivalent number for the period 1971–76 was 108 (Aspe and Beristain 1984a).[33] The government also expanded significantly the areas in which it operated. And while arguments could easily be found to justify these actions,[34] we interpret them as the pragmatic response of the government in pursuit of its political interests rather than as a conscious decision to take over the role of the private sector as the main producer of goods and services (or to take the "commanding heights" of the economy). Such a short-term pragmatic response, nevertheless, had important implications: the larger role of the government as producer and investor imposed further burdens on its already over-stretched finances and administrative capacity.

To put it differently, we argue that by 1973–74 events had acquired a dynamic of their own. Rather than following a tightly preconceived plan, the government pursued its own objectives through what we might label as "the path of least resistance": a mix of foreign borrowing and inflationary finance. Once this process began, however, it created a vicious circle. Willy-nilly, larger budget deficits and increasing devaluation expectations slowed private investment.[35] At the same time, the political objectives of the government

32. Tello (1979, p. 205) quotes an ex-president of COPARMEX (an association of business employers) as follows: "One can assert that few regimes as this one [Echeverría's] have been more concerned with promoting private initiatives. In just three years, more decrees, laws and regulations promoting entrepreneurial activity have been passed than during the whole of the prior *sexenio*" (our translation). In addition, Sigmund (1984) argues that the law regulating direct foreign investment, introduced in May 1973, requiring a majority of Mexican participation in all new foreign ventures enhanced the strategic position of Mexican vis-à-vis foreign investors.

33. Many of these enterprises, however, were quite small, and included a large number of funds and special trusts with little economic impact.

34. Flores de la Pena, who was minister of national patrimony during the Echeverría regime, argues that the Mexico public investment is preferable to private (1976, pp. 35, 41, and 51).

35. See Lizondo (1983) on the behavior of future prices for the Mexican peso during that time. In terms of the slowing of private investment, this was particularly the case after 1974; with the exception of that year, the rates of growth of private investment were lower than those of public investment for the period under study (see table 8.5).

Table 8.5   Total Investment (in Constant Prices)[a]

Year	Total	Growth Rate (%)	Public	Growth Rate (%)	Private	Growth Rate (%)
1960	38,606.0		. . .		. . .	
1961	38,965.9	0.9	. . .		. . .	
1962	39,840.5	2.2	. . .		. . .	
1963	45,085.5	13.2	. . .		. . .	
1964	54,857.9	21.7	. . .		. . .	
1965	57,047.3	4.0	. . .		. . .	
1966	62,616.5	9.8	. . .		. . .	
1967	69,861.5	11.6	. . .		. . .	
1968	76,731.5	9.8	. . .		. . .	
1969	82,016.9	6.9	. . .		. . .	
1970	88,660.6	8.1	29,249.9		59,410.7	
1971	87,142.2	−1.7	22,451.2	−23.2	64,691.0	8.9
1972	97,805.8	12.2	31,484.4	40.2	66,321.4	2.5
1973	112,227.7	14.7	43,938.2	39.6	68,289.5	3.0
1974	121,095.8	7.9	45,009.6	2.4	76,086.2	11.4
1975	132,316.1	9.3	54,732.9	21.6	77,583.2	2.0
1976	132,909.6	0.4	50,597.2	−7.6	82,312.4	6.1
1977	123,986.5	−6.7	47,212.4	−6.7	76,774.1	−6.7
1978	142,799.3	15.2	62,122.2	31.6	80,677.1	5.1
1979	171,714.2	20.2	72,753.3	17.1	98,960.9	22.7
1980	197,364.5	14.9	84,870.3	16.7	112,494.2	13.7
1981	228,975.0	16.0	103,930.7	22.4	125,044.3	11.1
1982	190,526.0	−16.8	84,289.7	−18.9	106,236.3	−15.1
1983	136,644.0	−28.2	53,928.4	−36.0	82,715.6	−22.1
1984	145,427.0	6.4	56,142.4	4.1	89,284.6	7.9
1985	156,846.0	7.8	56,641.2	.8	100,204.8	12.2
1986	138,341.0	−11.8	48,576.4	−14.2	89,864.6	−11.6
1987	137,476.0	−.6	43,830.5	−9.8	93,645.5	4.3

Sources: SPP, National Accounts.
[a]In millions of 1970 pesos.

called for a larger role in the economy. But as the government stepped up
public investment, it would further deteriorate its financial position, closing
the circle: private investors would see growing fiscal deficits together with
larger foreign borrowing as unambiguous signals of the unsustainability of the
macro configuration, and would wait for events to change with their capital
safely tucked away abroad.

The historically high inflation rates of 1973–74 began to permeate economic life. Investors hedged in foreign assets and real estate; the length of
contracts shortened: as of 1973 minimum wages were to be set annually, as
opposed to the biannual convention. Trust in the currency, which can be
thought of as a public good, eroded. The public tried to avoid the inflation tax
as a process of currency substitution increased the share of dollar-
denominated deposits in the total obligations of the financial system from 17%

Table 8.6   Total Investment (% of GDP)

Year	Total	Public	Private	Year	Total	Public	Private
1955	15.5	...	...	1972	19.0	6.1	12.9
1956	17.7	...	...	1973	19.3	7.5	11.8
1957	17.9	...	...	1974	19.9	7.5	12.3
1958	15.7	...	...	1975	21.4	5.0	12.4
1959	15.2	...	...	1976	21.0	8.2	12.9
1960	16.0	...	...	1977	19.6	7.8	11.8
1961	14.8	...	...	1978	21.1	9.5	11.6
1962	14.7	...	...	1979	23.4	10.3	13.2
1963	15.7	...	...	1980	24.8	10.7	14.1
1964	16.2	...	...	1981	26.4	12.1	14.3
1965	16.6	4.9	11.7	1982	23.0	10.2	12.8
1966	16.9	5.2	11.7	1983	17.5	6.6	11.0
1967	18.2	6.5	11.7	1984	17.9	6.6	11.3
1968	18.2	6.5	11.8	1985	19.1	6.5	12.5
1969	18.3	6.6	11.7	1986	19.4	6.5	12.9
1970	20.0	6.6	13.4	1987	18.9	5.5	13.4
1971	18.0	4.6	13.3				

Sources: Data for 1965–69: Economia Mexicana en Cifras, NAFINSA (1986). Data for 1970–87: Cuentas Nacionales, SPP.

in 1970 to 40% in 1976 (Solis 1981). In addition to the figures on the current account, these were all clear signs of the need for stabilization. And, indeed, such a program was announced: as of 1975 monetary policy became more restrictive and a tighter fiscal stance was signaled.[36] In fact, and despite the absence of a fiscal reform, fiscal revenues began growing quite rapidly due to improvements in the tax collection system (see table 8.2). But this increase arrived too late; public expenditures by then were growing even faster.

The stabilization program did not go far. Efforts at inflation control were pursued through, once again, the "path of least resistance": the exchange rate was kept nominally fixed and controls on imports increased, while price controls were tightened on key commodities provided by public enterprises: the resulting implicit subsidies further fed the fiscal deficit. In addition, government spending was not cut, although its rate of growth did slow somewhat (see table 8.3): it was argued that inflation would be cut by "increasing supply" with more public investment in key bottleneck areas, without recognition of gestation lags, or of the fact that the immediate effect of investment is to increase demand. The inflation rate fell slightly in 1975, but rose again in 1976. As tables 8.2 and 8.7 show, neither the budget nor the current account deficit showed any improvement.

36. The private sector's beliefs about the viability of Echeverría's economic program were also influenced by announcements made in 1975 of the discovery of large oil deposits in the south of Mexico. These discoveries would facilitate access to foreign borrowing, which was needed to finance the growing trade deficit. Although capital flight continued, it did not accelerate at that time, an event that gave Echeverría's program an additional breath of life.

Table 8.7   Indicators for the External Sector (% of GDP)

Year	Total Exports (goods & nfs) % GDP	Oil Exports/ Total Exports	Total Imports (goods & nfs)	Current Account Deficit	Current Account Deficit (in Millions of U.S. Dollars)
1955	16.6	. . .	17.2	1.1	−1.7
1956	15.9	. . .	17.9	2.5	183.1
1957	13.2	. . .	16.8	3.9	359.9
1958	12.0	. . .	14.9	3.3	385.5
1959	11.6	. . .	13.2	2.1	232.1
1960	9.7	. . .	11.9	3.2	419.7
1961	9.7	. . .	10.8	2.3	343.7
1962	9.8	. . .	10.2	1.6	249.6
1963	9.5	. . .	10.1	1.6	226.1
1964	8.8	. . .	10.0	2.4	444.7
1965	8.8	. . .	9.7	2.0	442.9
1966	8.6	. . .	9.2	1.8	477.8
1967	7.9	. . .	9.2	2.5	603.0
1968	8.1	. . .	9.5	2.7	775.4
1969	8.7	. . .	9.4	2.2	708.4
1970	7.7	.3	9.7	3.0	1,187.9
1971	7.6	.1	8.7	.2	928.9
1972	8.1	.1	8.8	1.9	1,005.7
1973	8.4	.0	9.5	2.4	1,528.8
1974	8.4	.4	10.6	3.7	3,226.0
1975	6.9	7.2	9.6	4.2	4,442.6
1976	8.5	7.2	9.9	3.3	3,683.3
1977	10.3	11.7	10.2	2.0	1,596.4
1978	10.5	16.5	11.0	2.6	2,693.0
1979	11.2	25.0	12.5	3.6	4,870.5
1980	10.7	47.5	13.0	5.0	10,739.7
1981	10.4	53.1	12.9	6.0	16,052.1
1982	15.3	62.7	10.3	.5	6,221.0
1983	19.0	53.6	9.4	−3.9	−5,418.4
1984	17.4	49.7	9.6	−2.6	−4,238.5
1985	15.4	47.1	10.3	−1.3	−1,236.7
1986	17.2	25.3	12.6	.4	1,672.7
1987	19.7	28.3	12.6	−3.1	−3,966.5

Sources: Indicadores Economicos, Banco de Mexico, and Cuentas Nacionales, SPP.

Various reasons explain why the efforts at stabilization in 1975 failed. At the technical level there were obvious flaws in trying to "cover up" inflation via higher subsidies and an overvalued exchange rate. But this probably misses the point. The Echeverría administration did not believe in the need for stabilization. To seriously attempt to do so would require undoing many of the policies (and rhetoric) of the previous years, since the political inertia of the administration—and the personal prestige of the president—was built on the idea of an expanding government with social and infrastructure investments. Reversing that inertia was politically difficult. Moreover, as the basis of political support for the government (or the president?) eroded within the private sector and some of the middle classes were hurt by inflation, it turned to the organized urban working class for political support. Spending cuts and a real devaluation would not enhance its standing there. The government had cornered itself into an inconsistent set of demands.

Two factors determined the final denouement of this process. One, Mexico's ample access to international finance. Two, the absence of any institutional mechanism in the Mexican political system that could counterbalance, in the short run, the power of the government. The accommodating variable to the inconsistent set of demands was foreign borrowing: the foreign debt almost doubled between 1974 and 1976. This was not borrowing to accommodate a temporary downturn in the terms of trade. Rather, it served to finance the large public-sector deficits and, increasingly, capital flight, as the government engaged in a forlorn attempt to "defend" the currency. The process came to a halt in September 1976, when the exchange rate, which had been nominally fixed since 1954, was devalued by 59%. Faced with no alternatives, with depleted reserves, with inflation of 22%, a foreign debt of $29.5 billion (U.S. dollars) and rather strained relations with the private sector,[37] the Echeverría administration terminated with an agreement with the International Monetary Fund (IMF).

8.4.2 The López Portillo Regime

The repair of strained relations between the government and the private sector was the first order of business for the new administration. The Alliance for Production was announced as the new accord under which all social groups would participate in the process of economic recovery and political healing (under the tutelage of the government, comme il faut). The rhetoric changed accordingly: fiscal prudence was (shortly) in vogue again. Thus, macroeconomic policy for 1977 was quite orthodox. As table 8.1 shows, GDP growth for that year was the lowest in decades, barely above population growth. Economic contraction was engineered by classical means: real public expenditures and the real money supply fell by 4% and 2%, respectively. The current account improved by over $2 billion, given a sharp drop in imports and a mild recovery of exports (see table 8.7).

Macro policy was carried out under the auspices of the IMF and, as a distinguishing characteristic, brought along changes in trade policy. Imports, 100% of which were subject to permits by the end of 1976, were to be liberalized.[38]

---

37. In what could perhaps ex post be seen as a precedent-setting action, the president also nationalized large tracts of land in the northern state of Sonora. The next *sexenio* would end with a similar action but on a larger scale with the nationalization of the domestic banking industry.

38. It is difficult to determine to what extent the change in trade policy at that time was perceived as permanent, so as to induce investments in the exportable sectors. Import liberalization

In addition to the intended removal of the domestic bias of the trade regime, other reforms were initiated later on. Tax policy was changed, and a value-added tax replaced the cascading system of indirect taxes; additional adjustments to corporate and personal income taxation followed, although the special tax treatment granted to agriculture and transportation continued (Gil Diaz 1984, p. 18). We can speculate: perhaps if oil had not been discovered the Mexican economy might have returned to the macro policies of stabilizing development, but with the added lesson that the structural reforms of taxation, trade, and regional policy could be postponed no longer. Oil, however, was discovered; it changed all. With the benefit of hindsight we can see the unfortunate event: a temporary terms of trade improvement in a commodity that had recently been discovered to be in abundant supply turned the government's attention away from structural reforms.[39]

López Portillo and his advisers believed that oil offered "financial self-sufficiency" (*autodeterminacion financiera*) and a historical opportunity to carry out a "structural transformation" of the economy; the task of the *sexenio* was not to shy away from such opportunity.[40] The government, in its role as leader, wanted a great leap forward and would, simultaneously, attack many problems: from the development of the capital goods industry to the elimination of poverty and malnutrition, on to the enlargement of the country's infrastructure, the promotion of tourism, and the achievement of self-sufficiency in energy and basic grains. And together with the financial resources to do so, the government felt, implicitly, that it also had the administrative capability to carry it out.

There was nothing truly novel in the government's taking such a gigantic role in the economy. As discussed, the foundations for substantial government participation in the economy were laid in the institutional arrangements of the 1930s. But there is a second factor that furthered this process connected, if we may say so, with a political culture that also sees the government *as a provider*. And oil, in this culture, removed any reasons why the government should not provide. The outburst of public spending was not the outcome of a single individual intoxicated by a terms of trade shock: it was also produced by a set of institutions that simultaneously placed great expectations on what the government should provide and few restraints on the nature of its intervention in the economy.

López Portillo and his advisers not only wanted a large public sector; they

---

proceeded by replacing quantitative restrictions and permits by tariffs, but the process was reversed later on.

39. Many observers, of course, saw this danger; e.g., Solis (1980, pp. 59–72).

40. "Either we exploit the oil right now, today, without further delays and infantile fears and use it to be truly self-sufficient and sovereign—given, of course, what our forces and intelligence allow—or soon we will be sorry for not being up to the historical moment that we are living"; from the speech given by Diaz Serrano, the general director of PEMEX, on 18 March 1978 (our translation).

also wanted an economy that would be immune to the vagaries of private investment. An objective of policy would be to build a public sector capable of producing its own inputs,[41] or at least capable of generating the foreign exchange required to buy these inputs, without running the risk of being "blackmailed" by the private sector. This rather odd idea of quasi self-sufficiency was partly motivated by fears that toward the end of the *sexenio* the government might face the same kind of economic blackmail (capital flight) experienced by Echeverría.[42] In a separate vein, others welcomed the growth of the public sector as a step in the direction of socialism (Tello 1987).

During the first two years of the oil boom, 1978 and 1979, macroeconomic policy was characterized by strong expansion of aggregate demand, triggered by government expenditures. As table 8.3 shows, the latter grew 13.7% in real terms in 1978 and 14.1% in 1979 (and continued to grow at high rates through 1981). Yet inflation, at rates of around 18% for those two years, was not accelerating. This was due partly to the opening of the economy, which allowed excess demand to spill more easily into imports. But three additional effects were also present. First, agricultural production had a much better performance, growing on average 4.5% during the López Portillo *sexenio* versus 2.6% during Echeverría's; this reduced some of the inflationary pressures that this sector had caused over the last decade.[43] Second, private investment responded quite positively to the government led expansion in aggregate demand: it grew by 5.1% in 1978 and by 22.7% in 1979. The official rhetoric was different; but, in addition, a domestic market growing at around 8% annually offered large profit opportunities at a time in which devaluation risks were perceived as minimal given the expected volume of foreign exchange earnings coming from oil. Third, a policy of "price contention" based on controls on nominal wages and public enterprise prices was followed, based partly on a (self-serving) belief of complete independence between the inflation rate, on the one hand, and aggregate demand and the budget deficit on the other.

A second oil shock in late 1979, associated with turbulence in the Middle East,[44] provided a sense of euphoria and affected the psychology of the coun-

41. A careful reading of the Plan Nacional de Desarollo Industrial reveals the objective of building a public sector less dependent on private investment for its inputs.

42. López Portillo, as any other politician, could mainly explain the events at the end of 1976—capital flight and the run on the banks—in terms of a carefully premeditated aggression on the part of organizations acting on behalf of the private sector.

43. The relationship between food supply and inflation is an old theme in Latin America. The issue is more generally related to the income redistribution that must occur when demand expands under an inelastic supply. One of the earliest analysis of this problem was by the Mexican economist Noyola, who argued that inflation was the result of a "social stalemate" where no group was willing or could be forced to absorb an income loss (see Bazdresch 1984). More recently, Cardoso (1981) shows how, under a passive money supply and markup pricing in the manufacturing sector, an inelastic supply of food can generate an inflationary process.

44. In 1979 the Shah of Iran was dethroned; the associated uncertainty produced a temporary increase in the world price of oil; see fig. 8.2.

try, and perhaps the president. (In fact, the president expressed the view that the country's economic problem was "the management of abundance.") The second oil shock further undermined fiscal discipline as well as attention to relative prices. Two factors then account for a substantial increase of the fiscal deficit. One, very large projects were undertaken by the government in infrastructure, health and nutrition, and productive public enterprises. Among these, the Mexican Food System (SAM, Sistema Alimentario Mexicano) deserves mention as a very ambitious effort to reduce poverty and improve nutrition of lower income groups, while at the same time raising incomes of the rural poor through guaranteed prices for basic grains. The second factor concerns the price contention policies for public enterprises which, as noted earlier, resulted in huge subsidies.

And while government revenues, principally from oil, grew substantially, the growth in expenditures—as table 8.2 and 8.3 show—was dramatic. Such growth further enlarged the range of sectors where the government intervened in the economy, provided ample opportunities for graft, and generated large inefficiencies given the speed with which resources were being spent. But more important from a short-term macroeconomic viewpoint, it generated unprecedented deficits in the fiscal and current accounts (tables 8.2 and 8.7). The latter account also reflected real exchange rate appreciation, as the rate of crawl of the nominal exchange rate was lower than that of prices (fig. 8.1). Tourism and border transactions lost competitiveness; merchandise exports actually fell in real terms. The current account deficit jumped from $2.7 billion in 1978 to $16 billion in 1981, a sixfold increase. Such an explosive growth of the current account deficit was met by foreign borrowing. Despite the positive terms of trade shock, the foreign debt increased from $36.4 billion in 1978 to $74.4 billion in 1981.

Circumstances began to change in 1981 and did so very rapidly. Economic policy was tied to the price of a single commodity. The short-run effects of real exchange rate misalignment and budget deficits could be ignored as long as oil resources kept growing. When the oil market weakened in mid-1981, there was a realization that the increase in the price of oil could be just a temporary phenomenon (fig. 8.2). This, together with the sheer magnitude of the underlying macroeconomic disequilibriums and the perspective of change that naturally arises when the administration comes to an end, rapidly changed the economic outlook.[45] Expectations adjusted rather quickly as the sustainability of current policies came increasingly into question; capital flight began in sizable magnitudes. The timing of events was politically unfortunate; capital flight began at the moment when the López Portillo presidency was ending, with only a few months remaining in the complicated process of naming a

45. This is an important side effect of a political system like the Mexican one, where presidents are barred from reelection. As the end of the *sexenio* approaches the current administration may fail to internalize fully the medium-term effects of economic policies, thus shortening the planning horizon for other agents.

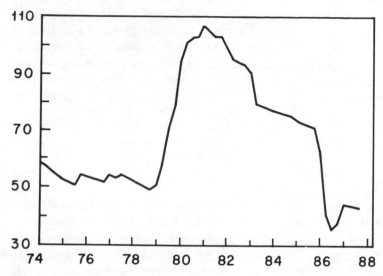

Fig. 8.2   Real oil price index (1980 = 100)
Source: Dornbusch (1988).

successor. The president faced the very situation he hoped to avoid: a negative vote of confidence by the private sector.

An appropriate response to dramatically changed circumstances was lacking. The need for adjustment was not in dispute in mid-1981: the oil boom was over and it was time to restore balance to the key macro variables, principally the fiscal stance of the government and the real exchange rate. But the measures taken were patently insufficient to deal with the magnitude of the crisis: the rate of devaluation of the peso was accelerated somewhat, and most of the import controls which had been removed since 1977 were reimposed.[46] As it occurred towards the end of the Echeverría regime, an attempt was made to solve macroeconomic imbalances with a patchy combination of trade policy adjustments and noncredible commitments to reduce expenditures.[47]

46. The situation at the time generated a debate centered on whether spending cuts, a real devaluation, or import controls were called for (see, e.g., Eatwell and Singh 1982). From our point of view, the essence of the problem was a fiscal imbalance which, given private savings and investment, was reflected as a current account deficit. In addition, the exchange rate appeared overvalued, and there was little evidence of excess capacity (Eatwell and Singh 1982 show average rates of capacity utilization in the manufacturing sector of over 95%; no data for the nontradable sectors is presented). Import controls would not help with the problem of exchange rate overvaluation; by cutting a source of supply, they would increase inflationary pressures. Moreover, it can be shown that even in a model that allows for markup pricing and excess capacity, import controls in general need not improve the trade deficit, while they will reduce the real wage (see Levy 1987). In addition, the use of trade policy to correct macroeconomic imbalances seemed inappropriate: it reversed the signals for investment in the exportable sector and probably generated an additional surge of imports as consumers anticipated higher obstacles to importing.

47. In particular, different members of the cabinet at that time were expressing divergent opinions on the nature of the crisis and the appropriate policy response. The underlying message was that the executive branch was not under full understanding and control of the process.

The government's response to the crisis was based on various considerations. First, to them it was not obvious that the fall in the price of oil was not a temporary phenomenon. Until they were convinced that this was not so, there was an understandable reluctance to change direction. In addition, the fact that, at least through the second half of 1981, foreign commercial banks continued to lend to Mexico could also be interpreted as a sign that they also saw the fall in the oil price as temporary. Second, there was perhaps a hope that, as in 1976, the American government would come to the rescue.[48] And while clearly these factors played a role, it is equally true that the political voluntarism so characteristic of the Mexican political system strongly pushed it against any major attempt at stabilization.

The ensuing response to the lack of serious adjustment and the uncertain policy signals devastated the Mexican economy. Massive capital flight was the private sector's response to the unsustainable policies. Yet at the same time, and in the face of a strong speculative attack against the currency, the government decided against any major jump in the exchange rate, maintaining the slow rate of crawl. Devaluation and stabilization were seen as equivalent to a surrender to its enemies, as these measures implied a substantial revision of the government's growth strategy. Such backing down of the powers-to-be was an unacceptable situation for any political authority.

Access to foreign borrowing played again a key role, but with a vengeance. Incredibly enough, in a single year, 1981, the country's foreign debt increased from $49 billion to $75 billion, with the bulk of the increase occurring during the last six months of the year. Most of this debt was contracted with private banks, with relatively short maturities, and with variable interest rates, just when world interest rates edged upward and monetary policy tightened in the United States. Après moi, le deluge.

The remainder of the López Portillo administration was characterized by intensely acrimonious relations between the government and the private sector. Policy was determined by the need to reduce a fiscal deficit of major proportions, in a context where the external conditions were now working against Mexico: world interest rates were increasing and the oil market weakening. At the same time, the supply of foreign resources turned inelastic as foreign creditors realized the magnitude of Mexico's obligations and its deteriorated economic conditions. This combination of events implied that foreign borrowing was procyclical with the price of oil, precisely the opposite of what should occur had there been any attempts at consumption smoothing.

Faced with the need to change policy, the government needed a new rheto-

48. We can only speculate why the initial response of the American government to Mexico's crisis, particularly during the first half of 1982, was different to that of 1976. Perhaps this was due to the differences in administration (Carter vs. Reagan); perhaps to the fact that in this occasion the crisis was of a much larger magnitude (involving other Latin American countries); perhaps also the response was due to the previous differences in foreign policy between Mexico and the United States, particularly over Nicaragua. It was only later, in August 1982, when there was a risk of substantial default with direct repercussions on the large American commercial banks, that the American government became fully involved in the crisis.

ric. It reluctantly had to adjust, but was not quite willing to hear the prescriptions of orthodox macroeconomic management. As events unfolded since mid-1981, the government turned, as it had done in the past, to those segments of the bureaucracy attuned to a heterodox perspective. But the magnitude of the crisis left almost no room for maneuver, and actions followed accordingly: toward the end of 1981 some public-sector prices were raised; in early 1982 the government ran out of reserves and could no longer support the exchange rate, generating a nominal devaluation of 470%.[49] All imports were subject to controls, and the rate of growth of public expenditures was reduced from 25% in 1981 to 3.7% in 1982. Nominal wage rates were also increased. Later a system of dual exchange rates was announced.[50] Subsequently, in a much-debated action, the president introduced exchange controls and nationalized the domestic banking industry. With depleted reserves, an inflation rate of almost 100%, a decline in real GDP of 0.5%, a public-sector deficit of almost 18% of GDP and a foreign debt of $92.4 billion dollars the *sexenio* ended, just like the previous one, by signing a stabilization program with the International Monetary Fund.

8.5 Concluding Observations

The sketch of macroeconomic events during 1970–82 presented above provides a background against which some further remarks on the nature of "populist economic policies" in Mexico can be made. We begin by noting some important differences between the two *sexenios*. First, and most obviously, López Portillo's was blessed with a much larger import capacity. In addition, since oil was publicly owned, the revenue position of the government was substantially improved. The underlying circumstances were very different.

Second and more important, the motives behind policies were different. Echeverría's main objective was to solve a political crisis: larger government participation and a reassertion of control of the economy were seen as the medium through which the crisis would be solved. This implied an almost unavoidable conflict between the government and the private sector. In contrast, at least through the first half of López Portillo's *sexenio,* policy could be characterized simply as an attempt to "please all," rather than a situation where the interests of the private sector and the government were in conflict. Thus, urban workers (or at least their unions) were pleased since even though the real wage fell slightly, employment grew at above-average trends; the middle classes were pleased by price subsidies and an overvalued exchange rate; the bureaucracy was pleased by the greater influence it derived from the

49. The nominal exchange rate had discrete jumps at various times during 1982. The figure in the text is obtained by comparing the December 1981 to December 1982 exchange rate.

50. Given the emphasis of this paper, and space constraints, we just list here the major events during that time. A fuller analysis of the crisis can be found elsewhere (see Taylor 1985 and Bazdresch, n.d., for contrasting views).

larger involvement of the government in the economy; the private sector was pleased by an overvalued exchange rate and the sizable profits that could be made in the domestic market; and rural Mexico was beginning to be pleased through large increases in employment, infrastructure investments, and SAM. It was only after the crisis erupted, when pleasing all was no longer feasible and the situation appeared explosive, that actions that attempted to reassert political power and control (exchange controls and bank nationalization) were taken.

A third difference relates to rhetoric. Echeverría's was quite militant, with entrepreneurs being the object of continuous criticisms. In contrast, during most of López Portillo's regime, the atmosphere of acrimony and political crisis that characterized shared development subsided significantly. Of course, after the crisis erupted in mid-1981 López Portillo's rhetoric changed dramatically (and rapidly), illustrating the little association that exists between the ideological proclivities of the president in turn and populist policies: populist policies are not a monopoly of "leftist-leaning" presidents (assuming such a term is meaningful in Mexico).

Differences between the two populist episodes notwithstanding, we emphasize that, on the whole, they did not result from incompetence, nor from the fact that either president did not have technically trained economists among their trusted advisers. This does not mean, of course, that some specific populist policies cannot result from mistakes, or from misunderstandings of the nature of markets or of the type of interventions that can increase welfare. Economics is not an exact science, and there is plenty of room for error and differences of opinions. In addition, ideology matters; sometimes the rejection of the distributional implications of undiluted markets leads some economists to reject tools of analysis that emphasize the allocative role of prices; paraphrasing Sheahan (see n. 3 above), rejection of efficiency criteria becomes a principle.[51]

But there is a wide gap between, on the one hand, individual populist policies that may arise from policy mistakes and, on the other hand, the systematic violation of economywide budget constraints and the persistence of government interventions against the logic of markets. While certainly mistakes matter (and are difficult to correct given inertia, vested interests, and prestige), the appearance of populist episodes under very different circumstances shows that other factors play a more central role. Our argument is that populist *episodes* are, at heart, the results of circumstances where policymakers be-

51. We note also that in rejecting tools of analysis that emphasize the importance of markets, policymakers create a vicious circle: the measures introduced end up strengthening monopolies and distorting prices further, then proving, ex post facto, that markets lead to undesirable outcomes. As an example, consider the issue of industrial policy. Many analysts have pointed out the oligopolistic structure of some sectors of manufacturing, with obvious welfare costs. Yet at the same time the same analysts will recommend import controls and other trade barriers that, among their many effects, certainly promote oligopolistic concentration in industry (see Cordera and Tello 1989, pp. 36–37).

lieve that their political goals can only be achieved by interventions that restrict the operation of markets and increased the degree of state intervention. From Echeverría's perspective, how else but with a return to the state was he going to convince left-wing intellectuals to abandon violent means? From López Portillo's perspective, how else but with exchange controls and bank nationalization was he to "punish" the private sector for capital flight and reassert the primacy of the government in the economy?

We posit that while distributional considerations are important (given the government's role as "referee of social conflict"), populist episodes are a reflection of a deeper phenomenon: the underlying weakness of governments who engage in populist policies because, so to speak, they have no other cards to play. Under our interpretation, therefore, populist episodes in Mexico occur when the government engages in "last-resort" policies that it believes will strengthen it. These policies can be deficit finance that results partly from pursuing some distributional objectives and partly larger influence through a greater presence and control of economic activity (as was most often the case with Echeverría); but they can also be policies that have no direct distributional objective but rather try to tilt the balance of power in favor of the government (as was the case with López Portillo's bank nationalization).

From a strictly technical point of view, the case against populist policies is simple and overwhelming: because they ignore the reaction of agents to the incentive structure, and the underlying resource constraints, they cannot be sustained. And, moreover, when the short-term economic benefits that they can potentially yield are exhausted, the unavoidable correction that follows has economic costs that erode the initial economic gains; in present value terms, populist policies are welfare reducing.

But policies must be evaluated by their ability to reach their underlying objectives. If populist episodes occur partly as a result of the weakness of the government, an important metric (though not the only one) for evaluating them must be their effectiveness in strengthening the government or solving the political crisis which was their initial raison d'etre.[52] Thus, as shown in section 8.4, there is no doubt that Echeverría's and López Portillo's regimes faired badly in the economic front; the dynamic equilibrium which had been so carefully preserved during stabilizing development was lost.[53] But during Echeverría's regime there were some notable improvements in the political front. Though hesitantly, the door was opened for extensive political reforms, political repression became a thing of the past, a potentially dangerous guerrilla movement was diffused, freedom of the press was established. With the beginning of the dismantling of the closed corporate political system of the

---

52. From this perspective, orthodox economists who criticize populist governments on the grounds that the same distributional objectives that those governments claim to pursue can be achieved at lower cost and/or by more efficient means, while technically correct, may be missing the point.

53. To this day, policymakers are still struggling to lower the inflation rate and raise the growth rate; those who signaled the dangers of breaking macroeconomic equilibrium were basically right.

fifties and sixties, Mexico initiated a transformation toward a politically plural society. Echeverría was a key element in this process.

With López Portillo the situation is also mixed. There was a substantial political reform that consolidated Echeverría's initial moves toward a less repressive state; political parties on the left were legalized. This certainly strengthened civil society. On the other hand, and perhaps paradoxically, López Portillo's populism failed to reach its political objectives, as the huge debt buildup, the bank nationalization, and the exchange controls did not strengthen but instead further weakened the government. Strength cannot derive from the inheritance of a huge public debt, a financial sector that escapes government control as banks reduce their importance as financial intermediaries, while foreign exchange transactions continue unabated.[54] And while distributional considerations were obviously not the motives for these actions, it is clear that (*i*) the poor people in Mexico did not benefit from them,[55] and (*ii*) the poor have borne, at least in absolute terms, the economic costs of the unavoidable adjustment to the large macroeconomic disequilibriums.

We thus find that populist policies, aside from their obvious economic shortcomings, generally fail to strengthen the government. And, after the populist episode comes to an end, the economic incentives required to increase private investment are larger, as investors require higher returns to compensate for the observed uncertainty and higher risks. The use of economic policy to pursue the short-term political interests of the government is hence doubly costly; not only do the episodes end in a need for macroeconomic stabilization, but the underlying increase in generalized uncertainty acts like a tax on new investment, which depresses the prospects for long-term growth.

Given their undesirable welfare consequences, how can populist episodes be avoided? The answer is complex, but we feel that two elements must play a dominant role. First, civil society—the set of nongovernment institutions that together with the central government bureaucracy shape the nation—

---

54. Proponents of exchange controls (see Tello 1987) argued that controls would give more "degrees of freedom" to economic policy by delinking the domestic interest rate from the foreign and allowing the government to pursue more aggressive tax reforms without the fear of capital flight. The nationalization of the banks was then required to help implement the said controls (while at the same time reducing the political power of the "financial sector"). As one of us has argued elsewhere, however, these arguments are unconvincing (Bazdresch 1985). Given Mexico's proximity to the United States, exchange controls would not serve to reduce the mobility of capital. As a result, if domestic savings were to be kept in the domestic financial system, exchange controls would not succeed in delinking the domestic rate of interest from the world rate of interest. It is not obvious, moreover, how proponents of exchange controls would set domestic interest rates even if the economy was closed to capital movements; the point here is that the interest rate is an intertemporal price that plays a key role in distributing consumption through time and cannot be set independently of agents preferences.

55. Moreover, some policies associated with the bank nationalization were certainly regressive. While the nominal exchange rate was set at 70.00 pesos per dollar, a special exchange rate of 50.00 pesos per dollar was instituted for firms with dollar-denominated debts (so as to "protect" the productive apparatus). This created the need for significant subsidies to cover the losses by the Central Bank on this type of operations. But, clearly, not many poor people had dollar-denominated debts.

must be strengthened. The government has, at present, too much room for arbitrary actions (either repressing the population as did Diaz Ordaz or suddenly nationalizing the private banks as did López Portillo). To some extent, the protagonistic role played by the government must be diminished. Upon reflection, it should be clear that strengthening civil society will, in turn, strengthen the government, because the latter will then have a legitimate mandate from the former to carry out reforms. And while a "strong" government is an operationally difficult concept, we mean by this a situation where the government has, among other things, the ability to decree and enforce reasonable tax structures, to develop institutional settings where conflicts are settled by law, and where there is no need to make unsustainable promises or engage in special deals with specific groups to obtain legitimacy and support. If populist episodes occur when governments have no further cards to play, then strong governments might not feel the need for populist policies or may be able to correct them before they produce long-term damages. But, more important, under a strengthened civil society governments will not have the possibility to lead the country into populist economic episodes.

The second element concerns the social perception about market-oriented policies. The fact that societies allow governments to pursue policies that systematically go against the logic of markets reflects the fact that they are not fully convinced about their benefits. As we have argued, there are substantial reasons why this has been so in Mexico. We are convinced that, on the whole, market-oriented policies are desirable and beneficial; there seems to be no other mechanism to produce an efficient allocation of resources. And yet, while markets do produce relatively more efficient outcomes than direct government allocations, efficiency is not enough. Market outcomes must also be distributionally acceptable.

Developing a social consensus in favor of market-oriented policies is also important. To do this, not only must the benefits of markets become clear, particularly the associated distribution of income, but the conditions under which markets do indeed produce better outcomes also requires elucidation: markets have desirable properties under a certain set of conditions. At the same time, however, we must also come to realize that while certain market outcomes may not be Pareto efficient, this need not imply that the situation can be improved by government action. It is necessary to understand that, given problems of bounded rationality, availability of information, and incentive compatibility, there are limits to what government interventions can achieve, even if well-intentioned.[56] In addition, the implicit connection that is made between markets and privilege must disappear.[57]

---

56. A case in point is the market for credit. It is now generally understood that credit rationing may arise even in contexts where the interest rate is free to vary (Stiglitz 1988). But the root of the problem is a moral hazard problem arising from the fact that information is asymmetric and costly. This type of informational failure, however, cannot generally be solved by governments.

57. Language is revealing about this problem in Mexico: the term *private sector* (or, misleadingly, entrepreneurial sector) generally denotes large firms in manufacturing and finance and is

Market-oriented policies will produce benefits when they are perceived by all agents to be permanent. There is now a substantial body of literature to show that noncredible or unsustainable market reforms may reduce welfare and, in doing so, reduce the reputation of markets. From a different perspective, imposing a market-oriented outcome may, to some extent, be sowing the seeds for a latter populist episode. The permanency of market-oriented policies is thus directly linked to the social consensus behind them. If the latter is developed, the associated economic outcome, while obviously not a Pareto optimum, is likely nonetheless to be better than the current situation. But, of course, a Pareto optimum, or anything coming closer to that, might not be what society desires. The arguments of the "social welfare function" might include elements other than physical goods. Society has the right to choose an alternative set of policies—as long as it is aware of the associated economic costs of those policies.

But the lesson from all this must be obtained by looking not only at Echeverría's and López Portillo's regimes, but also at stabilizing development. Stabilizing development can be criticized for paying scant attention to political development. Echeverría probably tried to redress the balance by focusing on political development, although in doing so he, in turn, paid scant attention to economic constraints. Neither strategy, in the end, was permanent. So the lesson is simply that societies cannot develop under either a purely economic or political track. One cannot focus only on one set of variables at the expense of the other, and perhaps Mexico has been suffering, since at least the 1950s, from wide swings in a pendulum that goes from concentration in economic matters at the expense of political development to concentration in economic development at the expense of politics. Populism is, from this perspective, just one of the two types of errors that policymakers can fall into.

References

Aspe, P., and J. Beristain. 1984a. The Evolution of Income Distribution Policies during the Post-Revolutionary Period in Mexico. In *The Political Economy of Income Distribution in Mexico*, ed. P. Aspe and P. Sigmund. New York: Holmes & Meier.

---

evocative of privilege and elite. In turn, the term *social sector* (or, misleadingly, popular sector), denotes an amorphous collection of agents (some rural workers, small vendors, and self-employed in the urban areas) and is evocative of destitution and poverty. Yet there is nothing more private (or social) in the activities of a large oligopolistic firm producing, say, fertilizers, than in an individual vendor in the streets of Mexico City selling, say, candy. Presumably both agents (entrepreneurs?) maximize profits and respond to current and expected relative prices. And while there are obvious differences of size, access to credit, tax obligations, etc., policies can either improve the functioning of markets for both (removing barriers to entry in fertilizers to lower price-cost margins and, say, granting credit to the street vendor) or, alternatively, suppress them (nationalizing the fertilizer producer, say, and giving a government-guaranteed job to the street vendor). The dichotomy private-social sector is not analytically useful but generates a background against which populist policies, regardless of their medium-term effects, seem immediately (we hesitate to use the term) "popular."

————. 1984b. Towards a First Estimate of the Evolution of Inequality in Mexico. In *The Political Economy of Income Distribution in Mexico,* ed. P. Aspe and P. Sigmund. New York: Holmes & Meier.

Bardhan, P. 1988. Alternative Approaches to Development Economics. In *Handbook of Development Economics,* ed. T. N. Srinivasan and H. Chenery. Amsterdam: North-Holland.

Bazdresch, C. 1985. La Nacionalizacion Bancaria. *Nexos* (January): 49–56.

————. 1984. *El Pensamiento de Juan F. Novola.* Mexico City: Fondo de Cultura Economica.

————. No date. Las causas de la Crisis. Mexico City. Mimeograph.

Cardoso, E. 1981. Food Supply and Inflation. *Journal of Development Economics* 8:269–84.

Cordera, R., and C. Tello. 1989. *Mexico, La Disputa por la Nacion.* Mexico City: Siglo XXI.

Cordoba, A. 1974. *La Politica de Masas del Cadenismo.* Mexico City: Serie Popular Era.

————. 1973. *La Ideologia de la Revolucion Mexicana; Formacion del Nuevo Regimen.* Mexico City: Ediciones Era.

Cosio Villegas, D. 1973. *El Sistema Politico Mexicano.* Mexico City: Joaquin Mortiz.

Dornbusch, R. 1988. Mexico: Estabilizacion, Deuda y Crecimiento. *El Trimestre Economico* 55, no. 220: 879–938.

Dornbusch, R., and S. Edwards. 1989. The Macroeconomics of Populism in Latin America. Massachusetts Institute of Technology, Cambridge, Mass. Mimeograph.

Eatwell, J., and A. Singh. 1982. Se Encuentra Sobre-calentada la Economia Mexicana? Un Analisis de los Problemas de Politica Economica a Corto y Mediano Plazo. *Economia Mexicana* 3:253–69.

Flores de la Pena, H. 1975. *Teoria y Practica del Desarollo.* Mexico City: Fondo de Cultura Economica.

Gil Diaz, F. 1984. The Incidence of Taxes in Mexico: A Before and After Comparison. In *The Political Economy of Income Distribution in Mexico,* ed. P. Aspe and P. Sigmund. New York: Holmes & Meier.

Gil Diaz, F., and R. Ramos. 1988. Lecciones desde Mexico. In *Inflacion y Estabilizacion,* ed. M. Bruno, G. Di Tella, R. Dornbusch, and S. Fisher. Mexico City: Fondo de Cultura Economica.

Green, R. 1977. La Politica Exterior del Nuevo Regimen. *Foro Internacional,* vol. 69. El colegio de Mexico.

Gregory, P. 1986. *The Myth of Market Failure: Employment and the Labor Market in Mexico.* Baltimore: Johns Hopkins University Press.

Grupo de Estudio del Problema del Empleo. No date. El Problema Ocupacional en Mexico: Magnitud y Recomendaciones. Mexico City. Mimeograph.

Hansen, R. 1974. *La Politica del Desarollo Mexicano.* Mexico City: Siglo XXI.

Ianni, O. 1983. *El Estado capitalista de cardenas.* Mexico City: Serie Popular Era.

Ibarra, D., I. Navarrete, L. Solis, and V. Urquidi. 1972. *El Perfil de Mexico en 1980,* vol. 1. Mexico City: Siglo XXI.

Levy, S. 1988. Los Efectos Macroeconomicos de los controles de Precios: Un Analisis de Equilibrio General de Corto Plazo. *Estudios Economicos de El Colegio de Mexico* 3:27–56.

————. 1987. Short Run Responses to Foreign Exchange Crises. *Journal of Policy Modellino* 9:577–615.

————. 1979. *El Problema del empleo en Mexico.* Mexico City: Banco Nacional de Mexico.

Little, I., T. Scitovsky, and M. Scott. 1975. *Industria y comerico en Alounos Paises en Desarollo.* Mexico City: Fondo de Cultura Economica.

Lipton, M. 1977. *Why Poor People Stay Poor: A Study of Urban Bias in World Development*. London: Temple Smith.

Lizondo, S. 1983. Foreign Exchange Futures Prices under Fixed Exchange Rates. *Journal of International Economics* 14:69–84.

Meyer, L. 1974. El Estado Mexicano Contemporaneo. In *Lecturas de Politica Mexicana*. Mexico City: El Colegio de Mexico.

Middlebrook, K. 1986. Political Liberalization in an Authoritarian Regime: The Case of Mexico. In *Transition from Authoritarian Rule*, ed. Guillermo O'Donnel et al. Baltimore: Johns Hopkins University Press.

Moore, R. 1984. Urbanization and Housing Policy in Mexico. In *The Political Economy of Income Distribution in Mexico*, ed. P. Aspe and P. Sigmund. New York: Holmes & Meier.

Ortiz Mena, A. 1970. El Desarollo Estabilizador. *El Trimestre Economico*, no. 146.

Sachs, J. 1989. Social Conflict and Populist Policies in Latin America. NBER Working Paper no. 2897. Cambridge, Mass., March.

Secretaria de Agricultura y Recursos Hidraulicos. 1983. *Econotecnia Agricola*. Mexico City.

Sheahan, J. 1987. *Patterns of Development in Latin America: Poverty, Repression and Economic Strategy*. Princeton, N.J.: Princeton University Press.

Sigmund, P. 1984. The Regulation of Foreign Investment in Mexico and Its Impact on Income Distribution. In *The Political Economy of Income Distribution in Mexico*, ed. P. Aspe and P. Sigmund. New York: Holmes & Meier.

Solis, L. 1981. *Economic Policy Reform in Mexico: A Case Study for Developing Countries*. New York: Pergamon Press.

———. 1980. *Alternativas Para el Desarrollo*. Mexico City: Joaquin Mortiz.

Stiglitz, J. 1988. Economic Organization, Information, and Development. In *Handbook of Development Economics*, ed. T. N. Srinivasan and H. Chenery. Amsterdam: North-Holland.

Taylor, L. 1985. The Crisis and Thereafter: Macroeconomic Policy Problems in Mexico. In *Mexico and the United States: Studies in Economic Interaction*, ed. P. Musgrave. Boulder, Colo.: Westview Press.

Tello, C. 1987. *La Nacionalizacion de la Banca en Mexico*. Mexico City: Siglo XXI.

———. 1979. *La Politica Economica en Mexico, 1970–1976*. Mexico City: Siglo XXI.

Yates, P. 1981. *Mexico's Agricultural Dilemma*. Tucson: University of Arizona Press.

Comment   Enrique Cárdenas

Bazdresch and Levy's paper is a well-structured and researched piece that deals with the economy's development from the late 1950s until the crisis of 1982. The authors also review briefly the immediate postrevolutionary years and emphasize the role of the revolutionary ideology as the seed of subsequent populist periods that have repeated themselves sporadically. However, they review very deeply the policies of the Echeverría (1970–76) and López Portillo (1976–82) administrations.

The first part intends to demonstrate that the revolution ideology created a

Enrique Cárdenas is rector and professor of economics at Universidad de la Américas-Puebla.

strong, interventionist, and large state with the power to influence and direct economic activity. In my view, although this is true to some degree—the 1917 Constitution that emanated from the revolution included many economic articles along those lines—the Mexican state "developed" its instruments of economic policy at about the same time as most other countries: during the 1930s. Indeed, in the 1920s, the Mexican government had as its only policy expedient the import tariff to affect relative prices; by the mid-1930s, the recently created Central Bank began to function as a real monetary authority, and fiscal policy began to be implemented very cautiously to counteract economic recessions. But all this was happening at the same time in all the major Latin American countries. Indeed, it is usually argued that the Great Depression throughout Latin America and elsewhere was the major force behind the idea of an interventionist government. This was not only through economic policy; the general atmosphere pointed in that direction.

The authors also consider that in contemporary Mexico there were two episodes of populist polices: Cárdenas and Echeverría—López Portillo. I have no doubt that they are right, but I would only mention that Cárdenas was careful not to ignore the macro constraints that his successors did. During the most expansionist years of the Cárdenas period, the fiscal deficit was about 1% or 2% of GDP. During the Echeverría period the deficit reached 10% of GDP, while during the López Portillo administration, the fiscal deficit reached a peak of almost 17% of GDP. Naturally, Echeverría and López Portillo would love to be placed in the same package as Cárdenas, but I do not think that should be the case.

With regard to the stabilizing development period, the authors follow the mainstream, noting that fiscal discipline was the reason that inflation and the nominal exchange rate were stable during those years. I firmly believe they are right, but that this was a necessary, but not sufficient, condition for such an outcome. New research has recently shown that the absence of foreign shocks also played a significant role in that respect. That is to say, "stabilizing development" was possible because the government was well disciplined in its finances *and* because there were no external shocks that disturbed the economy during that period.

Their approach to analyzing the 1970–82 years is by reviewing the various economic policies undertaken by those regimes. The authors conclude that these governments adopted populist policies to reach high-priority political objectives that, moreover, could not be reached through market-oriented interventions. They arrive at this conclusion by saying that Echeverría had no other choice than to increase the role of the state in the economy if he wished to attract the support of leftist intellectuals. However, when they review that period, they imply that the failure of Echeverría, as measured by the 1976 crisis, was largely due to his lack of fiscal discipline as well as to the pernicious interplay of foreign economic shocks, such as the oil embargo and high international inflation rates. This fact, with which I personally agree, points to a major ingredient of populist policies. It is true that they are pursued for political reasons of high priority, which tend to benefit a specific social group, sometimes at the expense of another. But what is equally true and important is that a populist regime is not willing to pay the whole cost of its policy. Echeverría, for instance, decided to redistribute wealth and enlarge the size of the state by spending resources that he actually did not have and *was unwilling to make the fiscal reforms that would provide such funds.* If he had done so, there would be a discussion on ideology (having a large vs. a small state) and not a discussion on populism. The consequence of that decision had disastrous effects, as Bazdresch and Levy well point out, which could have been avoided or at least could have served to turn the public's attention to the basic underlining factor: the weak structure of the economy.

Such an unwillingness to "pay the price" is also a reflection of a basic ingredient of populist policies: The utmost concern for the short run as opposed to the long term. Naturally, political objectives usually imply, at the end, the aim to control power. In modern regimes, holding power (and political prestige) is a concern for just a few years, especially in a nonrenewable six year term that the president serves in Mexico. In other cases, such a term is even shorter. Consequently, political objectives are usually concerned with the short term, and therefore populist policies are also usually concerned with immediate impact. That is why it is not difficult to understand why populist regimes are not prepared to pay the whole price and tend to overlook the macroeconomic constraints that any economy faces.

In the case of Echeverría, if he had made the fiscal reforms needed to pay for the additional expenditures required to pursue his political objectives, it is possible to speculate that the crisis would have arrived anyway, probably later. It would have come, however, not because of fiscal indiscipline but because the structure of the economy remained weak, uncompetitive, and highly vulnerable to external economic shocks, which were particularly strong in the 1970s.

López Portillo's populism, I believe, is of a different sort. He was blessed with the oil boom and a tremendous inflow of foreign exchange. At first the government thought that it had finally overcome its endemic financial constraint that the scarcity of hard currency imposes on the balance of payments. During its first years, the López Portillo regime simply wanted to distribute wealth that was pouring from the oil revenues, not necessarily redistribute it. José López Portillo's populism was for the poor and the rich. There was so much wealth that it seemed that there was enough for everybody. All enjoyed inexpensive public goods and services, cheap dollars, and extensive subsidies at all levels. It was like manna coming from heaven, but it became the virus of a "Dutch disease" type of macroeconomic problem. The sudden inflow of vast amounts of dollars distorted relative prices and increased income. The result was a growing import bias and high domestic rates of inflation, which exerted pressure on the balance of payments, given a fixed exchange rate policy. Consequently, the economy's structure became even weaker and more vulnerable to any type of shock.

It should be mentioned that, during López Portillo's regime, a segment of the government tried to enter the GATT in an attempt to force the economy to become more efficient and competitive. The impact of the Dutch disease was beginning to be felt, and concern was expressed in terms of the disastrous macroeconomic outcome if the status quo were maintained. The refusal to join GATT was a reflection of a generalized feeling of self-sufficiency, not only in the executive branch but also in most of the private sector. At the same time, there was no government recognition of the fact that the economy was becoming weaker.

Actually, it can be speculated that, if the price of oil had continued to climb as was forecasted by most analysts at the time, and assuming that overall macroeconomic policy would have continued the way it was, the Dutch disease would have become a cancer and a larger segment of the society would become a *rentier* class, very much in the same way the Spaniards in the sixteenth century were affected by the gold and silver inflows from their American colonies. Income was growing much faster than actual productivity, and the relative price increase of domestically produced goods with relatively open imports inhibited domestic investment on productive activities. To allow such a situation, with the concomitant impact in public finances and the budgetary deficit, was another form of populism. To make people believe that they were rich (because they truly believed it) when they actually are not is a certain way to spoil one's future.

The authors rightly argue that in order to "immunize" a country against populist policies it is necessary to strengthen the role of the civil society and to create a social consensus in favor of economic policies that do not clash directly with the logic of markets. They also indicate, with good reason, that it is important that institutions should be created in order to prevent a government from ignoring macroeconomic constraints. I would simply extend this thought to mention that governments and the "social consensus" alike must not forget that it is impossible to obtain something from nothing, that one cannot indefinitely consume more than what one produces, that a country cannot live from borrowing forever. Perhaps this is the most painful lesson that Mexico has learned from the recent economic crisis, a lesson that is now shared by the government and the common people alike. This is another kind of immunization, at least for one generation, I hope; that is, just having the disease.

Indeed, the prolonged crisis and the more recent opening of the economy to foreign competition has had a tremendous impact on people's mentality. Apparently governments learn and people also learn. In my opinion, there is a growing and widespread feeling today, at least among the middle and upper classes, that one has to be more productive and competitive in order to enjoy a better life, that it is no longer possible to spend beyond one's means indefinitely.

9   The Illusion of Pursuing Redistribution through Macropolicy: Peru's Heterodox Experience, 1985–1990

Ricardo Lago

9.1. Introduction

From the Inca empire to the viceroyalty and then to the Republic, Peru has enjoyed both international prominence and open opportunities for economic development. The "guano era" in the nineteenth century gave Peru considerable surpluses, as did mining, fishing, and petroleum in more recent times. Yet, despite its generous resource endowment, Peru has failed to find its way to a stable political, social, and economic environment in which to prompt balanced growth and equitable development. Economic decline has been particularly notorious over the last three decades, when Peru's income per capita fell from the eighth highest in Latin America in the 1960s, to the fourteenth position in the late 1980s.[1] At the turn of the decade, Peru's economic retrogression can be gauged by an income per capita equal to that of 1960 and by a level of exports 40 percent lower than that of 1979. Peru's frustrated economic and social expectations were eloquently described by its leading historian, Jorge Basadre, who defined Peru as a "beautiful promise yet to be fulfilled."

The object of this paper is to analyze the economic process undergone by Peru during the period 1985–90 during which the legendary APRA party (American Popular Revolutionary Alliance) assumed presidential office, for the first time, under President Alán García. Following closely the methodol-

Ricardo Lago is senior economist at the World Bank.

The views of the author do not necessarily reflect those of the World Bank or its affiliates. Efficient research assistance from Alberto Aza, Cesar Burga, Ignacio Cosentino, and Gillete Hall, editing by William Woodward, and comments from Paul Beckerman, Augusto Blacker, Vitorio Corbo, Rudiger Dornbusch, Sebastian Edwards, Carol Graham, Javier Iguiniz, Miguel Kiguel, Ignacio Mas, Javier Nogales, Felipe Ortiz de Zevallos, Carlos Paredes, Miguel Savastano, Alfredo Thorne, William Tyler, and Steve Webb are greatly appreciated.

1. *World Development Report*, various issues (Washington, D.C.: World Bank).

ogy recently developed by Dornbusch and Edwards (1990), the paper is organized as follows.

The next section provides a brief background on Peru's economy and recent
history. The third section analyzes the "heterodox" economic policies of the
period 1985–90 an their results. The section opens with a description of the
macroeconomic legacy—of high inflation and low income, but also of competitive exchange rate, high public tariffs, and sizable international reserves—
left by the second administration of Fernando Belaúnde. This legacy represents the initial conditions of the period under examination. The section
continues with a discussion of the analytical framework underlying the macroeconomic program launched in August 1985. The focus then shifts to an
analysis of the expansionary phase of the heterodox experiment (1985–87),
starting with a description of the economic measures—of demand expansion,
price freeze, and unilateral default—contained in the 1985 policy package,
and following with an examination of the dynamics of the consumption boom,
in which GDP expanded by a cumulative 16 percent and inflation initially
declined but at the expense of mounting financial and external disequilibria.

This main section closes with a detailed analysis of the recessionary phase
(1988–90) during which, after three unsuccessful corrective attempts, the
economy lapsed into an incipient hyperinflation and a major recession and real
wage decline. Particular attention is given to the period September 1988
through June 1989 in which the Central Bank took an independent course of
credit restraint, whereby it managed to partially hold back the hyperinflationary course and to accumulate a considerable level of international reserves.
This trend, however, was later reversed in 1989 when economic policy engaged again in another round of expansionary policies in an attempt to reactivate economic activity through depletion of international reserves.

The fourth section sums up some of the devastating effects of the experiment on income distribution, other welfare indicators, resource allocation,
rural incomes, the tax system, public infrastructure, and the financial viability
of the public sector.

Finally, the fifth and last section contains a few thoughts and concluding
remarks on demand-led experiments in the light of Peru's recent experience.
The main ones are the following. First, the phases of the Peruvian process of
1985–90 match closely those of the paradigm established by Dornbusch and
Edwards (1990). Second, the idea of finding strategies for rapid reactivation
of severely depressed economies—typically coming out of a previous stabilization phase—has indeed long appealed to politicians and economists alike.
However, the recent Peruvian experience proves, as many others have, that
this type of policy course almost inevitably implies disregard for the constraints imposed by flow of funds accounting and thus leads to macroeconomic failure. On the other hand, the policies utilized to prompt the recovery—comprising typically a broad array of subsidies, controls, and import
restrictions—are diametrically at variance with the incentive structure re-

quired to move the economy into the desired follow-up phase of investment and export growth. Therefore, demand-led macroeconomic booms have an inevitable and devastating aftermath of high inflation and decline. Third, of the different theories that attempt to explain why politicians launch self-defeating policies, Peru's recent experience provides some evidence supporting the hypotheses of high discount rate and faulty economic framework. However, these explanations are partial and somewhat naive and therefore, a more thorough consideration of political agents and factors is probably called for. Finally, Peru's very unequal income distribution and acutely diverging interests between urban and rural groups, on the one hand, and labor and capital, on the other, makes it particularly prone to unstable stop-and-go economic policy cycles.

9.2 Background and Recent History

Efforts to forge physical, economic, linguistic, and cultural links between Peru's three distinct regions—the highlands (*sierra*), the rain-forest (*selva*), and the coast—have long confronted the formidable natural barrier of the Andean mountains. About half of Peru's population of about 22 million live in the coastal region, while 40 percent live in the Andean highlands and the rest in the Amazon region. Income per capita, which has declined steadily since the mid-1970s, is now about $1,000 (in U.S. dollars). Income distribution is one of the most uneven in Latin America, and other welfare indicators, such as life expectancy and infant mortality, are among the worst in the region (see table 9.1). More than half of Peru's poorest 30 percent live in the Andean highlands and are self-employed peasants. Agriculture and mining have long lost their predominance in the economy due to the import substitution model

Table 9.1　　　　　**Income Distribution (% of Total Income)**

Percentile	1961 (Earners)	1972 (Household Consumption)	1985–86 (Household Consumption per Capita)
Poorest			
20%	2.5	3.2	4.1
21%–40%	5.5	7.3	8.9
41%–60%	10.2	13.3	14.0
61%–80%	17.4	21.5	21.6
81%–90%	15.2	17.7	16.2
Wealthiest 10%	49.2	37.0	35.2

Source: Data for 1961: Webb (1975); for 1972: Amat y Leon (1979); for 1985–86: Glewwe (1987), based on data from Peru's 1985–86 "Living Standard Measurement Survey," The World Bank.

Note: Figures are not comparable across years due to different methods.

followed since the sixties that gradually made manufacturing the mainstay of the economy.

Peru's modern history has been marked by political and economic instability. Single-term democratically elected governments have usually been followed by periods of military juntas and vice versa, in an almost alternating sequence. In turn, recurrent expansionary macroeconomic policies have ultimately run into foreign exchange crises and subsequent stabilization episodes. The Peru of the 1950s has been characterized as a laissez-faire economy. The country was open to foreign trade; exports of raw minerals, mostly exploited by foreign interests, and fish meal paid for imported manufactures. In turn, the government had little direct participation in the economy, and economic activities were largely unregulated. Industrialization by import substitution and government spending in the infrastructure started with the first government of Fernando Belaúnde (1963–68). A long-pursued tax reform needed to restore macroeconomic stability was systematically opposed by an uncooperative Congress, and Belaúnde's first term ended with an economic crisis and a military coup.

During the nationalistic rule of General Velasco Alvarado (1968–75), the government embarked on an inward-looking growth strategy, established a broad array of controls on economic activity, nationalized foreign corporations—particularly in mining and hydrocarbons—gave workers participation in ownership and management of private firms, and undertook a global agrarian reform. Large-scale public investment projects and a rapidly growing state enterprise sector brought about a mounting foreign debt.

Favorable external conditions during 1970–74 allowed rapid expansion of employment and incomes. In fact, income per capita had grown steadily, at an average annual rate of about 2.7 percent, during the entire 1950–74 period, with the exception of the years 1968–69. In parallel, inflation during that period had been moderate but growing. It rose from an annual average of 7 percent in the 1950s to the teens in the 1960s and early 1970s (table 9.2).

Starting in 1974, a deep downswing in the terms of trade together with a sudden withdrawal of foreign financing sources, in the wake of overly expansionary public spending, set the ground for a long recession. In that process, General Velasco Alvarado was forced out of office in 1975 by an internal coup that put his prime minister, General Morales Bermúdez, into the presidency. Income per capita stagnated in 1974–76 and then dropped, for two consecutive years, 1976–78, by a cumulative 5 percent, while inflation accelerated from single-digit rates early in the decade to nearly 70 percent in 1978.

A strong stabilization attempt was initiated in 1978–79, with the help of favorable terms of trade. In 1979, confident that economic growth had resumed and international reserves had been restored, the government initiated an import liberalization program. In that year, general elections were held and Fernando Belaúnde was voted back into the presidency. Belaúnde enjoyed massive international support but inherited a country with formidable social

Table 9.2   Public-Sector Finances and Overall Economic Performance

Years	Public Sector (% of GDP)			Annual Inflation Rate (%)	Annual Rate of GDP Growth (%)	Total External Debt (in Millions of U.S. dollars)[b]
	Gross Expenditure[a]	Investment	Deficit			
1950–62	12.5		.2	7.0	5.3	158
1953–68	19.1		2.1	11.6	4.4	737
1969–73	22.0	5.1	1.8	7.4	4.4	3,835
1974–75	35.9	8.3	7.0	21.6	6.3	5,748
1976–77	39.1	7.1	8.7	38.6	1.2	7,976
1978–79	39.6	5.2	3.2	70.2	3.1	9,329
1980–82	40.5	7.8	6.0	68.8	3.1	10,222
1983–85	43.1	7.3	6.1	131.6	− 1.7	13,974
1986	36.7	5.2	9.1[c]	62.9	9.5	14,976
1987	30.6	4.0	12.9[c]	114.5	7.8	16,263
1988	28.3	3.0	15.6[c]	1,722.3	− 8.8	18,018
1989	19.9	2.0	9.8[c]	2,775.3	− 10.4	19,156

Source: Central Reserve Bank, National Statistical Institute; Paredes and Pasco-Font (1987).

[a]Results from adding central government expenditures (excluding transfers to state enterprises) and state enterprises' gross expenditures.

[b]End of period, includes imputed interest on arrears.

[c]Includes Central Bank financial and foreign exchange losses, as well as transfers to development banks.

problems, an income per capita below its 1974 level, and major economic distortions. However, during its first three years, his government engaged in expansionary fiscal and monetary policies, which caused inflation to double to 100-plus percent in 1983. Subsequently, the foreign trade liberalization process was reversed. Likewise, the parceling out of land plots that had been granted to cooperatives by the military rulers was effected in a less than orderly fashion. In 1983, after frustrated negotiations on foreign debt rescheduling and fresh financing with commercial creditors, the government switched into a policy of "undeclared" arrears. As explained below, efforts to stabilize the economy were made in 1984–85.

9.2.1   Brief History of the Traditional Economic Program of the APRA

Carol Graham (1990) argues that Peru's age-old paradox is "an extremely poor record of social reform in spite of the long-term presence of a strong reformist party." The APRA is one of the oldest mass-based reform-oriented parties in Latin America. Originally inspired by the Mexican Revolution, the APRA experienced a significant transformation both ideologically and tactically from a radical and revolutionary party in the 1930s and 1940s to become a more compromising and pragmatic party in the 1950s and 1960s. The

APRA's history and ideology are intertwined with the life of its founder and main exponent, Victor Raúl Haya de la Torre, who died in 1979.

Throughout its history, the three central tenets of the APRA have been: establishment of an anti-imperialist state; creation of a multiclass coalition of the oppressed (*Frente Unico de las Clases Explotadas*); and pursuit of the unification of Latin America. The APRA's economic strategy has traditionally swung from the sometimes radical and occasionally socializing proposals of the *Programa maximo* to the more moderate *Programa minimo*. The *Programa maximo* included the nationalization of some resource-based industries in the hands of foreign firms; agrarian reform, whereby large latifundia would be expropriated and given to peasant cooperatives; and the creation of a sector of state-owned firms and worker-owned cooperatives. But at the same time it also recognized the need for private property.[2] By contrast, the *Programa minimo*, approved by the first party congress in 1931 as the platform for that year's general elections, attempted to rule out any socializing fear by emphasizing respect for private property and recognizing the need for properly regulated foreign capital.

The APRA's most original proposal is the creation of the "Democratic State of the Four Powers": executive, judiciary, legislative, and economic. The economic or "fourth power" would be exercised by a National Economic Congress made up of representatives of the state, labor, and capital as a device to conciliate the interests of the different classes (*planificacion concertada*). The National Economic Congress would be a colegislative chamber and the supreme authority for economic policy planning and design.

The *Programa minimo* of 1931 established that the intervention of the state in economic activity would consist of:[3]

* control over production conditions, prices, and firms' profits;
* repression of speculative maneuvers of monopolies and oligopolies;
* surveillance of industrial and economic activities;
* reform of banking legislation;
* adjustments to private and public utility tariffs;
* regulation of rents;
* guarantees of "fair" wages and employment conditions.

The APRA suffered persecution at different times in the 1930s, early 1940s, and again in the first half of the 1950s. After the general elections of 1962, the possibility that the APRA could assume the presidential office was ruled out by a preemptive military coup (Tamayo Herrera 1986, p. 356). The APRA assumed presidential office for the first time in July 1985, after its candidate for president, Alán García, obtained 48 percent of the popular vote in the first round of the presidential elections that had taken place in April of that year.

2. V. R. Haya de la Torre, *Obras Completas*, vol. 4, pp. 110, 156, 169, 171, 192, 193; vol. 5, pp. 17, 18, 19, 34, 73 (as cited by Vasquez Bazan 1987, pp. 37–47).
3. V. R. Haya de la Torre (n. 2 above, vol. 5, pp. 11–29; in Vasquez Bazan 1987, p. 45).

The runner-up candidate, Alfonso Barrantes of the United Left, who had obtained 24 percent of the vote in the first round, declined to contend in the runoff election in view of the popularity ratings of Alán García. In the legislative elections the APRA also obtained absolute majority in both chambers of Congress.

9.3   The Heterodox Experiment

9.3.1   The State of the Country Inherited in 1985: The Initial Conditions

At the time Alán García was sworn in as president in July 1985, Peru's income per capita was comparable to what it had been in the late sixties, more than half of the labor force was registered by official statistics as not properly employed,[4] and inflation was nearing 200 percent in the 12-month period ending in August 1985. Although the official tenet of the second Belaúnde administration (1980–85) had been orthodox public finance and free markets, it undertook, during its first three years, ambitious infrastructural investments that required inflationary financing. Macroeconomic imbalances were compounded by the international recession, the drying up of voluntary external financing due to the onset of the debt crisis in 1982, and a severe natural disaster in 1983, when *El Nino* caused floods in the north and droughts in the south. These factors materialized in a 13 percent decline in GDP per capita in 1983–85.

Against this economic background, the sociopolitical situation had quickly deteriorated with continuous labor strikes and frequent attacks by Peru's two terrorist movements (the sierra-based and Maoist *Sendero Luminoso,* a Shining Path, and the urban, Cuban-style guerrilla group, MRTA). A further complication was constituted by the flourishing of drug cropping in the Upper Huallaga Valley where cocaine growers and *Sendero* had reached a morbid symbiosis. *Sendero* provides cocaine growers with protection against the government and, in return, the growers provide *Sendero* with a tax base. Export revenues from drug exports have been conservatively estimated at $1 billion per year or about 4 percent of GDP (Abusada 1987).

In its last two years (1984–85), the Belaúnde administration engaged in a serious effort to stabilize the economy. Public-sector prices were raised significantly and an aggressive exchange rate policy was pursued. The Central Bank took an independent stance from the executive and forced the latter to effect expenditure cuts and seek genuine sources of revenues. This policy course left a good legacy for the incoming APRA government in terms of a competitive

---

4. Official statistics estimated unemployment at 12 percent and "underemployment" at 54 percent of the labor force. Of course, underemployment is an imprecise, arbitrary concept. The Peruvian Ministry of Labor classifies workers as underemployed if their incomes are lower than the minimum real wage of 1967 or if they are working part-time involuntarily.

exchange rate, high public-sector prices, and relatively strong international reserve position.

These initial conditions, which characterize the end of a recessionary phase in Latin America's chronic stop-and-go economic policy cycles, provided one of the basic premises, as stated in Dornbusch and Edwards (1990) and Sachs (1989), for a short-lived consumption-led boom. The other basic premise is, of course, a poverty-stricken country with unsettled and mounting social and political conflicts, of which Peru is a good example. An additional ingredient for a populist course was suitably offered by the preexistence of an incipient and undeclared policy of external arrears, which had been initiated by the Belaúnde administration in late 1983. At the time of the changeover of administrations, external arrears on Peru's then-$14 billion debt had surpassed $2 billion. The preexistence of de facto arrears also provided a convenient departure point for a policy of confrontation with Peru's creditors.

9.3.2 Theoretical Underpinnings: Does Demand Create Its Own Supply?

A problem confronting the APRA party since the Velasco years had been that many of the reforms implemented unsuccessfully by the latter in the late 1960s and early 1970s—such as the nationalization of foreign firms, worker participation in firm ownership and management, and agrarian reform—had preempted many key issues of the APRA's traditional reform agenda. Moreover, the rhetoric of Alán García in the electoral campaign had been sufficiently conciliatory to gain support from business and the middle class, a key element emphasized by Drake (1982) in his characterization of populism. The nationalization of private banks—which accounted for about half of total deposits, but only one-third of credit—had been ruled out by the then–presidential candidate in his book *El Futuro Diferente*.

On the other hand, many influential advisers shared the view that the neoliberal agenda had been repeatedly tested, in Peru and elsewhere in Latin America, with an overwhelming evidence of failure. This was a basic claim of the book *El Peru Heterodoxo* (Carbonetto et al. 1987), written by the architects of the "heterodox program" launched in August 1985. As a result, the absence of an agenda for structural reforms, coupled with the distrust on the functioning of markets, resulted almost inevitably in a policy of intervention and widespread, haphazard subsidies. The following two excerpts summarize these views:

> When we took over, orthodox economists wanted us to tell semi-paralyzed companies they ought to be saving! Existing theories are no good. One difference between us and them is that we believe in controls rather than "opening up" to a historically unequal world market. Our approach is also more micro-economic.[5]

5. Interviews with D. Carbonetto (Peru Reporting EIRL 1987a, p. 11).

It's a response to the failure of traditional models. It draws on attempts in South America, the USA and England during the 1970s to rethink the workings of the capitalist system under conditions of oligopoly and heterogeneous development. . . . In heterogeneous economies, the way prices are formed varies tremendously according to particular markets. All this conduces to a different vision of how to control inflation. . . . Another thesis we have abandoned is the appropriateness of the exchange rate as the main, generalized and almost automatic instrument to regulate the foreign sector. We have gone in for planned, selective, differential exchange rates.[6]

Several macroeconomic beliefs were broadly held by the economic team. One was that demand management policies were both recession inducing and ineffective in dealing with inflation. The widespread existence of excess industrial capacity was interpreted as indicating that excess demand was not a problem. Aggregate demand expansion would only cause inflation beyond full employment of both labor and capital. In other words, aggregate supply was thought to follow a reversed L-shaped curve against the price level. Further, a reactivation of aggregate demand would lead to higher firm activity levels and thus to lower per-unit-of-output costs, thereby contributing to deflation rather than inflation. Hence, it was argued that periods of expansion of aggregate demand are associated with low inflation and vice versa. No distinction was drawn between real and nominal aggregate demand. Thus, it was noted that:

It is necessary to spend, even at the cost of a fiscal deficit, because, if the deficit is the result of transferring public resources to consumption of the poor so as they can demand more products and firms are able to reduce unitary costs, this deficit will not create inflationary pressures, but all the contrary. . . . This constitutes our major departure with respect to the previous strategy of demand restraint. (Carbonetto et al. 1987, p. 82)

Inflation was viewed as being exclusively a "cost-push" phenomenon. Hence, setting or, more generally, managing adequately the key prices—exchange rate, interest rates, and public-sector prices and tariffs—in combination with controls on private-sector prices, would provide a solid cure for inflation. Initially, a price freeze would brake inflationary expectations and dynamics. Another belief was that domestic consumption patterns were unduly dependent on imported goods. Therefore, import restrictions were required to change consumption patterns into local goods so as to reactivate internal activity and improve the balance of payments. Furthermore, scarce foreign exchange could not be wasted in sumptuary imports. Beyond import restrictions, a policy of "relative prices," so as to make goods with high direct or indirect import content more expensive, was suggested as a tool to change

6. D. Carbonetto (Peru Reporting EIRL 1987b, p. 24).

consumption patterns and ease pressure on the balance of payments (Instituto Nacional de Planificacion 1986, pp. 75–86).

In sum, the macroeconomic model the team had in mind was a static one in which a "Keynesian cross" determines the level of output and a "mark-up" equation determines the price level—very much in the tradition of the first Wharton models seasoned with import-substitution thinking. The econometric macromodel utilized for policy-making along with the aforementioned beliefs are fully documented in the book *El Peru Heterodoxo* (Carbonetto et al. 1987).

The effectiveness of multiple exchange rates for exports, among other incentives, as a device for export promotion was a long-standing claim of some Peruvian heterodox economists.[7] According to this theory, export commodities with higher supply elasticities should be given higher exchange rates— and other stimuli—in order to maximize export levels. Thus, manufacturing exports were to be granted a more competitive exchange rate than minerals and other traditional exports. This rationale led at some point in 1986 to attempts to establish contract programs with each major export firm. Under these programs the firm would commit itself to a certain export target and in return the Central Bank would grant the firm its own tailored real exchange rate (in terms of the firm's own cost formula). The essence of multiple exchange rates as a policy tool can be captured in the following paragraph:

> Multiple exchange rates are a kind of laser beam, allowing for greater flexibility. As a whole, though, we are aiming at a balance between the degree of devaluation created by the whole set of devaluatory instruments at our disposal and increases in exporters' costs. We are out to ensure exporter's profitability. At the moment, the incentives are concentrated in a few lines that we know are especially beneficial for Peru, like garments and fish for human consumption. Others are being studied by the Institute of Foreign Trade.[8]

Rules-versus-discretion debaters would find a good test case study in the economic policy of the period 1985–90. Indeed, most "prices" were subject to some sort of administrative regulation. Adjustments by decree in the structure of exchange rates, controlled prices, wages, interest rates, import tariffs, and so on, became a daily event. Over the period 1985–89, there were 186 decrees (about one per week) modifying the rules and structure of the exchange rates (Banco Central 1986–90). This continuous maneuvering with policy instruments stemmed from a wholehearted belief in *fine-tuning* as a means of allocating resources better than the market, promoting specific sec-

7. The debate on export promotion instruments acquired particular resonance in Peru since 1983 when the Association of Peruvian Exporters issued a report on export promotion prepared by Schydlowsky, Hunt, and Mezzera (1983). This report argued, along "second-best" lines, that export promotion incentives should be used to compensate for distortions so as to conciliate private and social costs.

8. Interview with D. Carbonetto (Peru Reporting EIRL 1987a, p. 11).

tors, benefiting the poor, and as a vehicle for negotiations with business groups (the so-called *concertacion*). The essence of *concertacion* was defined as follows:

> [This process enables parties] to agree on how much to produce, export or import and at what prices (including agreements on input prices), and under what conditions the State would provide the necessary *approval* (in the case of social returns not very low and high private returns), *support* (in the case in which social and private returns are high), or *subsidy* (in the case of high social returns and low private returns). The support and/or subsidy can be effected through preferential credit, tax and/or tariff exemptions, guarantees of provision of foreign exchange, outright subsidies, profit guarantees, etc. The agreements on investments should include amounts, location, and terms as well as the conditions for approval, support and or subsidy by the State. (Ferrari 1986, p. 522)

The unilateral default on the foreign debt is undoubtedly the best-known policy of President Alán García. The 10-percent-of-exports ceiling on debt service payments was announced by the president at his inauguration. The belief that debt servicing was putting undue pressure on Peru's meager savings capacity was, at the time, shared by business and parties of the left and right alike. The net resource transfer had been negative since 1984 and was unlikely to become positive any time soon.

9.3.3   Contentment and Contentiousness: The Expansionary Phase of the Experiment, 1985–87

The Strategy

In August 1985, President Alán García launched an economic recovery program based on this set of unconventional economic premises and guidelines. As Ortiz de Zevallos (1989) describes, the program had been assembled in a three-day emergency summit shortly before the inauguration. The negotiated program represented a compromise between a "cautious" group of advisers, the APRA's own economic campaign team, and a group of "audacious" heterodox advisers of President García.

The compromise strategy was to prompt a quick economic recovery by boosting consumption demand, which would be accommodated by existing slack industrial capacity. Consumption demand would be fueled by increasing real wages, implementing direct subsidy programs and temporary employment-generating public works in marginal areas, and transferring disposable income from the public sector to the private sector. The latter was effected through reducing taxes and freezing public sector prices and tariffs. The use of slack capacity would be guaranteed by closing the domestic market to imports competing with domestic production. In addition, the government instituted a price, cost, interest rate, and exchange rate freeze geared to breaking inflationary expectations. The main policy measures included in the program are presented in table 9.3.

Table 9.3   Main Policy Measures of "Plan de Emergencia" from August 1985 to December 1986

Wages and Employment	Exchange Rate	Interest Rates	Taxes and Public-Sector Tariffs and Prices	Private-Sector Prices	Public Expenditure and Social Programs
Periodic nominal hikes so as to reach a 7% annual increase in real terms. In practice, minimum real wages rose 34% in the 17-month period. Tax exemption to employees on the share of income tax paid by them. Two one-time interest-free loans to civil servants. Reduction of *probation* period from three years to three months. Establishment of PROEM allowing firms to hire temporary workers for up to two years without adhering to labor stability laws.	Initial 12% devaluation and subsequent freeze of official rate. Later, introduction of multiple exchange rates; first, only for exports and then for imports as well.	Lending rate of commercial banks: gradual reduction from 280% to 40% annual rate. Saving rate (one year deposits): gradual reduction from 107% to 31%. Lending rate by Agrarian Bank: *a)* Regular rate reduced from 116% to 25% *b)* Establishment facility at *zero* interest rate for the Andean highlands farmers.	Reduction of sales tax rate from 11% to 6%. Enhanced tax exemptions to selected sectors on sales tax, import tariffs, and other taxes. Freeze of public-sector prices and tariffs. In February 1986, reduction of water and electricity tariffs by 20% and of prices of petroleum products by 10%.	Freeze of all prices. Later periodic adjustment and/or liberalization of most agricultural prices. Creation of a price authority (CIPA) coordinated by the Ministry of Finance.	Establishment of the following programs totalling expenditures of about 2% of GDP: *a)* FRASA: to fund price support schemes and subsidies for agricultural products. *b)* PAIT: temporary labor-works programs in marginal areas. *c)* Support to peasant communities. *d)* Microregional development in emergency zones. *e)* PAD: direct support program to provide social services and food in the *pueblos jovenes* (shanty towns). Establishment of credit lines and /or credit guarantee facilities for microentrepreneurs by the newly created IDESI, Peru's Development Finance Corporation (COFIDE), and the Industrial Bank.

Peru's pervasive and often romanticized informal sector would be instrumental in both the output recovery and employment generation. The demand boost, together with the establishment of several credit and credit-guarantee programs for microentrepreneurs, would stimulate the informal sector. The agricultural sector was also made a high priority: guaranteed prices to producers of the main staples were significantly raised, input subsidies increased, and lines of agricultural credit on preferential terms considerably expanded. The poor *campesinos* of the sierra, the most backward part of the country, would be the main beneficiaries. Raising incomes in the sierra also had the key purpose of pacifying this terrorism-stricken part of the country.

The necessary resources to finance the strategy were to become available from reductions in external debt payments and from Central Bank financing. The political rhetoric was confrontational with external creditors and conciliatory with domestic economic agents—designed to bring about contentment at home and contentiousness abroad.

The government's heterodox economic program, officially termed the *Plan de Emergencia,* was expected to last 12 months, from August 1985 to July 1986, but was subsequently extended through December 1986. The authorities stated that this recovery program, based on consumption-led expansion, could only last insofar as there was unutilized capacity. Therefore, the government envisaged a second phase for the postrecovery era where the focus would be on investment and exports, so as to make the transition from short-run output expansion to long-run sustainable growth. However, the economic strategy to be followed in the second phase was never consistently developed. Furthermore, the measures implemented to prompt the recovery were at variance with the rules of the game required to promote investment, exports, and growth. It was assumed that the government would be able to negotiate (*concertar*) with business groups the reinvestment of the profits accrued during the boom into export industries.

The Consumption Boom

After a few months of initial sluggishness, the response of the economy to the program was an unprecedented output expansion. The GDP expanded 9.5 percent in 1986 and 7.8 percent in 1987 (fig. 9.1 and table 9.4). Along with output, employment in the formal sector of the economy grew by a cumulative 12 percent in the two-year period (fig. 9.2), mainly through temporary recruitment under the newly instituted temporary employment program (PROEM). This program enabled employers to circumvent the government's decision of reducing probation from three years to three months as well as other restrictive layoff procedures in Peru's labor legislation. The price-cost freeze, coupled with initially moderate monetary policy, reduced inflation from 200 percent in the 12-month period immediately preceding the freeze to 63 percent in 1986 (fig. 9.3). Real wages grew 24 percent over the two-year period. During 1985–87, the combination of price controls for industrial products, generous

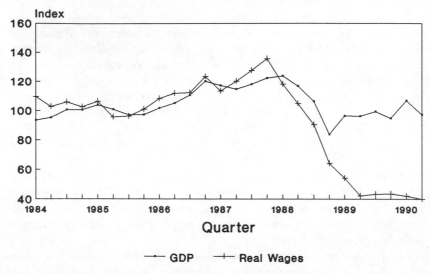

Fig. 9.1   Evolution of real GDP and real wages (1985 = 100)

agricultural price guarantees, and huge input and credit subsidies for agriculture translated into a 90 percent improvement in rural-urban terms of trade and a corresponding significant improvement of agricultural incomes. Some basic macroeconomic indicators are presented in table 9.4.

These results, however, were reached at the expense of growing financial and external imbalances and of increasing misalignments in key relative prices. These imbalances, in turn, signaled that the model being followed was unsustainable and that the economy would lapse into an open crisis if corrective measures were not adopted. *First,* total public-sector revenues dropped by a cumulative 18 percent of GDP in 1985–87.[9] In turn, foreign exchange and financial losses of the Central Bank—resulting from the operation of the multiple exchange rate system and interest rate subsidies, respectively—grew rapidly to a level equal to 3.7 percent of GDP in 1987. As a result, and notwithstanding a reduction in public investment, the public-sector imbalance—as gauged by the domestic financing of the public-sector deficit—jumped from 0.6 percent of GDP in 1985 to 10.5 percent in 1987. The decline in the ratio of public investment to GDP was largely a "cost of default," rather than a conscious decision, because many projects depended on either foreign technology or were linked to foreign financing. The minister of planning put it this way:

9. Here we refer to public-sector revenues as defined by simply adding tax revenues and state enterprise gross revenues (excluding transfers from the government). Obviously, there is double counting and other problems with this measure, but it provides a very good rough graphical indicator of the total revenue loss.

Table 9.4   Main Economic Indicators, 1980–89

	Average, 1980–84	1985	1986	1987	1988	1989
Real GDP growth (%)	− 1.0	2.4	9.5	7.8	− 8.8	− 10.4
Real per capital GDP growth (%)	− 3.6	− .2	6.9	5.2	− 11.4	− 13.0
Real consumption growth (%)	− .4	2.3	13.3	8.3	− 11.5	− 7.5
Inflation rate (%)	87.0	158.3	62.9	114.5	1,722.3	2,775.3
Broad money supply growth (%)	94.0	122.4	64.4	113.0	585.1	2,028.7
Public-sector borrowing require- ments (% of GDP)	7.8	5.8	9.1	12.9	15.6	9.8
Tax revenues/GDP (%)	13.5	14.9	12.4	8.9	9.1	5.4
Public enterprises revenue/GDP (%)	25.3	26.1	18.4	14.1	8.9	7.2
Current account deficit/GDP (%)[a,b]	3.9	.3	6.0	7.2	7.4	1.0
Gross international reserves (in Millions of U.S. dollars)	. . .	2,283.0	1,861.0	1,130.0	1,125.0	1,512.0
Foreign debt/GDP (%)[a]	51.0	76.8	67.8	62.4	77.0	103.5
Accrued debt service ratio (%)	61.1	69.8	77.9	77.0	79.3	64.0
Paid debt service ratio (%)	53.7	22.5	19.6	13.4	5.4	5.6
Real exchange rate (December 1978 = 100)[c,d]	77.1	99.6	86.8	74.9	91.2	59.0
Terms of trade (1978 = 100)	118.4	90.6	66.4	66.9	72.8	68.9
Real wage (1979 = 100)	95	64	73	79	60	29
Employment growth (%)	2.2	1.9	6.4	4.7	− 6.5	− 3.6
Utilized capacity index (%)	56.0	45.0	71.0	79.0	59.0	46.0

Source: National Statistical Institute, Central Reserve Bank, Ministry of Finance and author's estimates.
[a]Ratios obtained using the July 1985–based purchasing power parity exchange rate.
[b]Includes interest imputed on arrears.
[c]Evaluated at the weighted average of all current commercial exchange rates (intis per US$).
[d]An increase in the series means real depreciation of the effective exchange rate for trade accounts transactions.

The deficit, including unpaid interest due on the foreign debt, was the equivalent of about 5.6 percent of Gross Domestic Product in 1986. One reason why it was not larger is that the state companies have spent less than they were supposed to. Up to the end of September, the figures show state companies using only 30 percent of their budget, partly because of problems getting foreign financing, quarrels with foreign companies contracted by previous governments, investigations and so on. It was a disaster.[10]

Second, the real exchange rate appreciated 26 percent between July 1985 and October 1987. This, together with booming aggregate demand, made the GDP expansion highly import intensive contrary to the initial designs of the

10. Interview with J. Tantalean (Peru Reporting EIRL 1987a, p. 13).

Fig. 9.2   Evolution of real GDP and employment (1985 = 100)

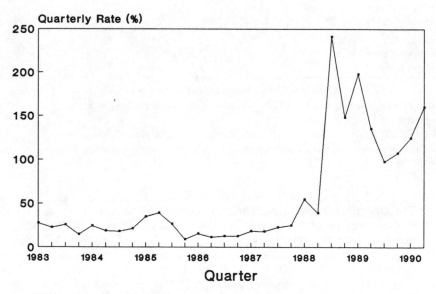

Fig. 9.3   Inflation rates by quarters (1983–90)

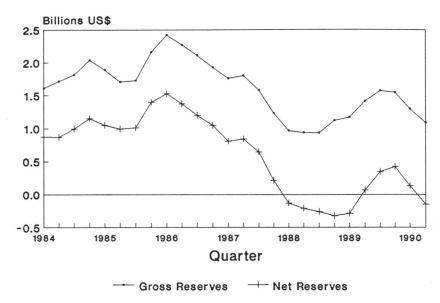

Fig. 9.4   **International reserves of the Central Bank**

government. With the parallel decline in exports, the external current account went from near equilibrium in 1985 to a deficit of about 6.5 percent of GDP in 1986–87. The ultimate effect of this was a sustained drop of net international reserves from a peak of $1.5 billion in March 1986 to roughly zero in December 1987 (fig. 9.4).[11] *Third, the focus on* boosting consumption reduced the potential for investing the surplus gained by the external moratorium, thereby trading off short-run expansion for future sustainable growth.

It should be noted that the demand-led course was initially counteracted to some extent by the Central Bank. During its first five months, the new administration had maintained the governor of the Central Bank of the previous administration. In this period, monetary policy was reasonably restrictive in an attempt, on the one hand, to sterilize the huge balance of payments surpluses (reserve inflows) originating from the limitation on foreign debt service payments, and, on the other hand, to decelerate the growth of monetary aggregates in accordance with the lower rate of inflation achieved with the price freeze (table 9.5). To this end, tighter legal reserve requirements were imposed on commercial banks' deposits, and although interest rates were scaled down, initially this reduction was matched by a similar decline in inflation, and thus real interest rates did not fall further. In August 1985, foreign cur-

11. However, gross reserves reported by the Central Bank in December 1987 still totaled $1.1 billion (with $800 million in gold). But Peru needed a large carryover of reserves to finance imports because the default had caused a withdrawal of external trade finance.

Table 9.5   Financial Survey: Uses and Sources of Broad Money[a] (Percentage Changes with Respect to the Stock of Broad Money Outstanding at the End of the Previous Period, Six-Month Rates)

	1985 I	1985 II	1986 I	1986 II	1987 I	1987 II	1988 I	1988 II	1989 I	1989 II	1990 I
A. Broad Money Supply (Uses)	50.7	46.2	22.5	35.4	34.3	58.5	45.4	371.2	443.1	292.0	278.6
1. Money	6.4	31.8	12.7	20.5	12.6	37.9	26.8	152.5	113.1	107.4	96.3
2. Near money	44.3	14.4	9.8	14.9	21.7	20.6	18.6	218.7	330.0	184.6	182.3
Domestic currency	7.1	27.3	17.5	17.9	21.7	13.2	17.1	76.4	175.9	132.8	97.2
Foreign currency	37.2	−12.9	−7.7	−3.0	.0	7.4	1.5	142.3	154.1	51.8	85.1
B. Broad Money Supply (Sources)	50.7	46.2	22.5	35.4	34.3	58.5	45.4	371.2	443.1	292.0	278.6
1. Net international reserves	10.1	26.5	−3.8	−7.6	−2.0	−14.2	−7.8	−86.1	87.1	42.4	−34.6
2. Domestic credit to nonfinancial public sector	9.5	−9.8	−5.2	22.0	11.7	34.7	4.1	69.8	27.5	63.7	156.8
3. Domestic credit to private sector	48.4	25.6	19.0	33.0	32.0	40.3	32.1	245.0	290.8	149.5	191.6
4. Net unclassified assets	−17.3	3.9	12.4	−11.9	−7.3	−2.3	17.0	142.5	37.7	36.3	−35.6
Memo items:											
Base money growth[b]	54.8	90.4	23.0	13.3	27.1	67.6	54.0	373.6	365.8	226.2	394.5
Inflation rate[c]	87.7	37.6	28.5	26.8	40.1	53.1	115.2	746.5	601.2	310.0	484.0
Money supply multiplier[d]	1.9	1.4	1.4	1.7	1.8	1.7	1.6	1.6	1.9	2.2	1.7
Income velocity of broad money:											
Including dollar-indexed deposits	3.1	3.3	3.3	3.6	3.7	3.8	4.9	6.4	9.5	9.8	n.a.
Excluding dollar-indexed deposits	6.8	5.6	4.3	4.2	4.1	4.2	5.3	8.8	14.3	13.0	n.a.

Sources: Central Reserve Bank and author's estimates.

[a]Includes all financial operations of financial institutions of the formal sector (banks and other nonbank) with economic agents.

[b]As a percentage of the previous period's base money (six-month rate).

[c]Inflation for the semester (six-month rate).

[d]The ratio of broad money to the base money.

rency deposits were made redeemable only in local currency at the official exchange rate plus a small premium. Monetary policy eased in the first half of 1986 and became overtly expansionary in the second half.

When the price and cost freeze was lifted in December 1986, price controls on several groups of products were eased somewhat. In January 1987, a mild crawling peg for the two benchmark exchange rates was instituted. The "crawl" was halted in July 1987 following concerns over inflationary pressures.

The Rise and Fall of Private-Sector Confidence

Prior to 1987, private-sector confidence in and support of the government's economic policy could only be described as being unanimous. In his July 1986 presidential address, President Alán García reaffirmed the partnership with the private sector and ruled out expropriation or other statist measures. Negotiations (*concertacion*) were continuously carried out during the second half of 1986 to persuade the principal industrial groups (the so-called twelve apostles) to invest in export-oriented businesses. Virtually every incentive was open for negotiation: preferential exchange rates, credit subsidies, tax exemptions, and so on.

The troubles started in 1987, when some sources began claiming that the private sector, while benefiting from the boom, was not delivering the quid pro quo of reinvesting surpluses so as to contribute to exports and growth. As this view was not corroborated by provisional Central Bank estimates— which indicated that private investment had grown 18 percent between 1985 and 1986—the National Planning Institute commissioned an independent study in early 1987 to analyze investment data from the financial statements of 62 firms listed in the stock exchange (Thorne 1986). The study found that in 1986 gross fixed investment had grown at most 7 percent and that most of this increase could be accounted for by inventory accumulation. Moreover, the firms that were investing more were those oriented to the internal market—just the contrary to the government's wishes.

The paradox was that, in practice, while seeking to induce firms to switch into export-oriented investments, the government was shifting all incentives toward the internal market. Indeed, by 1987 all imports were made subject to both an import license and a foreign exchange license, whereas in 1985, 61 percent of all tariff code items stood free from quantitative restrictions. Similarly, the maximum tariff rate had been raised from 91 percent in 1985 to 155 percent in 1987.

Table 9.6 shows that the claim of unresponsive private investment turned out to be unfounded. Final official data revealed that private investment doubled between 1985 and 1987, although it is true that the major share of new investment was in construction and inventories rather than in equipment. In the wake of the contention over private investment, the government tried

Table 9.6   **GDP and Aggregate Demand[a] (Index Numbers in Real Terms)**

	1980–84	1985	1986	1987	1988	1989
Aggregate supply	123.3	113.9	126.4	137.4	124.5	109.7
GDP	100.0	99.0	108.4	116.9	106.6	95.5
Imports	23.3	14.9	18.0	20.5	17.9	14.2
Aggregate demand	123.3	113.9	126.4	137.4	124.5	109.7
Consumption	72.9	72.4	82.1	88.9	78.6	72.8
Private	62.6	62.2	71.4	78.1	70.4	69.1
Public	10.3	10.2	10.6	10.8	8.2	3.6
Investment	26.4	16.0	21.4	26.5	25.5	12.9
Equipment	10.6	6.1	7.0	7.9	5.7	N.A.
Construction	13.1	10.4	12.8	14.8	14.0	N.A.
Inventories	2.7	− .5	1.6	3.8	5.8	N.A.
Exports	23.9	25.5	22.9	22.0	20.3	24.0
Memo items						
Private investment	19.2	10.1	15.8	21.8	22.3	11.0
Public investment	7.2	5.9	5.6	4.7	3.2	1.9

Source: National Statistical Institute and Central Reserve Bank.
[a]The average GDP for 1980–84 was taken as the base (GDP in 1980–84 = 100). As a result, all figures in the table are index numbers refered to the average GDP of 1980–84 and should be read as proportions of GDP of that period.

first a highly subsidized investment scheme,[12] and, shortly thereafter, devised a compulsory program aimed at forcing private firms to invest in export activities. Under this program, a large percentage of firms' profits had to be traded for compulsory investment bonds.

The honeymoon was finally over when President García launched his initiative to nationalize private commercial banks and insurance companies and to establish foreign exchange controls. These measures were announced in his second annual address to the nation in July 1987. These political events, together with the emerging concerns on the sustainability of the economic program as exemplified by the free fall of international reserves, triggered the onset of the crisis, with the free market exchange rate commanding growing spreads over the official rate (figs. 9.4 and 9.5).

The "10 Percent Default": Rhetoric and Practice

President García's announcement, in July 1985, of the 10 percent of exports cap on debt payments broke with the arrears-cum-best-effort-to-pay tenet of the last Belaúnde years. Shortly thereafter, Peru's debt was declared value impaired by the United States. The government attempted unsuccessfully to convince credits that *new debt* commitments would be fully serviced while *old debt* would, as a rule, be serviced only when creditors provided a positive

12. The *Fondo de Inversion y Empleo* granted prospective investors of approved export projects, largely located outside Lima, a cost-free equity contribution from the government equal to one-third of the project cost.

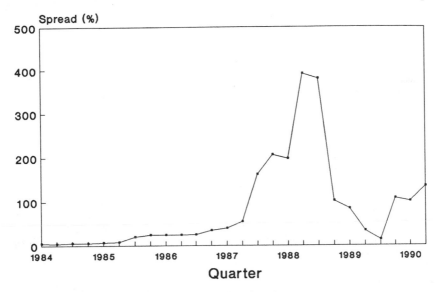

Fig. 9.5   **Spread between parallel and official exchange rates**

net transfer to Peru. Therefore, the trick with the 10 percent rule was that Peru would only pay as long as creditors provided the money to pay themselves. The reality was that, rhetoric to the contrary, from July 1985 to December 1986 Peru's actual debt service to creditors was around 20 percent of exports for public debt alone (table 9.7) and over 25 percent of exports for total debt, and the negative net transfer was almost as high as it had been in the last two Belaúnde years. The assumption, later proven erroneous, that Peru could selectively default against some creditors while obtaining financing from others led progressively to defaults with initially nontargeted creditor groups. It was only in 1988 that total debt service descended to the 10 percent limit.

In August 1986, Peru was declared ineligible for IMF lending, and one year later was placed on "nonaccrual" status by the World Bank. In early 1989, the Inter-American Development Bank also took the step of classifying Peru as a nonaccrual country due to protracted default. In 1986, the external debt moratorium was extended to private-sector liabilities. In his second presidential address to the nation in July 1986, President García announced the suspension for two years of both private debt service and profit repatriation by foreign corporations.

Another contentious issue was the renegotiation of exploration and production contracts with the three multinationals operating in Peru's hydrocarbons sector. Arguing that the hydrocarbons law issued by the previous Belaúnde administration had not paid due regard to the interests of the nation, the authorities forced renegotiation of the contracts under less favorable conditions. One of the three multilaterals, Belco, refused to accept the new conditions,

Table 9.7   **Debt Service Payments on Public External Debt[a]**
                         (In Millions of U.S. Dollars)

	1985	1986	1987	1988	1989
Central bank debt	236	165	58	42	71
Rest of public sector	617	495	422	158	183
Bilateral creditors	43	71	108	45	56
Commercial					
banks	133	27	5	3	5
Multilaterals	171	226	155	74	28
Socialist coun-					
tries	170	111	94	11	63
Suppliers	100	60	60	25	31
Total debt service	853	660	480	200	254
Debt service ratio[b]	22.5	19.6	13.4	5.4	5.6

Source: Central Reserve Bank and author's estimates.
[a]Debt service is defined as the sum of interest and amortization actually paid.
[b]Amount paid as a percentage of exports of good and nonfactor sevices.

leading to termination of the contract in 1986 and de facto, to expropriation of the assets without compensation.

    Growing isolation from creditors and foreign investors inevitably meant growing isolation from trading partners, rendering Peru particularly vulnerable to import restrictions in creditor nations and contributing to vanishing domestic confidence.

9.3.4   Decline and Despair: The Recessionary Phase of the Experiment, 1988–90

    By late 1987, the dynamics of the economics and the politics of the experiment turned an originally "well-orchestrated," center-right, "demand-led boom" into an openly confrontational, both abroad and at home, populist experiment. Net international reserves had reached "the red," Central Bank external deposits had to be moved from one country to another to avoid potential seizure by creditors, letters of credit for imports had to be collateralized with cash, and the Central Bank had to start drawing down gold reserves.[13] Public-sector real prices and tariffs, running on average at less than half of their levels of July 1985, were adjusted infrequently and insufficiently. The number of exchange rate categories increased from three in 1985 to nine in mid-1987. The Agrarian Bank continued allocating low- or zero-interest loans to farmers, and wage increases continued to be granted by decree every four months. Meanwhile, the domestic financing of the public-sector imbalance had soared from 0.6 percent of GDP in 1985 to close to 10.5 percent in 1987 (table 9.8).

---

13. In January 1988 the business newsletter "Eficacia" published the names of the international banks in which Peru's Central Bank maintained its reserves at the time. During the following days the Central Bank had to redeploy its reserves elsewhere (Peru Reporting EIRL 1988a).

In a country with a very narrow financial system, this represented a huge burden for the Central Bank to finance. Hence, an inflationary momentum was set in motion, with inflation jumping from 64 percent in 1986 to 115 percent in 1987.

Despite the unfolding crisis, policymakers still remained unconvinced of the need for macroeconomic stabilization. Some sectors maintained that although high capacity utilization had been achieved in several industrial sectors, other sectors still registered slack capacity. Since, on average, capacity use was still 70 percent, the doubling of inflation could not be attributed to excess demand pressures. Measuring excess demand *in real and static* Keynesian effective demand instead of *in nominal and dynamic* terms was a

Table 9.8	Public Finance, 1984–87 (% of GDP)					
	1984	1985	1986	1987	1988	1989
1. Public-sector revenues	39.7	41.0	30.8	23.0	18.0	12.6
Tax revenues	15.8	14.9	12.4	8.9	9.1	5.4
State enterprises revenues	23.9	26.1	18.4	14.1	8.9	7.2
2. Public-sector expenditures	45.5	44.6	36.7	30.6	28.3	19.9
of which, investment	7.4	6.0	5.2	4.0	3.0	2.0
of which, wages	8.9	7.9	8.5	9.0	6.8	5.5
3. Nonfinancial public-sector deficit (2–1)	5.8	3.6	5.9	7.6	10.3	7.3
4. Central bank losses	. . .	1.9	1.8	3.7	3.8	0.6
5. Overall deficit (3+4)	5.8	5.5	7.7	11.3	14.1	7.9
6. Central bank transfers to development banks	1.4	0.3	1.4	1.6	1.5	1.9
7. Total public-sector borrowing requirements (PSBR)	7.2	5.8	9.1	12.9	15.6	9.8
8. Financing of PSBR	7.2	5.8	9.1	12.9	15.6	9.8
Foreign PSBR	5.1	5.2	3.4	2.4	4.3	2.9
of which, extant international arrears	2.5	4.4	2.9	2.0	4.2	2.7
Domestic credit	2.1	.6	5.7	10.5	11.3	7.1
of which, domestic arrears	.5	1.3	1.6	1.1	3.2	2.8

Source: Central Reserve Bank and author's estimates.
Note: The reason why gross revenues of state enterprises and gross expenditures of the public sector are used here is to show the reader the phenomenal decline of the ratios to GDP of both items. We are, however, aware of the imperfections implied by these measures. In particular, adding tax revenues and state enterprise revenues (item 1) implies double counting of taxes paid by state enterprises. Besides, state enterprise revenues are gross and thus not strictly income. The same occurs with item 2, which is the sum of central government expenditures and public enterprise gross expenditures (the latter including intermediate expenditures and therefore not strictly comparable with Central Government expenditures, which are final aggregate demand). Double counting, however, affects equally both revenues and expenditures and therefore does not alter the deficit figures.

very common analytical framework used at the time (Postigo de la Motta 1988, p. 21). Some sources even suggested selectively "targeting" aggregate demand to sectors with slack capacity, while others came to defend that industrial capacity was still underutilized in most sectors since industry was operating on average at less than two shifts while full use was at three shifts of eight hours each.

On the eve of its collapse, the designers of the program published the book *El Peru Heterodoxo* (Carbonetto et al. 1987), in which they claimed to have discovered a new policy approach and recommended the application of their model to other countries:

> At the time of sending this book to print we are witnessing the first one and a half years of the implementation of Peru's reactivation policy. The results obtained prove most of the guiding thesis according to which it is possible to reactivate (in the presence of slack capacity) and simultaneously reduce inflation. (p. 16)

> We trust the book will be a useful tool for developing countries confronting similar problems to ours. (p. i)

The glamorous boom seduced even some foreign academics. In June 1987, a few months before the devastating collapse, Rosemary Thorp, after an in situ examination of the evolution of the program, and notwithstanding a few disclaimers, wrote:

> Gradually both the thinking behind the policy approach and its actual implementation have become more coherent, more interesting and more audacious. It is too early still to define phases, since the development has been continuous, marked by the appearance of coherent planning models for the Planning Institute (the first dated May 1986) and by the beginning of thinking on how reactivation should become growth and resulting policy initiatives in the second half of 1986. . . . The three areas in which new thinking has been most conspicuous and impressive are closely interrelated: *concertacion*, the external sector, and the issue of long run structural change. Short-term price and exchange rate management have also evolved—less confidently. (Thorp 1987, p. 5)

The Failed Stabilization Attempts

With the pressure of rapidly vanishing international reserves (fig. 9.4), failure to have adjusted the exchange rates for exporters as well as the fact of having channeled subsidies indiscriminately to all sectors, instead of a few priority sectors, were made the culprits for all troubles. The increasingly meager fiscal and foreign exchange resources prompted the National Planning Institute to launch its proposal for "selective growth" in late 1987. Subsidies channeled through foreign exchange, taxes, tariffs, credit, or any other means would, from then on, be addressed exclusively to predefined priority sectors. The problem was not the size of the subsidies per se, but rather that a large part had been wasted on promoting undeserving sectors (Postigo de la Motta 1988, pp. 28–31). Also in late 1987, the Ministry of Economy proposed a *Programa Trienal* that set the policies and targets for the next three years in the areas of increasing the tax-burden ratio, simplifying the exchange rate structure, and divesting several public enterprises. These measures sought to partially reverse the precarious financial situation and cumbersome incentive structure, but were to a larger degree designed as a strategy for resumed dialogue with multilateral credit agencies. This rapprochement to the multilaterals has been viewed as an application of President García's theory of the two fronts: the country could be in contentiousness either on the external front or the domestic front, but not simultaneously in both. Since the nationalization of the banking system had damaged relations at home, it was necessary to portray improved attitudes abroad. Nevertheless, neither selective growth nor the *Programa Trienal* were carried through. Instead, a sequence of destabilizing economic measures started to unfold.

Since late 1987, the Central Bank started systematically to adjust the exchange rates for exporters without passing on the higher price of dollars on to importers. The best of both worlds was being pursued. By August 1988, the Central Bank was on average selling foreign exchange to importers at half the price it paid to exporters. Thus, foreign exchange losses in 1988 reached 3.8 percent of GDP, adding to an already precarious budget imbalance.

Three major one-shot economic packages were implemented during 1988: in March, September, and November. Table 9.9 presents the key elements of these packages. In the three cases the measures finally announced, although they embedded the same approach to adjustment as the technical proposal prepared by the economic team, had undergone a tough political filter.[14] The three announced packages were very similar. Namely, they decreed adjustments in public prices, exchange rates, interest rates, and wages. In addition, the first two included a follow-up 120-day freeze on prices, wages, and the exchange rate, and the second declared the unification of the exchange rates for commercial transactions (thereby transferring subsidies for several highly subsidized food and agricultural imports to the budget).

With the exception of the November package, nominal wage hikes were, in general, granted at higher rates than those decreed for regulated prices and exchange rates. In the March package the highest price adjustment was set at 51 percent while minimum wages were raised by 60 percent; in turn, in the September package the effective exchange rate was devalued by 95 percent— although the largely irrelevant official rate was devalued by 600-plus percent—while minimum wages were raised by 150 percent. Economic policymaking had, thus, engaged in the impossible task of trying to narrow the

14. Peru Reporting EIRL (1988a, 1988b, 1988c) and weekly magazines: *Sí* (28 November 1988, pp. 6, 7) and *Oiga* (12 December 1988, pp. 13–15). These press accounts illustrate President García's personal involvement, in great detail, in economic policy-making.

Table 9.9   Packages of Economic Measures, October 1987 through November 1988

	1987		1988		
	October	December	March	September	November
PRICES, WAGES AND EXCHANGE RATE			+Adjustment & 120-day freeze (export exchange rate excluded from freeze)	+Adjustment & 120-day freeze (freeze lifted 3 weeks later)	+Adjustment & 120-day freeze (freeze lifted 3 weeks later)
Effective rate (devaluation) (%)	29	47	15	95	82
Number of exchange rates:					
Imports	3	7	6	1	1
Exports	3	2	3	1	1
Total	5	9	8	1	1
Minimum wage increases (%)	29	...	60	150	40
Public sector wage increases (%)	25	...	40	95	40
Private sector wage increases (%)	25	...	45	94	50
Increase of public tariffs:					
Gasoline (%)	0	0	51	296	140
Electricity (%)	24	12	29	136	114
Rice (%)	0	0	39	140	100
Increases of prices of controlled products (%)	5	6	15	148	40
TAXES					
Changes in existing taxes	+Increase in surcharge on imports: 4%	+Sales tax from 6% to 10% +Increase in all excise taxes +Indexation to inflation of prepayments of corporate profit taxes +Elimination of exemptions under import surcharge	+Sales tax to 10.5%	+Increase of excise tax rates on beer and cigarettes +Reduction of exemptions on import tariffs +Reduction in tax collection lags	+Partial indexation of tax liabilities to inflation +Reduction of excise taxes (cigarettes and liquors) +Ad-valorem custom duties: from 10% to 16% +On exports: 10%

New taxes	+ On purchases of foreign exchange: 25%	+ Minimum duty to imports: 5% + Tax on personal property: 1–4%		+ On exports: 4%	
IMPORT TARIFFS AND RESTRICTIONS	+ All imports subject to licenses	+ Import licenses need approval of Institute of Foreign Trade (ICE) and Central Reserve Bank	+ Some imports can be financed with the importer's own foreign exchange	+ Shift of 35% of imports from official exchange rate market	
Evolution of quantitative restrictions (QRs) (% of total of tariff categories):					
Free from QRs (%)		.0		.0	
License required (%)		89.7		89.7	
Import prohibitions (%)		10.3		47.3	
Evolution of tariffs:					
Average tariff (%)		67.0		70	
Maximum tariff (%)		155.0		108	
EXPORTS MEASURES				CLDª from 10 to 30	
INTEREST RATE					
Lending rate (%)		From 32 to 40	To 55	To 255	20 per month
Deposit rate (%)		From 22 to 35.5		To 219	17 per month

ªThe Certificados de Libre Disponibilidad (CLD) is a tradable dollar certificate given to exporters for a share of their export porceeds that can be used by an importer.

internal and external imbalances without requiring economic agents to adjust ex ante their budget constraints.

Indeed, narrowing the budgetary gap required, in addition to tax measures, an increase in the relative prices of goods and services provided by the public sector in terms of nominal wages. At the same time, correcting the external imbalance required an increase in the ratio of the nominal exchange rate to nominal wages. Moreover, reducing inflation required that the adjustment of these two key relative prices be effected with at most a moderate escalation of these three key sets of prices. The policy course taken was just the opposite, namely, small adjustments in the relative prices with high nominal escalation of absolute prices. The paradox was that the September package was officially termed the "double-zero" plan, for it was intended to eliminate both the fiscal deficit and Central Bank inflationary financing. But, as explained below, the president of the Central Bank took the plan seriously.

The Trigger Point of Hyperinflation: Laffer Curves, Snowballs, and Social Turmoil

Monetarists think of inflation as too much money chasing too few goods, while flow of funds believers view inflation as a dirty transfer of real resources from individuals and firms to the public sector and other favored sectors, and yet structuralists think of it as the result of a race between prices, wages, and exchange rates reflecting the struggle for the distribution of income.

The three aforementioned packages failed the three tests: the monetarist, the structuralist and the flow of funds consistency. Indeed, by the second quarter of 1988 inflation had surpassed the level that would generate the "maximum-inflation tax" (fig. 9.6).[15] Furthermore, gross real resources raised by the government through inflation did not contribute much to closing the non-financial public-sector gap, for these resources were largely transferred back as foreign exchange and financial subsidies, the latter particularly, but not exclusively, to peasants (table 9.10). Even worse, the dynamics were explosive since, as the gross inflation tax was sliding down the inefficient portion of the Laffer curve, real financial subsidies were rising because nominal interest rates lagged increasingly behind inflation. In parallel, the evolution of wages, prices, and exchange rates was setting into motion a snowball, which aggravated inflationary dynamics and expectations.

By late 1988, the economy had taken off on a hyperinflationary path, with inflation accelerating from an annual rate of 360 percent in the first half to nearly 7,000 percent in the second half, and real money plummeting to one-third of its level one year earlier (figs. 9.3 and 9.7). Economic agents had

15. The trade-off between inflation and real resources raised through inflation presented in fig. 9.6 was calculated by Lago (1989). It results from fitting the path followed by inflation and real money, from the second semester of 1987 to the first of 1988, into Philip Cagan's demand for money. It is therefore an arch estimate and not a regression result. It is presented only as an illustration of the Laffer curve.

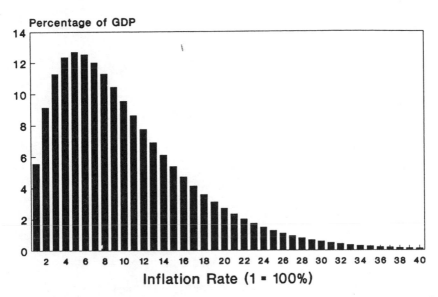

Fig. 9.6   Laffer curve: Revenues from inflation/GDP

Table 9.10   Inflation Tax, Inflation Subsidy, and Net Inflation Tax (% of GDP)

Year	Inflation Tax	Inflation Subsidy	Net Inflation Tax
1980	2.6	1.4	1.2
1981	2.1	1.4	.7
1982	.9	1.7	− .8
1983	2.1	3.0	− .9
1984	.9	1.9	− 1.0
1985	3.2	2.9	.3
1986	3.6	1.8	1.8
1987	4.3	3.0	1.3
1988	5.2	4.3	.9

Source: Based on a very detailed calculation performed by Oks (1989) of the effect of inflation on financial assets and liabilities of the consolidated public sector (including the Central Bank and all public banks).

interpreted the government's corrective attempts as destabilizing, prompting a massive rush to the dollar, unprecedented black market premia (up to 400%) and the continuation of a free fall of both GDP and real wages that had initiated in early 1988 (fig. 9.1). Hyperrecession walked hand in hand with hyperinflation.

The recession was prompted by the collapse of private investment—brought about by the unstable inflationary trend—and also by the downfall of

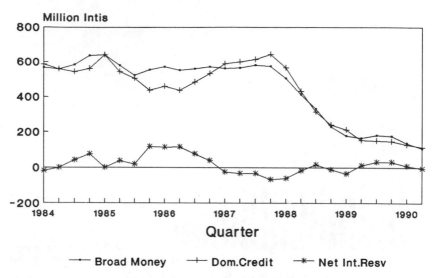

Fig. 9.7   **Broad money supply and its sources (in real terms)**

public-sector real aggregate demand. The latter resulted from the increasingly
diminished expenditure capability, in real terms, of the public sector, in turn a
consequence of shrinking real tax returns and state-enterprise revenues, and a
vanishing real demand for money. These recessionary effects of falling investment and government expenditures were compounded by the dirty work of
second-round multiplier effects on real consumption.

The sharp decline of labor incomes resulted from the procyclical character
of real wages and the reduced scope and imperfection of wage indexation.
Indeed, only unionized workers—about half a million of a total labor force of
over six million—were subject to indexation clauses, and even for these quarterly indexation adjustments were significantly below inflation because the
government established by law nominal inti ceilings to any indexed adjustment, which soon became binding. Regarding minimum wages, public-sector
wages, and wages of nonunion workers, the government decreed frequent adjustments, but inflation always kept a faster pace. Escalating inflation depressed real wages so fast that soon private employers started to pay higher
wages than those resulting from contractual or regulatory obligations. The
low degree of wage indexation acted as a stabilizing force of the hyperinflationary trend.

Labor unrest soared amid widespread protests by unions, prompted by imperfect indexation of wages, and shortages of basic foodstuffs. Hours lost in
strikes increased tenfold and were particularly acute in the two largest mining
firms, the multinational Southern Copper Peru and the state-owned Centromin
(fig. 9.8). Peru's terrorist Shining Path found in the crisis a promising breed-

ing ground. The situation at the time has been described by Smith (1989) as follows:

> In November, 1988, guerrilla units of the Communist Party of Peru, better known as Sendero Luminoso (Shining Path), laid the final crossbeam in an Andes-spanning strategy. They knocked down a vital power line between Lima and the Mantaro hydroelectric plant in the central Sierra. When the state electricity company moved to repair the downed pylons, Sendero quickly blasted others. Sendero also sabotaged the rail line between the mining center of Cerro de Pasco and Lima. Senderista columns moved viciously into the campesino communities and agrarian cooperatives in the countryside around Huancayo, the breadbasket of the national capital.
>
> Lima tottered on the verge of social and economic disarray. Already reeling from Peru's worst depression, the city and most of the coast sputtered on rationed electrical power and rotated blackouts and brownouts for six weeks. The troubled government of President Alan García declared a state of emergency in Junín, joining seven other departments under military control. Across a broad swath of Andean Sierra and Amazon jungle, roughly 750 miles long and 200 miles wide, the government recognized that it could not maintain a semblance of authority and order.

News reports claimed that the miners' strikes could not be settled by merely yielding on wage demands because the Shining Path was blackmailing union leaders. The type of demands made by unions included some of a very political nature, such as asking the government not to engage in any dealings with

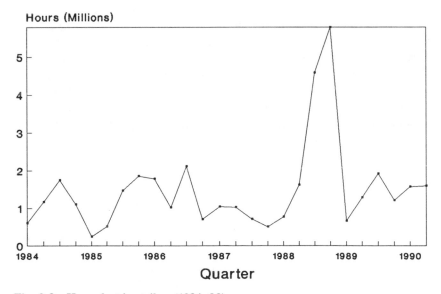

Fig. 9.8   Hours lost in strikes (1984–90)

the multilateral credit institution. The miners' strike lasted two and a half months, paralyzing Peru's main foreign exchange earning sector and thus aggravating the foreign exchange crisis and inflationary expectations.

Coronado and the Monetary Approach to the Balance of Payments

Central Bankers witness the hard way the correlation between money, the free market exchange rate, reserve losses, and inflation. Peru's Central Bank charter provides for a very independent Central Bank. Credit outstanding to the government is restricted to one-twelfth of the year's tax revenues, and net international reserves are subject to a minimum legal reserve requirement equal to one and a half months of imports (based on the average of the two previous years).[16] Central Bank independence is protected by the Constitution (Article 151) by providing that its president and board members, once appointed, can be impeached only by the Senate. In addition, Article 149 of the Constitution obliges the Central Bank to publish very detailed information on the economic and financial situation of the country, which the Central Bank does, inter alia, with a weekly publication called the "Nota Semanal."

During the last two Belaúnde years Central Bank Governor Richard Webb had already used the charter at its potential and succeeded in moderating the government's public spending plans. History repeats itself. Pedro Coronado, a lawyer appointed governor in late 1987 and who had presided over the Central Bank during the inherited nightmare of multiple exchange rates, cheap credit windows, and frequent recourse to government financing, took the step of regaining Central Bank independence at the time of the so-called double-zero plan of September 1988.

The tight new credit rule was to have been coordinated with the September and November adjustment measures which, at their original technical design, had been intended to reduce the government's deficit. This was particularly the case with the adjustment designed by then–finance minister Abel Salinas, who resigned in late November when his original proposal was turned down by President García. Despite the fact that the actual approved packages left unchecked the underlying budget imbalance, the Central Bank pursued a tight credit policy from September 1988 to July 1989. Only a fraction of the credit requests by the Treasury and public enterprises were accommodated, on occasion in exchange for price adjustments or other policy measures. The public sector was forced to adjust expenditures and resort to domestic arrears.

In November 1988, cargo ships loaded with wheat and corn supplied by USAID on grant terms waited idly day after day at Lima's Callao Harbor for their freight charges to be paid by ENCI (Peru's agricultural marketing board). The Central Bank was refusing to advance the funds to ENCI unless this institution would reduce subsidies. The rumor was spreading that there was no bread in Lima because of the Central Bank's monetarist policies.

16. Ley Organica del B.C.R.P., Articles 46, 47, 48, and 80, 82, respectively.

The credit crunch and its effects are illustrated in table 9.11. The effective flow of Central Bank domestic credit declined in nominal terms in several months and grew by very little in others. However, since an important share of both the monetary base and the money supply was in dollar-indexed accounts—which revalued whenever the exchange rate depreciated, as it did almost every month—the domestic "source" of the money supply continued to grow. The credit crunch managed to progressively drive down the free market premium of the inti and international reserves started to build up. By mid-1989, net international reserves had increased by $500 million, or 2 percent of GDP.

The Four-Months-Ahead Tablita

Despite the credit squeeze, inflation did not decline significantly during the first half of 1989. In January 1989 a new minister of finance announced a *tablita* or schedule of monthly changes of key prices for the next four months (table 9.12). Again, the strategy was one of almost equiproportional albeit declining overtime, escalation of the exchange rate, prices, and wages, much in the same vein as the one-shot packages of the previous year but with more frequent, and thus smaller, changes. As it turned out, actual adjustments to wages were higher than those for the exchange rate and public prices. Preannounced cost escalation, together with the credit squeeze, maintained the economy in stagnation at the hyperrecessed plateau reached in late 1988, without helping on the inflation front. By June 1989, real wages and GDP had dropped by 67 percent and 23 percent, respectively, in comparison to December 1987, while inflation hovered at 45 percent between December 1988 and April 1989. Eventually, however, the monetary cure produced its effects: since May 1989 monthly inflation receded to around 30 percent for 12 consecutive months.

As the recession drove down import levels and some dynamic domestic producers shifted from the depressed internal market to exports, the economy started to run a large trade surplus (figs. 9.9 and 9.10). To a large extent, the inti counterpart of this surplus was absorbed in people's portfolios because the free market exchange rate was appreciating in real terms (following the overshooting in late 1988) and the Central Bank was not supplying domestic credit. Devaluation expectations of late 1988 and early 1989 became frustrated by the crunch and thus ex post returns in dollars of inti deposits, at the now-higher domestic interest rates, turned out to be higher than "betting on the dollar." A significant part of the trade surplus, thus, went into intis instead of capital flight. The depressed level of output and imports translated into an unprecedented real appreciation of the official and parallel exchange rates. From late 1988 to mid-1989, the official exchange rate appreciated 50 percent and the parallel rate appreciated 75 percent, in real terms, while the spread between both became virtually zero (figs. 9.5 and 9.11 and table 9.13).

In hindsight, the paradox of the period from September 1988 to June 1989

Table 9.11   The Credit Crunch: September 1988 through June 1989

	September	October	November	December	January	February	March	April	May	June
Central bank domestic credit (%)[a]	-34.0	7.4	-13.2	19.6	-5.5	4.2	-.7	-6.5	1.2	3.3
Central bank net international reserves (in millions of U. S. dollars)	-293	-317	-304	-352	-319	-323	-213	-45	79	176
Broad money growth (%)[b]	22.7	19.5	15.4	38.6	17.8	31.3	37.9	33.7	41.6	27.9
Inflation spread (%)	114	41	24	42	47	43	42	49	29	23
Free exchange rate/official exchange rate (%)	71	97	79	130	190	56	9	13	44	47
Interest rates on deposits (monthly rates) (%)	10	10	17	17	17	21	21	21	21	21
Real GDP (1979 = 100)	107	93	84	82	103	96	99	99	99	99
Real wage (July 1985 = 100)	81	64	78	72	66	60	55	46	47	48

[a]Monthly growth rate. Excluding losses arising from valuation adjustments on net dollars liabilities due to exchange rate devaluations.
[b]A significant part of it indexed to the official exchange rate.

Table 9.12   **The Preannouncement of Key Prices Four Months Ahead,
February–May 1989**

	January	February	March	April	May
Exchange rate devaluation					
Announced	. . .	31	20	12	12
Actual	40	31	30	37	24
Gasoline price increase					
Announced	. . .	29	20	13	12
Actual	62	29	28	44	0
Minimum wage increase					
Announced	. . .	24	18	12	10
Actual	41	24	31	26	40

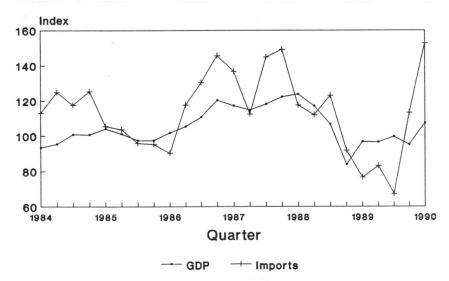

Fig. 9.9   Evolution of real GDP and real imports (1985 = 100)

is that the Central Bank's squeeze led to a massive buildup of international reserves, perhaps the least convenient avenue to have a good case to make with external creditors for the continuation of a unilateral default.

The monetary squeeze ended in July 1989 in the midst of strong arm-twisting between the Central Bank and the executive. The issue under dispute was the use of the foreign exchange reserves for yet another reactivation run with a view to the upcoming municipal elections in November 1989 and presidential elections in early 1990. Of the seven members of the Central Bank board, Coronado lost the one-vote margin that had permitted him to pursue credit restraint since September 1988; he resigned. From then on, Luis Guiulfo, who had systematically opposed any violation to the charter all along

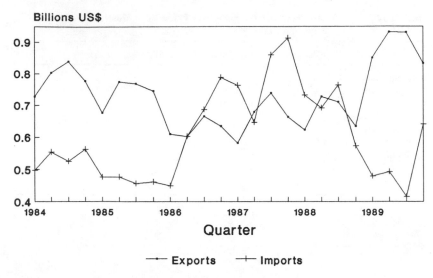

Fig. 9.10   Exports and imports of goods (1984–89)

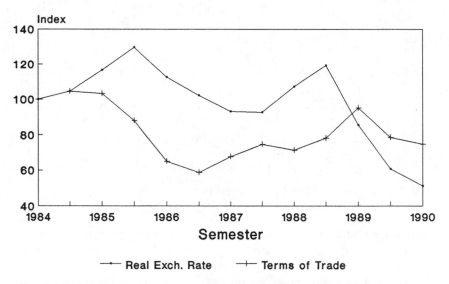

Fig. 9.11   Real exchange rate and terms of trade (first half of 1984 = 100)
Note: An increase in the Index of Real Exchange Rate means real depreciation. The index refers to the effective exchange rate.

Table 9.13 Nominal and Real Exchange Rates, 1985–90

| | Official Exchange Market | | | | | | Parallel Exchange Market | | |
| | Official Exchange Rate[a] | | | Average Effective Rate[b] | | | | | |
	Intis/ U.S. Dollars	Nominal Devaluation[c]	Real Exchange Rate Index[d]	Intis/ U.S. Dollars	Nominal Devaluation[c]	Real Exchange Rate Index[d]	Intis/ U.S. Dollars	Nominal Devaluation[c]	Real Exchange Rate Index[d]
1985:									
July	11.9	. . .	102.1	11.9	. . .	102.2	13.3	. . .	105.0
August	13.9	17.1	109.0	14.0	17.6	109.5	17.4	30.7	125.1
September	13.9	.0	106.3	14.0	.0	106.8	17.4	.1	122.2
October	13.9	.0	104.3	14.1	.5	105.3	17.4	.2	120.0
November	13.9	.0	102.5	14.1	.0	103.5	17.4	-.1	117.8
December	13.9	.0	100.7	14.1	.0	101.7	17.4	-.1	115.6
1986:									
January	13.9	.0	96.8	14.1	.0	97.7	17.4	.1	111.2
February	13.9	.0	95.3	14.1	.4	96.6	17.4	-.1	109.4
March	13.9	.0	92.3	14.1	.0	93.6	17.4	.0	106.0
April	13.9	.0	87.1	14.1	.0	88.4	17.4	.1	100.2
May	13.9	.0	85.1	14.1	.0	86.3	17.4	.0	97.8
June	13.9	.0	82.4	14.1	.0	83.5	17.4	.0	94.7
July	13.9	.0	80.5	14.2	.7	82.2	17.4	-.1	92.5
August	13.9	.0	78.8	14.3	.2	80.6	17.5	.7	91.2
September	13.9	.0	76.4	15.9	11.6	87.2	17.7	1.1	89.5
October	13.9	.0	73.3	15.9	.0	83.6	18.5	4.4	89.4
November	13.9	.0	70.5	15.9	.0	80.5	19.0	3.0	88.6
December	13.9	.0	68.0	16.6	4.1	80.8	20.0	5.3	90.0

(continued)

Table 9.13   (continued)

| | Official Exchange Market | | | | | | Parallel Exchange Market | | |
| | Official Exchange Rate[a] | | | Average Effective Rate[b] | | | | | |
	Intis/ U.S. Dollars	Nominal Devaluation[c]	Real Exchange Rate Index[d]	Intis/ U.S. Dollars	Nominal Devaluation[c]	Real Exchange Rate Index[d]	Intis/ U.S. Dollars	Nominal Devaluation[c]	Real Exchange Rate Index[d]
1987:									
January	14.2	2.2	66.8	16.9	2.2	79.3	20.2	.9	87.3
February	14.6	2.2	65.2	17.3	2.2	77.5	20.2	-.1	83.3
March	14.9	2.2	63.8	17.7	2.2	75.8	20.7	2.4	81.6
April	15.2	2.2	62.1	18.1	2.2	73.7	26.2	26.7	98.4
May	15.5	2.2	60.3	18.5	2.2	71.7	32.7	25.0	117.0
June	15.9	2.5	58.8	19.6	5.9	72.2	33.0	.6	112.1
July	15.9	.0	54.3	20.5	5.0	70.0	40.8	23.7	128.0
August	15.9	.0	50.6	20.5	.0	65.2	45.0	10.4	131.6
September	15.9	.0	48.1	20.5	.1	62.0	50.0	11.1	139.0
October	15.9	.0	45.6	26.5	28.8	75.7	61.8	23.5	162.8
November	15.9	.0	44.1	26.5	.0	73.3	63.5	2.8	162.0
December	33.0	107.2	86.5	38.9	46.9	101.8	92.0	44.9	222.1
1988:									
January	33.0	.0	76.6	40.3	3.8	93.6	89.5	-2.7	191.3
February	33.0	.0	67.8	43.0	6.6	88.3	102.0	14.0	193.1
March	33.0	.0	55.8	49.2	14.5	83.2	105.0	2.9	163.6
April	33.0	.0	47.7	55.9	13.5	80.7	150.5	43.3	200.3
May	33.0	.0	44.2	61.3	9.7	82.1	176.5	17.3	217.8
June	33.0	.0	40.2	74.1	20.9	90.2	177.5	.6	198.9
July	33.0	.0	29.9	89.0	20.1	80.7	204.0	14.9	170.3
August	33.0	.0	24.4	142.7	60.3	105.5	283.5	39.0	193.0
September	250.0	657.6	87.5	278.6	95.2	97.6	425.0	49.9	137.1

October	250.0	.0	63.1	292.1	4.8	73.8	508.6	19.7	118.3
November	500.0	100.0	103.0	532.5	82.3	109.7	700.0	37.6	132.8
December	500.0	.0	73.4	744.3	39.8	109.2	1660.0	137.1	224.4
1989:									
January	700.0	40.0	68.8	965.0	29.7	95.0	1740.0	4.8	156.6
February	920.0	31.4	63.4	1,062.0	10.0	73.2	1300.0	−25.3	82.5
March	1,200.0	30.4	58.2	1,339.2	26.1	64.9	1560.0	20.0	69.7
April	1,640.0	36.7	53.8	1,944.2	45.2	63.7	2177.0	39.6	65.7
May	2,025.0	23.5	50.9	2,584.0	32.9	64.9	3250.0	49.3	75.2
June	2,395.4	18.3	48.3	2,622.6	1.5	52.9	3070.3	−5.5	57.1
July	2,942.5	22.8	48.6	3,003.6	14.5	49.6	3094.7	.8	47.1
August	3,570.6	21.3	46.9	3,751.3	24.9	49.3	4061.1	31.2	49.2
September	4,132.2	15.7	42.6	5,012.3	33.6	51.7	5829.5	43.5	55.4
October	4,394.4	6.3	37.5	5,234.1	4.4	44.7	6241.9	7.1	49.1
November	4,701.2	7.0	32.1	7,900.9	51.0	54.0	12128.9	94.3	76.3
December	5,261.4	11.9	27.3	8,667.5	9.7	45.0	12821.3	5.7	61.3
1990:									
January	6,392.7	21.5	26.0	9,260.0	6.8	37.6	12,362.5	−3.6	46.3
February	8,146.2	27.4	25.4	11,039.9	19.2	34.4	13,920.2	12.6	39.9
March	11,225.4	37.8	26.3	17,215.0	55.9	40.4	23,098.0	65.9	49.9
April	15,892.8	41.6	27.3	21,806.4	26.7	37.4	28,133.3	21.8	44.4
May	22,501.0	41.6	29.4	30,944.7	41.9	40.5	49,624.6	76.4	59.8
June	33,720.6	49.9	31.0	63,891.7	106.5	58.7	103,268.4	106.1	87.3

Sources: Central Reserve Bank and author's estimates.

a MUC stands for Mercado Unico de Cambios and is the official exchange rate.

b Weighted average rate for all commercial transactions. There were multiple exchange rates.

c Percentage increase over previous month.

d An increase in the Real Exchange Rate Index means real depreciation. The base is December 1978.

since 1985, became the only member of the board favoring credit restraint. In the month of July, money printing for government financing (a traditional *maquinazo* in the local jargon) increased by 21 percent, compared to roughly zero in the previous semester (table 9.14).

The "30-percent Monthly Inflation" Knife's Edge Equilibrium

In May 1989, President Alán García had appointed his sixth minister of finance, a young economist of the left-wing of the APRA party. In his book entitled *The Forgotten Proposal* (1988), Vasquez Bazan had been critical of the government's economic policies, deeming them as a repetition of the traditional Latin American populist paradigm and at odds with APRA's traditional structural reform agenda. Notwithstanding this criticism, economic policy during the following 12 months engaged in an erratic sequence of ad hoc measures driven by short-run developments. In general, measures followed a "zig-zag" pattern, with later measures running in opposite direction to earlier ones in an attempt to correct their destabilizing effects. The initial new policies included, inter alia, introduction of a crawling peg (at a continuously fine-tuned rate), monthly wage increases, sporadic public price adjustments, and a few exotic tax measures, including a new tax on the turnover of checks (tables 9.15 and 9.16). Since July 1989, the Central Bank started to accommodate again government credit requests (tables 9.5 and 9.14). On the other hand, an increasing number of categories of imports were made eligible for foreign exchange at the highly subsidized official exchange rate. By December 1989, 72 percent of total imports were given access to the official market. The policy goal was to prompt a quick recovery by boosting import levels.

The free market exchange rate, however, very soon reflected expansionary financial policies. By the end of the year the spread over the official rate had surpassed 100 percent. At this point, the authorities switched into a containment effort aimed at avoiding a further explosion of the exchange rate and prices before the forthcoming presidential elections of 8 April 1990.[17] As part of this strategy, the Central Bank started to provide dollar loans to exporters and to sell term promissory dollar notes to importers in an attempt to depress the free market exchange rate. The Central Bank's financing of the government's deficit in 1989 was small, about 4.3 percent of GDP—most of it during the second half of the year (table 9.8). But, as often happens with high inflation processes, the pressure of just a little Central Bank financing on a tiny financial system was enough to sustain hyperinflation. Thus, the year 1989 ended with an inflation rate of 2,800 percent (after having peaked at nearly 6,000 percent during the 12 months ending in August 1989). Moreover, GDP dropped by 10 percent, adding to the 9 percent decline in 1988, and international reserves started to destock at a fast pace beginning in November 1989.

17. As explained in the publication *Peru Economico* of December 1989 (Apoyo 1989).

Table 9.14   Monthly Economic Indicators, 1985–90

	Real GDP (1979 = 100)	Inflation Rate[a]	Employment (1979 = 100)	Real Wage (July 1985 = 100)	Hours Lost in Strikes[b]	Broad Money (Nominal Growth Rate)[a,c]	Central Bank Domestic Credit (Nominal Growth Rate)[a]		Central Bank Net International Reserves (in Millions of U.S. Dollars)
							Total	Adjusted[d]	
1985:									
January	106.2	13.9	92.0	121	74.3	-.7	8.4		1,001
February	104.6	9.5	92.2	118	-81.9	.7	5.4		1,102
March	104.2	8.1	92.1	117	-81.0	7.7	23.6		1,048
April	102.3	12.2	91.7	111	-74.9	11.5	3.9		1,018
May	102.6	10.9	91.7	105	59.1	-1.9	6.9		997
June	102.6	11.8	91.6	104	-77.1	7.8	.3		971
July	104.0	10.3	91.5	100	44.9	13.7	9.5		894
August	98.7	10.8	91.4	111	-33.6	23.4	8.9		1,003
September	98.2	3.5	91.5	111	-47.6	17.2	3.1		1,144
October	100.9	3.0	91.7	112	-1.4	9.7	-3.9		1,310
November	105.3	2.7	92.3	113	139.0	9.8	18.4		1,388
December	104.7	2.8	93.8	113	69.8	20.3	15.6		1,493
1986:									
January	102.0	5.2	93.4	110	79.9	5.7	18.0		1,539
February	103.0	4.2	93.8	127	689.0	9.6	14.2		1,500
March	98.9	5.3	94.5	125	2,482.8	10.5	7.9		1,541
April	106.6	4.1	94.7	124	911.7	.7	7.3		1,434
May	108.7	3.3	94.6	123	-57.3	4.9	6.7		1,407
June	112.4	3.6	95.1	127	-34.2	6.1	11.5		1,278
July	114.0	4.6	95.9	125	-57.1	7.3	6.5		1,234

(*continued*)

Table 9.14 (continued)

	Real GDP (1979 = 100)	Inflation Rate[a]	Employment (1979 = 100)	Real Wage (July 1985 = 100)	Hours Lost in Strikes[b]	Broad Money (Nominal Growth Rate)[a,c]	Central Bank Domestic Credit (Nominal Growth Rate)[a]		Central Bank Net International Reserves (in Millions of U.S. Dollars)
							Total	Adjusted[d]	
August	114.4	4.0	96.3	125	−28.6	6.5	6.8		1,135
September	116.3	3.6	96.8	125	744.2	2.9	−3.5		1,239
October	122.2	4.0	97.7	140	−65.7	6.4	5.9		1,201
November	124.6	3.6	98.8	138	−85.4	4.9	13.5		992
December	128.4	4.6	99.8	134	−74.4	10.5	9.5		958
1987:									
January	118.1	6.6	98.7	129	−32.4	2.4	5.8		833
February	116.5	5.6	99.2	126	47.4	5.0	1.4		791
March	119.8	5.3	100.5	124	−77.7	7.7	2.5		820
April	121.8	6.6	100.8	138	−56.0	6.6	6.7		858
May	117.8	5.9	100.9	133	296.2	7.5	7.8		892
June	121.6	4.7	101.4	130	93.1	6.0	10.5		790
July	121.7	7.3	101.3	147	−22.7	13.1	12.7		765
August	124.0	7.4	101.6	141	−46.2	6.3	16.3		649
September	127.1	6.5	101.9	138	−82.0	4.0	7.1		533
October	128.5	6.1	102.7	152	16.1	5.9	10.6		405
November	130.5	7.1	103.7	155	79.5	6.6	11.9		194
December	128.6	9.6	104.5	146	−34.5	10.6	24.4		43
1988:									
January	122.1	12.8	101.8	134	157.5	.8	4.8	4.8	−50
February	130.8	11.8	101.6	126	−73.1	9.1	9.4	9.4	−153
March	129.5	22.6	102.1	135	−45.8	13.0	10.6	10.6	−194
April	122.9	22.9	102.0	121	−29.6	9.1	10.4	10.4	−237
May	120.1	8.5	101.5	117	−85.0	5.1	7.3	7.3	−219
June	118.2	8.8	101.1	113	146.3	4.4	8.6	8.6	−180
July	110.7	30.9	101.1	118	843.5	24.8	20.6	20.6	−222

August	110.8	21.7	100.9	104	714.2	15.6	18.4	18.4	−266
September	107.2	114.1	101.3	81	105.4	22.7	101.4	−34.0	−293
October	93.3	40.6	99.5	64	686.3	19.5	7.4	7.4	−317
November	83.9	24.4	97.4	78	1,095.5	15.4	58.2	−13.2	−304
December	81.8	41.9	97.7	72	1,767.7	38.6	19.6	19.6	−352
1989:									
January	103.4	47.3	95.9	66	146.2	17.8	24.8	−5.5	−319
February	95.7	42.5	95.1	60	94.7	31.3	30.5	4.2	−323
March	99.2	42.0	94.5	55	85.7	37.9	22.4	−.7	−213
April	99.0	48.6	94.0	46	40.4	33.7	26.9	−6.5	−45
May	99.3	28.6	93.4	47	−77.9	41.6	9.3	1.2	79
June	99.4	23.1	92.8	48	53.7	27.9	14.4	3.3	176
July	105.2	24.6	92.4	49	−75.7	40.8	32.3	21.0	222
August	98.8	25.1	92.8	48	−47.0	26.5	15.0	8.8	373
September	103.5	26.9	92.5	48	−32.9	30.7	16.8	13.6	450
October	97.1	23.3	93.5	51	−64.3	32.1	19.9	19.0	457
November	97.2	25.8	93.8	49	−85.3	28.3	14.8	14.1	453
December	99.0	33.8	94.2	46	−84.0	23.3	24.4	22.3	357
1990:									
January	113.7	29.8	94.1	46	314.4	13.5	27.3	22.4	301
February	109.9	30.5	94.4	46	87.8	17.6	29.0	19.7	131
March	107.1	32.6	94.4	44	131.5	27.8	57.2	38.8	−37
April	100.8	37.3	N.A.	44	86.1	22.2	25.9	7.0	−119
May	100.0	32.8	N.A.	44	125.1	31.8	38.8	17.4	−152
June	N.A.	42.6	N.A.	N.A.	N.A.	44.0	55.6	29.0	−143

[a]Percentage increase over previous month.

[b]Percent increase over same month of previous year.

[c]Excludes deposits denominated in dollars.

[d]Central Bank Credit netted out of losses arising from valuation adjustments due to exchange rate devaluation.

Table 9.15   **Packages of Economic Measures, January–June 1989**

	January	February	March	April	May	June
PRICES, WAGES, AND EXCHANGE RATE		+ *Tablita*: preannouncement for next four months of official exchange rate, gasoline price, and minimum wage				
Effective rate (devaluation) (%)	30	10	26	45	33	2
Number of exchange rates:						
Imports	1	1	1	1	1	1
Exports	2	2	2	2	2	2
Total	3	3	3	3	3	3
Minimum wage increases (%)	41	24	31	26	40	29
Public-sector wage increases (%)	46	15	35	24	30	38
Private-sector wage increases (%)	33	21	27	25	30	25
Increases of public tariffs:						
Gasoline (%)	62	29	28	44	0	0
Electricity (%)	60	25	30	27	0	0
Rice (%)	62	35	34	20	4	10
Increase of price of controlled products (%)	55	42	28	26	19	7
TAXES						
Changes in existing taxes	+ Decrease export tax from 10% to 6%			Reduction of excise taxes (cigarettes, beer, and soft drinks)		
New taxes						
IMPORT TARIFFS AND RESTRICTIONS		Reduction of % of imports eligible to the official market (from 65% to 50%)				
Evolution of quantitative restrictions (QRs) (% of total of tariff categories)						
Free from QRs						7.1
License required						82.7
Import prohibitions						10.2
Evolution of tariffs						
Average tariff						
Maximum tariff						
EXPORTS MEASURES	+ 127 of official exchange rate for Nontraditional Exports				+ CLD[a] from 30% to 40%	+ CLD[a] from 40% 50%
INTEREST RATE						
Lending rate (%)		25 per month				
Deposit rate (%)		21 per month				

[a]The Certificados de Libre Disponibilidad (CLD) is a tradable dollar certificate given to exporters for a share of their export proceeds that can be used by an importer.

Table 9.16   Packages of Economic Measures, July–December 1989

	July	August	September	October	November	December
PRICES, WAGES, AND EXCHANGE RATE						
Effective rate (devaluation) (%)	15	25	34	4	51	10
Number of exchange rates:						
Imports	1	1	1	1	1	1
Exports	2	2	2	2	2	3
Total	3	3	3	3	3	4
Minimum wage increases (%)	30	25	25	19	22	37
Public-sector wage increases (%)	15	57	18	61	24	28
Private-sector wage increases (%)	29	25	25	18	22	25
Increase of public tariffs:						
Gasoline (%)	11	0	25	5	6	18
Electricity (%)	10	25	31	13	0	42
Rice (%)	96	13	45	47	57	4
Increase of price of controlled products (%)	19	23	41	33	27	21
TAXES						
Changes in existing taxes				+ Reduction of excise taxes		
New taxes		+ Tax of 1% on checking account transactions	+ 2.5% of September sales for Social Compensation Fund and army		+ 1% of imports and 2% of traditional exports for National Defense Fund	
IMPORT TARIFFS AND RESTRICTIONS					+ Increase of % of imports eligible for the official exchange market (from 50% to 69%)	+ Further increase of % of imports eligible for the official exchange market (from 69% to 72%)

(continued)

Table 9.16   (continued)

	July	August	September	October	November	December
Evolution of quantitative restrictions (QRs) (% of total of tariff categories)						
Free from QRs						79.6
License required						10.2
Import prohibitions						10.2
Evolution of tariffs						
Average tariff						66
Maximum tariff						110
EXPORTS MEASURES			+CLDᵃ from 50% to 55%	+CLDᵃ from 55% to 45% but 10% in cash (U.S.$)	+CLDᵃ from 45% to 35% but 20% in cash (U.S.$)	+ Nontraditional exporters receive advance accounts (FENT) in U.S.$
INTEREST RATE						
Lending rate (%)				23.5 per month	21.5 per month	
Deposit rate (%)					19.0 per month	

ᵃThe Certificados de Libre Disponibilidad (CLD) is a tradable dollar certificate given to exporters for a share of their export proceeds that can be used by an importer.

Table 9.17   Packages of Economic Measures, January–June 1990

	January	February	March	April	May	June
PRICES, WAGES, AND EXCHANGE RATE						
Effective rate (devaluation) (%)	7	19	56	27	42	107
Number of exchange rates:						
Imports	1	1	1	1	1	1
Exports	3	3	3	3	3	3
Total	4	4	4	4	4	4
Minimum wage increases (%)	31	37	30	38	36	34
Public sector wage increases (%)	20	35	25	33	30	31
Private sector wage increases (%)	28	30	30	30	35	36
Increase of public tariffs:						
Gasoline (%)	12	38	0	29	31	96
Electricity (%)	29	42	30	38	36	34
Rice (%)	2	−2	9	42	64	24
Increase of price of controlled products (%)	18	24	21	36	25	32
TAXES						
Changes in existing taxes	Exemption on 1990 tax income for PETROPERU	+ Increase of excise taxes + Sales tax from 10.5% to 15%				
New Taxes					+ Tax on checking accounts from 1% to 2% + Tax on loans from 10% to 20%	

(continued)

Table 9.17 (continued)

	January	February	March	April	May	June
IMPORT TARIFFS AND RESTRICTIONS	+ Reduction of % of imports eligible to the official exchange market (from 72% to 67%)	+ Further decrease of % of imports eligible for the official exchange market (from 67% to 61%)	+ Additional decrease of % of imports eligible for the official exchange market (from 61% to 43%)			
Evolution of quantitative restrictions (QRs) (% of total of tariff categories)						
Free from QRs						
License required						
Import prohibitions						
Total number of tariffs categories						
Evolution of tariffs:						
Average tariff						
Maximum tariff						
EXPORTS MEASURES		+ CLD[a] from 35% to 45% but 10% in cash	+ CLD[a] from 45% to 35%	+ Advance accounts to exporters in intis		+ CLD[a] from 60% to 70%
			+ Elimination of advance accounts in U.S. dollars			
INTEREST RATE						
Lending rate	23.0% per month		29.0% per month		39.0% per month	
Deposit rate	21.0% per month		25.0% per month		32.0% per month	

[a]The Certificados de Libre Disponibilidad (CLD) is a tradable dollar certificate given to exporters for a share of their export proceeds that can be used by an importer.

In December 1989, following a warning by the IMF that it would initiate procedures that could ultimately lead to Peru's expulsion from the institution, the government resumed payments of current debt service to the IMF—thereby freezing arrears with this institution at the level of September 1989. The authorities came to terms with the institution against which they had been most vociferously confrontational, while continuing the default with the rest of the creditors.

The containment effort continued during the first half of 1990. But, as international reserves evaporated, imports were progressively transferred back from the official market to the free foreign exchange market and dollars supplied by the Central Bank for other transactions started to be tightly rationed. Hence, the burden of "controlling" the free exchange rate was now placed on monetary policy. Credit to the private sector was dried up, through increased reserve requirements on deposits. In parallel, the Treasury stretched payments of expenditures and incurred more domestic arrears rather than resort to price and tariff hikes and/or larger Central Bank financing. In this context, effective lending interest rates to the private sector reached 15-plus percent per month in real terms. To limit the pace of reserve depletion the authorities took the unprecedented step of going into a de facto default on ALADI (Latin American Trade Area), clearing payments owed to other Latin American Central Banks and requesting rescheduling of settlements so that the payments would fall due under the next presidential term. In spite of these efforts, reserves continued to decline—by June 1990, reported gross reserves totaled barely $600 million (most of them nonliquid), 1 billion less than in August 1989. After 12 consecutive months with an inflation rate of around 30 percent per month, inflation picked up again in June 1990, reaching 43 percent. In parallel, the free exchange rate took off in late June at spreads of 200 percent over the official rate. By late July, inflation was running at 6 percent per day.

To compound these formidable problems, that were handed over to president-elect Alberto Fujimori on 28 July 1990, a number of other obstacles to economic management during the next presidential term were established by the outgoing administration. Among them are a policy of active employment in public-sector entities launched in January 1990 and the issuance of a number of laws that will complicate some of the structural reforms that the next government may wish to embark upon. One of these laws affects the transfer of several key public enterprises to local governments, thereby preventing the central government from effective control over them.

9.4 Summing Up the Experience

Beyond its macroeconomic debacle, the policies of 1985–90 had devastating effects on income distribution, agricultural incomes, the financial system, the tax system, the financial viability of public enterprises, resource allocation, public infrastructure, and the health and nutrition of the poor. For a government whose main objectives were to expand the role of the state in the economy and to benefit the poor, the ultimate paradoxes were twofold. On the one hand, hyperinflation forced an ex post shrinkage of the size of the government by more than half—as gauged by the share of public expenditures on GDP—even though public-sector employment increased 30 percent. And, on the other hand, the poor ended up being hurt the most.

The government's attempts to protect wages notwithstanding, average real wages declined by a cumulative 60 percent in 1987–89, about three times the 20 percent output loss experienced in the period (fig. 9.1 and table 9.14). Peruvian workers and organized labor—in particular the left-wing CGTP, Peru's largest union—showed a considerable degree of pragmatism and restraint in accepting phenomenal real wage cuts in the form of imperfect wage indexation formulas, apparently in exchange for much less drastic reductions in employment levels. The reported cumulative decline of employment in 1987–89 was about 10 percent. By early 1990, however, 8 percent of the labor force was reported unemployed and 74 percent underemployed.[18]

Income distribution definitely worsened. As shown in table 9.18, the income shares of working-class recipients, after having experienced significant improvements in 1986–87 at the tie of the boom, went back in 1988 to levels lower than those of 1985. The Gini coefficient in 1988 had regressed to that of 1985. Moreover, as fig. 9.1 shows, the formidable widening of the gap between the paths of real GDP and real wages occurred after the fourth quarter of 1988, which indicates that probably the income shares of civil servants and nonagricultural workers must have deteriorated further in 1989. Likewise, as figure 9.12 shows, the rural-urban terms of trade plunged starting in 1988—in the wake of the fast real appreciation of the exchange rate and the impossibility of maintaining the subsidy levels of 1986–1987—leading to a decline in the share of agricultural incomes in GNP from 12.1 percent in 1986 to 9.3 percent in 1988. A probable further decline occurred in 1989 in view of the continued drop of the terms of trade. (At this writing, data on income distribution for 1989 was not available.)

On the other hand, most subsidies provided through low public-sector prices and tariffs—by June 1990, most of these were at 30 percent or less of their levels, in real terms, of July 1985 (table 9.19)—tended to benefit relatively more the less poor, the urban, and the rich consumers. The regressiveness of most of these subsidies is illustrated in table 9.20, in which it can be noted that Peru's 30 percent poorest barely purchase gasoline, electricity, and water or use telephone and transport, and, to the extent that they purchase or use these, they consume relatively less than the less poor consumers. Paradoxically, the price of rice, the poor's main staple, rose by far more than, say, gasoline, despite the clear progressiveness of the rice subsidy and the regressiveness of the gasoline subsidy. All this indicates that the deterioration in

18. See n. 4 above for the definition of underemployment.

Table 9.18   Income (at Factor Cost) Distribution by Groups of Recipients

Income Groups	Percentage of Income				Percentage of Recipients			
	1985	1986	1987	1988	1985	1986	1987	1988
Agricultural workers	10.8	12.1	10.9	9.3	36.3	35.5	35.0	35.2
Nonagricultural self-employed	15.7	17.9	16.7	19.7	23.2	23.3	23.2	23.8
Nonagricultural workers	21.3	22.8	22.3	19.5	26.0	26.3	26.3	25.1
Civil servants	11.0	11.8	12.4	7.2	11.6	12.0	12.0	13.0
Employers	41.2	35.5	37.7	44.3	2.8	2.9	2.9	2.9
Total	100.0	100.0	100.0	100.0	100.0	100.0	100.0	100.0
Gini coefficient	0.50	0.41	0.43	0.50	. . .	. . .	. . .	. . .

Source: National Statistical Institute.

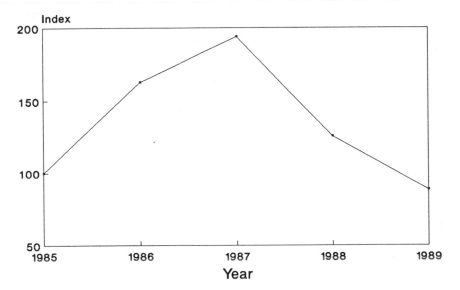

Fig. 9.12   Rural-urban terms of trade, 1985–89 (1985 = 100)

income redistribution, as portrayed in table 9.18, probably understates the
real magnitude of the problem. Indeed, subsidies via prices and tariffs seem
to have worsened distribution even further.

Lagging public-sector prices—a permanent key feature of the government's strategy to fight "cost-push diagnosed" inflation—resulted in a fall of
public enterprises' revenues from 26 percent of GDP in 1985 to 7 percent in
1989, and to a corresponding decline in investment expenditures from 6 percent of GDP to 2 percent (table 9.8). In parallel, the policy of discretionary
tax exemptions together with collection lags—of three months on average—
and imperfect indexation of the tax base gave rise to a caricaturized Tanzi

Table 9.19   **Relative Prices of Selected Goods and Services Provided by Public Enterprises (July 1985 = 100)**

	Average				June
	1986	1987	1988	1989	1990
Gasoline 84	81	57	47	35	12
Kerosene	54	32	26	31	21
Electricity:					
Residential	70	52	40	12	7
Industrial	76	60	48	28	24
Telephone	81	82	46	12	6
Public transportation	79	66	65	54	N.A.
Water					
Residential	112	100	69	38	33
Industrial	92	84	67	37	39
Rice	73	65	53	57	44

Source: Ministry of Finance and author's estimates.

Table 9.20   **Budget Shares of Selected Items (%)**

	Poorest 10%	Poorest 30%		Rest 70%	All Peru
Item		All	Urban		
Fuel and oil for vehicles	.0	.0	.0	1.9	1.7
(% who purchase)	(.8)	(1.1)	(.5)	(11.2)	(8.2)
Kerosene	.7	1.3	3.1	.9	.9
Electricity	.3	.5	1.4	1.0	.9
(% who purchase)	(11.7)	(21.6)	(56.1)	(58.8)	(47.8)
Water service	.3	.4	1.1	.5	.5
(% who purchase)	(11.7)	(26.8)	(65.3)	(51.5)	(44.2)
Telephone	.0	.1	.1	.4	.3
(% who purchase)	(.4)	(1.4)	(4.2)	(12.0)	(8.8)
Public transport					
Local	.8	1.7	3.6	2.3	2.2
Long distance	1.0	.9	.9	1.2	1.2
Rice	5.7	5.3	5.2	2.2	2.9

Source: Glewwe (1988), drawing on data from Peru's 1985–86 "Living Standard Measurement Survey," carried out by Peru's National Statistical Institute and the World Bank.

effect (fig. 9.13). In 1989, tax revenues barely totaled 5 percent of GDP, down from 15 percent in 1985, just sufficient to cover the public sector's payroll. In total, combined gross revenues of the consolidated public sector dropped to one-third of the 1985 level. Inadequate expenditures on investment and maintenance of infrastructure, together with the drought of 1989 and terrorist attacks on electrical networks (in 1988 the number of electrical facilities damaged by terrorist strikes increased 100% compared to 1987), made electrical

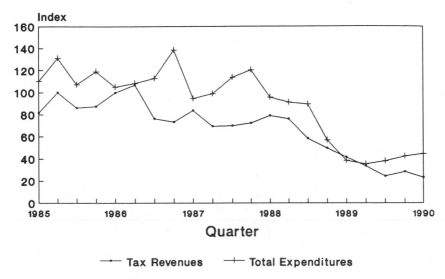

Quarter

——— Tax Revenues   ——+—— Total Expenditures

Fig. 9.13   Central government: Taxes and expenditures
(real index 1985-II = 100)

shortages and acute water scarcity a daily event in Lima and other cities. Private electricity-generating systems became one of the fastest growing lines of business.

Even theoretically, it is difficult to quantify output and welfare losses resulting from price distortions. Indeed, it is even difficult to measure price distortions, more so in a hyperinflationary setting. Nonetheless, two illustrations of the problem can be provided. The first is price volatility, and the second consists of deviations from border pricing. Price volatility rises with the level of inflation, thus blurring the genuine informative content of prices and increasing information and transaction costs. All this leads to resource misallocation, uncertainty, and low investment levels. Table 9.21 provides information on price dispersion derived from the inflation indices of the eight broad categories of consumption "carried" in the CPI basket. The coefficient of variation of contemporaneous monthly inflation indices jumped fourfold from 1985 to 1989.

A second illustration of distorted price signals is provided by the "potential" deviations of domestic relative prices from border prices resulting from the tariff code, multiple exchange rates and quantitative restrictions. Table 9.22 presents the combined effects on nominal protection of the tariff structure and multiple exchange rates alone at two points in late 1987. It can be noticed that the relative price between a highly protected good and a highly unprotected good could potentially rise as high as nine times over the corresponding international relative price. It is also remarkable that in only two months both the levels of protection and the dispersion of protection rates increased signif-

Table 9.21   Price Dispersion[a]

Year	Dispersion[b]	Maximum Increase[c] (%)	Minimum Increase[c] (%)	Interval[d] (%)
1984	89.8	134.7	103.5	31.2
1985	100.0	214.3	137.8	76.5
1986	114.1	113.2	33.7	79.5
1987	139.2	177.9	66.6	111.3
1988	290.2	2,454.2	1,231.3	1,222.9
1989	426.9	10,017.9	1,632.9	8,385.3

Source: Apoyo (1990).
[a]Price indices of eight broad categories of the CPI.
[b]As measured by the ratio of the standard deviation to the mean of monthly inflation rates of eight categories. Index number (1985 = 100) reported is the average of 12 months of the year.
[c]Of annual inflation rate for each category of goods.
[d]Derived from (maximum increase) − (minimum increase).

Table 9.22   Combined Nominal Protection from Tariffs and Multiple Exchange Rate (Unweighted Rates in %)

	Exchange Rate as of 10/26/87				Exchange Rate as of 12/21/87			
	Minimum	Maximum	Mean	SD	Minimum	Maximum	Mean	SD
The whole economy	− 35.3	237.4	95.5	56.6	− 57.4	300.7	99.4	72.6
Agriculture	− 35.3	187.0	79.9	55.5	− 57.4	240.9	79.6	70.6
Mining	12.0	114.2	76.3	28.4	− 26.0	154.4	51.9	28.3
Manufacturing	− 19.2	237.4	96.6	56.8	− 47.2	300.7	101.2	72.8
Consumer goods	− 19.2	237.4	141.3	58.3	− 46.6	300.7	166.3	79.0
Intermediate imports	− 19.2	189.8	75.5	44.5	− 44.4	244.2	56.6	43.2
Capital goods	.8	189.8	90.5	51.2	− 47.2	244.2	108.7	57.7

Sources: Calculated by Lachler (1989) at the eight-digit tariff code level. Arancel Integrado de Aduanas del Peru 1987 and Diario Oficial "El Peruano," 10/26/87 and 12/21/87.

icantly (the maximum rate rose from 237 to 301 percent, while the standard deviation went from 57 to 73).

The formal financial system shrunk to less than one-quarter of its size in 1985. Indeed, while in 1985 total financial-sector internal liabilities amounted to 21 percent of GDP, by mid-1990 they barely represented 5 percent. About two-thirds of total credit was either utilized by the public sector or redirected to public development banks to be on loan to the private sector.

Economists hide behind what common people view as abstract magnitudes (GDP, inflation, etc.). These magnitudes are in general subject to considerable measurement error. However, the real ultimate effects of economic decline and more regressive income redistribution are best assessed by "impact," more precise variables such as infant mortality. The destruction of the revenue base—and thus of the expenditure capability—of the government led to a decline in public social expenditures from \$40 per capita in 1981 to \$14 in 1989. Declining social expenditures and falling real wages provoked a marked deterioration of health and nutrition indicators, particularly among the poor. Comparable surveys undertaken by PRISMA, a Peruvian NGO, in a peri-urban Lima settlement, show that infant mortality for children five years old or younger increased 50 percent between 1987 and 1989, while the index of adequacy to the norm of weight and height of children under three years old worsened substantially.[19]

9.5 Concluding Remarks

Peru's economic policy between 1985–90 fits all the elements of the Dornbusch and Edwards (1990) paradigm: a stagnant economy with highly skewed income distribution and consistently unfulfilled expectations. The latter had been particularly frustrated with the failure of the sweeping social reforms attempted by military dictator Juan Velasco Alvarado in 1968–75, who had hoped to integrate this fragmented country.

The policy goals of the 1985–90 experiment were indeed reactivation and improvement of incomes of workers and peasants by use of macroeconomic policy. It was, however, believed—or at least the official rhetoric stated—that the improvement of real wages would not have to come necessarily at the expense of lower profit margins. Slack capacity and abundant foreign exchange reserves could allow everybody's income to expand. Moreover, the profits of firms in the "reactivation" phase were thought to provide the government with a good bargaining tool to use in negotiating private firms' reinvestment in exporting sectors during the subsequent "restructuring" phase. It was the dispute over private investment that seems to have prompted the initiative to nationalize banks and insurance companies and embark on a left-leaning agenda.

The nationalization of the banking system was the only social "reformist" step attempted by the government. The reality of the nationalization is, however, that it was de facto never implemented. It was contested in the courts and actively resisted by mass mobilization. When the law was finally issued by Congress in October 1987—three months after the presidential initiative—it permitted 51 percent employee-owned banks to remain nonpublic and offered banks the possibility of becoming private regional banks. The owners of Peru's largest private bank, Banco de Credito, rushed to block sell 51 percent of its shares to workers, with financing provided by a subsidiary of the same bank. As for the remaining banks, the process ended up in a precarious legal

---

19. Surveys undertaken in Pampas de San Juan by the Grupo de Trabajo A.B. PRISMA/UPCH. Report presented to UNICEF, September 1989.

status: banks were de facto allowed to continue in private hands but the Nationalization Law was not repealed.

The phases of the experiment match closely those described by Dornbusch and Edwards (1990). The expansionary phase was as spectacular—and indeed the government was fully vindicated even by big business—as the recessionary phase which ended in hyperinflation was formidable. Two striking features of Peru's hyperinflation were the rapid deindexation and real decline of wages and the independent course pursued by the Central Bank during 10 months in the middle of the process. These two factors reversed the explosive hyperinflationary trend and helped accumulate sizable international reserves. Two central lessons can be learned from Peru's experience. First, the devastating decline in real wages and agricultural incomes shows that populist experiments end up hurting most those whom they are intended to benefit. Second, clear rules of the game embodied in the laws, like charters that provide for an independent Central Bank, are a desirable commodity even in countries where laws are loosely enforced, as is the case in many developing nations. Somebody might come and use the laws!

Of the major Latin American debtors, Peru was the first one to embark on a broad-scale unilateral default. Unlike the cases of the other debtors, Peru's default was deliberately confrontational beginning in 1985 and was later extended to the multilateral credit institutions. Although assessing costs of default is beyond the scope of this paper, suffice it here to say that they were significant in terms of paralyzed development projects, reluctant new foreign investments, increased trade restrictions abroad, reduced aid flows, and, above all, a major macroeconomic failure. By early 1990, about 70 percent of Peru's $20 billion external debt was in arrears, and Peruvian commercial debt traded at 7¢ on the dollar in the secondary market. The ultimate debacle of the economic policies has been viewed by some as the example to prove that foreign debt is not the problem of Latin American countries, yet others have claimed that a debt overhang acts as a tax on the debtor country's predisposition to embark on sound policies (Sachs 1987). Peru's experience, however, appears to prove both, often presented as conflicting, theories: a debt overhang does not reward good performance and yet the burden of the debt is just only one of the many problems faced by Latin American countries.

Theoreticians of the now-fashionable topic of the economics of populism struggle to set forth theories attempting to explain why politicians engage in such adventurous experiments and why populist episodes have been a recurrent them in many Latin American countries. Several hypothesis put forward recently can be analyzed in light of Peru's recent experience.

The first hypothesis is that of a high discount rate. The policymaker prefers an early high payoff—at the cost of a later decline—to a steady path of improvement in incomes. Under this hypothesis, the policymaker is viewed as a rational agent, aware of the key interrelations and constraints among the economic variables, who tries to maximize an intertemporal income stream at a high discount rate. To assess the relevance of this hypothesis in the Peruvian case the following simple exercise was performed: a comparison between the present value of the actual monthly real wage index for the period July 1985 to June 1990 (actual scenario) and the monthly real wage index that would have resulted from a sustained annual real growth of 2 percent (alternative scenario).[20] It can be seen in figures 9.14 and 9.15 that the actual scenario is preferable to the alternative one at annual real discount rates higher than 19 percent. This line of reasoning, however, does not explain why high rates of discount are indeed high. Political and social dimensions need to be considered to provide an explanation. Among these, Kaufman and Stallings (in this volume) have emphasized several factors that appear to shorten policy makers' time horizons. These include (1) political and social instability that may render the tenure of office insecure and (2) the arrival to power of parties after long periods of political exclusion. Both factors clearly apply to the Peruvian case. Moreover, Kaufman and Stallings also argue that in politically unstable societies it is more difficult for the people to assign responsibilities, and that politicians themselves might use this circumstance to put the blame for economic failures on "exogenous forces." In April 1990 President García declared that terrorism was responsible for hyperinflation.

The second hypothesis is "bad economics": policymakers do not know the real constraints imposed by macroeconomic variables and behavioral relations, and they act accordingly. Ample evidence was provided in this paper (section 9.3.2) of the departure from received mainstream economics of most economic beliefs of the team that designed the 1985 heterodox program. However, it is, in principle, difficult to know whether those theories are an exotic tailored rationalization of a set of inconsistent policy objectives established "a priori" by politicians or if they are indeed genuine guiding theories. In the case under analysis, it appears that the dominant line of thought in policy-making was misled most of the time, but this seems to have been overshadowed by the prevalence of a firm political agenda. In fact, once the crisis had already unraveled, the corrective attempts proposed by Coronado and Salinas were frustrated by political constraints.

The third hypothesis, proposed by Drake (1982), is that populism starts as a calculated effort to gain political support and momentum but subsequently fails to switch into orthodoxy at the right time. In this case, populism would be a combination of a high discount rate and bad economics. This explanation, however, raises the questions of why most if not all populist experiments end in macroeconomic disaster and why there is a failure to learn from previous similar experiences.

20. We are aware of the limitations of this exercise. Among others, real wages might not be the only variable to be maximized, and the planning horizon might go beyond the five-year presidential term.

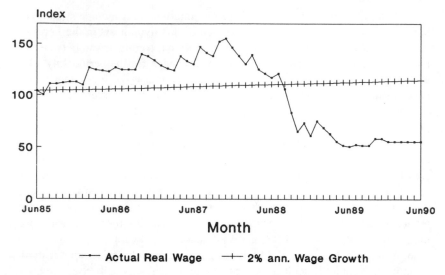

Fig. 9.14   Real wage: Actual versus 2% per year alternative (June 1985 through June 1990)

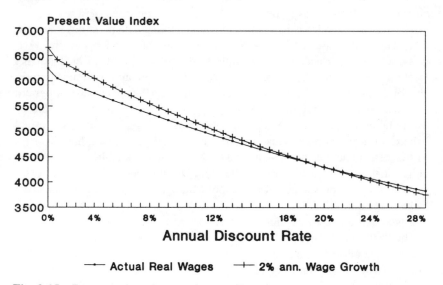

Fig. 9.15   Present value of real wages at different discount rates, demand-led boom versus stable 2% per year growth rate

The fourth explanation is that populism is a deliberate attempt to favor the interests of specific groups at the expense of other sectors. However, as noted above, the intended beneficiaries (i.e., workers and poor farmers) end up being major losers. Again, perhaps this comes as a consequence of a combination of a miscalculated effort, bad economics, and a high discount rate.

Sachs (1989) has established a formal dynamic framework aimed at explaining recurrent stop-and-go economic cycles in Latin American countries. He argues that secularly skewed income distribution and pressure from powerful urban lobbies, represented by inward-looking businesses and urban labor unions, are two key elements that prompt politicians to engage in an expansionary cycle at the end of a yet-not-totally-completed previous stabilization phase. Expansionary cycles seek to benefit urban groups at the expense of the incomes of resource-based exporting groups. The model fits Peru's characteristics well: (i) income distribution is worse than the average for Latin America (the ratio between the income shares of the top and poorest quintiles is 25 compared to an average of 21 for the region) and (ii) the development model followed since the sixties is perhaps the most inward-looking of the region (in 1989 Peru was still the Latin American country with the highest average and maximum tariff rates, as well as the one with the largest share of imports under licenses). In a sense, however, recurrent economic policies can be viewed as a particular case of the more general theme portrayed by modern Latin American novel writers. In his masterpiece *One Hundred Years of Solitude*, Gabriel García Marquez depicts a world in which the cast of characters changes, but everything else remains the same. History repeats itself over and over again. Therefore, the absence of an effective "learning process" from previous economic failures probably has cultural and other roots deeper than those purely economical or political.

Finally, a note on reactivation programs. At a time when the old Keynesian paradigm is being reincarnated into new fashionable and rigorous theories of "multiple real equilibria," the issue of the viability of recovery programs for severely depressed economies needs to be given consideration. The question is whether it is possible for an economy, which has undergone an unbalanced previous stabilization, to successfully run a demand-led experiment for a while and, from then on, return to orthodoxy. In other words, if during stabilization there was "excessive" hoarding of international reserves reached at the expense of overadjustment of real wages and depressed domestic real demand, it is possible for a "credible" incoming government to return real wages and GDP to more normal levels and then to switch into an orthodox approach?

It is conceivable that this may be possible at least in theory. The economics and politics of Peru in 1985 were particularly prone for such an experiment. But the easy part is the recovery, the difficult part is maintaining macroeconomic stability and resuming sustainable growth. More specifically, the difficult issue is to find consistency between the policies implemented for the recovery and the policies needed for stability and growth. The designers of Peru's program were certain that the limits of the recovery were set by international reserves and slack capacity, but they were not aware that the strategy followed to prompt the recovery—subsidies, controls, and import restrictions—were the antithesis of the incentive environment required to move the economy into the desirable second phase of investment and export growth.

Moreover, ideology aside, economic programs that rely heavily on naive "multiplier-accelerator" Keynesian models and price controls and, at the same time, disregard the inevitable restrictions imposed by budget constraints ultimately lead to macroeconomic collapse. While it is often argued that there is no agreement within the profession on economic theories—an argument often put forth by the designers of populist programs—disagreement on flow of funds accounting is nothing less than "bad economics." And populist programs end with macroeconomic failure because of their disregard for accounting constraints.

A country's economy is a complex system. Belief in virtuous-cycle policy interventions to improve the dynamics of complex systems is a dangerous strategy. Jay Forrester's (1972) two basic principles on the "counterintuitive behavior of complex systems" need to be borne in mind. The first is that complex systems have a few sensitive points of entry at which a small effort can yield a significantly larger return. The second is that a complex system tends to draw our attention to the very points at which an attempt to intervene will fail. It is far too simple to believe that the intricacies of "multiple real equilibria" could be exploited with price controls and public deficit financing.

References

Abusada, R. 1987. Final Report on the Evaluation of AID Project no. 527-0244. Development of the Alta Huallaga Area. Lima: ECONSULT S.A.

Amat y Leon, C. 1979. *La Distribucion del Ingreso en el Peru*. Lima: Universidad del Pacifico, Centro de Investigacion.

Apoyo, S. A. 1989. *Peru Economico*, vol. 12, no. 12. Lima: Editora Grafica Pacific Press S. A.

———. Measures of Price Dispersion in Peru 1984–89. Manuscript.

Banco Central de Reserva del Peru. 1986. *Memoria 1985*. Lima: BCRP.

———. 1987. *Memoria 1986*. Lima: BCRP.

———. 1988. *Memoria 1987*. Lima: BCRP.

———. 1989. *Memoria 1988*. Lima: BCRP.

———. 1990. *Memoria 1989*. Lima: BCRP.

Carbonetto, D., I. de Cabellos, O. Dancourt, C. Ferrari, D. Martinez, J. Mezzera, G. Saberbein, J. Tantalean, and P. Vigier. 1987. *El Peru Heterodoxo: Un Modelo Economico*. Lima: Instituto Nacional de Planificacion.

Dornbusch, R., and S. Edwards. 1990. The Macroeconomics of Populism in Latin America. *Journal of Development Economics* 32, no. 2 (April): 247–77.

Drake, P. 1982. Conclusion: Requiem for Populism? In *Latin American Populism in Comparative Perspective*, ed. M. Conniff. Albuquerque: University of New Mexico Press.

Ferrari, C. 1986. La Heterodoxia en Politica Economica (o la nueva Politica Economica Peruana). In *Establizacion y Ajuste Estructural en America Latina*, ed. S. Roca. Lima: Universo.

———. 1989. *Politica Economica. Teoria y Practica en el Peru*. Lima: Fundación Friedrich Ebert.

Forrester, J. 1972. Understanding the Counterintuitive Behaviour of Complex Systems. In *Systems Behaviour,* ed. J. Beisham and G. Peters. London: Harper & Row.

Glewwe, P. 1987. The Distribution of Welfare in Peru in 1985–86. LSMS Working Paper no. 42. Washington, D.C.: World Bank.

———. 1988. The Poor in Latin America during Adjustment: A Case Study of Peru. World Bank working paper. Washington, D.C.: World Bank.

Graham, C. 1990. Peru's APRA Party and Power: Impossible Revolution Relinquished Reform. *Journal of Inter-American Studies and World Affairs.*

Instituto Nacional de Planificación. 1986. *Plan Nacional de Desarrollo.* Lima: Instituto Nacional de Planificación.

Lachler, U. 1989. The Interaction of Tariffs and Multiple Exchange Rates. In *Peru: Policies to Stop Hyperinflation and Initiate Economic Recovery.* Washington, D.C.: World Bank.

Lago, R. 1989. Inflation and Inflationary Finance. In *Peru: Policies to Stop Hyperinflation and Initiate Economic Recovery.* Washington, D.C.: World Bank.

Oks, D. 1989. The Inflation Tax: Theoretical Derivation and Calculation for 1980–87. In *Peru: Policies to Stop Hyperinflation and Initiate Economic Recovery.* Washington, D.C.: World Bank.

Ortiz de Zevallos, F. 1989. *The Peruvian Puzzle.* New York: Twentieth Century Fund, Inc.

Paredes, C., and A. Pasco-Font. 1987. The Behavior of the Public Sector in Peru, 1970–84: A Macroeconomic Approach. Washington, D.C.: World Bank.

Peru Reporting EIRL. 1987a. *The Peru Report,* vol. 1, no. 1. Lima.

———. 1987b. *The Peru Report,* vol. 1, no. 2. Lima.

———. 1987c. *The Peru Report,* vol. 1, no. 8. Lima.

———. 1988a. *The Peru Report,* vol. 2, no. 2. Lima.

———. 1988b. *The Peru Report,* vol. 2, no. 4. Lima.

———. 1988c. *The Peru Report,* vol. 2, no. 10. Lima.

———. 1988d. *The Peru Report,* vol. 2, no. 12. Lima.

Postigo de la Motta, W. 1988. *Crecimiento Selectivo y Viabilidad de la Politica Economica del Peru.* Lima: Instituto Nacional de Planificacion.

Sachs, J. 1987. Efficient Debt Reduction. NBER Working Paper. Cambridge, Mass.

———. 1989. Social Conflict and Populist Policies in Latin America. NBER Working Paper no. 2897. Cambridge, Mass.

Schydlowsky, M., J. Hunt, and S. Mezzera. 1983. *La Promocion de Exportaciones No Tradicionales en el Peru.* Lima: Asociacion de Exportadores del Peru.

Smith, M. L. 1989. Taking the High Ground: Peru's Sendero Luminoso and the Andes. Manuscript.

Tamayo Herrera, J. 1986. *Nuevo Compendio de Historia del Peru.* Lima: Editorial Osiris.

Thorne, A. 1986. Proyecto de Estimacion y Seguimiento de la Inversion Privada en el Ano 1986. Manuscript.

Thorp, R. 1987. The APRA Alternative in Peru. *The Peru Report,* vol. 1, no. 6. Lima: Peru Reporting EIRL.

Vasquez Bazan, C. 1987. *La Propuesta Olvidada.* Lima: Okura.

Webb, R. 1975. *Distribucion del Ingrreso en el Peru.* Lima: Instituto de Estudios Peruano.

Comment   Javier Iguíñiz-Echeverría

The title of Ricardo Lago's paper is misleading. It would seem to suggest that, in general, pursuing redistribution through macropolicy is an illusion. In that respect, I would like to say, first of all, that redistribution is a common feature of macropolicy, not an illusion. We all know, for instance, that exchange rate policies or, more precisely, real devaluation, a key element of almost any macropolicy, has fairly systematic regressive redistributive effects.

After reading the paper, a second possible meaning of the title came to my mind. Lago's main thesis seems to be that government attempts to prevent regressive income redistribution by, for instance, raising wages by the same amount as other price increments, are self-defeating. Its main policy conclusion appears to be that the best way to protect wage earners during an adjustment process is to increase wages by amounts less than exchange rate and public price increments. Actually, I think this is a well-known method for reducing aggregate demand while trying to establish a new structure of relative prices and income distribution. Before going into a more detailed analysis of the arguments supporting this thesis in the case of Peru, however, I would like to comment on some less technical and more historical matters in order to improve, I hope, descriptions of recent Peruvian experience.

I particularly feel that Lago's paper builds a stylized image of García's government that fits a well-structured and coherent "economic villain" model. García—or heterodoxy—is the obvious enemy, while on the other side of the (theoretical) coin are the friends or "heroes" at the Central Bank (Webb and Coronado) waving the flag of the monetary approach to the balance of payments. The main problem with this view is that García has been, above all, a noneconomic man with no economic program and with no stable class or social allegiances. He was at first antilabor, because organized workers were "the privileged," and also anti-industry, because this activity was imitative of Western production and consumption patterns and geographically concentrated in the capital city. Austerity at the top 25% of the income pyramid and reactivation from below (peasants as producers and shanty-town dwellers as direct consumers) were his stated goals, given that he considered himself the president of the lower 75%. The key issues were food and decentralization. This was his first redistributive program. Accordingly, he explicitly rejected any reactivation plan based on the growth of the modern sector of the country. At that time, García stressed the need to undergo sacrifices. This period coincided with the application of a variant of the Austral Plan that was incorporated into García's economic policy options a few days before he assumed office, and was influenced by the enormous popularity of Alfonsín in Argentina.

Javier Iguíñiz-Echeverría is professor of economics at the Universidad Católica del Peru and a researcher of the Centro de Estudios y Promoción del Desarrollo (DESCO) in Lima.

From this mix of physiocratic polpotianism and practical short-run neo-structuralist and truly heterodox view of reactivation, he was transformed (after a summer inflationary fever due to difficulties in the food area) into a proponent of urban consumption-led growth, modern agriculture, easy food importation, and easier import subsidies. His first redistributive project was discarded, heterodoxy was also abandoned and an old-fashioned Keynesian demand-led program was put in place. This second model is the one extensively considered by Lago in his paper. Mentioning the original project in spite of its short life span is meant to recall that García was never a prolabor politician, and that, therefore, once the recession started, his adjustment measures were antilabor ex ante, from the beginning. This viewpoint appears to run against Lago's thesis about the ex ante attempt to avoid the redistributive effects of adjustment measures. Let me examine this aspect of García's successive stabilization attempts.

According to table 9.9, for instance, Lago suggests that the economic "packages" attempted to keep the earnings/wages (e/w) ratio more or less constant. That is not right. In October 1987, measures of the increases in public-sector wages (25%) and private-sector wages (25%) appear more or less equal to the effective devaluation rate (29%); something similar can be found in the case of the March, September, and November 1988 measures. This information, however, is in fact misleading, because in practically all cases there were upper limits to the wage hikes that made the ex ante effective increase in those wages smaller than the devaluation rate. The important rise of the e/w ratio is not, as Lago suggests, an ex post result of the attempt to do otherwise; there was a conscious and very successful redistributive attempt. For instance, in the October 1987 measures, the 25% increase in private-sector wages applied, according to Decree 016-87-TR, only to those that were receiving at that time an income of 3,200 intis or less. The rest received less than that percentage since the maximum increment allowed was 800 intis. Moreover, the increment was due to become effective only in November. Something similar happened with the public-sector wages. The raise in wages was granted in July and there was an absolute limit imposed that month by Decree 077-87-PCM. Moreover, the 25% raise applied only to the "basic" income, which is smaller than the "net" or total "liquid" income to which workers are entitled. In October, the only raise in wages was 10% received by public blue-collar workers. It is true that the minimum legal wage rose from 1,710 to 2,200 intis, but the other wages were increased by less than the devaluation rate. In the March 1988 measures, the 45% increase in private-sector wages applied to wages of up to 5,000 intis per month, while the rest received a raise of only 2,250 intis. The 40% increase applied to public-sector wages also had a limit. The same type of rule was applied in the November measures. The rule has therefore been, to raise those wages at the bottom more and to set absolute ceilings to the increment. As we know, more or less three-fourths of the mass of wages is received by the upper one-quarter of wage earners. On the other hand, around

20% of the labor force received the minimum wage. In June 1988 there was a devaluation of the inti, and in July there was a raise in wages. These measures do not appear in Lago's table. This time the nominal increase in private-sector wages, established by Decree 021-88-EF, was 60% and was applied to those wages up to 6,000 intis per month. Those with larger salaries received an increment of only 3,600 intis. In the case of the public sector the raise was 51% of the "basic" income of those workers that had an effective wage of up to 20,000 intis. Those with wages between 20,001 and 25,000 intis received 40%, and smaller percentages were applied to higher wages. In September 1988 the measures were somewhat different. There were no wage hikes, and the policy was to give first an exceptional nominal bonus of 3,000 intis to both the private and public sectors and one of 9,000 intis, fifteen days later, to the public sector alone. In the case of the unionized workers of the private sector the 9,000 intis increase that was also granted to them would be an advance payment, anticipating the next general increment or individual pact. The same type of wage containment measures were to be found in the November measures.

All these measures and several other details suggest that the purpose of wage policies was to reduce aggregate demand and to alter income distribution between capital and wage labor as well as among laborers. The ex ante containment of wages was absolutely transparent and coherent with the structure of the successive adjustment "packages" that were implemented.

Several other aspects of the paper are worth commenting upon, but I will concentrate on some general views that require greater insight or at least some polishing. The first one refers to the interventionist nature of the Peruvian government. I feel that Lago applies to García some much-repeated features that are part of an abstract model of intervention that can be characterized by the use of multiple exchange rates, import restrictions, and expansionary policies and which appear in most critical evaluations by multilateral organizations. How important these specific features were in generating the crisis is open to question, as is the relative importance of these types of interventions within the whole set of García's manipulations. The lesson, in any case, would seem to be that if you unify exchange rates, eliminate import restrictions, and avoid growth, you are on the right track. Is it so simple? Are those necessary conditions to stabilize the economy? I do not think so, nor, much less, that they are sufficient. We know those policies become critically important and particularly dangerous in those cases in which you lack a long-term development program, state administrative capabilities, and a solid institutional base, all of which were the deeper weaknesses of García's government. In fact, in Colombia or Korea, for instance, those interventions have not been so dangerous.

Another aspect of the paper that would require a more sophisticated analysis is related to the government's objective with respect to the State. Lago says that it was to "expand the role of the state." Two comments may be relevant.

First, García has never been characterized by his prostatist ideology. He made explicit from the beginning that he was against planning and state control. What he wanted and practiced was the expansion of his own personal role. Second, Alán García ravaged the state to its roots. His most systematic behavior was to bleed public enterprises to death, decapitalizing them "at the service of particular interest groups." The attempted nationalization of the financial system had little to do with his vision about the state and, even less, as the official version states, with the resistance to invest on the part of the "12 apostles"; much more important was his political conflict within the party and his need to recover its leadership. This critical aspect of the problem explains the chaotic implementation of the measure, its extremely short preparation period, and the small size of the team that designed the nationalization attempt. García did not strengthen the National Planning Institute, did not establish any institution with enough power to coordinate state activities; he sucked resources from every corner of the state in order to empower himself and announced that the Social Security System would be privatized. His more common statements about the state stressed its mild regulatory function and always rejected its role as planner.

A final questionable aspect of Lago's view is the one related to the autonomy of the Central Bank with respect to the president. The argument goes as if the monetary approach to the balance of payments was the enemy of the Belaúnde government first and of the García presidency afterward.

Again, evidence shows that the problem was more complex than "Webb against Belaúnde's populist policies." In fact, the president himself was not totally innocent in relation to the poor electoral results of his own party because, as with García before the attempted nationalization, he had lost the control of his party and the new candidate of his party had to be destroyed, as, in fact, happened. A strict monetary policy was useful to him. This does not imply absence of conflicts between the Central Bank and the president, but it is not easy to reduce the conflict to the populist-versus-monetarist paradigm.

With respect to the Coronado versus García chapter, things are even more complex. During the first four months of 1989, Rivas Dávila, the secretary of economy and finance (MEF), did not demand a cent from the Central Bank. Monetary restriction was not strictly speaking a Coronado affair, since others in government backed that policy. One component of this policy was, by the way, the reduction in subsidies from $70 (in U.S. dollars) per month in November 1988 to $4 in April 1989. In December 1988 and January 1989, impact of several key products such as canned milk and corn were moved to the free exchange rate market. Summarizing, Coronado's policy was mainly part of government's policy. His conflicts with the executive were real, but not as significant as Lago considers.

The important question, however, is about populism. My impression is that the economic policy definition of "populism" does not appear to add anything new to the traditional policy recommendations of the Bretton Woods institutions. I feel that the definition of several Latin American governments as "populist" helps to show that some basic macroeconomic rules should never be forgotten. This is, I think, the best application of that concept, but I do not believe we should go much further with it. To use that sensible recommendation in order to push for just one way of abiding by those rules is not helpful because the concrete economic and political methods and institutions cannot be derived from them. Perhaps that is why the problem is so stubborn.

Comment   Miguel A. Savastano

Ricardo Lago has presented a very illustrative and well-documented description of Peru's heterodox experiment of the past five years. He shows in a detailed way how the recent Peruvian experience fits most of the elements of the populist paradigm described by Dornbusch and Edwards,[1] from the initial conditions to the different phases of the experiment, with the probable exception of the apocalyptic final phase predicted for Peru in that article. Although I find it hard to disagree with most of what Lago has said about the main features and flaws of this experience, I think that he has overlooked—or at least not emphasized sufficiently—some elements that turn out to be crucial for understanding the emergence and the chaotic results of President García's administration.

In the first place, regarding the initial conditions found by the APRA government, it is necessary to have clear the fact that populist regimes of different vintages have been the norm rather than the exception in Peru during the last 30 years. The degree of government intervention in almost all the spheres of economic activity has increased steadily since the first Belaúnde government—as reflected by the share of total public-sector expenditures on GDP that rose from 26% in 1968 to 58% in 1985—and the revealed preference for discretionary and short-lasting measures has been the commonplace of almost all finance ministers and Central Bank governors during this period. Even the second Belaúnde administration (from 1980–85) carried out mild populist policies, in spite of its initial rhetoric and its quickly aborted trade liberalization program. Public investment reached its highest level in Peruvian history in 1982 (10.5% of GDP), no privatization of the more than 200 public enterprises was even attempted—except for newspapers and TV stations—and the fiscal deficit averaged 7.5% of GDP during this period. The reader of this

Miguel A. Savastano was a doctoral candidate at the University of California, Los Angeles, when this comment was first prepared. He is now an economist at the International Monetary Fund.
1. R. Dornbusch and S. Edwards, "Macroeconomic Populism in Latin America," *Journal of Development Economics* 32, no. 2 (April 1990): 247–77.

paper, then, should not be surprised to find out that the "only" reformist step taken by President García was the failed nationalization of the banking system. There was not (or is not, for that matter) much else to nationalize in Peru without the risk of transforming the country into an outright socialist economy.

On the other hand, I think that one has to be more careful before characterizing the stabilization attempts undertaken from 1980 to 1985 as "orthodox" or "serious." The continuous adjustment of the exchange rate and of public-sector prices during the last two years of Belaúnde's government represented isolated measures that reflected a concern for the deteriorating external position of the country in the midst of the debt crisis, but they were far from constituting a consistent strategy to stabilize the economy. In fact, it would not be difficult to show that the "overwhelming evidence of failure of orthodox policies" cited so effusively by the proponents of the heterodox plan and by many other economic advisors, including former Central Bank President Richard Webb,[2] was more the natural consequence of a badly implemented partial stabilization program than the reflection of the negative effects of an "overdone" stabilization as Lago seems to suggest.

Moving now to the initial phase of the APRA experiment, I think that—besides the price-cost freeze and the depressed domestic market—an important and downplayed factor that facilitated the disinflation achieved in the first two years was the forced conversion of dollar deposits that was decreed in August 1985. The "dollarization" of the domestic financial system had reached very significant levels during the Belaúnde administration (more than 70% of the private sector's financial assets were held in foreign currency by 1985), and the confiscation of these deposits represented for the government a sudden increase in the base of the inflation tax and the ready availability of approximately $1 billion. Indeed, the figures reported in table 9.5 of the paper show that the income velocity of money experienced almost a 40% decrease from June 1985 to June 1986. It is this forced increase in the demand for domestic money, and not the suggested independent stance of the Central Bank, that explains the lack of an aggressive expansion of monetary aggregates in the first phase of the experiment.

Another potential source of confusion that I have found in Lago's paper—as well as in the few other accounts of this experience—is the tendency to identify the turning point of the experiment with the government's attempt to nationalize the private banking system in July 1987. In spite of the great political, and not economic, significance of this move, one has to be emphatic in asserting that the anachronic and pernicious inward-oriented strategy adopted was deemed to fail even in the absence of this nationalization attempt. Perhaps

---

2. R. Webb, "La Gestacion del Plan Antinflacionario del Peru," in *Planes Antinflacionarios Recientes en la America Latina,* ed. J. A. Ocampo (*El Trimestre Economico,* special issue [September 1987]).

the eruption of the crisis would not have been as abrupt as it was, but the huge fiscal and current account deficits and the steady appreciation of the real exchange rate could not have been sustained much longer without some serious adjustment.

Finally, I think that a very interesting feature of the Peruvian experiment is that it ran out of steam without taking the economy to an open hyperinflation. Lago assigns the responsibility of this result to the independent stance adopted by the Central Bank's Governor Pedro Coronado from September 1988 to June 1989. Even if one is willing to be as generous as the author in describing Coronado's performance—leaving aside the fact that he maintained most of the pervasive foreign exchange controls as well as the credit and interest rates regulations—it seems to me that his partial and insufficient measures only contributed to jeopardize the success of the comprehensive stabilization program that is urgently required in Peru.

Undoubtedly the credit crunch of early 1989, together with the imperfect indexation of wages and the systematic delay in adjusting controlled prices, prevented the explosion of a hyperinflationary spiral at the cost of an enormous recession. However, it is also true that by mid-1989 inflation remained high and the private sector became an active supporter of the executive's demands for a looser credit policy. In this context, the fact that the so-called *maquinazo* of July 1989 (21% of the monetary base) did not have any noticeable effect on the inflation rate of the following six months ended up vindicating the president's position regarding the irrelevance of "monetarist" or "orthodox" predicaments. Moreover, the "bad" steady-state equilibrium in which the Peruvian economy appears to be currently trapped (which is documented in tables 9.6 and 9.7) has affected the general consensus regarding the need to stabilize the economy and is reviving the very same arguments of "lack of excess aggregate demand" that were used in late 1985 to justify the heterodox program.

To me this is just another illustration of the fact that the partial and ill-conceived stabilization attempts that are so common in recent Peruvian history do more harm than good by damaging the effectiveness of crucial policy instruments and by adding more noise to the perverse dynamics of high inflations. It also shows that the design of a coherent set of instruments capable of, among other things, enforcing the legally contemplated independence of the Central Bank is even more important than the laws themselves for avoiding what I see as the inevitable repetition of another populist blast. Sadly enough, however, even today I am not sure that Peruvians have learned this basic lesson.

10   Collapse and (Incomplete) Stabilization of the Nicaraguan Economy

José Antonio Ocampo

10.1   Introduction

In the 1980s, the Nicaraguan economy faced massive macroeconomic disequilibria. Economic activity never recovered the large losses incurred during the 1979 revolution that brought the Sandinistas to power. Moreover, GDP fell steadily from 1983 to 1989. As a result of production losses and rapid population growth, by the latter year GDP per capita had returned to levels comparable to the 1940s. Due to the financial needs generated by a continuing war effort, private consumption per capita and real wages fell even more.

This process was accompanied by massive external disequilibria. As a result of these imbalances, the country had accumulated at the end of 1989 a foreign debt of $9,741 million, equivalent to 33 times the exports of goods, and more than four times the GDP, the worst debt ratios in the heavily indebted region (República de Nicaragua 1990). Finally, the collapse of real economic activity has been accompanied by equally massive domestic financial disequilibria, which exploded into hyperinflation in 1988. From January 1988 to January 1989, when this process was at its peak, inflation reached an astonishing 43,000%, the record so far in Latin America and one of the highest in world history.

Macroeconomic management faced a complex set of constraints, quite different from those confronted by other Latin American countries in the 1980s. Through the decade, Nicaragua continued to receive massive financing from abroad. Also, according to ECLAC estimates, the terms of trade did not fare badly, either.[1] However, these favorable events were overwhelmed by the impacts on production and resource availability of the revolution and the Contra

José Antonio Ocampo is senior researcher at Fedesarrollo, in Bogotá, Colombia, and head of the WIDER/SIDA Mission to Nicaragua.

1. This is not true according to alternative estimates by Bulmer-Thomas (1987, table A.14).

war, the U.S. trade embargo and veto on multilateral lending, excessive reliance on relatively inflexible bilateral assistance from the socialist countries, and a series of natural disasters.

The buildup of macroeconomic disequilibria was also closely associated with economic policy. In the first years of the revolution, the government adopted an expansionary public expenditure program to improve the poor social record inherited from the Somoza years and to accelerate economic growth. These goals, particularly the latter, were sacrificed when the government was forced to increase defense expenditure to face the Contra war. Up to 1988, the central government ran massive budget deficits. Monetary financing of the deficit, together with equally massive subsidies on the use of foreign exchange and credit resulted, with a lag, in hyperinflation.

The magnitude of existing disequilibria forced the government to adopt more ambitious adjustment programs in 1988 and 1989. In the former year, the program emphasized the correction of relative price distortions, particularly the simplification of the inefficient and costly multiple exchange rate system. In 1989, continuing efforts to correct exchange rate overvaluation were combined with a contractionary fiscal policy.

As this general characterization indicates, macroeconomic events in Nicaragua over the 1980s largely coincide with the concept of "populism," as defined by Dornbusch and Edwards (1990). In particular, following their definition, the approach of the Sandinistas to macroeconomic policy emphasized growth and income distribution and disregarded "the risks of inflation and deficit finance, external constraints and the reaction of economic agents to aggressive non-market policies." The sequence of events from expansionary aggregate demand policies to collapse and orthodox adjustment was also similar to the prototypical phases defined by these authors.

Nonetheless, the term "populism" seems somewhat inadequate to characterize the Sandinista period. Most important, some of the structural reforms adopted in the first years of the revolution and the very nature of political mobilization were typical of socialist rather populist regimes. On the other hand, contrary to Dornbusch and Edwards's definition, the major constraints faced by the Sandinistas were U.S. intervention and the Contra war rather than external financing. Finally, some of the typical policies of "populist" regimes were absent in the Nicaraguan experience. In particular, the Sandinistas never adopted an expansionary wage policy, and a series of tax reforms increased the domestic resources made available to the central government to finance the expansion of social services and investment.

This paper analyzes macroeconomic policies and performance in Nicaragua in the 1980s. It is divided in six sections, the first of which is this introduction. The second summarizes some features of the Nicaraguan economy prior to the revolution. The third considers the effects of revolution and the period of recovery which followed it. The fourth analyzes the buildup of macroeconomic disequilibria during the transition to and full-fledged war economy. The fifth

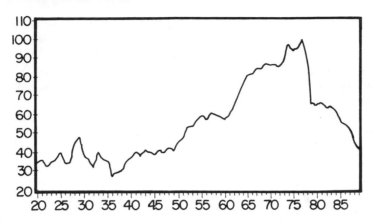

Fig. 10.1   Per capita income of Nicaragua, 1920–89 (1977 = 100)

shows the characteristics of the 1988 adjustment program and the hyperinflation that accompanied it. The paper ends with a close look at the 1989 stabilization program. The defeat of the Sandinistas in the February 1990 elections
is taken as the closing date of the analysis.

10.2   The Nicaraguan Economy prior to the Revolution

The recent study by Bulmer-Thomas (1987) indicates that there was little
growth in GDP per capita in Nicaragua from the 1920s to the late 1940s (see
fig. 10.1). This period of relative stagnation was followed, however, by an
export-led boom from the 1950s to just before the revolution. GDP per capita
multiplied by 2.5 during this period. As this process was matched by rapid
population growth, GDP expanded at an average rate of some 6% a year, the
fastest in Central America. The rapid growth of cotton exports was the initial
basis for expansion. Later on, the process was reinforced by new primary
exports (beef, sugar, shellfish, etc.) and a boom of agroindustrial and other
manufacturing exports to members of the Central American Common Market,
or CACM (Bulmer-Thomas 1987; CEPAL 1981; Gibson 1987a).

Rapid economic expansion was not translated into an equally rapid improvement of social indicators. At the end of the boom, illiteracy, child mortality, and life-expectancy levels were among the worst in Latin America—
comparable, however, to other Central American countries, excluding Costa
Rica and Panama.[2] Income distribution remained highly skewed, at levels also
similar to Nicaragua's Central American neighbors (Brundenius 1987, table
2). There is little evidence on how distribution evolved during the period of
expansion. However, available data on labor incomes indicate that real wages

2. See CEPAL (1988a, pp. 13, 45, 50) and n. 4 below.

were basically trendless in the 1960s and 1970s.[3] As this was accompanied by widespread and growing informality in the labor market (Gibson 1987a, table 2), it may indicate that income distribution deteriorated in the last phases of the boom. On the other hand, the concentration of wealth in hands of the Somoza family and his political clique was remarkable, as the data on nationalizations following the revolution later revealed.

Economic management was fairly orthodox throughout the boom. From the late 1950s to just before the revolution, the exchange rate was pegged at a rate of seven cordobas per U.S. dollar. Since 1963, the currency was freely convertible. Orthodox fiscal and monetary policies guaranteed low inflation rates but also the transmission of external shocks to the domestic economy. As a reflection of limited fiscal and current account deficits, foreign indebtedness remained within close bounds (Gibson 1987a, 1987b).

The economy and economic management experienced, however, increasing hardships in the 1970s (CEPAL 1981). Reconstruction efforts after the 1972 earthquake broke the tradition of fiscal conservatism. In the last years of the Somoza regime, budget deficits increased to an average of over 5% of GDP (see table 10.2 below). This was also reflected in increasing foreign indebtedness. According to ECLAC estimates, the external public-sector debt quadrupled from 1972 to 1979 (from $230 to $961 million). The counterpart of this process was persistent current-account disequilibria, enhanced by the adverse effects of the 1973 oil shock, the slowing down of growth of trade within the CACM, growing overvaluation of the cordoba, and capital flight in the months before the victory of the Sandinistas (see below). To face growing disequilibria, the Somoza government established mild exchange controls in late 1978. In April, 1979, it devalued the basic exchange rate to 10 cordobas per dollar and introduced a multiple rate system.

10.3   Revolution and Recovery, 1979–81

The economic legacy of the last years of the Somoza regime and the revolutionary uprising was complex. Economic activity severely contracted in 1978 and 1979, by an accumulated 34.4% (table 10.1). The capital stock was also severely affected. Losses associated with the destruction of buildings, equipment, and stocks, the looting of inventories, the slaughter of immature beef cattle, and the smuggling of herds were estimated by ECLAC at $381 million (CEPAL 1981), equivalent to 18% of 1980 GDP. National Accounts records indicate that the loss of inventories in 1978–79 was equivalent to 14.4% of GDP (see table 10.1). To these, we must add capital flight for $535 million in the 18 months preceding the revolution (CEPAL 1981), portfolio

3. Using the average wage estimated by INSSBII, and the GDP deflator as a price index, real wages (1981 = 100) increased slightly from 1960–64 to 1965–69 (from 100.2 to 107.0) but then stagnated and declined (106.0 in 1970–74 and 103.2 and 1975–79).

Table 10.1   Macroeconomic Indicators, 1978–89

	GDP Growth Rate (%)	GDP (1977 = 100)	GDP per Capita (1977 = 100) (%)	Investment as % of GDP (Constant Prices)	Fixed Investment (%)	Change of Inventories (%)	Private Consumption per Capita (1977 = 100)	Real Wages (1985 = 100) Using GDP Deflator	Real Wages (1985 = 100) Using CPI	Average Monthly Inflation (CPI) (%)
1978	−7.9	92.1	89.4	10.7	12.7	−2.0	93.2	139.9		.4
1979	−26.5	67.7	65.0	−6.4	6.1	−12.4	67.9	126.7		4.5
1980	4.6	70.9	64.9	16.8	14.6	2.2	80.0	119.4		1.9
1981	5.4	74.7	66.2	24.4	22.2	2.2	68.7	120.8	186.0	1.8
1982	−.8	74.1	63.6	20.2	18.0	2.2	59.9	116.9	165.5	1.7
1983	4.6	77.5	64.3	21.0	18.1	3.0	56.5	114.6	142.9	2.4
1984	−1.6	76.3	61.2	21.6	18.7	2.8	53.6	112.0	135.9	3.4
1985	−4.1	73.1	56.7	22.3	19.8	2.6	49.3	100.0	100.0	13.0
1986	−1.0	72.4	54.3	22.3	18.7	3.5	45.3	101.4	59.5	19.5
1987	−.7	71.9	52.1	22.1	19.1	3.0	42.9	73.9	24.6	24.9
1988	−10.9	64.0	44.9	24.9	21.0	3.9	33.8	50.5	14.9	62.4
1989	−2.9	62.2	42.1	22.7	14.0	8.7	41.7	33.3	11.6	27.2

Sources: SPP, INSBII, and INEC.

losses by industrial and commercial firms and, of course, the casualties in-flicted by the war.

The revolutionary government brought with it some emergency measures and a plan for economic recovery but, above all, an agenda for structural change. The latter was presented as a program for a "mixed economy," in which the state would assume control of the properties of the Somoza family and his clique and some "key" economic sectors and considerably expand social expenditure and its contribution to capital accumulation. The state would also encourage the organization of the popular classes through union-ization in urban areas and cooperativization in the countryside. As a result of the enhanced role of the public sector, new rules of the game for the private sector would be designed.

One of the first decrees issued by the government after the military victory on 19 July 1979 was the nationalization of the properties of the Somoza family and their allies who fled the country. It was followed by the nationalization of the financial system, foreign trade, large-scale (particularly gold) mining, for-estry, and fishing. Few other important nationalizations took place in the fol-lowing years, but the government periodically exercised the right to confiscate the properties of capitalists suspected of counterrevolutionary activities or practices that led to the decapitalization of their businesses (Stahler-Sholk et al. 1989). Government's share in GDP rose from 15% to 40% in the early 1980s, but then stabilized. The private sector retained a dominant share of agriculture, manufacturing, domestic commerce, and most services (World Bank 1981; Baumeister and Neira 1986; Ruccio 1987; Brundenius 1987).

The initial nationalization decrees also brought some 20% of land property under state control. Land redistribution accelerated as a result of the Agrarian Reform Decree issued at the second anniversary of the revolution. As a result of both measures, more that 50% of rural property was affected in the years following the revolution. During its first phases, the government emphasized the development of parastatals and cooperatives, but soon evolved into en-couraging small-scale farming. The redirection of agrarian policy was largely induced by the need to erode peasant support for the Contras in some regions of the country. Nonetheless, it also reflected the social programs of the revo-lution and the policy of self-sufficiency in food staples (Enriquez and Spalding 1987; Neira 1988; Wheelock 1989).

The initial nationalizations created a large parastatal sector. As in most countries undergoing similar processes, the management problems generated by such a sudden expansion of the state sector were costly (Colborn 1990). On the other hand, the redesign of new rules of the game for the private sector proved difficult and in fact led, rather early in the process, to violent confron-tations (Vilas 1987). At a purely economic level, the private sector resented excessive state intervention in their businesses and government predilection for public-sector enterprises. More important, however, the exclusion of the bourgeoisie from political power and the practice of intermittent political confiscations generated a general sense of insecurity about property rights.

The inadequate functioning of state enterprises and confrontations with the private sector may explain the failure of economic activity to recover rapidly in the years following the revolution. A partial recovery was, nonetheless, experienced, based on an expansionary demand policy and an ample supply of external financing (Fitzgerald 1989). By 1981, central government expenditure, as a share of GDP, had doubled with respect to levels typical before the revolution. The initial fiscal expansion included many social programs—which induced a rapid improvement in key social indicators[4]—but also defense and general bureaucratic expenditures. A large part of this expansion was financed by rising taxes. The resulting deficit, of some 9% of GDP, was, nonetheless, reasonable in the short run, given the ample supply of external financing (table 10.2).

In fact, other domestic macroeconomic indicators were not particularly troublesome. As a result of the disruption of the domestic distribution network during the last stage of the revolutionary uprising, inflation peaked at 70% in 1979. As supplies stabilized, this price surge was followed by moderate inflation in the early 1980s—some 20% a year (see table 10.1). Domestic liquidity ratios increased with respect to those typical before the revolution,[5] but were stable (table 10.2). finally, nominal wages increased, but there was no attempt to raise them in real terms (see table 10.1 and n. 3 above). This required, in fact, a significant political effort by the Sandinistas to control labor demands (Vilas 1987). The policy strategy adopted by the government thus implied that workers would receive increasing real income through government services—a "social wage", as it was called—but would contribute, through wage restraint, to the recovery of economic activity.

The core external sector indicators moved, however, in the wrong direction. Neither traditional nor nontraditional exports ever reached prerevolutionary levels (table 10.3). The reduction of exports as combined in the early years with a deterioration of the terms of trade. On the other hand, the revolutionary government inherited a clearly overvalued cordoba and a rate of inflation clearly incompatible with a fixed exchange rate. There was no attempt to correct such imbalances. A steady real appreciation of the cordoba then ensued. It was accompanied by a strong depreciation of the black market rate (fig. 10.2

4. Life expectancy at birth increased from 56.3 years in 1975–80 to 62.3 years in 1985–90, as child mortality fell from 9.3% to 6.2%. At the same time, the illiteracy rate fell from 42.5% in 1970 (and a similar figure just before the revolution) to 13.0% in 1985 (see CEPAL 1988a, pp. 13, 45, 50).

5. Estimated on the basis of end-of-year monetary aggregates, the ratio M1/GDP increased from 13.1% in 1974–1978 to 22.6% in 1980, whereas M2/GDP increased from 20.7 to 30.5% (see IMF, *International Financial Statistics*). The methodology used in table 10.2 puts such liquidity indicators at 20.9% and 33.0% in 1980.

Table 10.2   Fiscal and Monetary Indicators (% of GDP at current prices)

	1974–78	1979	1980	1981	1982	1983	1984	1985	1986	1987	1988	1989
Central government accounts:												
Current income[a]	12.5	14.0	22.2	24.4	25.7	31.2	35.2	32.3	32.4	27.7	20.6	18.9
Total expenditure	17.7	21.2	31.2	33.3	38.1	52.9	58.7	54.8	49.6	44.2	46.4	21.4
Deficit	−5.2	−7.2	−9.0	−8.9	−12.4	−21.7	−23.5	−22.5	−17.2	−16.5	−25.8	−2.5
Central government expenditure[b]				34.5	39.2	61.0	59.7	55.6	50.0	44.3	46.4	19.6
Social services				10.2	9.5	11.4	13.0	12.1	11.9	10.9	11.2	4.8
Infrastructure and production				7.6	10.1	24.7	16.9	9.5	6.7	4.8	4.9	2.1
Defense				7.6	7.4	11.0	12.4	17.6	18.5	18.1	18.5	8.0
Public administration				9.1	12.2	14.0	17.4	16.5	12.9	10.5	11.7	4.6
Consolidated public sector deficit (IMF) [c]						−25.1	−26.6	−25.0	−21.0	−21.7	−31.3	−10.2
Public-sector enterprises, excluding utilities						−10.7	−5.3	−13.1	−11.2	−10.1	−6.7	−10.1
Unpaid foreign interest						−4.1	−4.4	−5.3	−5.8	−4.6	−6.8	−5.7
Monetary stocks as proportion of GDP:[d]												
Means of payment			20.9	20.0	21.8	27.2	36.4	36.8	35.0	28.2	16.6	7.5
Quasi money			12.1	12.5	11.9	12.7	15.4	10.4	5.9	3.6	1.2	1.1

Sources: Ministry of Finance, SPP, IMF, and Central Bank.

[a]Excludes foreign transfers.

[b]Total expenditure according to these figures is apparently based on budgets and, thus, does not coincide with expenditure according to the central government accounts.

[c]Excludes unpaid foreign interest and deficit of public sector enterprises (excluding utilities).

[d]Average monthly ratio between aggregate and annual GDP.

Table 10.3   External Sector Indicators (Millions of dollars unless otherwise indicated)

	1974	1975	1976	1977	1978	1979	1980	1981
Exports:								
Traditional[a]	236.8	240.8	370.6	449.5	459.4	449.0	354.1	418.5
Nontraditional	144.1	134.3	168.3	187.3	186.6	117.6	91.0	95.3
Total	380.9	375.2	538.9	636.8	646.0	566.6	445.1	513.8
Real exports of goods and services (1977 = 100)	92.2	99.0	102.9	100.0	109.0	124.8	74.1	85.1
Import coefficient	30.6	22.7	22.1	27.5	22.6	24.9	43.3	39.3
Current account balance:								
Global	-257.2	-185.0	-39.3	-181.9	-24.9	180.2	-430.1	-590.6
Excluding unpaid interest							-397.8	-504.
External debt (ECLAC)[c]	456.0	598.0	655.0	864.0	961.0	1136.0	1825.0	2566.0
External resources contracted						363.2	678.7	803.0
% from socialist countries						1.8	25.6	23.0
Terms of trade (ECLAC, 1980 = 100)	109.9	92.0	113.5	129.8	118.1	107.0	100.0	90.2
Real exchange rate (1980 = 100)[d]								
Official							100.0	85.2
Black							100.0	139.7
Ratios:								
Black/official rate							1.73	2.85
Parallel/official rate								

(*continued*)

Table 10.3   (continued)

	1982	1983	1984	1985	1986	1987	1988	1989
Exports:								
Traditional[a]	339.5	387.8	355.0	268.5	217.9	254.9	201.3	232.0
Nontraditional	69.1	64.1	57.4	36.6	39.3	40.1	34.4	47.1[b]
Total	408.6	451.9	412.4	305.1	257.2	295.0	235.7	279.1[b]
Real exports of goods and services								
(1977 = 100)	78.3	83.8	66.4	58.6	48.3	47.2	41.5	56.3
Import coefficient	28.8	32.2	32.3	33.8	29.2	30.5	32.3	28.2
Current account balance:								
Global	−491.6	−507.4	−596.8	−725.7	−687.8	−679.1	−594.9	−455.3
Excluding unpaid interest	−448.4	−353.6	−378.8	−500.1	−461.5	−450.7	−359.8	−249.7
External debt (ECLAC)[c]	3139.0	3788.0	4362.0	4936.0	5760.0	6270.0	7220.0	7570.0
External resources contracted	597.7	619.2	772.5	1196.6	517.9	386.3	801.6	
% from socialist countries	48.1	50.6	77.3	89.3	75.0	69.2	65.3	
Terms of trade (ECLAC, 1980 = 100)	85.1	82.0	102.8	94.0	99.4	95.6	94.6	87.0
Real exchange rate (1980 = 100)[d]								
Official	74.1	63.7	48.8	52.1	35.3	9.8	69.4	105.2
Black	236.9	443.8	753.8	819.2	631.2	556.7	202.1	81.9
Ratios								
Black/official rate	5.54	12.29	27.58	27.43	32.83	177.14	4.61	1.28
Parallel/official rate					19.61	93.93	3.44	1.22

[a] Coffee, cotton, sugar, meat, shellfish, bananas, sesame seeds, molasses and gold.
[b] Excluding re-exports.
[c] Excludes interest arrears and some short-term debt.
[d] Using GDP deflator.

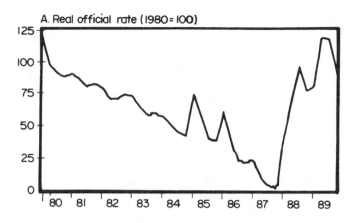

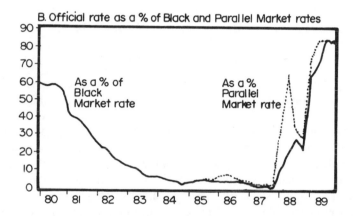

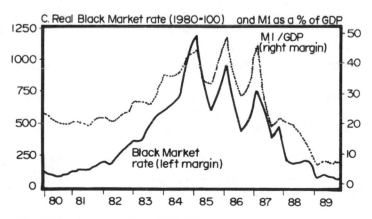

Fig. 10.2   Exchange rate policy, 1980–89

and table 10.3). The political climate generated by growing confrontations between the Sandinistas and the private sector accentuated this trend.

Although strong import and exchange controls became a central feature of external sector management during the first years of the revolutionary government, the former were not particularly harsh. Indeed, the import coefficient reached a historical peak in 1980 and 1981 (table 10.3). Growing external imbalances generated by record imports and weakening exports were financed by record capital inflows. Thus, as outstanding debts were renegotiated, the country had ample access to new financing. Resources came from multilateral agencies and bilateral sources, both in the developed countries (including the United States) and the Third World (Mexico in particular), and only secondarily from socialist countries (see Stahler-Sholk 1987; Arana et al. 1987; and table 10.3). The result of this strategy was, of course, the rapid growth of the external debt. By 1981, the debt had already reached extremely critical levels (table 10.3).

10.4 War Economy and Macroeconomic Disequilibria, 1982–87

10.4.1 General Features of Macroeconomic Management[6]

The expansionary demand policy adopted during the first years of the revolutionary government could be defended on the grounds that the access to external financing should be used to ensure a fast turnaround of economic activity and an equally rapid improvement in key social indicators. On the other hand, as we have seen, the macroeconomic package typical of the first years revealed some prudence on behalf of the government, as reflected in its wage and tax policies. Nonetheless, by itself, external disequilibria would have called for a significant policy shift as early as 1981.

The government did not grasp the urgent need for action. Indeed, the systematic lag in the adoption of the stabilization policies and the partial nature of such efforts once they were adopted became central features of Sandinista macroeconomic management early in the postrevolutionary period. "Voluntarism" and economic ideologies go a long way to explain some of these features—particularly the strong preference for intricate government intervention rather than traditional orthodox macroeconomic management. However, political dynamics played an equally important role.

As one would expect, the government was unwilling to give up what it thought to be the essential goals of the revolution or to adopt policies that it thought would affect the economic recovery and, even more, risk military

6. For a more extensive analysis of this period, see Arana et al. (1987), Fitzgerald (1989), Gibson (1987b), IMF (1988), Medal (1988), Pizarro (1987), Taylor et al. (1989), and the World Bank (1986). Stahler-Sholk et al. (1989) presents also a very useful chronology, which would be extensively used below.

defeat. Nonetheless, the political process worked in peculiar directions. Understandably, defense and social expenditure became the most inflexible components of the budget. Paradoxically, however, the government was, at the end, more willing to sacrifice real wages and capital accumulation than to reduce the massive subsidies to the productive sector. Its strong political control of the labor movement and public-sector enterprises and, on the contrary, its feeble relations with the private sector and the need to guarantee the support of the peasants in the Contra war, go a long way to explain this paradox.

Although the first signs of government concern for the balance of payments—the adoption of export-promotion policies—came as early as 1982; the "populist" dynamics of expenditure policies were in full swing up to 1984. By then, domestic disequilibria had reached clearly explosive levels. Forced by the circumstances, the government adopted the first important stabilization measures in 1985, including cuts in nondefense expenditure, readjustment of government-regulated prices, and devaluation. This was followed by similar steps in the subsequent years. However, the inconsistency of the stabilization packages implemented from 1985 to 1987 enhanced macroeconomic disequilibria. Particularly, rising inflation eroded the tax base, and attempts to repress inflation and defend exporters against official exchange rate overvaluation led to massive relative price distortions and booming black markets. As a consequence of these imbalances, the government was finally forced to adopt more drastic stabilization measures in 1988 and 1989.

On top of the dynamics generated by "populist" expenditure policies and inconsistent macroeconomic management, the revolutionary government also had to face during this period the destabilizing impact of the Contra war and the U.S. anti-Sandinista campaign. The war had additional demand effects, as it forced a further expansion of government expenditure. However, the war and the U.S. campaign had also significant supply effects (Fitzgerald 1987; Gibson 1987b). Aside from the destruction of resources and production generated by the war, it created multiple labor shortages associated with the diversion of young workers into military service, rural-urban migration, scarcity of labor in some crucial (particularly coffee-producing) regions, and the flight of skilled workers abroad. On the other hand, the 1985 U.S. embargo forced an inefficient substitution of trading partners. Finally, the suspension of direct U.S. aid soon after Reagan was inaugurated in 1981 and the American veto on multilateral lending in the following years, forced the country to rely increasingly on inflexible bilateral assistance from socialist countries (table 10.3; see also Stahler-Shock 1987).

10.4.2 Fiscal and Monetary Disequilibria and the First Stabilization Efforts

As a reflection of policy decisions and defense needs, central government expenditure continued to increase rapidly after 1981, peaking at 58.7% in

1984.[7] As table 10.2 indicates, the most dynamic element from 1982 to 1984 was the expenditure in infrastructure and production (largely investment outlays). However, all components of central government expenditure continued to increase at rapid rates. Efforts to raise government revenues were successful, and by 1984 the country had one of the highest tax rates of Latin America. Nonetheless, the growth of expenditure clearly outstripped the tax effort. In the same year, the central government deficit reached 23.5% of GDP—26.6% for the consolidated public-sector deficit, according to a partial estimate using IMF data.[8]

Growing pressures generated by macroeconomic disequilibria and the Contra war led the government to undertake significant expenditures cuts starting in 1985. However, the war forced a further increase in defense expenditure, which peaked over 18% of GDP in 1986–88. Thus, the government was forced to concentrate cuts in civil expenditure. From 1984 to 1987, expenditure on infrastructure and production fell to very modest levels, and foreign interest payments were all but suspended, as the expansion of public administration costs earlier in the decade was reversed. Expenditure in social services was maintained, however, at historically peak levels.

Overall, central government expenditure was reduced from 58.7% to 44.1% of GDP from 1984 to 1987. Noninterest civil expenditure fell even more, by some 18% of GDP, but remained slightly above 1980–81 levels. Unfortunately, most of the expenditure cuts were defeated by the adverse Olivera-Tanzi effect on government revenues.[9] Thus, the central government deficit remained at 16.5% of GDP in 1987. As we will see shortly, other major components of the public-sector deficit, particularly Central Bank losses, were even more inflexible. Thus, the overall public-sector deficit never fell below 20% of GDP, even if unpaid interests on the external debt and the deficit of several public-sector enterprises are excluded.

The monetary impact of deficit financing was dramatic. However, up to 1984, the economy absorbed it through an impressive increase in liquidity,

---

7. As pointed out in note *b* of table 10.2, total expenditure according to central government accounts does not coincide with data on destination of expenditure by ministries, which is used to make up the breakdown shown in the second part of the same table. The former figures are used in the text when referring to total spending.

8. We have excluded from this figure both unpaid foreign interest and deficit estimates for the "rest of the public sector." The former are unlikely to ever be paid. The latter have been estimated by the IMF on the basis of domestic lending, which is a poor approach in a highly inflationary economy. The estimates of central bank losses in recent years are also subject to controversy.

9. This was the dominant element in the erosion of tax revenues in 1984–87 and through 1988. Given a month's lag in the collection of tax and other current incomes (a lag that seems to have been reached by the end of this period), the 1984 share of current government income in GDP would have fallen to 29.1% in 1987 and 22.4% in 1988 as a result of faster inflation. Thus, additional effects on government income, such as domestic recession, had a secondary role in the erosion of the tax base. They may be important, however, as an explanation of the recent stabilization of the tax rate at fairly low levels.

with only a modest acceleration of inflation (see tables 10.1 and 10.2). Although the lack of an inflationary tradition goes a long way to explain this result, it was also supported by a fixed exchange rate and strong price controls. The importance of these latter factors is supported by the significant role played by explicit adjustments in the official exchange rate and other controlled prices in the inflationary dynamics after 1985 (see below).

Oddly enough, the demand for money grew faster than that for term deposits up to 1984 (table 10.2). Several factors may explain this result. First of all, nominal interest rates were hardly readjusted with inflation up to late 1988.[10] With rising inflation, this meant that term deposits became a close, *though illiquid,* substitute for money. In a more orthodox pattern, excess domestic liquidity was reflected in the increasing demand for black market dollars, as the evolution of the relevant real exchange rate indicates (fig. 10.2, part C). The demand for dollars was enhanced by political instability and the growing overvaluation of the official exchange rate (fig. 10.2, part A, and table 10.3). The role of political factors may explain why devaluation in the black market overshot the rapid increase in liquidity levels and monetary aggregates actually collapsed in terms of (black) dollars (table 10.3).

By 1984 the official exchange rate was only a minimal fraction of the black market rate (table 10.3 and fig. 10.2, part B). This finally convinced the government to devalue the official rate from 10 to 28 cordobas per dollar in February 1985. As we have seen, the devaluation was accompanied by some austerity measures in the fiscal area. The need for fiscal austerity also led the government to massively readjust controlled prices (basic consumer goods and gasoline) at the same time.

In an attempt to regulate the wage structure, the government decreed in 1984 a complete wage scale (SNOTS), to which, theoretically, public and private firms were to abide. As a result of the price adjustments adopted in the first months of 1985, the government then attempted to defend them against inflation, and thus adjusted the scale three times from February to May 1985, increasing the average wage by 146%. The adjustment was slightly higher than inflation during these months, but not enough to compensate for the fall in real wages in previous years. Nonetheless, returning to its otherwise "unpopulist" wage policy, this attempt to index wages was soon abandoned. In the following months and years, wage policy was ineffective and in fact did not seriously try to avert the collapse in real wages that accompanied the explosive inflationary dynamics (table 10.1). Under these conditions, and with the increased demand for labor generated by growing black markets, incentives to work in the "formal" sector (including the government) were reduced.

---

10. The most important increase in interest rates took place in early 1986. Most lending rates were then established in the 20%–30% range. The highest rate (for loans to commercial firms) was then placed at 45% a year (Medal 1988, table 32).

The result of this process was a general fall in labor productivity, high labor rotation, and growing payments in kind.[11]

10.4.3   The Outburst of Inflationary Pressures

The stabilization package adopted in early 1985 clearly induced a "regime" change: from an "atypical" excess liquidity/low domestic inflation/rapidly rising black-official exchange rate differentials, to a more "classical" flight against the currency and explosive inflationary effects of monetary expansion. The former regime was undoubtedly one of "repressed inflation" (cum foreign exchange speculation). The "fundamentals" were thus bound to prevail at some point. However, in the *transition* from one regime to the other, the *explicit* pricing decisions adopted by the government in the first months of 1985 played the crucial role. In fact, as figure 10.3 shows, the first dramatic acceleration of inflation in the postrevolutionary period came as the direct effect of these policy decisions.

After this turning point, the price-monetary dynamics became explosive. The average monthly inflation rate constantly accelerated until it reached hyperinflation in 1989 (table 10.1). Under these conditions, price controls became totally ineffective and only led to widening differentials between the legal and the free markets for goods subject to regulation.[12] The monetary fuel was provided by the budget deficit, but also by the losses of the Central Bank in foreign exchange transactions and the need to finance most of the nominal expansion in domestic credit through money creation. The latter was made necessary by the decision to fix nominal interest rates at artificially low levels. Moreover, as the official exchange rate was only devaluated once more during the period under analysis (in February 1986, when the official rate was devalued to 70 cordobas per dollar), the costs of dollar-denominated domestic debts (foreign trade financing) were also kept at very modest levels.

Accelerating inflation was accompanied by a great variability in monthly rates. Moreover, as figure 10.3 indicates, rather than the stepwise acceleration typical of "inertial" inflationary processes, it adopted a neat cyclical pattern. The length of the cycle was annual from 1985 to 1987. Hyperinflation was basically associated with the dramatic shortening in the length of the cycle to some four to five months in 1989. What is more interesting, *some* turning points, *but not the intensity of the cycles,* were associated with explicit deci-

11. In 1986 labor rotation in the central government was 50%. As a result, 44% of government employees in 1987 had one year or less in service (Secreteria de Planificacion y Presupuesto 1989). For payments in kind in the government, see n. 18 below. In mid-1989, some private entrepreneurs informed the SIDA Mission that the costs of different payments in kind were three times the costs of the nominal wage bill.

12. In May 1989, just before the major liberalization of domestic prices (see sec. 10.5), the ratio of black market to official market prices was the following for some important consumer goods: rice 5.5, kidney beans 5.2, soap 12.7, detergent 16.6, and toilet paper 2.4 (Secreteria de Planificacion y Presupuesto 1988b).

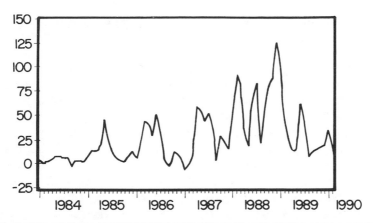

Fig. 10.3   Monthly inflation rate, 1984–90

sions to correct basic pricing imbalances: February 1985, the same month in 1986 and, as we will see below, February and June 1988.

As traditional monetary theory predicts, accelerating inflation was accompanied by falling demand for domestic liquid assets. For reasons that have already been mentioned, the demand for term deposits declined ahead of that for money. The latter remained, in fact, surprisingly high even at fairly advanced stages of the hyperinflationary process (table 10.2). The strong underdevelopment of the domestic financial market goes a long way to explain this result. Finally, despite the gross and increasing overvaluation of the official exchange rate (fig. 10.2, part A) and the dramatic widening in black/official rate differentials (table 10.3 and fig. 10.2, part B), falling liquidity was accompanied by an appreciation of the real black market rate (fig. 10.2, part C). Some policy measures may have supported the process, particularly the creation of a "grey" (parallel) foreign exchange market in 1985,[13] where foreign remittances and a fraction of export earnings could be legally sold. Massive U.S. aid to the Contras may have also supported this paradoxical outcome.

The parallel market was actually part of a more general multiple exchange rate regime. Since 1982, this regime became increasingly complex, reflecting the decision to defend exporters against the growing overvaluation of the cordoba. It included two basic mechanisms: exporters were authorized to keep part of the foreign exchange earned, and domestic support prices for export crops were fixed at levels higher than those compatible with prevailing international prices and the official exchange rate. The basic difference between the two systems was the mechanism by which the implicit "export incentive"

13. As part of the package of February 1985, foreign exchange houses were allowed to operate, under the regulation (and, in fact, ownership) of the Central Bank. The first and most important of the two existing houses, NECSA, started to operate in June of that year. BICSA started to so in August 1988.

was financed. In the first case, it was paid by importers of goods and services who bought the foreign exchange in the parallel market. In the second, it was financed by the Central Bank.

As table 10.4 indicates, both mechanisms were quite effective in raising the average exchange rate for exports significantly above the official rate (to almost 100 times greater by January 1988). The latter was increasingly relevant only for a few exports (mainly from state enterprises) and most imports. Under these conditions, the government had to rely on direct import controls to ration import demand. As most imports were sold by parastatals, the massive subsidy implicit in the grossly overvalued official rate was, to a large extent, passed on to the final user, subject, in any case, to significant resource misallocation, rationing, and growing secondary black markets. Late in the process (June 1987), the government adopted a surcharge for most imports (the *tasa de estabilización monetaria,* or TEM) to finance the foreign exchange losses of the Central Bank. By January 1988, this mechanism had raised the average import rate significantly above the official rate; still, the average export rate was almost 13 times higher than that applicable to imports.

Given the features of the multiple rate system, the collapse of exports that took place through most of this period (table 10.3) was only partly associated to exchange rate policies. A myriad of factors, affecting both the domestic supply and the external demand, account for the collapse of exports: the effects of war in some areas of the country; lack of confidence by the private sector; stronger incentives (price and, particularly, credit) given to food crops; inefficiencies of state enterprises; the exodus of skilled labor and other labor-supply shortages; and the collapse of the CACM, which was decisive for nontraditional exports. These same factors were responsible for the decline in economic activity since 1984 (table 10.1), as production for the domestic market continued to grow at moderate rates up to 1987 (1.2% a year in the period 1984–87).

Although imports fell with respect to the early postrevolutionary peak, they remained at historically high levels. In any case, the country was able to finance its record external deficits, despite skyrocketing debt ratios and the interruption of capital flows (table 10.3). Three sources were basically used to finance the deficits: mounting payments arrears, bilateral assistance from socialist countries, and prefinancing of export crops.

10.5 1988 Stabilization and Hyperinflation[14]

By early 1988, economic conditions were critical. The most transparent to all economic observers were the massive distortions associated with the mul-

14. For a more extensive analysis of the 1988 and 1989 stabilization packages, see Arana (1990), Ocampo and Taylor (1990), and Taylor et al. (1989).

Table 10.4   Differential Exchange Rates, 1980 through January 1988

	1980	1981	1982	1983	1984	1985	1986	1987	January 1988
Official market	10.00	10.00	10.00	10.00	10.00	28.00	70.00	70	70
Black market	17.33	28.47	55.40	122.90	275.80	716.70	2,183.30	12,400	40,000
Exports:									
Coffee	7.18	8.40	9.79	16.82	25.25	110.15	179.89	1,611	18,400
Cotton	11.79	11.19	12.28	12.50	12.50	144.30	733.32	2,118	10,509
Sesame seeds	5.59	6.96	8.35	7.73	13.58	64.09	177.70	2,209	7,158
Bananas	10.00	10.00	10.00	10.00	10.00	28.00	70.00	2,021	5,053
Meat	10.00	10.00	12.00	12.00	12.00	28.00	70.00	70	70
Shellfish	10.00	10.00	10.00	10.00	10.00	28.00	70.00	70	70
Other agricultural	10.00	10.00	12.40	12.40	12.40	28.00	70.00	3,415	10,035
Manufacturing	10.00	10.00	13.20	13.20	13.30	28.00	70.00	2,021	5,053
Average export rate[a]	8.89	9.64	10.64	13.15	16.03	106.12	267.63	1,978	6,840
Imports:									
Oil and derivatives								70	70
Subject to TEM[b]								306	269
Financed in the parallel market								7,856	21,000
Average import rate[a]	10.00	10.00	10.00	10.00	10.00	28.00	70.00	191	536
Average exchange rate	9.70	9.90	10.18	10.89	11.45	42.72	101.78	516	1,920
Ratios:									
Average export/import rate	0.89	0.96	1.06	1.32	1.60	3.79	3.82	10.36	12.76
Average export/official rate	0.89	0.96	1.06	1.32	1.60	3.79	3.82	28.26	97.71
Average import/official rate	1.00	1.00	1.00	1.00	1.00	1.00	1.00	2.73	7.66

Source: Central Bank.
[a]Goods and services.
[b]Monetary stabilization rate.

tiple exchange rate system (table 10.4). However, this was only a manifestation of generalized macroeconomic disequilibria. Monetary and fiscal imbalances were already reflected in extremely high inflation rates—an average monthly rate of 24.9% in 1987 (see table 10.1)—which had led to the virtual collapse of price controls. External deficits had also resulted in near generalized moratoria on the foreign debt. Finally, the country had already experienced a substantial fall in GDP per capita and an even stronger contraction of real wages and private consumption per head. This dramatic deterioration in economic conditions were combined by clear signs that the Contras were in disarray, that the war was losing intensity, and that peace talks among Central American presidents were being successful, as reflected in the Esquipulas I Accord of August 1987.

These conditions were the background to the two massive stabilization packages implemented in February and June 1988. The goals of these programs were multiple and ambitious (Secretaria de Planificacion y Presupuesto 1988a). They included (1) the realignment of relative prices; (2) a reduction of inflation rates by austere fiscal and monetary policies; it was stated early in the year that the central government deficit would be reduced to 10% of GDP in 1988 and eliminated altogether by 1990; (3) reversing the deterioration of the formal sector of the economy generated by price controls and falling real wages; and (4) reconstituting the normal economic functions of the wage payments system. Wage policy aside—which was explicitly conceived as a *supply-side* policy—the objectives and instruments of the stabilization plan were fairly orthodox, as the IMF (1988) acknowledged later in the year.

Although these stabilization packages were more ambitious than any previous effort, they tended to reproduce patterns that had been common to macroeconomic policy since 1984. Particularly, the different goals were not pursued with the same vigor, nor were the packages globally consistent. Emphasis was placed on relative price realignment. This fact was reflected in the outcomes of the programs, as we will see below. On the contrary, fiscal and monetary policies were not made consistent with the inflation targets. Also, as in 1985, the attempt to defend or even increase real wages was soon abandoned, giving way to a different policy later in the year.

The February package included five major provisions. The first was a monetary reform, by which 1,000 old monetary units were converted into one new cordoba. This reform included the demonetization of some 20% of existing liquid assets, which had, attached to it, explicit political goals.[15] The monetary reform was accompanied by the consolidation of all explicit and implicit exchange rates into two legal rates: 10 new cordobas in the "official" and

15. The short period necessary to make the conversion in the banks (three days) was planned to leave the Contra with a sizable stock of useless bills. It was also determined that households converting more than 10 million old cordobas had to leave their money in deposit at the banks for 12–14 months. This was aimed at speculators and black market arbitrageurs holding sizable amounts of cash.

10.25 in the "parallel" market. In relation to January levels (table 10.4), this implied that the official and average import rates were multiplied by 143 and 19, respectively, and the average export rate was devalued by 46%. However, the new legal rates were set significantly below the black market rate. Third, the government decreed significant increases in controlled prices. This was accompanied by a 675% increase in the average SNOTS wage level. Finally, it announced a 10% cut in central government expenditure.

The major successes of this package were associated with exchange rate policies: the official rate was massively devalued in real terms, as the black market rate appreciated and exchange rate differentials narrowed (fig. 10.2, parts A and C). Nonetheless, the official rate remained clearly overvalued, and no mechanism was adopted to avert its further real appreciation (only two minor devaluations of one new cordoba per dollar each were adopted in April and May).

The major weaknesses of the February package were related, however, to fiscal and, particularly, monetary policies. The initial cut in central government expenditure was clearly insufficient to reach the target deficit, as the Olivera-Tanzi effect was eroding the tax base at a fairly rapid rate (see n. 9 above). On the other hand, the maximum domestic lending rate was kept at 45% *a year,* and the government decided that the devaluation of the official rate would not be passed on to dollar-denominated liabilities. Under prevailing conditions, these decisions were equivalent to a generalized debt forgiveness. They also implied that the Central Bank would continue to incur in massive losses in foreign exchange transactions and that any *nominal* increase of domestic credit would have to be financed by money creation.

The mix of massive exchange rate, price and wage adjustments, and weak demand policies initiated a new inflationary cycle, more intense than those experienced in previous years (fig. 10.3). Under these conditions, price controls were totally ineffective and real wages soon fell below 1987 levels (see table 10.1 and table 10.6 below). The government then abandoned any attempt to arrest the fall in real wages.

The June package liberalized most prices and wages, decreed massive increases in those prices that remained under the government's control (particularly gasoline), and deepened the exchange rate reforms but did little to make the global stabilization policy more consistent. The official exchange rate was then devalued by 700%, and the parallel/black market differential considerably narrowed. In the following months, the parallel and, since late August, the official rate were devalued more frequently (the latter five times between 31 August 1988 and 4 January 1989). As a result, the overvaluation of the official rate was considerably reduced. Although the black/official exchange rate differential remained substantial, it narrowed considerably with respect to previous years.

Nonetheless, fiscal policy was not significantly affected by the June decisions. There was also no attempt to control the growth of credit. However, two important reforms in monetary policy took place in June. First, the government did not assume the exchange rate risks on dollar-denominated domestic debts. Given devaluation policy, this decision considerably raised the costs of such debts, if contracted after February.[16] Second, authorities decided to index domestic interest rates. However, the "indexing rule" used was imperfect, particularly in the first few months.[17] Thus, from mid-June to mid-September, the maximum effective lending interest rate was set at 14.9% a month. Beginning in mid-September, the rule was improved. Still, in the last months of the year, interest rates ran significantly below inflation levels (see table 10.5).

In June, government wages were adjusted by 30%. Given massive price increases accumulated since February (790%), this was an extremely moderate rise. They were adjusted more frequently after September (monthly, except in December) but at a level systematically below inflation rates. To compensate for this fact, government employees were granted a food subsidy (AFA) in August.[18]

The series of maxidevaluations and massive adjustments in regulated prices, together with the inability of the authorities to control the major sources of monetary growth were the fundamental sources of the 1988 hyperinflation. As figure 10.3 indicates, the economy underwent three distinct price cycles between January 1988 and the first moths of 1989. The first two of them were clearly unleashed by the adjustment programs of February and June. The third was more closely associated with the effects of Hurricane Joan, which hit the country in October, generating losses estimated by ECLAC at $840 million (CEPAL 1988b). The third cycle was the most intense. In total, the inflation rate ran close to 100% a month between September 1988 and January 1989.

Overall, the monthly inflation rate was 64.5% between December 1987 and January 1989. It was led by public-regulated prices (public utilities and transportation), which increased by more than 80% a month during this period. Following a classical pattern, this process was accompanied by rapid demonetization. By January 1989, M1 as a share of GDP had fallen to 6.5% (table 10.5). On the other hand, reductions in aggregate demand, relative price changes induced by the adjustment programs (real devaluation and wage cuts, in particular), and supply shocks (the hurricane and electric supply failures during the first semester) led to a 10.9% fall in GDP. This was accompanied by a renewed deterioration of exports and the balance of payments.

16. For a debt contracted just after the February devaluation and paid in mid-January 1989, the monthly interest rate was 61.9%, somewhat below inflation (63.7% a month in the same period). However, the closer the debt was contracted before the June devaluation, the higher the implicit interest rate. Thus, a liability contracted just before that devaluation and paid in January 1989 had a monthly cost of 107.7%, or 19.3% in real terms.
17. An annual interest rate was determined by *adding up* the monthly inflation rates.
18. The subsidy took the form of the right to buy a basket of basic food products (10 lbs. of rice, 10 lbs. of beans, and 5 lbs. of sugar) paying between 5% and 10% of their nominal wages.

Table 10.5 1989 Adjustment Program

	1988		1989					
	Average	Last Quarter	January	February	March	April	May	June
Fiscal/monetary connection (% of GDP):								
Central government deficit[a]	24.9	21.6	2.7	6.4	4.1	1.9	-.8	-6.9
Monetary emission—Deficit	6.6	3.5	2.9	.4	5.7	6.4	9.4	13.8
Total monetary emission	31.5	25.1	5.6	6.8	9.7	8.2	8.7	6.8
Monetary aggregates (% of GDP):								
Means of payments	16.6	11.6	6.5	5.7	7.4	8.5	8.8	6.9
Quasi money	1.2	.5	.4	.6	.9	1.0	1.2	.8
Real exchange rate (1980 = 100):								
Official	69.4	77.5	68.4	70.4	93.3	105.6	102.6	135.4
Black	202.1	213.2	109.7	67.4	58.9	68.5	73.0	124.2
Differentials:								
Black/official rate	361.3	375.5	177.5	59.6	9.1	10.6	22.9	58.5
Parallel/official rate	243.5	257.8	128.8	41.3	2.9	3.1	9.0	32.6
Monthly inflation (CPI)	65.7	97.7	91.8	45.8	20.1	12.6	15.5	62.2
Nominal monthly interest rates:								
Lending: agriculture		38.3	50.5	56.0	52.4	22.0	14.0	14.0
Lending: industry		35.8	50.8	58.0	54.0	26.0	15.0	18.0
Lending: commerce		44.4	80.4	86.3	68.9	28.0	19.0	20.0
Term deposits (3ms)		42.4	63.1	55.1	51.6	23.6	16.0	28.9

(continued)

Table 10.5 (continued)

	1989						1990	
	July	August	September	October	November	December	January	February
Fiscal/monetary connection (% of GDP):								
Central government deficit[a]	1.4	-4.0	-2.6	1.6	.6	.8	-3.1	3.4
Monetary emission—Deficit	8.3	8.0	8.6	4.9	11.1	14.8	13.2	10.1
Total monetary emission	9.7	4.0	6.0	6.5	11.7	15.6	10.0	13.5
Monetary aggregates (% of GDP):								
Means of payments	6.9	7.7	7.9	7.8	7.9	8.4	8.3	8.5
Quasi money	.8	1.1	1.4	1.5	1.3	1.5	1.5	1.4
Real exchange rate (1980 = 100):								
Official	126.2	118.2	111.7	103.5	103.5	104.1	104.7	94.0
Black	87.7	83.4	73.3	65.3	82.7	80.3	90.4	86.3
Differentials:								
Black/official rate	20.2	22.0	13.5	9.1	38.1	33.5	33.2	49.5
Parallel/official rate	25.0	22.0	13.5	7.7	29.2	24.4	19.2	22.2
Monthly inflation (CPI)	32.3	7.7	11.9	14.4	16.2	19.2	34.2	11.4
Nominal monthly interest rates:								
Lending: agriculture	14.9	15.0	14.1	10.0	10.0	13.0	15.0	13.0
Lending: industry	18.0	18.0	14.4	10.0	10.0	13.0	15.0	13.0
Lending: commerce	20.0	20.0	17.3	13.0	13.0	17.0	19.0	15.0
Term deposits (3ms)	33.8	27.2	24.0	19.6	23.4	26.0	21.1	16.0

Sources: SPP, Central Bank, and INEC.

[a]Negative sign indicates fiscal surplus. Excludes foreign transfers in 1988.

10.6   The 1989 Adjustment Program

If massive relative price distortions associated with the multiple exchange rates and price controls were the dominant economic feature of Nicaragua in January 1988, hyperinflation had taken over that place one year later. The urgent need for action was reflected in the rapid pace of demonetization and the generalized lack of confidence in government policies. Moreover, the authorities had few instruments to handle the explosive price dynamics. Price controls had collapsed in mid-1988 after several years during which they became increasingly ineffective. The official exchange rate was still overvalued and too distant from the parallel and black market rates to be used as an anti-inflationary weapon. Finally, scarce foreign exchange placed severe restrictions on any attempt to fix the exchange rate or liberalize imports.

Under these conditions, the government correctly understood that a very orthodox policy was called for, combining fiscal and monetary austerity with additional relative price adjustments. The package adopted by the authorities in January included six major provisions. First of all, central government expenditure was massively cut to reach an expected deficit of 5.6% of GDP (Ministerio de Finanzas 1989). In practice, expenditure was cut even further by transferring to the ministries in the first months of the year less resources than were demanded according to budget allocations.[19] An essential element of fiscal austerity was a significant cut in public-sector employment (*compactación*).

Second, the government adopted a restrictive credit policy, accompanied by active interest rate management. The authorities aimed at keeping positive real returns on term deposits and real costs for all (or most) types of credit. Third, a system of gradual devaluation was adopted in late January. In practice, this led to small or medium-size devaluations some three times a month. This was accompanied by important readjustment of real regulated prices in the first months of the year. On the other hand, as in 1988, the authorities stated the objective of arresting further deterioration of real wages in the public sector.

In the speech in which President Ortega made public the new program, he also announced willingness to establish new rules of the game for the private sector; as a first step in that direction, he informed that expropriations would cease.[20] Finally, the government adopted a financial programming system coordinated by the Planning Secretariat (SPP) and significantly improved the data base for short-term macroeconomic analysis.

In terms of some of its major targets, the stabilization program was initially

---

19. Transfers were cut by 33% in January, 25% in February, 20% in March, and 18% in April. See Secretaria de Planificacion y Presupuesto, *Síntesis evaluativa de las principales variables económicas de abril 1989 y programación de mayo 1989,* May 1989, p. 6 (similar documents will be quoted hereafter as *Síntesis evaluativa*).

20. See "Esfuerzo nacional por la Paz y la Reconstrucción," *Barricada* (31 January 1989, pp. 3–4).

very successful. Inflation rates fell rapidly (fig. 10.3). Actually, by March, the CPI increased by 8%, excluding public utilities and transportation. This implies, in turn, that the government was effective in increasing real regulated prices. On the other hand, the government was quite successful in devaluing the official exchange rate in real terms and in stabilizing the parallel and black markets. By March, differentials between the different foreign exchange markets had been reduced to less than 10%.

In the face of falling inflation rates, demonetization ceased in February (table 10.5). The demand for term deposits also increased since that month, but remained fairly low by historical standards. The government cut and maintained central government expenditure at low levels. Indeed, as table 10.2 indicates, such expenditure stabilized around 20%–23% of GDP, less than half the average 1988 level. Starting in June, the government actually ran fiscal surpluses in a few months. Finally, the fall in real wages was also arrested (table 10.6).

The major initial cost of stabilization was a strong recession. In the first quarter of the year, industrial production fell by 17% with respect to the same period in the previous year. However, it started to recover in the second quarter (table 10.6). Cattle production for the domestic market was also severely hurt. On the contrary, with a few exceptions (cotton), exportables experienced a boom. Other inward-oriented sectors (e.g., agricultural foodstuffs and electrical energy) were either stagnant or experienced some recovery.[21]

Employment effects were significant. By June, central government employment had fallen by 14.3% with respect to the same month in 1988—11,000 employees, approximately (Secretaria de Planificacion y Presupuesta 1989). Interestingly enough, there were also a significant number of unfilled vacancies in the central government, as the way budget allocations were transferred to the different ministries actually encouraged this phenomenon.[22] In the same month, 16,500 civil employees, including those in public-sector enterprises, had been affected by *compactación*. This figure had increased to 17,000 by October.[23] This was equivalent to 2% of the labor force of the country. Managua household surveys reflected this massive reduction of public-sector employment. However, they indicated that it did not lead to increased open unemployment (which remain surprisingly low, at 5%–6% of the labor force) but to growing informality (rising proportion of self-employment and workers in very small enterprises) and longer unemployment spells.[24]

The major problems faced by the stabilization program in the first months of the year were both related to monetary policy. Aside from the central government, other domestic agents were subject to a credit crunch (table 10.6).

21. *Síntesis evaluativa* (June 1989, and succeeding months).
22. The wage costs of vacant positions were transferred by the Ministry of Finance. The different ministries used them to selectively increase wages of existing employees.
23. *Síntesis evaluativa* (August 1989, p. 21; December 1989, p. 23).
24. *Síntesis evaluativa* (September 1989, App. 2).

Table 10.6   Additional Quarterly Indicators, 1988–89

	1988				1989				1990
	I	II	III	IV	I	II	III	IV	I
Domestic credit (millions of 1980 cordobas)[a]									
Short term	879.1	1,040.0	1,128.5	697.9	110.6	219.2	204.3	227.4	187.1
Long term	87.0	125.4	141.0	144.1	28.6	29.2	21.7	26.3	35.3
Trading companies	302.0	44.4	63.1	163.6	322.4	257.0	134.5	185.2	381.7
Total	1,268.1	1,209.8	1,332.6	1,005.6	461.6	505.4	360.6	438.9	604.1
Transactions in the foreign exchange houses (thousand dollars, monthly average):									
Purchases	1,344.5	604.5	1,782.1	1,452.4	4,824.1	5,955.2	11,989.8	13,221.0	12,654.7
Sales	1,171.0	715.5	1,689.4	1,627.1	4,459.0	5,062.0	9,093.6	17,176.7	12,787.2
Real wage (1985 = 100):									
With GDP deflator	94.8	55.4	26.5	25.4	30.2	36.5	33.2	38.5	41.9[b]
With CPI	28.0	16.0	7.8	7.9	10.0	12.7	12.1	14.8	16.7[b]
Manufacturing production (billions of May 1989 cordobas)	134.9	123.7	127.8	124.6	103.7	119.7	113.3	111.1	125.6

Sources: Central Bank, Ministry of Labor, and MEIC.
[a]Using GDP deflator as the price index.
[b]January and February.

The most important exception was found in the government trading companies, which, at the same time, continued to receive massively subsidized credit. The profits made by these companies by the joint effect of credit subsidies and real devaluation were transferred to the producers of export crops (particularly coffee and cotton) by periodic resettlement of accounts (*reliquidaciones*), fueling the money supply.

Interest rate policy became also a major source of complications. Nominal rates were raised effective 15 February. In the face of rapidly falling inflation, ex post real rates were extremely high from February to April (table 10.5). Pure backward indexation rules and significant lags in decisions—rates were adjusted only once a month—and information contributed to the same phenomenon. Some of these problems were eventually solved: "forward" indexation criteria were introduced in April and weekly readjustments in June. However, the political opposition to high interest rates led the government, in a meeting with agricultural producers on 17 and 18 April, to agree to stabilize lending rates, to establish ceilings on lending rates and new subsidized long-term rates, and to grant a mix of debt forgiveness and debt restructuring at low interest rates for foodstuffs and cotton producers. Starting in May, these agreements led the government to fix some and, in June, *all* lending rates *below* deposit rates (table 10.5).

More generally, the authorities were unable to control sources of monetary growth different to the central government (see "Monetary Emission—Deficit" in table 10.5). From March to May, this led to a sizable expansion of liquidity. Monetary expansion was reflected in moderately rising inflation rates in May and, particularly, in a speculatory wave in the foreign exchange market. The latter process was interpreted in some parts of the government as a sign that the official rate was still overvalued and that a maxidevaluation was called for. These sectors were apparently successful in restricting the official supply of dollars to the parallel market. Expectations of devaluation then became generalized and were reflected in massive speculation in the parallel and black markets. The authorities then decided to "follow the market" and devalued the official rate by 111% on June 12.

This devaluation was soon reflected in massive inflation, which rapidly eroded most of its real effects (see table 10.5). It also initiated a new "stop-go" cycle, not unlike that experienced during the first semester. Inflation came down fairly rapidly, reaching 8% in August. This was initially accompanied by a dramatic fall in liquidity. However, as the government was unable to control all sources of monetary expansion, liquidity and inflation started to pick up. Once more, this was reflected in speculation in the foreign exchange market in November. This time, the government maintained the system of gradual devaluation of the official rate, thus averting major foreign exchange speculation and a new inflationary shock. However, it also kept liquidity at high levels. Aside from this basic change in policy reactions, there were also two important changes with respect to the inflation cycle early in the year.

First, the negative interest rate margins widened (table 10.5). Second, the size of the parallel market doubled (table 10.6). This was equivalent, in fact, to an unplanned import liberalization.

Overall, the 1989 stabilization program was less contractionary and more effective in terms of the inflation and exchange rate targets than its 1988 predecessor. However, its inconsistency and fragility were apparent to many economic observers (see, e.g., Fishlow et al. 1990). First of all, it was clear that the cut in central government expenditure could not be indefinitely maintained. On the other hand, as we have seen, monetary and interest rate policies remained a source of considerable difficulties. The sensibility of the foreign exchange market continued to be a major source of instability. This reflected, in turn, the inability of the government to raise an adequate supply of liquid foreign aid. Indexation increased in 1989 to levels, which are incompatible with permanent reductions in the inflation rate. Finally, although the room for private initiative considerably widened, no major advance was made in terms of designing stable rules of the game for the private sector.

The February 1990 elections changed the course of macroeconomic events. Attempts to maintain previous stabilization efforts ceased altogether. By April, strong increases in government wages were reflected again in high fiscal deficits, rapid growth in the money supply and an imminent new wave of hyperinflation. Moreover, the official and parallel exchange rates were grossly overvalued and regulated domestic prices were considerably repressed. Massive macroeconomic disequilibria induced by these policy decisions forced the Chamorro administration, inaugurated on 25 April 1990, to undertake, once more, massive adjustment efforts. This time, however, they faced a strong labor union resistance. This, as well as other events at the outset of the new administration clearly indicate that the February elections had done so far little to overcome the political paralysis that affects the relations between the Sandinistas and the powerful private interests of Nicaragua.

References

Arana, M. 1990. Nicaragua: Estabilización, ajuste y estrategia económica. In *Politicas de ajuste en Nicaragua: Reflexiones sobre sus implicaciones estratégicas*, ed. M. Arana, R. Stahler-Sholk, and C. Vilas. Managua: CRIES.

Arana, M., R. Stahler-Sholk, G. Timossi, and C. López. 1987. *Deuda, estabilización y ajuste: La transformación de Nicaragua, 1979–1986*. Managua: CRIES.

Baumeister, E., and Oscar Neira. 1986. The making of a mixed economy: Class struggle and state policy in the Nicaraguan transition. In *Transition and development: Problems of third world socialism*, ed. R. R. Fagen, C. D. Deere, and J. L. Coraggio, pp. 171–91. New York: Monthly Review Press.

Brundenius, C. 1987. Industrial development strategies in revolutionary Nicaragua. In *The political economy of revolutionary Nicaragua*, ed. R. J. Spalding, chap. 4. Boston: George Allen & Unwin.

Bulmer-Thomas, V. 1987. *The political economy of Central America since 1920.* Cambridge: Cambridge University Press.

CEPAL. 1976. *América Latina: Relación de precios de intercambio.* Santiago: CEPAL.

———. 1981. *Nicaragua: El impacto de la mutación politica.* Santiago: CEPAL.

———. 1987. *América Latina: Indices de comercio exterior.* Santiago: CEPAL.

———. 1988a. *Anuario estadistico de América Latina y el Caribe.* Santiago: CEPAL.

———. 1988b. Damage caused by Hurricane Joan in Nicaragua. Santiago, December. Mimeograph.

Colborn, Forrest D. 1990. *Managing the commanding heights: Nicaraguas' state enterprises.* Berkeley: University of California Press.

Dornbusch, R., and S. Edwards. 1990. The macroeconomics of populism in Latin America. *Journal of Development Economics* 32, no. 2 (April): 247–77.

Enriquez, L. J., and R. J. Spalding. 1987. Banking systems and revolutionary change: The politics of agricultural credit in Nicaragua. In *The political economy of revolutionary Nicaragua,* ed. R. J. Spalding, chap. 5. Boston: George Allen & Unwin.

Fishlow, A., E. Bacha, G. Helleiner, and L. Velasco. 1990. Final report of the monitoring group. April. Mimeograph.

Fitzgerald, E. V. P. 1987. An evaluation of the economic costs to Nicaragua of U.S. Aggression: 1980–1984. In *The political economy of revolutionary Nicaragua,* ed. R. J. Spalding, chap. 9. Boston: George Allen & Unwin.

———. 1989. Problems in financing a revolution: Accumulation, defense and income distribution in Nicaragua, 1979–86. In *Financing economic development: A structural approach to monetary policy,* ed. E. V. P. Fitzgerald and R. Vos. Aldershot: Gower.

Gibson, B. 1987a. Structural overview of the Nicaraguan economy. In *The political economy of revolutionary Nicaragua,* ed. R. J. Spalding. Boston: George Allen & Unwin.

———. 1987b. Nicaragua. In *Stabilization and adjustment policies and programmes.* Country Study no. 3. Helsinki: WIDER.

IMF. 1988. *Nicaragua: Recent economic developments.* Washington, D.C., August.

Medal, J. L. 1988. *Nicaragua: Crisis, cambio social y politica económica.* Managua: CINASE.

Ministerio de Finanzas. 1989. *Proyecto del presupuesto general de la Republica.* Managua, January.

Neira, Oscar. 1988. La reforma agraria nicaraguense: Balance de ocho años. In *Nicaragua: Cambios, estructurales y politicas económicas, 1979–1987,* chap. 4. Managua: INIES.

Ocampo, J. A., and L. Taylor. 1990. La hiperinflación nicaraguense. In *Inflación rebelde en America Latina,* ed. José Pablo Arellano, pp. 71–108. Santiago: CIEPLAN-HACHETTE.

Pizarro, R. 1987. The new economic policy: A necessary readjustment. In *The political economy of revolutionary Nicaragua,* ed. R. J. Spalding, chap. 10. Boston: George Allen & Unwin.

República de Nicaragua. 1990. *Documento presentado ante la conferencia de donantes en Roma.* Managua, June.

Ruccio, D. 1987. The state and planning in Nicaragua. In *The political economy of revolutionary Nicaragua,* ed. R. J. Spalding, chap. 3. Boston: George Allen & Unwin.

Secretaria de Planificacion y Presupuesto. 1988a. Tesis centrales del plan de ajuste económico. Managua, February. Mimeograph.

———. 1988b. Analisis de los efectos de las medidas económicas. Managua, July. Mimeograph.

————. 1989. Situación de los salarios en el gobierno central. Managua, July. Mimeograph.

Stahler-Sholk, R. 1987. Foreign debt and economic stabilization policies in revolutionary Nicaragua. In *The political economy of revolutionary Nicaragua*, ed. R. J. Spalding, chap. 7. Boston: George Allen & Unwin.

Stahler-Sholk, R., C. López, G. Vunderink, and M. V. Frenkel. 1989. *La politica económica en Nicaragua, 1979–88*. Managua: CRIES.

Taylor, L., R. Aguilar, S. de Vylder, and J. A. Ocampo. 1989. *Nicaragua: The transition from economic chaos toward sustainable growth*. Stockholm: SIDA.

Vilas, C. M. 1987. *Perfiles de la revolución sandinista*. Managua: Editorial Nueva Nicaragua.

Wheelock, J. 1989. Diez años de transformación agraria sandinista. *Revolución y Desarrollo*, no. 5: 5–10.

World Bank. 1981. *Nicaragua: The challenge of reconstruction*. Washington, D.C.: World Bank, October.

————. 1986. *Nicaragua: Recent economic developments and prospects*. Washington, D.C.: World Bank, October.

Comment   Ann Helwege

Jose Antonio Ocampo's essay is rich in detail about economic policies pursued by the Sandinista regime. It also makes available data that has been virtually inaccessible to those outside the Nicaraguan government.

The paper presents the economy as one in a chronic state of disequilibrium. Ocampo describes a series of short-run policies aimed shoring up the economy, all of which ultimately failed. The paper is thorough and meticulous in its description of these policies. My main recommendation would be to highlight fundamental reasons for the instability and the failure of stabilization efforts, and to set these apart from less significant specific policies.

What Went Wrong?

At the risk of being a bit repetitive, let me emphasize arguments that Eliana Cardoso and I made earlier (see chap. 3, in this volume). The Sandinistas do not represent a classic case of populism. Urban wage earners lost throughout the regime's tenure. Real wages fell every year after 1981 and even 1979–81 wages were below prerevolution wages. Unlike classic populists who served employed workers, the Sandinista's redistributive efforts were directed toward the poor in the form of literacy campaigns, health programs, and agrarian reform. Although the regime meets Dornbusch and Edwards' criteria for "economic populism," namely, it ran large deficits leading to hyperinflation,

Ann Helwege is assistant professor at the Urban and Environmental Policy Department, Tufts University.

_it does not share populist characteristics common to Perón, Vargas, and Ve-
lasco._

There are several underlying reasons for the economic crisis that developed
under the Sandinistas.

From the start, socialist rhetoric and threats to expropriate property created
uncertainty for private producers, who were expected to generate the bulk of
output. This uncertainty made early consolidation of the economy difficult.

Second, overvaluation meant that investment was not only risky, but un-
profitable.

Third, world prices of cotton and coffee slumped. Uncertainty about property rights, overvaluation, the U.S. embargo, and low world prices made export production unattractive. Neither cotton nor coffee production ever recovered its prerevolution level.

Fourth, the large government deficit played a significant role in generating
hyperinflation once Contra activity began. Before then, massive foreign aid
financed social spending and kept inflationary pressure under control. With
the onset of the war, the deficit soared to 30% of GDP in 1983 and stayed in
the 15%–25% range thereafter. Foreign donors lost interest, and the printing
press took over as a major means of finance.

The war made a bad situation unmanageable. It forced the government to
devote half its budget to the military; it exacerbated labor shortages and destroyed infrastructure; and it diverted foreign exchange toward weapons, forcing industry and agriculture to struggle along without imported parts and fertilizers. It also made a mockery of Sandinista intentions to redistribute
income. Not only were social programs ultimately cut, but generous subsidies
were given to large agricultural producers in the hope of maintaining exports
to finance the war. By 1986, private consumption had fallen to only one-third
of its prerevolution level.

Parenthetically, I would add that it is a mistake to emphasize the role of bad
weather in the development of the economic crisis. Agricultural output was
depressed throughout the 1980s. FAO data show that even the best harvest,
that of 1982, fell 20% below that of 1978. Although the agrarian nature of the
Nicaraguan economy makes it unusually vulnerable to climatic shocks, the
factors described above are more important in explaining a decade of agricultural stagnation.

A massive stabilization effort was implemented in 1988. On a technical
level, its failure can be attributed to the fact that the devaluations did not keep
up with inflation, impressive as they were in nominal terms. Moreover, the
fiscal deficit remained excessive for reasons pointed out by Ocampo, including the effect of inflation on the tax base. New attempts at stabilization in 1989
also collapsed.

At a more basic level, the failure of stabilization programs can be attributed
to the inability of the Sandinistas to reduce uncertainty and to establish clear
rules of the game. Having challenged property rights, they could not restore

the confidence of private producers. Expropriation of a major sugar mill in July 1988 did not help. Compounding the uncertainty about property rights was concern that defense expenditures would continue to create fiscal imbalances.

Whither the Future of Socialism in Latin America?

I have argued elsewhere that the Allende regime faced problems that were quite different from those faced by the Sandinistas.[1] In contrast to Nicaraguans, Chileans were more urbanized, better educated, and enjoyed a markedly higher standard of living. Allende's challenge was to maintain industrial output to satisfy a large, politically powerful middle class. The agrarian nature of the Nicaraguan economy and the simple lifestyle of its people enabled the Sandinistas to build a constituency through land reform and basic social services. Nonetheless, both Allende and the Sandinistas challenged property rights while depending on a market economy.

Oscar Lange argued in 1938:

A socialist government really intent upon socialism has to decide to carry out its socialization program at one stroke or to give it up altogether. The very coming into power of such a government must cause a financial panic and economic collapse. Therefore, the socialist government must either guarantee the immunity of private property and private enterprise in order to enable the capitalist economy to function normally, in doing which it gives up its socialist aims, or it must go through with its socialization programs with maximum speed. Any hesitation, vacillation and indecision would provoke the inevitable economic catastrophe. Socialism is not an economic policy for the timid.[2]

The problem with massive expropriation is that a fully centralized economy is hard to manage and tends to lead to stagnation in poor countries. The Cubans have succeeded because of Soviet aid; neither Nicaragua nor Chile received enough aid to follow Cuba's path.

Is socialism in Latin America due for a requiem? Yes. The Soviets are no longer interested in supporting revolutions abroad. Two failures have tarnished the model's appeal regionally. It is possible that a socialist regime will again take power, in Peru or El Salvador, for example, but it is unlikely that it can succeed in meeting popular expectations.

The demise of socialism need not mark the end of serious efforts to redis-

1. A. Helwege, "Three Socialist Experiences in Latin America: Surviving U.S. Economic Pressure" (*Bulletin of Latin American Research* 8, no. 2 [1989]: 211–34). Also, see Helwege, "Is There any Hope for Nicaragua?" (*Challenge* [November/December, 1989]: 22–28).

2. See D. Morowitz, "Economic Lessons from Some Small Developing Countries" (World Development 8 [1980]: 337–69) for Lange quote. The original statement is found in O. Lange and F. Taylor, *On the Economic Theory of Socialism* (Minneapolis: University of Minnesota Press, 1938), p. 354.

tribute income. Income distribution in Latin America remains very inequi-table relative to the rest of the world. Capitalist growth requires clear rules of the game and secure property rights, but there is no evidence that growth depends on continued inequity.

Lessons for the Region

The Nicaraguan experience with unsuccessful stabilization efforts provides useful lessons for nonsocialist regimes.

First, the rules of the game with respect to private property need to be clear whether or not the government is socialist. By freezing bank assets, the Collor administration has created a major credibility problem for investors in Brazil. It takes years to regain the trust that is lost with one such freeze. The Mexi-cans learned this in 1982. Rudiger Dornbusch likens the move to wife beating: once done, the relationship is irrevocably changed, whether or not the beating occurs again.

One can make this argument somewhat more general. Having once let an economy spin out of control, it is difficult for a regime to regain public confi-dence. For this reason, a change in regime (not necessarily a coup) may be important for stabilization to succeed.

Second, for all the ease with which economists prescribe stabilization mea-sures, they are remarkably difficult to implement. If austerity were as easy as swallowing a bitter pill, we would see more of it today. Political pressure prevents cuts in government programs, and tax compliance is hard to enforce. We need more work by political scientists to understand how one builds a consensus to support stabilization. Karen Remmer's work comparing the ef-fectiveness of democratic and authoritarian regimes in stabilizing economies offers a useful starting point.[3]

A third lesson is that devaluations do not jumpstart an economy. They are effective in reducing external imbalances by cutting imports. They do not gen-erate growth unless they are accompanied by renewed confidence in economic stability. In theory, devaluations stimulate the production of tradable goods. Together with high interest rates, they also encourage the return of flight cap-ital. To do so effectively, however, investor trust is essential. No firm will expand its productive capacity if it expects continued instability and potential expropriation of assets. Devaluations may be the Latin American equivalent of "pushing on a string."

What Does the Future Hold for Nicaragua?

U.S. intervention and the Contra war have caused enduring damage. Most Nicaraguan professionals emigrated and are now unlikely to give up the new

3. K. Remmer, "Democracy and Economic Crisis: The Latin American Experience" (*World Politics* [April 1990]: 315–35).

lives they built in the United States. The war damaged a capital base that was weak to begin with: what industry existed in the 1970s depended on the Central American Common Market, which dissolved with regional hostilities. There is now very little industrial capacity in place. Furthermore, political polarization as a result of the Contra war leaves open the possibility of continued civil war. The new government will find it very difficult to attract investors.

Nicaragua is a poor agrarian society, made poorer by events of the past decade. Having shown that the Sandinistas could not match the strength of U.S. pressure, it remains for the United States to prove, through generous aid, whether the Nicaraguans have gained anything by crying uncle.

Comment   Arnold C. Harberger

It is hard for me to comment critically, maybe not even objectively, on the work of José Antonio Ocampo. For it is not an exaggeration to say that probably close to half of what I know about the Nicaraguan economy I learned from him (either through his writings or through contact with him in professional meetings and working sessions). My experience in other countries had led me to believe that populism on the political scene had bad economics as its handmaiden. In this I do not mean to equate populism with left-of-center politics—not by a long shot. Left-of-center governments have, in fact, run some quite good economic policies in recent years (Spain under Gonzalez, France under Mitterand, New Zealand under Lange, Australia under Hawke), but they have done so by trying to be consistent, to face reality, to live within budget constraints, to reduce economic distortions. In my opinion, left-wing governments, when they have succeeded in their economic policies, have done so precisely by eschewing populism.

Nothing in the Nicaragua story, as told by Ocampo, leads me to change the opinion expressed above. In the background we have the fact that prior to the Sandinista revolution, Nicaragua shared with other Central American countries the phenomenal economic boom of 1960–77. Indeed, Nicaragua tripled its GDP between 1959 and 1977, catching up to Guatemala and El Salvador and narrowing Costa Rica's lead in terms of per capita income. The boom did not bring an equally rapid improvement in social indicators, however, and undoubtedly the seeds of a successful revolution were sown by the Somoza family itself, in the virtually unbridled avarice with which it sought an ever-expanding control over the economic as well as the political arena.

Perhaps because of the professional nature of the forum in which his paper was presented, Ocampo does not dwell on the vast numbers of sheer blunders

Arnold C. Harberger is the Gustavus F. and Ann M. Swift Distinguished Service Professor, University of Chicago, and professor of economics, University of California, Los Angeles.

(at the microeconomic level) that underlay the patchwork quilt of economic policy put together by the Sandinistas. To be sure, he mentions the extensive nationalization, the agrarian reform, the rapid expansion of the public sector, and the widespread use of price controls. But in the main he focuses on the macroeconomic side. Fiscal deficits, monetary expansion, artificially low interest rates, Central Bank losses, exchange-rate maladjustments, import controls, and multiple exchange rates—these are the items that are grist for his mill. Ocampo does not overlook the mistakes implicit in the elements just listed, but the main message that comes through—at least to this reader—is one of surprise of how "traditional" were the measures taken to stabilize the economy, once the goal of stabilization was taken seriously. He mentions the dramatic reductions of government spending, the conscious efforts to raise the average real exchange rate facing exporters, and the freeing of many prices in June of 1988. He points out, too, the halving of government expenditure by 1989, the reduction of public employment, the application of a restrictive credit policy, the use of active interest rate management and the adoption of a sort of crawling-peg exchange rate system. All these are familiar components of "standard" Latin American stabilization.

This helps explain why a reaction of surprise is triggered in a professional audience. Why surprise? Because amid the jungle of policy mistakes there appears clear evidence that at least *some* voices were striving to bring about more rational economic policies. First, partial measures (starting in 1985), then more full-blown stabilization efforts (in 1988 and 1989) represent the fruits of their strivings. Central government expenditure reached its peak in 1984, at close to 60 percent of GDP, which was reduced to 44 percent by 1987 and to below 30 percent in 1989. An inflation which peaked at over 60 percent per month in 1988 was cut to some 27 percent per month in 1989. In the process, real wages were drastically reduced. By 1987 they were less than half their pre-revolutionary level; the stabilization programs led to still further drastic cuts.

Is this populism? To me, it certainly looks and tastes like something else. Yet a single visit to Nicaragua is enough to convince anyone with an economist's eye to see that the economy is in a shambles.

I do not have the basis (in either study of or experience with the Nicaraguan economy) to make sense out of the conflicting signals. What is clear to me is that the voices of reason did not prevail sufficiently, that vast uncorrected mistakes were still present in economic policy up through the passage of power from the Sandinistas to their loosely linked opposition, which presently controls the government.

What I would like to do now is concentrate on just one area—bank credit to the productive sector of the economy—in which I have had the occasion to work a bit, and to study the available data. Fortunately, this area is pregnant with lessons, both for economists and for policymakers.

We start with the story of the 1960s and 1970s. During this period, bank credit to the private sector was abundant, by normal LDC standards. The year-end data from *International Financial Statistics* show that at no point in these two decades did private-sector credit fall short of M2. How did such an unusual relationship prevail for so long a time? Through a pattern in which the banking system borrowed abroad (and from some domestic sources) to finance loans well beyond the level dictated solely by its deposits. How large in absolute magnitude were these loans to the private sector? The answer is, simply huge. Starting from about 15 percent of GDP in 1960, they grew to some 25 percent of GDP by 1970, and reached over 50 percent of GDP by 1980. This was all, so far as I can see, genuine financial intermediation. The savings of some were being transferred to others, who put those savings to productive use, and who paid for the right to do so.

The story changed swiftly. By 1984, the strictly *private* sector had loans equal to about 15 percent; by 1985 that went below 10, and from 1987 to 1989 below 1 percent of GDP. If we include credit to the so-called APP (nationalized productive) sector along with the strictly private sector, we find such credit at some 35 percent of GDP in 1984, some 15 percent in 1985, going down to less than 3 percent in 1987, and less than 2 percent in 1989.

It is clear that whatever the economic function that bank credit to the productive sector was performing, that function was incredibly eroded over the decade of the 1980s. With credit so scarce, one would think it would come to carry a huge price, in real terms. But no, the actual story is just the reverse. Instead of carrying a positive price, it carried a hugely negative one. And instead of functioning as a vehicle for financial intermediation, bank credit to the private (productive) sector was permuted into a mechanism of transfer payments.

How does such a mechanism work? Imagine an economy in which bank loans are made for a term of six months, at zero nominal interest, and in which prices double every quarter. Let new loans be issued each quarter in the amount of 2 percent of GDP. By next quarter they amount to 1 percent, and by the end of the following quarter they are worth only .5 percent of GDP and are paid off. Each quarterly "cohort" of bank loan recipients gets 2 percent of GDP in credit, and pays off something like .5 percent of GDP six months later. Total outstanding credit follows a sawtooth pattern going down from 3 percent of GDP at the beginning of each quarter (after the maturing loans have been paid off and the new ones extended,) down to 1.5 percent of GDP at the end of each quarter (before the maturing loans are paid off and before the new ones are extended).

The above example shows how, with a very low *ratio* of bank loans to GDP, substantial transfers can nonetheless be effectuated using the machinery of bank loans at vastly negative real interest rates. This is basically what Nicaragua's bank credit system has been doing over the past several years. The figures are not as neat as those of the example, but they can be found by simply taking each quarter's (or month's or week's) "gross lending" minus "interest plus amortization," deflating the resulting figure by the average price level of that period, and adding up the results for a year, to be then compared with that year's GDP in real terms.

The whole phenomenon of transfers via the credit mechanism deserves to be studied with care, its history chronicled, its causes sought. In the meantime let me note that what little evidence I have seen suggests a gross transfer of close to 4 percent of GDP being effectuated through the credit machinery in 1989, with about two-thirds of that sum going to what in the statistics are called "productive loan" borrowers (private sector plus APP), and the rest going to state marketing enterprises.

This vast deterioration of Nicaragua's credit system, and its conversion (I would say *per*version) into a mechanism of haphazard transfers must have some explanation, but explaining it does not signify defending it. I find it hard to imagine that a professional economist would want to try to defend it, or even know how to begin such an attempt. Certainly, Ocampo offers no defense for it, but neither does he explain such a tremendous deviation from solid economics and even from straight common sense, existing side by side with the nonpopulist, rationalizing efforts pointed out by Ocampo and cited earlier in this comment.

I certainly do not think that the rationalizing efforts cited by Ocampo are the cause (or the explanation) of the sorry state of the Nicaraguan economy today. To the contrary, I see in those efforts the professional hand of economists. But in the story of bank credit I find no professional touch at all. The new makers of economic policy in Nicaragua are essentially going to have to build a new system of bank (or financiera) credit from scratch. And if one seeks reasons in the realm of economic policy for the dismal performance of the Nicaraguan economy during the Sandinista years, one must, I think, look also for the causes of the other major mistakes, which, added to the monetary and credit debacle, created the problems that Ocampo's reformers in the post-1985 period were bravely struggling to surmount.

In my opinion, the Nicaraguan economy got to where it is through a series of policy blunders, of which the bank credit episode is just one example, simply the best example I know. It is gratifying to know that there were countercurrents of economic rationality during that period. But it is important to realize that the countercurrents were no more than just that (the counterculture to *Sandinismo,* as it were). The main currents were what swept the Nicaraguan economy into its present dismal situation. Whether those currents can be tagged with the label of populism I do not know and would not venture to guess. But that they can be accurately tagged with the label of bad economics I have not the slightest doubt.

11   On the Absence of Economic Populism in Colombia

Miguel Urrutia

11.1   Introduction

When I first discussed the organization of this volume with Rudiger Dorn-busch and Sebastian Edwards, I pointed out that populist macroeconomic policies had not been the norm in all of South America and supported that point of view by stating that in Colombia such policies had never been tried. The result of the discussion was that I was asked to write a paper showing the absence of populist macroeconomics in Colombia, and to explain that phenomenon. In the first part of this paper I try to show the absence of populist economics in Colombia, and in the second part I present some hypotheses of how this may have come about.

Colombia is an atypical Latin American country in many ways. Carlos Diaz Alejandro (1985, p. vii) wrote that "Social Scientists have had a difficult time fitting Colombian development experience of the last thirty years into fashionable categories such as monetarism, structuralism, bureaucratic-authoritarianism, and such." Indeed, except for two short periods of military government, it has been a democracy for over 160 years. While the rest of Latin America was grappling with the difficulties of redemocratization, Colombia celebrated the 100 years of its constitution by deepening democracy through the popular election of mayors, who had been until then appointed by provincial governors. At about the same time it was celebrating the twentieth birthday of the establishment of the present foreign trade and exchange regime and the system of the "crawling peg." In a continent characterized by very volatile economic policies, Colombia has had essentially the same economic policy since the late sixties. In the late 1970s, while foreign credit was inundating the region, Colombia, against the advice and pressure of international organizations and

Miguel Urrutia is executive director of Fedesarrollo, a private nonprofit economic policy research institute in Bogota, Colombia.

private bankers, actually decreased its foreign debt in order to facilitate monetary management during a period of high coffee prices. Finally, Colombia has not had populist economic macroeconomic policies in this century, and political groups with a populist agenda have never won the presidency or been able to obtain important minorities in Congress.[1]

Since populist economic policies have been followed by one or more administrations in most countries of Latin America, including Argentina, Brazil, Chile, Ecuador, Panama, Peru, Venezuela, and even Mexico, it is interesting to explore the reasons why populism has not been popular in Colombia.

11.2   The Macroeconomic Record

Dornbusch and Edwards (1989, p. 1) define "economic populism" as: "an approach to economics that emphasizes growth and income redistribution and de-emphasizes the risk of inflation and deficit finance, external constraints and the reaction of economic agents to aggressive nonmarket policies." They then describe the essential characteristics of populist programs as emphasizing three elements (p. 6): "reactivation, redistribution of income and restructuring of the economy. . . . The recommended policy is a redistribution of income, typically by large real wage increases. Inflation not withstanding, devaluation is rejected because of the inflationary impact and because it reduces living standards. The economy is to be restructured to save on foreign exchange and support higher levels of real wages and higher growth."

This definition of economic populism would include the economic policies of political regimes of a rather wide spectrum, going from the regimes of Velasco and García in Peru, Perón in Argentina, to that of Allende in Chile. There is no inconsistency, however, since the term "populism" has been used to cover a very wide spectrum of political phenomena. Margaret Canovan (1981), identifies as many as seven different types of populism: revolutionary intellectual populism, peasant populism, farmer's radicalism, populist dictatorship, populist democracy, reactionary populism, and politician's populism.

If we define populist macroeconomics as the attempt to utilize macroeconomic policies and government intervention in the price system in order to redistribute income, while deemphasizing the risk of inflation, the foreign

---

1. There have been, however, some close calls. After the devaluation of 1961, a much-debated decision, the government decreed a large wage increase, which accelerated inflation and wiped out many of the benefits of the devaluation. The wage increase was carried out with the announced purpose of insuring that workers would not be affected by the devaluation. The political close call was much more serious. In the presidential election of 1970, the former dictator, Gustavo Rojas Pinilla, lost the election by a few thousand votes after running a populist campaign. Interestingly enough, his main criticism of the government was its lack of decision in the control of inflation, and his promise was to stop price increases. In recent years inflation had been running at about 10% per year. It is significant that the populist political movement created by Rojas received much decreased support in the municipal elections two years later and practically disappeared by the next presidential election.

exchange constraint, and fiscal deficits, then evidence of economic populism should show up in the statistical series that deal with a country's major macro balances.

Dornbusch and Edwards (1989) utilize series on the black market exchange rate, real wages, and foreign reserves to illustrate populist processes and results in the case of Chile and Peru. Their tables show immense fluctuations in these variables and systematically show how populist economic policies improve real wages and employment in the first phase and then lead to balance of payment crises, dramatic increases in the black market exchange rate, and then sustained decreases in real wages, income per capita, and accelerated inflation.

The Colombian tables show, on the contrary, few large fluctuations. The smoothness of the curves is, I think, good evidence of the absence of economic populism. The most interesting table shows the black market exchange rate (table 11.1 and fig. 11.1). Not only is it usually very close to the official rate, but it has been below it in some periods. This shows clearly that the Colombian authorities have kept the exchange rate fairly close to equilibrium

Table 11.1   **Exchange Rates, International Reserves, and Imports, 1970–89**

Year	Exchange Rate	Black Market Exchange Rate	Black Market Rate/ Exchange Rate	International Reserves (in Millions of U.S. Dollars)	Imports (in Millions of U.S. Dollars)	International Reserves/Imports
1970	19.03	22.80	1.20	152.0	796.0	.191
1971	20.81	22.50	1.08	170.4	892.0	.191
1972	22.70	25.00	1.10	345.2	843.0	.409
1973	24.65	26.10	1.06	515.9	976.0	.529
1974	28.26	28.40	1.00	429.5	1,502.0	.286
1975	32.84	32.60	.99	547.3	1,415.0	.387
1976	36.20	35.80	.99	1,165.8	1.654.0	.705
1977	37.71	34.20	.91	1,829.6	1,969.0	.929
1978	40.79	36.80	.90	2,481.8	2,552.0	.972
1979	43.79	39.50	.90	4,105.9	2.978.0	1.379
1980	50.56	48.20	.95	5,416.0	4,283.0	1.265
1981	58.64	56.00	.95	5,630.2	4,730.0	1.190
1982	69.59	71.00	1.02	4,890.8	5,358.0	.913
1983	87.83	100.00	1.14	3,078.5	4,464.0	.690
1984	112.74	128.00	1.14	1,795.5	4,027.0	.446
1985	169.19	172.72	1.02	2,067.4	3,673.0	.563
1986	216.97	218.40	1.01	3,477.7	3,409.2	1020
1987	262.08	262.60	1.00	3,449.9	3,793.5	.909
1988	332.97	335.50	1.01	3,809.9	4,515.3	.844
1989	401.67	409.23	1.01	3.917.9		

Source: Fedesarrollo data base.

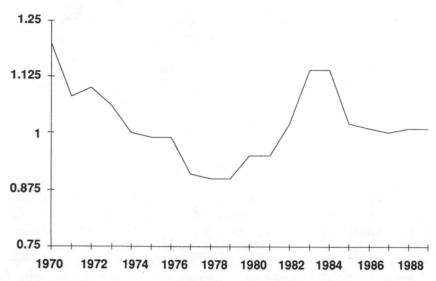

Fig. 11.1   Relation between black market exchange rate and official exchange rate
Source: Fedesarrollo

levels throughout the period and have not tried to use the exchange rate for redistributive purposes.

Table 11.2 shows the trend in the real exchange rate, the trade balance, and the fiscal deficit since 1970. Once again, one sees substantial stability in comparison to other Latin American countries. The real exchange rate became revalued at the time of the coffee and drug export boom, despite the efforts of the government to avoid this result through limits on foreign indebtedness, continuation of the crawling peg, and massive open market operations to control inflation. This revaluation was the source of a growing balance of payments problem at the end of the seventies, when commodity prices started to decrease after 1979, but which was postponed by increases in foreign indebtedness. Although adjustment was postponed during 1982 and 1983, when international reserves started to fall rapidly, in part due to a misjudgement concerning the possibility of obtaining foreign credit after the Mexican debt crisis, adjustment took place successfully in 1984.

If one of the characteristics of populist economics is the attempt to redistribute income through the expenditure side of the budget without a concurrent effort to increase tax revenues, then the fiscal deficit columns in table 11.2 show that Colombian governments have not been tempted by fiscal heterodoxy. In the last three decades there have also not been any wage freezes with price freezes, although there have been price controls in certain goods and implicit subsidies at different times for wheat, gasoline, milk, and cement. Public services tariffs for electricity and water have also been controlled at

Table 11.2   Real Exchange Rate, Tax Revenues, and Fiscal Deficit

Year	Real Exchange Rate	Trade Balance (in Millions of U.S. Dollars)	Current Account (in Millions of U.S. Dollars)	GDP (in Millions of U.S. Dollars)	Percentage with Respect to GDP		Fiscal Deficit
					Tax Revenues	Tax Revenues[a]	
1970	90.3	− 20	− 291.0	132,768	8.9	8.3	− 4.6
1971	95.8	− 150	− 456.0	155,886	9.2	8.7	− 4.7
1972	99.2	116	− 201.0	189,614	8.7	8.2	− 3.5
1973	97.5	260	− 77.0	243,160	8.5	7.7	− 3.3
1974	95.7	− 47	− 405.0	322,384	8.5	7.5	− 2.6
1975	100.0	297	− 127.0	405,108	10.0	9.1	− 2.0
1976	97.4	560	189.0	532,270	9.7	8.6	.1
1977	83.9	705	390.0	716,029	8.9	7.6	− .5
1978	84.5	667	330.0	909,487	9.5	8.0	− 1.3
1979	83.2	537	512.0	1,188,617	9.9	8.0	− 2.5
1980	82.8	13	104.0	1,579,130	10.7	8.1	.0
1981	77.7	− 1,333	− 1,722.0	1,982,773	10.6	7.8	− .9
1982	73.2	− 2,076	− 2,885.0	2,497,298	10.2	7.6	− 1.2
1983	75.1	− 1,317	− 2,826.0	3,054,137	9.8	7.8	− 1.5
1984	81.9	− 404	− 2,088.0	3,856,584	7.9	7.9	− 4.0
1985	94.8	109	− 1,586.0	4,965,883	9.2	9.2	− 2.0
1986	121.8	2,023.8	565.0	6,787,956	9.5	9.5	− .4
1987	133.5	1,460.5	− 70.9	8,779,383	10.5	10.5	.5
1988		824.0	− 364.6	11,681,819	10.6	10.6	− .1

Source: Fedesarrollo data, based on Central Bank and Tax Office statistics.
[a]Without exchange gains or losses at B.R.

levels below long-term marginal costs, with redistributive arguments, but re-distribution has been done more through large tariff differentials between rich and poor households than through a generalized subsidy.

Table 11.3 shows the gradual growth in real wages and cyclical increases and decreases that are much less abrupt than in those countries of the region that have experimented with populist economics. One does not see the 50% drop in real wages from 1971 to 1974 shown for Chile by Dornbusch and Edwards (1989), or the similar drop in real wages in Peru in 1988. The large real wage decreases during the recent adjustment in Mexico are also of a much larger magnitude than anything ever seen in Colombia.

Table 11.3 also shows the inflation record in Colombia, which, although high by international standards, is low by Latin American standards. The in-flation rate is also surprisingly constant, once one takes into account the up-ward ratchet of the early 1970s. The smoothness of all these statistical series is good evidence of the absence of populist economic policies.

Jeffrey Sachs (1989) has postulated a relationship between populist macro-economics and income distribution. He has argued that the bitterness of class and sectorial conflicts throughout Latin America reflects the extreme inequal-

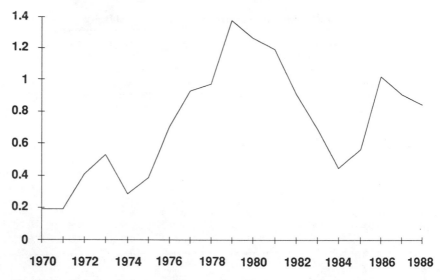

Fig. 11.2   Relation between net international reserves and imports in the same year
Source: Fedesarrollo

ities of income in the region, and that the large group of people that feel they are not benefiting from economic development tend to support those politicians that promise a different strategy for improving the general welfare. In Latin America, according to Sachs, that alternative strategy has been populist economics.

Colombia, like the majority of the countries of the region, has had a very unequal distribution of income. According to Chenery and Syrquin (1975), around 1965, the highest earning 20% of the labor force in Colombia received about 60% of total income, a proportion similar to that found in Mexico, Peru, and Brazil. Since then, however, while the income distribution has changed little or deteriorated in other countries of the region, it has improved substantially in Colombia. Londono (1989) has shown that the Colombian Ginis have decreased significantly both in the urban as well as the rural areas, and for the country as a whole. He shows a decrease in the Gini coefficient from 0.57 in 1964 to 0.45 in 1988. Even more interesting is his estimate that, according to international patterns, Colombia should have had a Gini of 0.47 in 1964, a figure much lower than that actually observed, while at the level of per capita income of 1988, the expected Gini was 47%, a level above the observed statistic. In summary, there seems to have been a significant improvement in income distribution in Colombia in the last two decades. We will come back to this phenomenon, since it may have something to do with the absence of populist economics in the country.

Table 11.3   **Real Wages and Unemployment**

Year	Yearly Change in Consumer Price Index	Real Wages, Industrial Workers (in 1978 $)	Real Wages, Agricultural Workers (in 1978 $)	Real Minimum Wages (in 1978 $)	Unemployment in Bogota	
					Month	Rate
1960	—	186.3	73.0	—	—	—
1961	5.7	—	76.9	—	—	—
1962	6.3	248.7	83.3	—	—	—
1963	33.7	266.5	84.1	—	June	8.7
1964	8.8	257.6	84.8	—	June	7.2
1965	15.1	281.8	84.3	—	June	8.8
1966	12.2	259.5	84.6	—	March	10.1
1967	7.2	265.4	83.3	—	June	12.7
1968	6.5	272.4	81.9	—	—	—
1969	8.6	279.4	87.8	—	—	—
1970	6.6	301.2	85.0	81.2	June	13.1
1971	14.1	295.3	81.1	70.7	July	9.2
1972	14.0	286.4	—	62.1	September	7.4
1973	24.1	262.6	—	49.6	October	10.7
1974	26.4	249.5	—	39.1	June	11.1
1975	17.8	244.7	—	76.7	March	10.2
1976	25.8	250.6	103.5	79.2	June	8.4
1977	28.7	236.7	116.4	69.5	June	7.8
1978	18.4	262.6	127.1	78.0	June	6.7
1979	28.8	280.3	126.2	88.6	June	6.1
1980	25.9	236.7	127.8	91.3	September	6.8
1981	26.3	210.7	122.4	91.3	June	4.9
1982	24.1	216.4	116.8	95.8	September	6.6
1983	16.6	229.5	120.0	102.6	June	9.3
1984	18.3	242.9	119.3	105.8	June	12.0
1985	22.4	243.4	117.5	103.5	June	13.1
1986	21.0	239.8	123.4	106.3	June	14.1
1987	24.0	236.5	134.0	104.1	June	11.8
1988	23.6	—	137.3	105.2	June	10.9
1989	26.1	—	—	105.9	June	8.5

Sources: Fedesarrollo data, based on National Department Office Statistics. Unemployment Bogota: 1963–1975, in Miguel Urrutia, "Los de arriba y los de abajo," Fedesarrollo, 1984.

11.3 Populism and Clientelism

We have defined populist economics as the attempt to redistribute income and power with the tools of macroeconomic management: the use of exchange rates, wage policy, price policy, and monetary policy. The political science literature would not find the use of the term populism inadequate to describe this phenomena, since there seems to be consensus in considering, as Nicos Mouzelis (1985, p. 330) does, that "All forms of populism without exception involve some form of exaltation of and appeal to the 'people' and all are in one sense or another anti-elitist."

Mouzelis (1985, p. 332) also writes that there are two fundamental modes of vertical political inclusion that are typical in the parliamentary semiperiphery: clientelism and populism. The argument I would like to make is that in Colombia political development has led to a rather sophisticated form of clientelism instead of toward populism.

Clientelism is one way to solve the problems created by political mobilization and enlarged political participation. It consists of the use of vertical networks of patron-client relationships for bringing lower-class strata into national politics. In its more advanced forms, the private patron–client network is expanded dramatically through the use of the government budget to multiply the patron's favors. Leal (1989), writing on clientelism in Colombia, differentiates its modern version from the more traditional basis of personal political power, which was also based on the exchange of favors and obligations. Traditionally, however, in the absence of a strong state with command over substantial economic resources, this relationship was of a private nature. Thus the large landowner was the patron, and he provided his clients favors out of his own command over economic resources. The political system that resulted from this network of favors versus political support at election time was known during the nineteen century as *gamonalismo* or *caciquismo*.

Loyalty and faithfulness, as the basis of the exchange of services, constituted the social values that supported and gave ideological content to the system. These values are still present now and are reflected in the strong allegiance of individuals to the political party of their families. In Colombia, it is still unacceptable for any politician to shift parties, and few individuals would in the past openly declare that they have voted for a candidate of a different party, although this is beginning to happen more frequently now.

Modern clientelism differs from the more traditional forms of political allegiance because politicians now do not have to finance the favors to their clients out of their own assets. The growth of the state has given politicians command over public funds, and these are used to maintain the political networks. Leal (1989, p. 12) correctly points out that the new political leader, born of modern clientelism, is no longer dependent on the prestige and economic power of his position in the productive system.

In other words, he no longer has to be a *latifundista,* or a prestigious professional. This has led to the development of a professional class of politicians specialized in intermediating between the state and the voter. As we will see, one of the results of the system is that in Colombia public expenditure is very redistributive, and the poor have greater access to public services and programs than in other countries of Latin America.

Ideologues and intellectuals find clientelistic democracy repugnant, and in Colombia clientelism has a very bad name. It is considered immoral to have a system in which the resources of the state are used in part in the interest of maximizing individual political support. Internationally, clientelism also has a bad name. Japanese democracy, which is very close to the ideal clientelistic regime, does not have a very good name in the international press or among Japanese intellectuals or the Japanese press, and yet the system has produced a very egalitarian society, spectacular economic growth, and the voters seem satisfied with the system.[2]

Mouzelis (1985) considers that the second major and often antagonistic mode of political inclusion prevalent in capitalist developing countries is populism. The most obvious, as well as the most-often discussed, difference between clientelism and populism stems from the ideological themes of populist discourse, which focus predominantly on the antagonism between the "people" and the "establishment," "the poor" and "the rich," which, as a rule, plays a lesser role in nonpopulist ideologies. Populism also emphasizes the leader's charisma and the necessity for direct, nonmediated rapport between the leader and his or her "people."

In this perspective, the Sachs hypothesis of a close relationship between unequal income distribution and the popularity of populism makes sense. It is therefore necessary to explain why in an unequal society such as that of Colombia populist politics have not prospered. Various factors may explain why Colombian politics have developed in the direction of clientelism and not populism.

11.4   The Impact of Clientelism on Economic Policy

The first factor that has worked against the development of populism has been the strength of the traditional political parties. Before the Colombian territory was integrated into a modern nation-state and a national market—the latter did not occur until the 1930s—there already existed two strong political parties. When the two parties emerged in the 1840s, the country was divided into fairly autonomous and economically independent regions. Before the complete consolidation of the nation-state and of a national market, one of the

2. The Japanese political system is also based on loyalty and networks of reciprocal favors, and politicians mobilize the vote through organized support groups of individuals who are tied to the individual politician by receiving favors from him. These may vary from the preence of the politician at a wedding of a relative, including the cash gift that he must provide, to the pressure on the Ministry of Public Works to build an expensive tunnel that will shorten substantially the distance from a village to the nearest provincial capital. Books and articles on the Japanese political system make fascinating reading for a Colombian, both because of the similarities but also because of the way clientelism in Japan seems to have achieved greater efficiency and respectability by being more closely integrated into aspects of the culture that are highly valued, such as loyalty and the system of mutual obligations. According to Dore (1958, p. 210), "The receipt of favours acknowledged to create an obligation of indebtedness but in no way detracting from the individual's sense of self respect, and the granting of favours in conscious expectation of a return in loyal service, the genuine and positive approval of the sentiments of personal loyalty to superiors and protective solicitude for inferiors, . . . all these features of the patron-client relationship . . . are a useful tool for 'getting on' in Japanese society." For more on Japanese politics and society, see Curtis (1983), Dore (1973), Fukutake (1982), Ike (1978), and Thayer (1973).

main integrating forces was the existence of the national political parties. These parties, in turn, were strengthened by the fact that access to political power occurred throughout the nineteenth century and the twentieth century through the ballot box.

Although the only way to gain control of the national government was through political parties that cut across provincial lines and class and occupational lines, the political power base was local. This meant that the political parties were a federation of local political bosses, and a national party political machine never developed. The presidential candidates of the parties have been chosen by the most powerful local political barons, who usually controlled blocks of senators and representatives, who in turn controlled the party nominating conventions.

Partisan newspapers and magazines played an important role in maintaining both unity and enthusiasm in the parties or party factions, and the owners of those newspapers were also influential in the choice of candidates and in the political agenda of the parties. Given the importance of the partisan press for the loosely organized and decentralized political parties, the principle of a free and independent press was maintained throughout the country's republican history. As we shall see, the existence of an independent press has been important for economic policy, because it has insured a permanent auditing of the government's economic decisions.

Although ideology played a part in the two traditional parties, the Liberal and Conservative parties, at election time the votes were mobilized by the local boss. He did this essentially by building a political machine that would reward him with votes at election time in return for favors rendered throughout the years. The boss's network of political debts is created by helping people get jobs, sometimes in the private sector but mostly in the public sector, by getting scholarships for the children of members of his support group, and by having the state build infrastructure or extend public services to the municipality or urban neighborhood where the clientele is being built up. In some cases, although they are less frequent than claimed by editorializers or opposition candidates, the local boss will actually pay for votes. More often, he has been expected to pay for food, drink, and musicians at political rallies.

As can be seen, the functions of the local political boss do not differ very much from those of the traditional urban political boss in the United States, and it must be remembered that the local political machines in that country played the important role of integrating immigrants and minorities to the economy. In the United States public works contracts not only created jobs for the immigrant minorities, and more recently the black minorities, but also helped to create businessmen and capitalists out of those minorities. In Colombia, politics has also been an important source of social mobility.

The local politician needs favors from the state in order to extend his clientele, but he also needs political conditions that will not drive that clientele to abandon him or the party out of exasperation with the prevailing state of the economy. In particular, inflation seems to be very unpopular with the voters. It affects everybody, at all times. Thus both the local politician, and the head of state, have a very limited tolerance for inflation. As has been mentioned, the one time that a populist candidate came close to winning a presidential election was in 1970, when General Gustavo Rojas Pinilla ran on a platform of diminishing the cost of living. Since within the political class there has been sufficient economic literacy for the spread of the belief that there is some relationship between money supply and fiscal deficits and inflation, neither local politicians or the head of state are willing to risk the wrath of the public by supporting expansionist fiscal or monetary policies in order to obtain the doubtful political gains generated by faster growth or less unemployment, if the possible cost is inflation. In fact, President Alfonso Lopez Michelsen, of the majority liberal party, ran and won on a platform of sound money (*moneda sana*), and the present presidential candidate of that party (Cesar Gaviria), declared in his acceptance speech at the party convention that sound money was one of the most important historical commitments of his party.

The Colombian system works with a well-defined division of labor. Industrialists, bankers, and traders produce goods and services in the private sector and sometimes lobby government for privileges, but they have little influence in Congress and with the political class, although this may be changing due to the increasing costs of waging political campaigns in a mass society. The division of labor is less clear between farmers and politicians, since in certain regions people have both occupations. But, in general, there is a political class quite distinct from the entrepreneurial class and from the labor unions. The business of this class is to get elected, and politics is its source of income.

The political class is therefore pragmatic and nonideological. In addition, since politics is a very efficient road to social advancement, the political class is not only not obsessed with ideology, but it also feels fairly committed to the system (*las instituciones*). Although often reformist, the politicians of the traditional parties, who always win over 80% of the vote, do not find leftist and populist calls for a radical restructuring of the economy attractive. Traditional politicians are not enthusiastic about radical income or asset redistribution plans, but do believe strongly in distributing the budget widely to reward their clientele.

Since there are clearly contradictory attitudes between entrepreneurs and politicians with respect to the way the government budget should be distributed, with entrepreneurs pushing for subsidies that will favor production, while politicians will prefer expenditures that will maximize the number of votes in their favor, it makes a difference which group has the most influence in government. When businessmen and labor unions have more influence, public expenditure will concentrate on subsidizing the rather small formal sector of the economy. When the local politicians have more influence, public expenditure will concentrate in subsidizing government services to the greatest number of poor voters. The Colombian political system concentrates power in the local politician, and therefore there are few subsidies to the private sector or state enterprises—if we do not count the implicit subsidies of the protection afforded by trade policy—while the government budget is spent in a fairly progressive way.

In the early seventies, (Urrutia and Berry 1976, pp. 172–73) I tried to calculate the redistributive impact of the public sector in Colombia and concluded that the tax system was slightly progressive and that public expenditure redistributed income significantly to the poorest 50% of the population. It would appear that, around 1966, the lowest quintile of the income distribution increased its income by 72% after taxes and the explicit and implicit subsidies of public expenditure, with respect to its pretax income.

Selowsky (1979) carried out special surveys in 1974 to determine the redistributive impact of government expenditures, and he too gets results that suggest that such expenditures benefit the poor more than proportionally. However, this may be the case in many countries, and Colombia may therefore not be exceptional. Comparing the impact of social expenditures in Colombia with similar estimates for other Latin American countries that have similar levels of development and different political systems would be interesting, but the data is not readily available, although it could, in the future, be put together. Table 11.4 is a first approximation. It shows that Colombia spent a smaller proportion of GDP on education than Argentina, Costa Rica, and Chile, but only Chile distributed that expenditure in a clearly more progressive way. Given that all of the countries in the table, with the exception of the Dominican Republic, have the most equitable income distributions in the region, and much better than that of Colombia, the progressiveness of public expenditure in education in Colombia is impressive. Expenditure on health, on the other hand, is both low and not particularly progressive.

However, in the discussion on the methods of clientelism, it was suggested that the government services that were used to expand the clientele were typically public services such as electricity, water, and telephone services, as well as the distribution of subsidized agricultural credit, scholarships, and employment in the public sector.

Selowsky (1979) explored who benefited from these types of public expenditures. The results of that research are interesting. Although the rich had more services in 1974, the proportion of households that received these services between 1970 and 1974 was much higher in the first quintile of the income distribution. While 11.3% of new connections to the electricity grid was for households in the upper quintile of the income distribution, the proportion reached 26% in the first quintile. Access to piped water was even better for the poor. While 31.4% of all new households receiving piped water belonged to the lowest quintile of the income distribution, only 5.6% of new connections benefited the top quintile in those four years.

Subsidized agricultural loans also benefited primarily small farmers. Fully 82.8% of the credit subsidy went to the first three quintiles of the income

Table 11.4   **The Impact of Social Expenditure on Income Distribution**

	Argentina (1980) (1)	Costa Rica (1982) (2)	Chile (1982) (3)	Dominican Republic (1980) (4)	Uruguay (1982) (5)	Colombia (1974) (6)
Proportion of educational subsidy with respect to pre-tax income: Income quintiles (poorest to richest):						
1	28.5	30.8	77.0	7.0	17.3	18.0
2	12.9	18.2	31.4	5.1	7.1	11.0
3	8.4	10.6	17.5	4.5	4.8	7.0
4	5.7	9.3	8.2	4.3	3.3	5.0
5	3.0	3.9	2.9	2.1	1.2	2.2
Average	7.6	9.2	9.9	3.4	4.0	5.0
Poorest quintile divided by the average	3.75	3.35	7.77	2.05	4.3	3.6
Proportion of health subsidy with respect to pretax income: Income quintiles (poorest to richest):						
1	15.6	42.1	31.5	23.8	16.5	5.0
2	3.4	14.0	19.1	5.3	8.8	2.5
3	2.7	12.0	9.7	4.4	3.8	1.6
4	.8	6.8	4.1	2.0	1.5	.9
5	.2	2.3	.9	.5	.9	.2
Average	2.3	8.4	4.7	3.0	3.5	1.0
Poorest quintile divided by average	6.8	5.0	6.7	7.9	4.7	5.0

Sources: Cols. 1–5, Petrei (1987); col. 6, Selowsky (1979).

distribution. Educational scholarships, on the other hand, did not seem to be distributed in a progressive manner. No analysis has been made of the social origins of public employees, but there is clear evidence that the different levels of government pay above labor-market rates for unskilled work, and below market rates for skilled and managerial public employment.

In summary, the Colombian political system, very dependent on clientelistic practices, is not admired by national and foreign intellectuals, but it receives support from more than 80% of the voters in election after election. In the last two decades it has produced economic growth, an improved income distribution, and fairly progressive government expenditures. Its very success is the main source of its weakness, since voters have systematically excluded minorities that want radical change from power, and this has driven such mi-

Table 11.5   **GDP Growth: 1965–86**

Year	Nominal GDP	Real GDP ($ DE 1975)	GDP Per Capita Nominal	GDP Per Capita Real
1965	60,488	235,051	3,191	12,399
1966	73,285	247,360	3,764	12,705
1967	84,504	257,588	4,230	12,895
1968	97,102	272,871	4,742	13,327
1969	111,728	289,523	5,329	13,809
1970	132,768	307,496	6,190	14,336
1971	155,886	325,825	7,108	14,857
1972	189,614	350,813	8,456	15,644
1973	243,160	374,398	10,611	16,338
1974	322,384	395,910	13,753	16,890
1975	405,108	405,108	16,902	16,902
1976	532,270	424,263	21,728	17,319
1977	716,029	441,906	28,610	17,657
1978	909,487	479,335	35,584	18,754
1979	1,188,817	505,119	45,565	19,360
1980	1,579,130	525,765	59,316	19,749
1981	1,982,773	537,736	73,021	19,803
1982	2,497,298	542,836	90,207	19,608
1983	3,054,137	551,380	108,252	19,543
1984	3,856,584	569,855	134,187	19,828
1985	4,965,883	587,561	169,684	20,077
1986	6,701,425	617,527	224,973	20,731

Source: National Department of Statistics.

norities to violence and guerrilla activity. Since many in the political class have experienced upward mobility, these political leaders have not been very eager to increase tax burdens and to increase public expenditure in social safety nets. What is clear, however, is that such a political class does not find the populist appeal to restructure the economy very attractive, and it prefers microeconomic redistribution of income through the budget to massive redistribution through macroeconomic policy and the radical restructuring of the economy.

11.5   The Political Process of Electing Presidents

To understand the absence of populism in Colombia, it is necessary to analyze the sources of power of the head of state, since populism is closely related to the charisma and the direct relationship of the head of state with "the people."

In Colombia it is very difficult for a politician to win a presidential election if he is not from one of the two traditional parties; the exception might arise if, for some reason, there emerge serious divisions within both parties, and they field various candidates. This is unlikely, but not impossible. Since the sixties, the liberal party has been a majority, and for a conservative to win the presidency he has to appeal to the uncommitted voters and to some liberals who may switch their allegiance, and therefore there is more of a tendency for the conservatives to field populist candidates.

However, since political power is dispersed among regional political barons who are jealous of their colleagues, these political operatives tend to choose presidential candidates at the party convention or support candidates during national primaries who are different from themselves and who will not create a personal power base at their expense. They need a sympathetic president, who will name their friends to positions of power and give them access to the budget, but they are not interested in a head of state who will create a power base of political leaders dependent directly on him, thus making it possible to bypass them. They tend to choose presidential candidates who have high prestige, and this usually means intellectuals or technocrats who have been in politics, but who have kept somewhat above the day-to-day clientelistic work.

The system, therefore, tends to produce presidential candidates who are very well read and informed, well traveled, but with some practical experience of politics. Although two or three presidents since the thirties have been more interested in poetry or international affairs than in economics, and have actually disliked having to deal with economic decision making, as a rule Colombian presidents are well versed in economics and understand that populist economics or postponing the political costs of certain inevitable economic decisions only produces short-term benefits.

The political structure of the parties produces a congress and city councils mostly interested in distributing the budget to the largest number of potential clients, but who are also aware that fiscal deficits are dangerous because of the unpopularity of inflation. Politicians love fiscal deficits in local governments or public enterprises that they control, if these can be transferred to the nation, since this is an efficient way of forcing a redistribution of the budget in their favor, but they expect the national government to avoid generating a fiscal deficit, since this will be inflationary, and it has been shown that inflation hurts incumbents. A good part of the job of a minister of finance is to avoid being forced to make unplanned expenditures to bail out local authorities who have managed to spend more than they have and then also manage to force the nation to come to their help by the application of political power or the threat of street disruptions or violence.

At the same time that the political structure creates a low tolerance for inflation, the system produces heads of state who are knowledgeable about economics and who will not try to create large new political movements on the basis of large-scale redistribution programs based on populist economics; after all, they are working within established political parties, and there is little chance of retaining influence without the support of the political barons. (As the conservative party becomes weaker among the voters, there is a phenomenon that is becoming more serious: that is, the temptation for a Conservative president, who has won an election against a divided liberal party or on a populist platform, to try to use populist economics to maintain the minority party in power and thus rebuild that party's clientele by producing short-term economic benefits before an election.)

On the contrary, the political class and the voters are very suspicious of excessive popularity. A good proof of this is that few presidents have been named for a second term; only one was elected for a second term since the 1920s and he had to resign halfway through that term due to lack of political support from his own party and very virulent opposition from the other party. Thus Colombian presidents have achieved the maximum of their power when elected, and they cannot increase it through the tools of populism. This is a large disincentive to populist economics. As a rule it is also more likely for a candidate to be elected through the support of the local political bosses than by appealing over their heads to "the people" in the populist tradition.

The optimistic hypothesis presented here is, therefore, that populist economic policies will not emerge in well-established democracies, where there is no possibility of rapidly consolidating a new political movement. In Argentina or Peru, where, in a democratization process, a head of state is willing to gamble in the short run with economic policy in order to consolidate a new political movement, populist economics, which produces short-term gains and long-term losses, may be more attractive than in Colombia, where no amount of short-term prosperity will transform a political system and political parties that have been in power for over 160 years.

11.6 The Role of Technocrats

In the Japanese system of political clientelism the role of the technocrats in economic policy has been important. Although the characteristics of the civil service and the system of recruitment is very different in Colombia, technocrats have played an important role in forming economic policy there as well.

One interesting feature of the Colombian system is that, given the danger of concentrating all of the clientelistic potential of the Ministry of Finance in the hands of a politician or a political faction, there has been, since the war, the practice of naming an industrialist or a technocrat as minister of finance. In addition, institutional innovations, such as the creation of the Monetary Board to handle monetary policy, and the contracts with the Coffee Federation have given the minister of finance virtually total power in the areas of monetary, fiscal, and exchange policy. These areas have therefore been isolated from day-to-day politics and put in the hands of technocrats. Since the early seventies many of the ministers of finance have had postgraduate degrees in economics, and the rest have worked at some time as economic consultants. Since the minister of finance is not a politician, and his capacity of building a power base from scratch at the ministry is limited, the temptations of populist economics are weak.

Another area where technocrats have dominated is the Planning Department, an agency that has been responsible for the government investment budget, the management of foreign credit (with the Ministry of Finance), and the production of the government's Development Plan, which serves as a framework for economic policy. When in 1967 the department was reformed, the precedent was set that recruitment to all high posts in the agency required postgraduate studies, and, to reach head of division, the candidate had to be at least a Ph.D. candidate. (Even now there are no Ph.D. programs in the country, so the candidates had to have done postgraduate work abroad.) Thus the Planning Agency has been essentially a technical department, advising the president on economic policy, and its officers by and large remain out of politics. Politicians often complain bitterly about the lack of realism and responsiveness of the planning department to "popular needs," but they have not pressured to make it a clientelistic bastion, and, as a rule, presidents have defended its decisions and used its staff in the process of economic decision making.

The role of the international institutions in strengthening and giving legitimacy to the technocrats in the economic area has also been important. The decisions of the technocrats gain legitimacy when they can produce loans to back them up.

11.7   The Role of the Fourth Estate

The other phenomenon that has worked against populist economics is the existence of complete freedom of the press. When populist economics is tried—as it often is at the micro level and sometimes economic policy does drift towards populist macroeconomics—there is substantial criticism, first from the specialized press, and then more generally from newspapers, television, and radio commentators.

If the criticism is justified, upon being alerted, private pressure groups mobilize against such policies. When independent experts criticize economic policy, private pressure groups can more legitimately attack the government since they are presumably not doing it from a narrow self-interest point of view, but are instead backed by independent, expert opinion.

Another factor that makes possible open debate of economic policies is that economists have alternative sources of income to the government. In the first place, some of the best universities are private, and so government censorship is more difficult. Second, the private pressure groups utilize independent economists to argue their case before the bureaucracy, and this is an alternative form of employment to the government. Finally, since the parties are not highly centralized, and different factions come to power at different times, economists that criticize the government now may be in the next government, and this makes the persecution of dissenters less attractive.

Finally, it must be admitted that governments that try to implement populist economic policies usually have economic advisors that justify those policies.

Although they may be in the fringe of the profession, they tell the populist politician what he wants to hear. The free press and frequent public debates in Colombia means that most economists have to face the market test for their ideas. By the time an economist reaches an important position in government or as advisor to a presidential candidate, he has had to explain his ideas in public, and his peers have had a chance to let people know whether those ideas are completely on the fringe or not. Foreign observers are therefore always surprised to find that Colombia's best-known economists are never those who held extreme ideological positions, and that although they disagree sometimes strongly on the specifics of economic policy, they continue to talk to each other. There are Colombian structuralists, but all of them dislike fiscal deficits of more than 3.5% of GNP.

Another factor that has made Colombian economists antipopulist is that many of them have had short experiences in the public sector and thus learned the limits of power of the state and how difficult it is to make government regulations effective. Due to low salaries, professionals cannot stay long in the public sector, and so there is a large pool of economists who have returned to the private and academic sector more than willing to use the press and specialized publications to discuss the latest changes in economic policy.

Criticism from abroad is also an additional factor that works against populist macroeconomics. Maybe due to the lack of control by foreign investment of important sectors of the economy, Colombia is not terribly nationalistic, and Colombians in general respect foreign opinion. Criticism of certain policies by international institutions such as the World Bank or Inter-American Development Bank does not generate support for those policies, as it does in other countries of Latin America. Foreign experts and academics also have prestige and are often used to legitimize reforms in which the president of the technocracy are interested. Since economic populism has not been fashionable among the foreign experts that deal with Colombia, this has been an additional factor that has created disincentives to populist economics.

11.8   Conclusion

In conclusion, the presence of well-established political parties, the clientelistic nature of politics, the concentration of political power at the local level, and the existence of a free press are factors that help explain the absence of populist macroeconomics in Colombia. This suggests the optimistic hypothesis that as democracy is consolidated in the region, the plague of populist macroeconomics will disappear. The process will be hastened, however, if the analysis of the inevitably disastrous effects of these policies by Latin American and foreign economists becomes more widely known.

References

Canovan, M. 1981. *Populism*. London: Junction Books.
Chenery, H., and M. Syrquin. 1975. *Patterns of Development: 1950–1970*. London: Oxford University Press.
Curtis, G. L. 1983. *Election Campaigning Japanese Style*. Tokyo: Kodansha International Limited.
Diaz Alejandro, Carlos. 1985. Foreword to *Winners and Losers in Colombia's Economic Growth of the 1970s* by Miguel Urrutia. New York: Oxford University Press.
Dore, R. P. 1978. *Shinohara: A Portrait of a Japanese Village*. New York: Pantheon Books.
———. 1973. *City Life in Japan*. Berkeley: University of California Press.
Dornbusch, R., and S. Edwards. 1989. The Macroeconomics of Populism in Latin America. Paper presented at the IASE meeting in Bogota, Colombia. Mimeograph.
Fukutake, Tadashi. 1982. *The Japanese Social Structure*. Tokyo: University of Tokyo Press.
Ike, Nobutaka. 1978. *A Theory of Japanese Democracy*. Boulder, Colo.: Westview Press.
Leal Buitrago, F. 1989. El Sistema Politico del Clientelismo. *Analisis Politico*, no. 8 (September-December).
Londono, J. L. 1989. Distribucion Nacional del Ingreso en Colombia: Una Mirada en Perspectiva. *Coyuntura Economica*, no. 1 (December).
Mouzelis, N. 1985. On the Concept of Populism: Populist and Clientelist Modes of Incorporation in Semiperipheral Polities. *Politics and Society* 14, no. 3.
Petrei, A. H. 1987. *El Gasto Publico Social y sus Efectos Distributivos*. Rio de Janeiro: Programa ECIEL.
Sachs, J. 1989. Social Conflict and Populist Policies in Latin America. NBER Working Paper. Cambridge, Mass.
Selowsky, M. 1979. *Who Benefits from Government Expenditure? A Case Study of Colombia*. New York: Oxford University Press.
Thayer, N. B. 1973. *How the Conservatives Rule Japan*. Princeton, N.J.: Princeton University Press.
Urrutia, M., and A. Berry. 1976. *Income Distribution in Colombia*. New Haven, Conn.: Yale University Press.

Comment   Juan L. Cariaga

With the twenty-first century fast approaching, it is incredible that in Latin America—not to mention elsewhere—some governments are still attempting to adopt populist policies. It is almost as though we were dealing with a more or less unconscious predisposition on the part of some politicians to treat government power as if it were there only to benefit one or more specific pressure groups. In the final analysis, this amounts to little more than an attempt to achieve a certain desired vote count in the next election, coupled with a pro-

Juan L. Cariaga is executive director for Bolivia, Paraguay, and Uruguay for the Inter-American Development Bank.

found ignorance of the rudiments of economics—not to mention the rules of common sense.

Consequently, it is not surprising to see that in some countries populist politicians who have realized their past mistakes are now returning to public life to apply more orthodox measures to the running of the government. The unfortunate thing is that this process of on-the-job training in the art of government has incurred high economic and social costs that the countries in question are now obliged to pay.

In his interesting and thorough paper, Miguel Urrutia takes up this subject to postulate that Colombia, unlike other Latin American countries, has been characterized by a lack of populism. Urrutia begins this task by gathering together various definitions of "macroeconomic populism" and eventually sketches out a definition of his own. He then goes on to evaluate the macroeconomic variables in Colombia. Given the conspicuous absence of fluctuation in the black market for foreign exchange, in real wages, or in foreign reserves, he concludes that this country does not represent a typical case of populist behavior like Chile or Peru. Urrutia also describes how, in Colombia, the expenditure side of the budget has not been used as a means of redistributing income and how even the most recalcitrant political circles have been ill-disposed toward the idea of inflation.

In addressing the subject of clientelism and its impact on the economy, Urrutia notes that the Colombian political system does depend upon clientelistic practices, but that the strength of the political parties, the clearly defined process for electing the president, the existence of complete freedom of the press, the educational level of the leadership, and the highly important role played by the technocrats have effectively precluded populism in Colombia.

Urrutia's paper is unquestionably of great interest and sheds a great deal of light upon the lessons that the rest of Latin America can learn from Colombia. I would like to contribute just a few brief comments on this subject:

1. First, a word about definitions. Urrutia in his paper reviews several definitions on macroeconomic populism and adds one of his own. It is on this basis that he concludes that there is an absence of populism in Colombia. The question then is: Are these definitions applicable to all other cases? For example, how populist are we to consider the so-called orthodox program in Bolivia, under which an ill-advised reactivation program was put into effect in 1987. The problem with definitions in general—and not just with this specific definition—is that they cannot specify precisely the essential nature of what they are defining. As a result, they leave gray or undefined zones in which their validity is limited, giving rise to a host of exceptions. On the other hand, I believe that Urrutia's claim that populism is entirely absent from Colombia may be a bit too rigid. This certainly appears to be the case when the author himself explains that Colombia still maintains price controls and implicit subsidies—practices that, as we all know, have as their fundamental purpose the redistribution of income for populist ends.

2. When Urrutia claims that there is a lack of populism in Colombia, but that the system depends upon clientelistic practices, it is pertinent to ask the following question: To what extent is clientelism a form of populism? Until an adequate answer can be found to this question, it is difficult to state categorically whether or not some form of populist expression has manifested itself in Colombia. This is all the more true when one considers the manner in which politicians in Colombia seek to bestow political favors with public money.

That being said, it is important to stress that Urrutia's description shows us that Colombia does constitute an atypical case in Latin America. It is as if one were dealing with a unique island in a region where uninhibited political dealing and irresponsible use of national budgets are time-honored traditions among political parties. In Colombia, the magic word is "gradualism." All the actions of pressure groups, whether they be trade unions or regional interests, have always been characterized by the gradual nature of their demands. These demands have always respected the principles of good government and shown a steadfast aversion to the risk of inflation. In this respect, Urrutia's paper is an important piece of work that allows us to describe a relatively durable and significantly long-lasting phenomenon atypical of Latin America as a whole.

3. Despite the fact that Colombia has made significant progress against populist economic practices, it still has some major barriers to surmount before it can truly accommodate itself to the new international economic order. For all its virtues, and for all the profound differences from the rest of Latin America described in Urrutia's paper, Colombia still has a legacy from the past. Among other things, this legacy manifests itself in domestic industrial protectionism, import prohibitions, tariff restrictions, and other such measures, which Colombia needs to change in light of what is transpiring elsewhere in the world.

Moreover, Colombia and Latin America will face a new challenge in the coming decade. This challenge is posed by the sweeping changes now underway in Eastern Europe and the Soviet Union. As these economies resolve their convertibility and stabilization problems and consolidate their free-market reforms, they will become a sizable market for the countries of Latin America. Once this large new market gets established, it will need agricultural commodities, foodstuffs, and energy-related products to support its development. Colombia and the other Latin American countries must prepare themselves for this eventuality. Doing so will require profound structural adjustments in their economies in order to breathe new life into the economic structures and orient them toward exporting the resources those emerging market may require.

Comment   Guillermo A. Calvo

Why has Colombia succeeded in avoiding the bouts of very high inflation that have beset its neighbors in the postwar era and, particularly, during the last decade? This is the central question that this most-inspiring paper by Miguel Urrutia attempts to answer.

Urrutia's thesis is that a country's institutional characteristics play a central role in policy making. For Colombia, he notes, for example, that: (1) politicians have a strong incentive to assure that the *party*, not themselves, be reelected; (2) the Central Bank and the Planning Institute have relatively high technical standards. Moreover, they are relatively free from political pressure or pressure from vested economic interests.

Thus, an implication of the paper is that politicians/economists ("policonomists," for short) tend to have a longer-term perspective than they would in the absence of the above type of institutional framework, which can help to explain Colombia's low inflation and low fiscal deficits relative to other Latin American countries.

However, typical populist experiments are characterized by *inflationary cycles:* inflation rises dramatically for a while and then comes down dramatically after a strong stabilization program is adopted. Why is Colombia relatively free from inflation cycles?

The absence of inflation cycles cannot be explained by the presence of low-subjective-discount-rate policonomists, as the Time Inconsistency literature shows.[1] Point 2 above, however, suggests the existence of a highly structured and bureaucratized class of policonomists in Colombia. The latter, in turn, is likely to contribute to the emergence of a relatively slow policy-making machinery, which makes it more difficult to implement "surprise-type" policies (like a surprise, not preannounced, devaluation). Since surprise-type policies appear to be at the heart of high-inflation episodes, the institutional aspects emphasized by Urrutia are, thus, potentially capable of explaining the lack of inflation cycles in Colombia. (Incidentally, the theorist should take note because there seems to be some interesting theory to be developed in this respect.)

I strongly feel that the institutional aspects stressed by Urrutia should go a long way into explaining cross-country inflation experiences. However, I think that a more complete explanation should also account for policy mistakes—either as a result of sheer incompetence or because of incomplete information. I suspect that policy mistakes leading to high inflation have become more prevalent in recent times. The reason being that financial

Guillermo A. Calvo is senior advisor at the Research Department of the International Monetary Fund. Formerly, he was professor of economics at Columbia University and the University of Pennsylvania.

1. See Torsten Persson and Guido Tabellini, "Macroeconomic Policy, Credibility and Politics," April 1989, typescript.

innovations may have shrunk the base of the inflation tax beyond the expectations of policymakers. Thus, the same budget deficit gives rise to larger inflation (like it is the case in Colombia, as shown in Urrutia's paper), and it may actually no longer be consistent with steady inflation. The latter would happen if the deficit to be monetized exceeded the maximum steady-state revenue from the inflation tax. Thus, a not-fully-expected shrinkage of the base of the inflation tax could place otherwise stable economies into an hyperinflationary path.

Policy mistakes are more likely to happen, the closer the government is from extracting the maximum steady-state revenue from inflation. Closeness from this maximum could be dictated by the institutional aspects emphasized by Urrutia, but it could also be the result of higher government expenditure due to, for instance, higher service on foreign debt or a deterioration in the country's terms of trade. Consequently, "size of government"—especially, the unanticipated part—could also be positively correlated with populist episodes, even when governments have the incentives not to utilize surprise-type policies.

Urrutia's paper opens new and very interesting vistas on the populism issue, and especially on high-inflation episodes. Let us hope that other similar studies will soon follow to be able to test more thoroughly the proposition that, as Urrutia's paper implies, "inflation is an institutional phenomenon" (with apologies to Milton Friedman).

Contributors

Alberto Alesina
Department of Economics
Littauer Center
Harvard University
Cambridge, MA 02138–5398

Carlos Bazdresch
Centro de Investigación y Docencia
  Económica
Carretera México—Toluca Km 16.5
Apartado Postal 10–883
Col. Lomas de Santa Fe
Del. Alvaro Obregón
01210 Mexico D.F., Mexico

Guillermo A. Calvo
Research Department
International Monetary Fund
700 19th Street, NW, Suite C-200
Washington, DC 20431

Enrique Cárdenas
Universidad de las Américas-Puebla
Sta. Catarina Mártir
Apartado Postal 100
72820 Cholula, Puebla, Mexico

Eliana Cardoso
The Fletcher School of Law and
  Diplomacy
The Cabot Intercultural Center,
  Room C505A
Tufts University
Medford, MA 02155

Juan L. Cariaga
Inter-American Development Bank
1300 New York Avenue, NW
Washington, DC 20577

William R. Cline
Institute for International Economics
11 DuPont Circle, NW
Washington, DC 20036

José De Gregorio
International Monetary Fund
Research Department, Room 10–320
700 19th Street, NW
Washington, DC 20431

Guido Di Tella
Esmeralda
1376 1° Piso
1007 Buenos Aires, Argentina

Rudiger Dornbusch
Department of Economics
Room E52–357
Massachusetts Institute of Technology
Cambridge, MA 02139

Paul W. Drake
Department of Political Science
University of California at San Diego
9500 Gilman Drive
La Jolla, CA 92093–0521

Sebastian Edwards
Department of Economics
8283 Bunche Hall
University of California
405 Hilgard Avenue
Los Angeles, CA 90024–1477

Roque B. Fernandez
President
Banco Central de la Replíca Argentina
Reconquista 266, 2°p. of. 208
1003 Buenos Aires, Argentina

Arnold C. Harberger
Department of Economics
University of California
2263 Bunche Hall
Los Angeles, CA 90024

Ann Helwege
Department of Urban and
  Environmental Policy
Tufts University
97 Talbot Avenue
Medford, MA 02155

Javier Iguíñiz-Echeverría
DESCO
Calle Huascar 1435, Jesus Maria
Lima 11, Peru

Robert Kaufman
Department of Political Science
Hickman Hall, Douglass College
Rutgers University
P.O. Box 270
New Brunswick, NJ 08903–0270

Ricardo Lago
The World Bank
1818 H Street, NW
Washington, DC 20433

Felipe Larraín
Departamento de Economía
Universidad Católica de Chile
Av. Vicuña Mackenna 4860
Santiago, Chile

Santiago Levy
Department of Economics
Boston University
270 Bay State Road
Boston, MA 02215

Patricio Meller
Corporacion de Investigaciones Econ-
  omicas Para Latinoamerica
Av. C. Colón 3494
Casilla 16496
Santiago 9, Chile

José Antonio Ocampo
Fundacion Para La Educacion Superior
  y El Desarrollo
Calle 78, #9–91
Bogotá, Colombia

Paulo Rabello de Castro
RC Consultores
Rua de Quitanda, 68–4°
Rio de Janeiro—RJ 20011, Brazil

Marcio Ronci
RC Consultores
Rua de Quitanada, 68–4°
Rio de Janeiro—RJ 20011, Brazil

Miguel A. Savastano
International Monetary Fund
700 19th Street, NW
Washington, DC 20431

Barbara Stallings
Department of Political Science
110 North Hall
University of Wisconsin
Madison, WI 53706

Federico A. Sturzenegger
Department of Economics
Massachusetts Institute of Technology
Cambridge, MA 02139

Simón Teitel
Inter-American Development Bank
1300 New York Avenue, NW,
  Room NW642
Washington, DC 20577

Miguel Urrutia
Executive Director
Fundacion Para La Educacion Superior
  y El Desarrollo
Calle 78, #9–91
Apartado Aereo 75074
Bogotá, Colombia

Name Index

Subject Index

AAA (Alianza Anticomunista Argentina), 78
AD (Acción Democratica), Venezuela, 22
Agrarian reform: Chile, 181, 217; limited policies for, 62–63. *See also* Land reform
Agrarian Reform Decree, Nicaragua, 336
Agricultural sector: Chile, 192–93; Colombia, 380; Peru, 275. *See also* Land reform
APRA (American Popular Revolutionary Alliance), Peru, 18, 263, 267–68
Assistance, economic, Nicaragua, 343, 347
Austral Plan, Argentina, 121–27, 146
Authoritarian regimes: Brazil, 153–58, 164; characteristics of, 26

Balance of payments: Chile, 176; factors contributing to crisis in, 116–17
Banking system: Chile, 181, 187–88, 191; Nicaragua, 366–68; Peru, 317–18
BB (Bunge Born Corporation) Plan, Argentina, 135–38
Black market: Argentina, 99–100, 103; Chile, 204; Nicaragua, 343, 345, 347–48
BONEX (treasury bond in U.S. dollars), Argentina, 133–35
Brazilian Coffee Institiute (IBC), 155
Brazil-USA Commission (1951–53), 155, 159
Bresser Plan, Brazil, 166

CACM. *See* Central American Common Market

Capital flows: Mexico, 239, 246, 249, 251; Nicaragua, 334, 348
Central American Common Market (CACM), 333–34, 348
Central Bank: Argentina, 98, 101–4, 125, 132–36; Brazil, 155, 158, 162; Chile, 198, 200, 203–4; Peru, 269, 294–95, 297, 302, 318, 327–30
Centralization, government, 157. *See also* Power concentration, Chile
CGE (Confederación General Económica), 91, 108
CGT (Confederación General del Trabajo), Argentina, 100, 108
Chamorro administration, Nicaragua, 359
Clientelism, Colombia, 376–77, 380–81
Contra war, Nicaragua, 55, 331–32, 343–44, 347
Controls, economic, 10–11. *See also* Price mechanism; Protectionism; Trade policy
COPEI, Venezuela, 22
Copper industry, Chile, 180–85
CORFO, Chile, 187–89
Corporation of National Enterprises, Argentina, 86, 93
Coups d'état: Argentina (1943, 1955, 1962, 1966, 1976), 81–82, 113; Brazil (1937, 1964), 154, 161, 165; Chile (1973), 206; Uruguay (1973), 25
Credibility of economic policy, Argentina, 123–24, 132, 143
Crowding-out effect, 140